U.S. Nuclear
Weapons Policy

U.S. Nuclear Weapons Policy

CONFRONTING TODAY'S THREATS

GEORGE BUNN AND CHRISTOPHER F. CHYBA, EDITORS

Foreword by William J. Perry

Center for International Security and Cooperation
Freeman Spogli Institute for International Studies
Stanford University
Stanford, California

Brookings Institution Press
Washington, D.C.

Copyright © 2006
CENTER FOR INTERNATIONAL SECURITY AND COOPERATION
STANFORD UNIVERSITY

U.S. Nuclear Weapons Policy: Confronting Today's Threats may be ordered from:
BROOKINGS INSTITUTION PRESS
c/o HFS, P.O. Box 50370, Baltimore, MD 21211-4370
Tel.: 800/537-5487; 410/516-6956; Fax: 410/516-6998
Internet: www.brookings.edu

Library of Congress Cataloging-in-Publication data

U.S. nuclear weapons policy : confronting today's threats / George Bunn, Christopher F. Chyba, editors ; foreword by William J. Perry.
    p. cm.
  Includes bibliographical references and index.
  ISBN-13: 978-0-8157-1365-4 (pbk : alk. paper)
  ISBN-10: 0-8157-1365-7 (pbk : alk. paper)
  1. Nuclear weapons—United States. 2. United States—Military policy. 3. World politics—21st century. I. Bunn, George, 1925– II. Chyba, Christopher F. III. Perry, William James, 1927– IV. Stanford University. Center for International Security and Cooperation. V. Title.

UA23.U78 2006
355.02'170973—dc22   2006020949

9 8 7 6 5 4 3 2 1

The paper used in this publication meets minimum requirements of the American National Standard for Information Sciences—Permanence of Paper for Printed Library Materials: ANSI Z39.48-1992.

Typeset in Minion

Composition by Cynthia Stock
Silver Spring, Maryland

Printed by R. R. Donnelley
Harrisonburg, Virginia

Contents

Foreword

For almost four decades during the cold war, the world was faced with the terrible prospect of a nuclear holocaust. The United States and the Soviet Union confronted each other with nuclear arsenals capable of destroying the world. Each year the size and the destructive power of these arsenals increased until they reached levels that could not have been imagined at the beginning of the cold war and to this day seem surreal. Moreover, because of the mutual suspicion and hostility of the two nations, each kept its arsenal on hair-trigger alert. Thus a deadly nuclear exchange could occur not only if one of these nations initiated an attack but if one of them mistakenly believed that the other had initiated an attack. This perilous state of affairs was rightly called a "balance of terror."

With the ending of the cold war, there also ended the geopolitical conditions that had led to the buildup of these arsenals and the concomitant balance of terror. The whole world breathed easier as this awful danger receded. But the end of the cold war was not the "end of history." New tensions and conflicts developed, and old ones reemerged. And it did not bring about the elimination of nuclear weapons. The two nuclear superpowers still have tens of thousands of nuclear weapons, and new nations, some of them dangerously unstable, are vying to become nuclear powers.

The new threat from nuclear weapons emerged in the late 1990s, described as "catastrophic terrorism" by Ashton B. Carter and William J. Perry in *Preventive Defense: A New Security Strategy for America* and by others. Many observers thought that such concern was fanciful, but with al Qaeda's attack on New York City and the Pentagon, it became clear that terror groups were trying to inflict the maximum casualties on their declared enemies. And Osama bin Laden's instructions to his followers that the acquisition of weapons of mass destruction was a "religious duty" confirmed that the threat of nuclear terrorism was all too real. If they get them, they will use them. U.S. strategy, well spelled out in Graham Allison's book *Nuclear Terrorism: The Ultimate Preventable Catastrophe*, must be to prevent that from happening.

For the second time since the detonation of the nuclear bomb, "Everything has changed except the way we think." Given the seriousness of the threat of nuclear terrorism, it is imperative that we change the way we think about nuclear weapons. We must recognize that the strategy and programs designed to prevent a nuclear holocaust during the cold war are inappropriate for preventing nuclear terrorism.

This book examines in some detail the current danger from nuclear weapons and outlines strategies and programs that are appropriate for dealing with this danger. It is written by a group of experts with decades of experience in nuclear weapons design and testing, nuclear policy, and arms control. The authors bring not only extensive experience to this difficult problem but considerable wisdom. The book is a unique and vital guide to dealing with the most serious security problem of our time.

WILLIAM J. PERRY
Stanford University

Preface

What role should U.S. nuclear weapons play in the world today? What related policies should the United States follow to promote international security while safeguarding its national interests? This volume addresses these questions.

The book first provides a baseline for this discussion through an analysis of current U.S. nuclear weapons policies and strategies. It includes those for deterring or preempting the use of nuclear weapons against the United States or its allies; those for preventing the spread of nuclear weapons to additional nations or to terrorists; those for defending against an actual nuclear attack on the United States; and those for developing modified nuclear weapons designs and revising the U.S. nuclear weapons posture.

After the cold war, U.S. nuclear weapons policies underwent major changes. For example, the first President Bush took steps toward the reciprocal reduction of U.S.-Russian tactical nuclear weapons, including the removal of most such weapons from their deployment locations in a way that did not require lengthy treaty negotiations. Congress financed the Nunn-Lugar program to assist Russia and new states born from the collapse of the Soviet Union in providing adequate protection to prevent terrorists and thieves from acquiring nuclear materials and technology that could be used to make nuclear weapons. In the Clinton administration, negotiations with Russia and three of its former republics resulted in the elimination of Soviet nuclear weapons from Belarus, Kazakhstan, and Ukraine. In addition, negotiations among many countries, including Russia, culminated in a treaty to ban future nuclear weapon testing. All of these changes required greater cooperation with Russia than had existed with the Soviet Union.

Further and more radical changes were made during the administration of the second President Bush. A new military strategy report, begun before the terrorist attacks of September 11, 2001, in response to a congressional mandate, was approved by Secretary of Defense Donald Rumsfeld in December of that year. Titled the Nuclear Posture Review, its leaked portions included more aggressive possible uses for nuclear weapons. In 2002 and 2003, the White House issued three reports stating post–September 11 U.S. policies for the use of military force (including nuclear weapons) against both terrorists and hostile states: the National Security Strategy of the United States of America, the National Strategy to Combat Weapons of Mass Destruction, and the National Strategy for Combating Terrorism. In March 2006, the White House issued a revised National Security Strategy of the United States of America.

This book analyzes these and related changes in U.S. strategies and policies as they apply to nuclear weapons and then asks where U.S. nuclear weapons policy and strategy should go now. It is organized around the following topics: the new international political and technical environment in which nuclear policies and strategies must now be formulated; key issues that need to be addressed, such as deterrence, preemption, and preventive war; the history and elements of the nuclear nonproliferation regime, the current challenges to that regime, and the U.S. responses to those challenges; various methods that might be considered for defense of the United States from nuclear attack; and the current U.S. nuclear weapons posture (including proposals for new nuclear weapons, what these new weapons would be used for, and whether they would be successful in these roles). The discussion concludes by drawing together the key findings of these analyses and suggesting a way forward for the United States.

The chapters in this book have been written by experts with experience in designing nuclear weapons at U.S. nuclear weapons laboratories; developing nuclear weapons policies as advisers to responsible U.S. agencies, U.S. contractors, or National Academy of Sciences advisory committees; participating in the negotiation of the Nuclear Non-Proliferation Treaty and other important treaties; and conducting research and teaching related to U.S. nuclear weapons policies. While the authors, collectively, have many decades of experience in these fields, they realize that neither they nor anyone else can claim to have the last word in the matter of dealing with weapons that pose both the greatest military threat to civilization and offer the greatest incentive to avoid major conflicts. Circumstances affecting some of the conclusions reached in this book changed even as the book was being written. The authors hope, however, that the discussion in the following pages will contribute to choosing the best policies for the future.

The authors and editors have benefited greatly from bipartisan critiques of this book's chapters. The book grew out of seminars convened at Stanford University's Center for International Security and Cooperation (CISAC) to analyze the meaning of the unfolding changes to U.S. nuclear policy. CISAC, a research center within Stanford's Freeman Spogli Institute for International Studies, invited administration critics and advocates alike to participate in the seminars and in reviews of the resulting chapter drafts. Formal reviews were solicited by the editors as part of a weeklong symposium in 2004, funded by the John D. and Catherine T. MacArthur Foundation, whose support we gratefully acknowledge. During that symposium, earlier versions of what became chapters 1 through 7 of this volume were criticized by formal respondents and then discussed by a wide-ranging group of experts. These individuals included Jay Davis, Laura Donohue, Sid Drell, Katya Drozdova, Lynn Eden, David Elliott, Hal Feiveson, Lew Franklin, Tom Graham, Keith Hansen, John Harvey, George Lewis, Ed Lyman, Clay Moltz, Pavel Podvig, Ted Postol, Bill Potter, Scott Sagan, and Michael Wheeler. Support provided to CISAC by Carnegie Corporation of New York was instrumental in completing this project as well. The editors and authors also thank Sharan Daniel for her great skill and assistance in getting the chapter manuscripts into proper form and in making arrangements with Brookings Institution Press for publication.

The editors note that no single chapter of this book enjoys the complete approval of every member of the summer symposium, or indeed, even of all the authors of the book—the individual chapters are, in the end, the responsibility of their particular authors.

U.S. Nuclear
Weapons Policy

one

A World of Risk: The Current Environment For U.S. Nuclear Weapons Policy

Christopher F. Chyba and Karthika Sasikumar

The United States currently has some 10,000 nuclear weapons in its stock-pile.[1] They are there because of a long chain of technical and political decisions made in the past. Although current U.S. nuclear weapons policy may be understood in light of this history, it should be assessed in the context of present international security risks. These risks include dangers left over from the cold war era, challenges posed by states that are newly growing in power, and the dramatic new presence of nonstate actors. The salient features of this new environment, the context of technology and international politics in which nuclear weapons decisions must now be made, are the subject of this chapter.

A New World of Risk

Shortly after the end of the cold war, a series of terrorist attacks in the 1990s, followed by those on September 11, 2001, emphasized the willingness of some individuals and groups to practice mass-casualty terrorism.[2] Some of the perpetrators were *nonstate* entities, operating without any significant state assistance; others were *substate* entities, meaning they did benefit from such assistance. Their aspirations included biological terrorism, such as the attempted anthrax attacks by the Japanese group Aum Shinrikyo in 1993, whose competence, fortunately, was not high.[3] Documents captured in 2001 showed that al Qaeda also had an interest in biological weapons (though a questionable capacity for pursuing them).[4] Many U.S. analysts and politicians believe that some groups would employ nuclear terrorism if that option were available to them.[5] How serious is this risk?

Nuclear Theft and Terrorism

It would be difficult to steal and smuggle a complete warhead from a state program, overcome whatever security measures might be installed on it, and then gain operational use of that warhead—but this possibility cannot be ruled out.[6] A more likely path to a terrorist nuclear weapon would be to steal nuclear explosive material (NEM) in the form of plutonium or highly enriched uranium (HEU); there are already anecdotal examples of thefts of kilogram quantities of HEU from Russian facilities.[7] In fact, HEU is present at hundreds of sites around the world, many of which contain enough HEU to make a nuclear weapon.[8] While in principle a nonstate group could produce a working fission nuclear warhead with either stolen plutonium or HEU, plutonium warheads would pose a greater challenge because they require spherical implosive compression with precision timing.[9] However, a gun-type HEU weapon (like the one used at Hiroshima) would be less demanding, and, according to a former director of a U.S. nuclear weapons laboratory, some substate groups could assemble such a weapon with relative ease if they had the HEU.[10]

Proliferation Rings

A terrorist group could already have access to plans for a more sophisticated, spherical implosion design. Apparently a nuclear equipment smuggling network put in place by A. Q. Khan—former director of the Khan Research Laboratory in Pakistan and leader of the uranium centrifuge enrichment program established to produce HEU for Pakistani atomic bombs—sold the design of a workable uranium implosion warhead to Libya.[11] The design is thought to be one originally provided to Pakistan by China and suitable for a missile warhead.[12] The Khan network may also have offered this design to Iraq in 1990, and to other nations.[13] The possibility that copies of this warhead design are now available elsewhere in the world, perhaps outside of state control, cannot be discounted.

The Khan network also provided North Korea (formally, the Democratic People's Republic of Korea) with blueprints and components for uranium-enrichment centrifuges, evidently in exchange for ballistic missile technology.[14] It also sold equipment to Libya, Iran, and perhaps other countries. Just as disturbing, it made use of firms in a variety of countries, including such nontraditional nuclear suppliers as Malaysia, to manufacture centrifuge components whose ultimate destination was camouflaged by transshipment. In the worst case, were such nuclear and missile "proliferation rings" to be further developed, a set of countries or substate actors in the developing world might be able to cut loose from traditional nuclear suppliers and trade among themselves for the capabilities that their individual programs lack. The result would be a world in which it is much harder to curtail the transfer of technology related to missiles and nuclear weapons.[15]

Latent Proliferation

The Nuclear Non-Proliferation Treaty (NPT) of 1968, which counts all but four countries (India, Israel, Pakistan, and North Korea) among its members, allows only five states to possess nuclear weapons: the United States, Russia, the United Kingdom, France, and China, defined as the nuclear weapon states (NWS).[16] The treaty prohibits all other members—the non-nuclear weapon states—from acquiring nuclear weapons.

A latent proliferator is an NPT member state that develops the capabilities needed for a nuclear weapons program, either within the limits of the treaty or under the façade of observing those limits.[17] (Indeed, any country that includes uranium enrichment or plutonium reprocessing in its nuclear program unavoidably attains some degree of latency.) A latent proliferator's strategy may be to withdraw from the NPT and build actual weapons on short notice, or simply to remain in the NPT while maintaining the capability for the rapid realization of nuclear weapons as a hedge against future threats. Over the past several decades, a number of countries in good standing with respect to the NPT have followed the hedging strategy, whereas North Korea chose to withdraw.[18] Many countries, including the United States, worry that Iran is now intentionally pursuing a latent proliferation strategy for acquiring nuclear weapons.[19]

The Rise of New Nuclear Powers

India and Pakistan each conducted a rapid series of nuclear weapons tests in 1998, confirming their nuclear weapons capability.[20] Israel is not known to have tested any nuclear weapons, but its capacity in this regard is unquestioned, even if details remain opaque.[21] Now to this list must be added North Korea, which has apparently produced enough plutonium for fewer than ten implosion weapons and has withdrawn from the NPT. Many have suspected that it has also manufactured the weapons themselves, and the North Korean Foreign Ministry has in fact made a claim to this effect.[22]

At the same time, South Africa, as well as three successor states to the Soviet Union (Belarus, Kazakhstan, and Ukraine), have renounced their nuclear weapons and joined the NPT. Libya and Iraq are no longer trying to acquire nuclear weapons.[23] The good news is that the world has avoided the nightmare of having "15 or 20 or 25" nuclear powers by 1975, as envisioned by President John F. Kennedy.[24] We do not yet face "life in a nuclear-armed crowd."[25] The bad news is that the potential for further nuclear proliferation and the possibility of a breakdown of the NPT regime clearly exists.[26]

The rise of new nuclear powers is dangerous for several reasons.[27] First, nuclear proliferation raises the specter of nuclear war between regional powers, or between any of the five nuclear weapons states and these new powers. Were war to break out on the Korean peninsula, it is possible that nuclear weapons would be used. They might also be used in the Persian Gulf if Iran were to acquire them. Iran has completed a test program of its Shahab-3 missile (in July 2003), which is thought to be capable of carrying a 1,000-kilogram payload (large enough for a nuclear warhead) for 1,500 kilometers.[28] And, of course, Israel already has a nuclear arsenal. Another region of great nuclear risk is South Asia. In both the Kargil conflict of 1999 and the border standoff in 2001–02 following an attack on the parliament in New Delhi (allegedly backed by Pakistan), both Indian and Pakistani leaders issued veiled threats.[29] Indeed, it is possible that nuclear weapons may have made limited conventional attacks more likely, since the risk of nuclear war may provide confidence that conventional attacks would not be allowed to escalate too far.[30] The danger that conventional conflict could escalate into nuclear war has now been mitigated by a ceasefire and a gradual improvement of the political situation in Kashmir.[31]

Second, weapons and technology in the possession of new nuclear powers may be especially vulnerable to threat or sabotage by terrorist groups. And third, the arsenals of new nuclear powers may be more likely to be used in error. The arsenals' small size makes them more vulnerable to a first strike. Fearing this, such powers may be swifter to use them, thereby increasing the chances of miscalculation. It may be especially difficult to resist the pressure to "use them or lose them" when missile flight times are short. Missiles can travel between India and Pakistan in less than ten minutes (compared with the cold war's thirty-minute flight times for ICBMs flying between the United States and the Soviet Union). Were India or Pakistan in the future to configure their nuclear weapons on missile systems that had to be launched rapidly in order to avoid destruction in a first strike, this would increase the risk that misperception could trigger an erroneous nuclear response.[32]

A Discontinuity in Nuclear Risk Assessment

All these factors—mass-casualty terrorism, the possibility of nuclear theft, nuclear smuggling by substate networks, and a gradual increase in the number of nuclear-armed states and in the potential for escalating regional conflicts—have led to a discontinuity in nuclear risk assessment compared with that of the cold war. U.S. nuclear strategy no longer hinges on being able to deter a single, comparably powerful, nuclear rival. Rather, the Bush administration's 2002 National Security Strategy embraced "preemptive" attacks against certain potential adversaries, rather than a strategy of deterrence, under the assumption that terrorist groups and even certain "rogue" states cannot be deterred.[33] The administration's 2006 National Security Strategy stated that the nation's "strong preference and common practice is to address proliferation concerns through international diplomacy, in concert with key allies and regional partners," but that if necessary, preventive attacks (called "preemption" in the strategy) would be used: "The place of preemption in our national security strategy remains the same."[34]

"Rogue" states are hardly a new challenge. During the cold war, the United States was deeply concerned about whether a nuclear-armed China could be deterred. Decisionmakers grappled with the same alternatives—preventive strike versus deterrence—now posed by states such as North Korea or Iran.[35] In addition, some cold war–era risks, such as that still posed by the Russian nuclear arsenal, remain relevant to U.S. security and cannot be ignored. For both reasons, certain cold war concepts, such as deterrence, will continue to play an important role in international security.

Global Strategic Trends

The constellation of new risks just described is not the only post–cold war trend of concern to U.S. nuclear weapons policy. Others include the changing U.S.-Russian relationship, the rise of China and India, the effects of globalization, and the overwhelming conventional military dominance of the United States itself.

The Changing U.S.-Russian Nuclear Relationship

With the thawing of cold war relations, the United States and Soviet Union made substantial reductions in their arsenals. Following the Soviet collapse, new negotiations envisioned cuts to even lower levels, where nuclear weapons would be counted in the thousands rather than the tens of thousands.[36]

But this does not mean that nuclear risk has disappeared from the U.S.-Russia relationship. Hundreds of nuclear-armed missiles on both sides remain on high alert, ready to launch on a few minutes' notice.[37] This alone prolongs the risk of an inadvertent launch during some future crisis. Furthermore, Russia's early warning system against nuclear surprise attack has deteriorated considerably since the end of the cold war. There are now trajectories by which a missile launched from a U.S. nuclear missile submarine could reach Moscow without being detected prior to detonation, and the Russian leadership is aware of this.[38] The possibility of a false warning of attack and subsequent Russian launch must therefore be taken seriously. At the same time, the improved relationship between Russia and the United States (compared with the Soviet-U.S. relationship during the cold war) makes it less likely that either country would precipitously assume the worst in response to some initial apparent warning of nuclear attack.

The U.S.-Russian strategic relationship continues to evolve. Some U.S. analysts argue that the trajectory of the two countries' nuclear arsenals is such that the United States is entering an era of "nuclear primacy" over Russia and China, in which it will be possible for the United States to destroy either country's long-range nuclear arsenals with a first strike.[39] In response, a Russian analyst formerly with the Soviet military intelligence agency has predicted President Putin would now "pull out all the stops and spend whatever necessary to modernize Russia's nuclear deterrent."[40] In his May 2006 annual address to the Federal Assembly, Putin spoke of a "new spiral" in the arms race and the need for new weapons to maintain the strategic balance.[41]

The Rise of China

Even as the cold war ended, some scholars and analysts in the United States began to express concern about the strategic challenge that China might pose. Some feared that China might become the next "peer competitor" to the United States, pointing to its rapid economic growth since Deng Xiaoping's economic reforms of the late 1970s.[42] Estimating China's gross domestic product (GDP) is difficult, but at present, China's GDP is perhaps about one-seventh that of the United States and one-third that of Japan. Average annual growth in GDP appears to have been about 8 percent over the past quarter century, with some slowing in 2005.[43] Were China to continue a steady 8 percent growth while the United States maintained its annual 3 percent growth of the last twenty-five years, China's GDP would pull even with that of the

United States in about 40 years.[44] For a host of reasons, though, China is unlikely to sustain such growth over that long a period.[45]

China's economic growth could bring with it a greater military challenge to the United States, particularly with respect to Taiwan, power projection beyond its borders, and its nuclear arsenal.[46] China asserted its changing global status in 2003 by becoming only the third nation to launch its own astronaut ("taikonaut") into space. Since then it has flown a two-astronaut capsule and announced ambitious plans for robotic missions to the Moon.[47]

A report by the Office of the Secretary of Defense recently concluded that "the future of a rising China is not set immutably on one course or another," but asserts that "China does not now face a direct threat from another nation. Yet it continues to invest heavily in its military, particularly in programs designed to improve power projection."[48] The report anticipates that China will move toward a larger, more survivable strategic nuclear force. The Chinese, for their part, argue that U.S. deployments in missile defense and growing interest in space weapons will undermine their country's nuclear deterrent.[49] A Council on Foreign Relations task force predicts that over the next ten to twenty years, Chinese strategic missile modernization, under way for decades and progressing slowly, will increase the number of Chinese nuclear warheads capable of reaching the United States to between "tens" and "75 to 100."[50] In 2005 the United States shifted two ballistic missile submarines from the Atlantic to the Pacific, apparently in order to improve its ability to target Chinese nuclear forces.[51]

Despite these concerns, the United States seeks cooperation from China in resolving the worrisome proliferation challenges from North Korea and Iran. The United States also counts on China to maintain restraint toward India, since the Indian government claims that its nuclear weapons program is substantially driven by the Chinese threat.[52] The future of the expansive and complex U.S.-China relationship is now an important factor in U.S. nuclear weapons policy thinking.

India and the United States: Natural Allies?

In a joint statement issued on July 18, 2005, Prime Minister Manmohan Singh of India and President George W. Bush agreed that "as a responsible state with advanced nuclear technology, India should acquire the same benefits and advantages as other such states."[53] This was widely taken to mean that the United States had de facto accepted India's self-declared status as a nuclear weapon state. Just seven years earlier, President Bush's predecessor, Bill Clinton, had reacted to India's nuclear tests with dismay, saying that India had put itself "on the wrong side of history."[54]

Today there is unprecedented enthusiasm for India seemingly across the U.S. political spectrum.[55] That such an alliance is "natural" was first asserted in September 1998 by India's prime minister at the time, A. B. Vajpayee.[56] In this vision of the future, the United States and India are loosely allied against terrorism on a global scale and, in the view of some, "as a hedge against a rising China" on the Asian continent.[57]

India and the United States do have much more in common than their tense cold war relationship would suggest. Both are large multicultural democracies, both are concerned about the threat of Islamist terrorism, and both worry about the rise of China—yet have strong security and economic interests with it. Like China, India is on the rise economically: India's GDP in 2004 calculated in terms of purchasing power parity amounted to $3.3 trillion, the sixth highest in the world.[58] The Indian economy is growing at about 7 percent annually and is an attractive market for the United States.[59] Indian firms now provide valuable business process services for American companies.

An October 2002 report from the U.S. Office of the Secretary of Defense reportedly states: "The U.S. military seeks a competent military partner that can take on more responsibility for low-end operations in Asia, such as peacekeeping operations, search and rescue, humanitarian assistance, disaster relief, and high-value cargo escort, which will allow the U.S. military to concentrate its resources on high-end fighting missions."[60] India seems to fit the bill for this outsourcing of military services. A month before the proposed nuclear deal, India and the United States signed a ten-year defense agreement to increase collaboration in intelligence, counterproliferation, and defense.[61]

India plans to launch Chandrayaan-1, its first robotic spacecraft to orbit the Moon, in late 2007 or 2008. In May 2006 NASA announced a memorandum of understanding with the Indian Space Research Organization to fly two U.S. scientific instruments on the spacecraft.[62]

On the other hand, the United States and India have divergent interests on a number of issues. As the global superpower, the United States would like to maintain stability in South Asia. Its cultivation of Pakistan to that end inevitably is in some tension with India's security. On the terrorism issue, India is grateful for U.S. support but is troubled by American reluctance to put greater pressure on Pakistan to curb cross-border terrorism.

By strengthening its ties with China and Russia, India is hedging its bets. Sino-Indian relations are, in fact, at their highest peak in several decades.

India is also interested in establishing a natural gas pipeline from Iran to satisfy its ratcheting energy needs.

The Indian economy may be booming, but it has a lot of growing to do before it can catch up with the leading economies. In 2003 India was only the twenty-fourth largest export market for the United States and eighteenth in the list of exporters to the United States.[63] Moreover, while India's GDP is impressive, its per capita income remains very low, at $3,100 in 2004, about a tenth of the U.S. figure.

Overwhelming U.S. Conventional Dominance

Whatever its fears of potential adversaries or hopes for potential allies, the United States continues to enjoy overwhelming dominance in the sophistication and global reach of its conventional armed forces.[64] Its crushing combat victories in the First and Second Persian Gulf Wars demonstrated to the world that the ongoing "revolution in military affairs" (RMA)—the incorporation of "smart" high-technology weapons (including precision-guided munitions, cruise missiles, surveillance, and stealth) into the armed forces and doctrine—had placed the U.S. military on an altogether different plane from that of its potential rivals.[65] This conventional dominance has important consequences for U.S. nuclear strategy.

By the 1990s, it was recognized that U.S. conventional dominance might lead some adversaries to pursue "asymmetric" warfare in response to the United States, rather than attempt the impossible task of meeting the U.S. military on its own terms.[66] After the First Gulf War, India's chief of army staff was famously quoted as saying that the lesson of the war was "Don't fight the Americans without nuclear weapons," the implication being that U.S. conventional military dominance might prompt nuclear proliferation in other countries.[67] As the U.S. secretaries of state, defense, and energy argued in a 2004 report to Congress:

> North Korea and Iran appear to seek WMD [weapons of mass destruction] in response to their own perceived security needs, in part, to deter the United States from taking steps to protect itself and allies in each of these regions. In this regard, their incentives to acquire WMD may be shaped more by U.S. advanced conventional weapons capabilities and our demonstrated will to employ them to great effect—in Bosnia, Kosovo, Afghanistan, and during both wars with Iraq—than to anything the United States has done, or is doing, in the nuclear weapons arena.[68]

The RMA may allow the United States to employ precision-targeted conventional weapons for military objectives where previously only nuclear weapons might have been sufficient, making it less dependent on nuclear capabilities. The Nuclear Posture Review has even envisioned the use of conventionally armed ballistic missiles against enemy nuclear forces.[69] In the Department of Defense's view, however, certain hard and deeply buried targets (HDBTs) will continue to lie beyond the reach of conventional weapons, so that nuclear weapons, and possibly new versions of earth-penetrating nuclear weapons, will be needed to be able to threaten these targets.[70] Indeed, increasing U.S. precision in striking targets protecting enemy leaders may spur potential enemies to build bunkers deeper underground, beyond the reach of conventional strikes. Accordingly, the Nuclear Posture Review has suggested that nuclear and conventional weapons be integrated into an offensive strike leg to be available for strategic operations, with the choice of weapon governed by the nature of the target. But then the United States risks the appearance of treating the nuclear weapon as "just another weapon" in the stockpile, rather than one of profound strategic significance.

Overwhelming conventional dominance allows the United States to depend less on nuclear weapons in military planning. But it may also invite nuclear proliferation and spur potential enemies to place hardened targets deeper underground.

The Globalization Trajectory

Another important factor affecting U.S. nuclear policy today is globalization—a phenomenon that is both concrete and amorphous. So many different global trends may be included in the bundle termed "globalization" that there is no standard definition.[71] Many aspects of the "new world of risk" discussed earlier in this chapter could be considered manifestations of globalization. The Defense Science Board in 1999 defined it as "the integration of the political, economic and cultural activities of geographically and/or nationally separated peoples," noting that it "is not a discernable event or challenge, and it is not new. What *is* new is the dramatic acceleration of global integration and the resulting political, economic, and technological change the world has seen over the last decade."[72]

Globalization affects nuclear policy and strategy in at least two ways. First, as already mentioned, the globalization of technology lowers the threshold for the acquisition, development, or production of nuclear, biological, chemical, or radiological weapons—so-called weapons of mass destruction—for states and perhaps even for substate or nonstate groups.[73] In the case of biological weapons, the biotechnological explosion and the fact that it is being driven not by states but by universities and private enterprise guarantees that biotechnologies of increasing power will be available to small technically competent groups; many of these technologies could be applied to weapons as well as to peaceful ends.[74] Nuclear weapons–related capabilities seem to be spreading in a similar, but far slower and more restrained, manner.[75] This is abetted by the spread of information technology and the consequent access to a great deal of technical data.[76]

Second, globalization draws national security attention to small states and even sub- and nonstate groups.[77] To the extent that nonstate groups are not easily deterred, nuclear deterrence is challenged as a cornerstone of U.S. strategy governing the purpose and use of its nuclear arsenal.[78] The Bush administration argues that threats from "rogue states" and nonstate actors underline the need for greater reliance on preemptive or even preventive attacks than on deterrence.[79]

Still a World of Offensive Dominance

If some enemies facing the United States are now harder to deter, one might hope that strengthening defenses offers a way out. There is some truth to this in the case of a biological, chemical, or radiological attack, in that better methods of civil defense (such as improved disease surveillance and response) could make a large difference in the severity of the consequences of an attack.[80] By contrast, civil defense offers only limited hope for mitigating the consequences of a nuclear attack.

The intercontinental ballistic missile defense system now under construction by the United States may ultimately prove capable of intercepting small numbers of ballistic missiles launched against it, although a realistic capability of that kind is not yet in place.[81] Moreover, a group intending to terrorize or strike the United States with a nuclear weapon could employ many easier methods to this end—smuggling it on board a ship, for example. Hence the utility of a missile defense system is limited, and the interdiction of an attack cannot be counted upon. In this sense, the world remains one of offensive dominance—as was the case in the cold war—meaning that those possessing nuclear weapons are disturbingly likely to be able to deliver them to their intended target.

Current Status of Nuclear Forces and Nuclear Use Doctrine throughout the World

U.S. nuclear decisionmaking must be alert to the size and employment doctrines of the world's other nuclear powers. All parties to the NPT, including the nuclear weapon states, are formally obligated by Article VI "to pursue negotiations in good faith on effective measures relating to cessation of the nuclear arms race at an early date and to nuclear disarmament, and on a treaty on general and complete disarmament under strict and effective international control."[82] Since the end of the cold war, the nuclear weapon states with the two largest arsenals, the United States and Russia, have substantially reduced their total number of warheads. They are committed by treaty—and, in the case of the United States, unilateral declaration—to further cuts. France and Britain have also reduced the size of their much smaller nuclear forces, apparently for financial reasons. Any discussion of nuclear arsenals and doctrines must also include India, Pakistan, Israel, and North Korea, the four additional states known or thought to have nuclear weapons outside the NPT framework.

Russian Federation

The Russian Federation inherited the nuclear stockpile of the former Soviet Union as well as its NWS status. (As already mentioned, the other successor states that inherited Soviet nuclear weapons—Belarus, Kazakhstan, and Ukraine—subsequently relinquished them.) The Soviet Union conducted its first nuclear weapon test in 1949, only four years after the United States first tested. The Soviet Union conducted 715 tests between 1949 and 1990; Russia has not conducted any tests since the union's fall. Russia has signed and ratified the Comprehensive Test Ban Treaty (CTBT). It is thought to have an arsenal of about 16,000 intact nuclear weapons, comprising perhaps 3,800 deployed strategic weapons, 3,400 operational nonstrategic (so-called tactical) warheads, and 8,800 intact warheads held in reserve or inactive stockpiles.[83]

Russia's strategic nuclear forces include weapons on bombers, intercontinental ballistic missiles (ICBMs), and submarine-launched ballistic missiles (SLBMs), although much of this force has been in rapid decline. Under the Treaty of Moscow (also called the Strategic Offensive Reductions Treaty, or SORT) signed between Russia and the United States in 2002, Russia agreed to reduce the number of its strategic warheads to between 1,700 and 2,200 offensively deployed strategic weapons by December 31, 2012.

The collapse of the Soviet Union engendered great concern in the West over the security of nuclear warheads and nuclear explosive materials; the United States has spent over $10 billion to assist the states of the former Soviet Union to secure these.[84] Although substantial progress has been made in this regard, as of early 2004 perhaps only half of the 150–210 sites in Russia where nuclear warheads are stored had received security upgrades with

U.S. government assistance.[85] By that date a similar fraction of the roughly 600 tons of potentially vulnerable nuclear material outside of nuclear weapons in Russia had had some form of security upgrades installed.[86]

Over the past two decades, Russia has actually increased the role of nuclear weapons in its security doctrine. In 1982 the general secretary of the Soviet Communist Party, Leonid Brezhnev, established a no-first-use nuclear policy, but Russia abandoned this policy in 1993, likely out of concern for its dwindling conventional capabilities.[87] In 1996 First Deputy Defense Minister Andrei Kokoshin acknowledged this explicitly.[88] In its 1997 statement of national security policy, the National Security Concept, Russia indicated that nuclear arms would be used only "in case of a threat to the existence of the Russian Federation."[89] But the January 2000 Concept signed by President Vladimir Putin provided a somewhat weaker criterion for first use of nuclear weapons, saying that they may be used "in case of the need to repel an armed aggression when all other means of settling the crisis situation have been exhausted or proved ineffective."[90] Russia's 2000 Military Doctrine gives a more expansive statement: "The Russian Federation keeps the right to use nuclear weapons in response to the use of nuclear weapons or other WMD against Russia or its allies, as well as in response to the large-scale conventional aggression in critical situations for the Russian national security."[91]

United Kingdom

The United Kingdom conducted its first nuclear test in 1952, the first of forty-four such tests it conducted through 1991. It is thought to have produced more than 800 nuclear warheads by 1992. It has signed and ratified the CTBT.[92] The United Kingdom's nuclear force structure now consists of four Trident nuclear missile submarines, one of which is on patrol at any time; the 1998 Strategic Defence Review (SDR) stipulated that each boat would carry forty-eight warheads when on patrol. By 1998 the U.K. arsenal's previous nuclear gravity bombs had been withdrawn from service. That is, the U.K. nuclear arsenal now relies on a single type of warhead and submarine delivery system. The SDR also stated that the future U.K. stockpile would consist of fewer than 200 operationally available warheads, a reduction of more than 70 percent of the potential explosive power of the arsenal since the end of the cold war.[93]

The SDR explicitly states that the United Kingdom's nuclear operating posture is such that its submarine missiles will not be targeted and will normally be at several days' notice to fire, "rather than the few minutes quick-reaction alert that we sustained throughout the Cold War."[94] The submarine force is viewed as a minimum deterrent "that does not depend on the size of other nation's arsenals but on the minimum necessary to deter any threat to our vital interests."[95] However, in 2002 Defence Minister Geoff Hoon told members of Parliament that some states willing to sacrifice their own people might not be deterrable, and that Britain would be willing to use nuclear weapons against certain states if they employed "weapons of mass destruction" against British soldiers in the field.[96]

Official British policy is to "press for multilateral negotiations towards mutual, balanced and verifiable reductions in nuclear weapons. British nuclear weapons will be included in such negotiations when the Government is satisfied with verified progress towards the goal of the global elimination of nuclear weapons."[97]

France

France conducted 210 nuclear tests between the time of its first test in 1960 and its last in 1996. It is thought to have produced over 1,100 nuclear warheads; it currently deploys about 350 nuclear weapons on 84 nuclear-capable aircraft and 48 submarine-launched ballistic missiles on four nuclear submarines, three of which are deployed at any given time. In 1995–96, President Jacques Chirac decided to dismantle two of France's ground-based short- and intermediate-range nuclear missile systems. France joined the NPT in 1991 and has signed and ratified the CTBT.[98]

In a speech delivered in June 2001, President Chirac made public the results of nuclear strategy decisions taken over a three-year period in meetings of the Conseil de Défense.[99] During the cold war, France's nuclear posture had focused on "deterrence by the weak of the strong," that is, on France's ability to deter the Soviet Union despite its relatively smaller military capacities. Now, as had been partly anticipated by a 1994 Defense White Paper, France might need its deterrent in cases where it was not the "weak" party:[100]

> I just now noted the development by certain states of ballistic missile capabilities that could give them the means, one day, to menace European territory with nuclear, biological, or chemical weapons. Were they moved by hostile intentions toward us, the leaders of these states should know that they would be exposing themselves to damage that would be absolutely unacceptable for them.
>
> And in this case, the choice would not be between the total annihilation of a country or inaction. The damage to which a possible aggressor would expose itself would be primarily directed against its centers

of political, economic, and military power. Of course, by its nature, the nuclear weapon is different and the world understands this. What I am affirming to you is that France, faithful to its concept of non-use, has, and will keep, the means to maintain the credibility of its deterrent in the face of all the new threats.[101]

Chirac's speech has been interpreted as a move away from an anti-cities strategy to one with a wider array of nuclear strike options of a more precise and discriminate nature.[102] In November 2001, Chirac declared that the September 11 terrorist attacks in the United States did not undermine France's deterrent, for nuclear deterrence "was never designed to work against individuals or terrorist groups. It is aimed at states."[103] Chirac's military adviser during the formulation of the new nuclear deterrent strategy confirmed in June 2003 that the threat of nuclear retaliation also applied to "any attack on a French city with chemical or biological weapons" by "a dictator in a 'rogue' state."[104]

In a speech in January 2006, said to reflect changes adopted in a routine five-year review of French nuclear doctrine, President Chirac expanded the circumstances under which France might use nuclear weapons, implying that France would consider a nuclear response to a large, state-sponsored terrorist attack even if that attack did not involve "weapons of mass destruction": "The leaders of states who would use terrorist means against us, as well as those who would consider using in one way or another weapons of mass destruction, must understand that they would lay themselves open to a firm and adapted response on our part. This response could be a conventional one. It could also be of a different kind." Chirac stated that "under no circumstances" would France use nuclear weapons for purely military, as opposed to strategic, purposes and reiterated that nuclear deterrence was not intended to be effective against "fanatical terrorists" operating independently of established governments.[105]

People's Republic of China

Since its first nuclear weapons test in 1964, China has conducted forty-five such explosions, with its last test in 1996. China has about 400 nuclear weapons, most on short- and medium-range ballistic missiles. About 20 Chinese intercontinental ballistic missiles are able to reach the western continental United States. China has nuclear weapons potentially deliverable by plane, missile, and submarine, although it has only one ballistic missile submarine, which has never left coastal waters and is not operational. China is modernizing its nuclear arsenal in all these areas but continues to do so slowly. In particular, it is developing and may have begun to deploy a mobile, three-stage, solid-fueled ICBM, the DF-31, which has an estimated range of 8,000 kilometers. China has signed but not ratified the CTBT.[106]

For about thirty years after China exploded its first atomic bomb, it had "no coherent, publicly articulated nuclear doctrine."[107] However, China's 1998 white paper on national defense stated: "From the first day it possessed nuclear weapons, China has solemnly declared its determination not to be the first to use such weapons at any time and in any circumstances, and later undertook unconditionally not to use or threaten to use nuclear weapons against non-nuclear-weapon states or nuclear-weapon-free zones."[108] That same document endorsed a 1996 Chinese proposal at the United Nations urging that "all nuclear-weapon states should commit themselves not to be the first to use nuclear weapons at any time and in any circumstances, [and] undertake unconditionally not to use or threaten to use nuclear weapons against non-nuclear-weapon states or nuclear-weapon-free zones."[109]

China reportedly follows a counter-city deterrent posture, with a small number of warheads sufficient to constitute a "minimum deterrent." This defensive posture has sometimes been referred to as an "anti-nuclear-blackmail" strategy.[110] In its 2005 white paper on arms control, China declared that nuclear weapon states should conclude at an early date "an international legal instrument on the complete prohibition and thorough destruction of nuclear weapons."[111]

Despite China's no-first-use policy, over the past decade occasional voices in the Chinese military have sent a different message. In 1995 Xiong Guangkai, now the deputy chief of the general staff of the People's Liberation Army, reportedly told a Pentagon official that China would consider using nuclear weapons in a conflict with the United States over Taiwan. Xiong was quoted as saying that Americans should worry more about Los Angeles than Taipei.[112] At an official briefing with a visiting delegation of correspondents in July 2005, Major General Zhu Chenghu, an active-duty officer, stated he believed the Chinese government was under internal pressure to change its no-first-use policy to make clear it would use nuclear weapons if need be in a Taiwan conflict. He stated that these were his personal views. China would need to use nuclear weapons, he explained, because "we have no capability to fight a conventional war against the United States. We can't win this kind of war."

General Zhu's remarks were played down by Beijing officials who characterized them as only his personal views.[113] Since then, Chinese strategists have strongly criticized Zhu's remarks. Retired Major General Pan Zhenqiang described them as "dead wrong" and "sure to do serious damage to the understanding of Beijing's nuclear policy by the international community," whereas the doctrine of no first use is in Beijing's "foremost security interests."[114] The 2005 Chinese white paper on arms control reaffirms the no-first-use policy.[115]

India

India has not signed either the NPT or the CTBT. It conducted a test of a "peaceful" nuclear device in 1974 and five tests of nuclear weapons in May 1998, after which it declared itself a nuclear weapon state. India is estimated to have produced enough plutonium for between 75 and 110 nuclear weapons, though the actual number of weapons manufactured is unknown. It has developed and deployed short- and intermediate-range ballistic missiles, but in a classified 2001 memorandum, the Indian Air Force reportedly concluded that until the end of the decade, India's fighter-bombers would remain the country's only feasible delivery system for nuclear weapons.[116]

India has not published an official nuclear doctrine, but within days of its May 1998 tests it announced that its nuclear doctrine would be guided by the principles of minimum nuclear deterrence and no-first-use against nuclear weapon states, and non-use against non-nuclear nations.[117] In 1999 it released a draft nuclear doctrine written by its National Security Advisory Board stating that "in the absence of global nuclear disarmament . . . India shall pursue a doctrine of credible minimum nuclear deterrence," and that "the fundamental purpose of Indian nuclear weapons is to deter the use and threat of use of nuclear weapons by any State or entity against India and its forces. India will not be the first to initiate a nuclear strike, but will respond with punitive retaliation should deterrence fail."[118] The draft's no-first-use and non-use pledges were modified by Prime Minister Vajpayee in 2003, however, when he reiterated India's no-first-use pledge but then retained the option to respond with nuclear weapons if India were attacked with biological or chemical weapons by a nuclear or non-nuclear weapon state. Indian news reports of this announcement noted that the retention of this option was similar to that claimed by the United States.[119]

Pakistan

Pakistan conducted a number of nuclear tests in May 1998, following the Indian tests, and declared itself to be a nuclear weapon state. Like India, Pakistan has not signed the NPT or the CTBT. It is estimated to have produced enough highly enriched uranium (along with much smaller amounts of plutonium) to produce 60 to 130 nuclear weapons, although the actual number manufactured is unknown and may be much smaller. President Pervez Musharraf has indicated that normally these weapons are maintained in a disassembled state, although the director of Pakistan's Army Strategic Plan Division, General Khalid Kidwai, has stated that they could be assembled "very quickly."[120] Pakistan has a variety of medium-range ballistic missiles and is developing longer-range options, but its primary nuclear delivery vehicle likely remains the fighter-bomber, particularly the F-16 bought from the United States.[121] Nonetheless, President Musharraf said in 2003 that the induction of the Ghauri missile into the army's Strategic Forces Command in January of that year would "radiate the necessary effects of deterrence."[122]

Pakistan has not made public a formal nuclear doctrine.[123] Foreign Minister Abdul Sattar stated in 1999 that "minimum nuclear deterrence will remain the guiding principle of our nuclear strategy," but that the number of warheads might have to change as India built up its nuclear force, to guarantee the survivability and credibility of Pakistan's deterrent. Nevertheless, "we shall not engage in any nuclear competition or arms race."[124] Pakistan rejects a no-first-use policy, likely because it lacks strategic depth and its conventional forces are at a disadvantage in relation to India.[125] General Kidwai reportedly cited the following scenarios among a number of unofficial thresholds for nuclear use: where India conquers a large part of Pakistan, India destroys a large part of Pakistan's land or air forces, India "proceeds to the economic strangling of Pakistan," or India "creates a large-scale internal subversion in Pakistan."[126]

Israel

Israel has maintained an "opaque" nuclear posture, never officially acknowledging that it is a nuclear weapon state.[127] Nonetheless, it is thought to possess enough nuclear material for between 100 and 170 weapons, deliverable by short- and medium-range ballistic missiles; it could also deliver nuclear weapons using fighter-bombers purchased from the United States. It may have tested sea-launched nuclear-capable cruise missiles.[128] Israel is not a member of the NPT but signed the CTBT in 1996.

The conditions under which Israel would choose to use its nuclear weapons are not known. A last-resort deterrent to prevent destruction by conventional military attack or chemical or biological attacks on its cities are widely cited rationales for its nuclear capability.[129] Israel's then foreign minister Ehud Barak stated in 1996 that without proven and reliable regional peace agreements, "Israel's nuclear policy, as it is perceived in the eyes of the Arabs, has not changed, will not change and cannot change, because it is a fundamental stand on a matter of survival which impacts all the generations to come."[130] Shimon Peres said in 1998 that the nuclear option was intended to provide a chance for peace: "not in order to have a Hiroshima, but to have an Oslo."[131] Some speculate that the rationale extends beyond deterrence to being capable of preemptive attack and nuclear warfighting.[132] Israel might also use the arsenal as a tool of both peacetime and wartime pressure on the United States.[133]

North Korea

North Korea appears to have reprocessed enough plutonium for fewer than ten nuclear weapons, although whether it has actually built these weapons remains unclear.[134] In February 2005 a spokesman for North Korea's Foreign Ministry claimed that it has manufactured such weapons, "in response to the Bush Administration's increasingly hostile policy towards North Korea."[135] Given the country's current plutonium production facilities, its nuclear stockpile will probably grow by about one warhead a year, unless the negotiations under way among North Korea, South Korea, China, Japan, Russia, and the United States put a halt to its program.[136]

Summary: The Proliferation Landscape

More than a quarter century has passed since President John F. Kennedy expressed the fear that the world would have "15 or 20 or 25" nuclear powers, "unless we are successful." Instead, five nuclear weapons states have been formally recognized by the NPT, another two states are known to have tested nuclear weapons and have declared themselves as nuclear weapons states, one state remains opaque about its nuclear status but is widely acknowledged to be a nuclear power, and one state has declared that it has manufactured nuclear weapons and may, in fact, have a small number of warheads. Three successor states to the former Soviet Union, as well as South Africa, gave up their nuclear weapons in the 1990s.[137]

Among the eight or nine nuclear powers, China is the only one that has made an unqualified pledge of no first use of nuclear weapons, although certain senior active-duty officers have suggested that first use has not been discounted. Most others have adopted a general no-first-use posture with possible exceptions for retaliation against the use of biological or chemical weapons, or have been ambiguous about the circumstances under which they would initiate first use of nuclear weapons.

Key Issues for U.S. Nuclear Policy

Recent trends in technology and international politics constitute the environment in which decisions about U.S. nuclear weapons must now be made. They inform the evolving U.S. nuclear weapons policy and are in turn affected by it. The subject matter of this book is primarily, though not exclusively, nuclear weapons *policy* rather than *strategy*. We distinguish between the two along the lines of the definition proposed by English military historian Liddell Hart: strategy is "the art of distributing and applying military means to fulfill the ends of policy."[138]

As the sole current superpower, the United States has immense influence on global affairs. In many respects, it is also the "norm leader," which means that its decisions may lead other governments to reconsider their own policies.[139] Decisionmakers are confronted by questions of the balance between multilateral initiatives and unilateral action, between long-term efforts to strengthen international cooperation and short-term imperatives, and between preparing for the worst-case scenario and encouraging positive trends that may sometimes seem intangible. Arms control and nonproliferation measures often involve trading a tangible unilateral capability (though one that may or may not actually be realizable) for gains that are more difficult to quantify, or are even diffuse, and that depend in part on the behavior of at least one other country. There is no general rule for weighing the potential benefits and drawbacks of the one course against the other.

Nevertheless, certain issues are crucial for the formulation of U.S. nuclear weapons policy. These include:

—The interactions and changing balance among strategies of dissuasion, deterrence, preemptive attack, and preventive war.

—The nuclear nonproliferation regime, its historical successes and failures, and the lessons to be drawn from this history.

—New challenges to the nonproliferation regime, especially those posed by the spread of weapons-related technologies, latent proliferation, and nuclear smuggling networks.

—Appropriate responses to these challenges, including to current "hard cases," particularly those of Iran and North Korea, and for very different reasons India, Israel, and Pakistan.

—The interdiction of the delivery of nuclear weapons, including the role of ballistic missile defense.

—The role of potential new nuclear weapons and choices to be made regarding nuclear use.

Some of these factors are discussed individually in the following chapters, while others receive attention throughout the book. Important among these is the evolution of U.S. nuclear weapons policy since the end of the cold war and its impact on the nuclear decisions of other countries.

Decisions about the construction and employment of nuclear weapons are among the most profound that any government, and any national leader, can possibly make. Hundreds of thousands, and possibly many millions of lives rest on making these decisions well. Today the margin for error may be as small as that during the cold war, and the context for these decisions is far different, as is the manner in which decisions made by any one power ramify through the entire system. The authors of this book endeavor to provide something better than a mere sketch of how the United States should choose to maneuver within this new context, but necessarily something less than a complete guide. The dynamic nature of the technical and political environment will require a regular assessment of the changing landscape. Certain long-standing principles have proven their worth and should not be abandoned on the basis of exaggerated claims of their irrelevance. Others will need to be updated, modified, or left behind. We have done our best in the following chapters to draw these distinctions and to point to their trajectories through time. Future decisionmakers will need to do better. We hope that we have helped.

Notes

1. For estimates of the size of the current U.S. nuclear weapon stockpile, see Joseph Cirincione, Jon B. Wolfsthal, and Miriam Rajkumar, *Deadly Arsenals: Nuclear, Biological, and Chemical Threats*, 2nd ed. (Washington: Carnegie Endowment for International Peace, 2005), pp. 203–17. For a definition of the term "nuclear weapon," see Committee on International Security and Arms Control, *Monitoring Nuclear Weapons and Nuclear-Explosive Materials* (Washington: National Academies Press, 2005), pp. 89–91.

2. Attempted mass-casualty terrorist attacks in the 1990s included the World Trade Center bombing in 1993, the Oklahoma City bombing in 1995, the Aum Shinrikyo's sarin nerve gas attack in Tokyo in 1995, and the Aum's attempted anthrax attacks in 1993. See C. F. Chyba, *Biological Terrorism, Emerging Diseases, and National Security* (New York: Rockefeller Brothers Fund Project on World Security, 1998) (206.135. 15.24/pws/Chyba_Bioterrorism.pdf), and "Biological Terrorism and Public Health," *Survival* 43 (Spring 2001): 94–106. Also, Richard Betts, "The New Threat of Mass Destruction," *Foreign Affairs* 77, no. 1 (1998): 26–41; Ashton B. Carter and William J. Perry, *Preventive Defense: A New Security Strategy for America* (Brookings, 1999), pp. 143–74; and Stephen Simon and Daniel Benjamin, "America and the New Terrorism," *Survival* 42 (Spring 2000): 59–75.

3. For a careful account of Aum's biological and other attacks, see D. E. Kaplan, "Aum Shinrikyo (1995)," in *Toxic Terror: Assessing Terrorist Use of Chemical and Biological Weapons,* edited by J. B. Tucker (Cambridge, Mass.: MIT Press, 2000), pp. 207–26. See also Milton Leitenberg, "The Experience of the Japanese Aum Shinrikyo Group and Biological Agents," in *Hype or Reality: The "New Terrorism" and Mass Casualty Attacks,* edited by Brad Roberts (Alexandria, Va.: Chemical and Biological Arms Control Institute, 2000), pp. 159–72.

4. See Mike Boettcher, "Evidence Suggests al Qaeda Pursuit of Biological, Chemical Weapons," November 14, 2001 (archives.cnn.com/2001/WORLD/asiapcf/central/11/14/chemical.bio/); *The 9/11 Commission Report: Final Report of the National Commission on Terrorist Attacks upon the United States* (New York: W. W. Norton, June 2004), p. 151; and *Report of the Commission on the Intelligence Capabilities of the United States Regarding Weapons of Mass Destruction,* Report to the President of the United States, March 31, 2005, pp. 267–78. See also the critical discussion in Milton Leitenberg, *Assessing the Biological Weapons and Bioterrorism Threat* (Carlisle, Pa.: U.S. Army War College Strategic Studies Institute, December 2005).

5. At their first presidential debate on September 30, 2004, Senator John Kerry and President George W. Bush concurred "that the biggest threat facing this country is weapons of mass destruction in the hands of a terrorist network." A transcript of the debate is available at www.debates.org/pages/trans2004a.html.

6. For a discussion of the security of Russian nuclear warheads, see Matthew Bunn and Anthony Wier, *Securing the Bomb: An Agenda for Action* (Harvard University, Project on Managing the Atom, May 2004), pp. 51–56. Evaluating the security of nuclear weapons in a number of other programs, especially in the Pakistani program, is more difficult. In January 2002, Pakistani general Khalid Kidwai reportedly stated that Pakistani warheads do not have permissive action links (or PALs, devices designed to prevent the explosion of the warhead by an unauthorized user), although the bombs are normally kept in a disassembled state. See Paolo Cotta-Ramusino and Maurizio Martellini, *Nuclear Safety, Nuclear Stability, and Nuclear Strategy in Pakistan* (Como, Italy: Landau Network, Centro Volta, February 11, 2002) (lxmi.mi.infn.it/~landnet/Doc/pakistan.pdf). See also Richard L. Garwin and Georges Charpak, *Megawatts and Megatons: A Turning Point in the Nuclear Age?* (New York: Alfred A. Knopf, 2001), p. 342. Garwin and Charpak state that PALs on a stolen warhead could eventually be overcome, but that this would be challenging for a nonstate or unsophisticated state program.

7. NEM refers to any mixture of materials that can be made to support an exponentially growing chain reaction triggered by "fast" neutrons. For a list of the most important such materials, see "Physics and Technology of Nuclear Explosive Materials," in Committee on International Security and Arms Control, *Monitoring Nuclear Weapons and Nuclear-Explosive Materials* (Washington: National Academies Press, 2005), app. A, pp. 221–44. This appendix also explains the difference between NEM and "fissile" material; all fissile material is NEM but not all NEM is fissile. According to Garwin and Charpak, *Megawatts and Megatons,* p. 59, the gun-type Hiroshima weapon contained about 60 kilograms of HEU. More complicated implosion designs require 25 kilograms of HEU, or as little as 15 kilograms or less for increasingly sophisticated designs. See Leonard Spector with Jacqueline Smith, *Nuclear Ambitions: The Spread of Nuclear Weapons 1989–1990* (Boulder, Colo.: Westview Press, 1990), app. A. For an account of

recent attempts of the theft of NEM, see "Anecdotes of Nuclear Insecurity," *Controlling Nuclear Warheads and Materials: A Report Card and Action Plan,* edited by Matthew Bunn, Anthony Wier, and John Holdren (Harvard University, Project on Managing the Atom, March 2003), pp. 166–78.

8. For example, there are 128 research reactors or associated facilities with 20 kilograms of HEU or more. See U.S. Government Accountability Office, *Nuclear Nonproliferation: DOE Needs to Take Action to Further Reduce the Use of Weapons-Usable Uranium in Civilian Research Reactors,* GAO-04-807 (2004) (www.gao.gov/new.items/d04807.pdf). Another compilation lists 350 facilities with HEU in at least fifty-eight countries; see Robert Schlesinger, "24 Sites Eyed for Uranium Seizure," *Boston Globe,* August 24, 2002. See also Bunn, Wier, and Holdren, *Controlling Nuclear Warheads and Materials,* pp. 15, 71–72.

9. See Garwin and Charpak, *Megawatts and Megatons,* pp. 347–50.

10. Albert Narath, "The Technical Opportunities for a Sub-National Group to Acquire Nuclear Weapons," in *XIV International Amaldi Conference on Problems of Global Security* (Rome: Accademia Nazionale Dei Lincei, 2003), pp. 19–32.

11. See, for example, Robin Wright and Glenn Kessler, "Iran, Libya, and Pakistan's Nuclear Supermarket," *Disarmament Diplomacy* 75 (January/February 2004): 39–42.

12. See references in Cirincione and others, *Deadly Arsenals,* p. 172; and John Pike, "Pakistan Nuclear Weapons," *GlobalSecurity.org* (www.globalsecurity.org/wmd/world/pakistan/nuke.htm).

13. See discussion and citations in Chaim Braun and Christopher F. Chyba, "Proliferation Rings: New Challenges to the Nuclear Nonproliferation Regime," *International Security* 29 (Fall 2004): 16.

14. In August 2005, President Pervez Musharraf of Pakistan confirmed that A. Q. Khan had provided North Korea with uranium centrifuges. See Salman Masood and David Rohde, "Pakistan Now Says Scientist Did Sell Koreans Nuclear Gear," *New York Times,* August 25, 2005.

15. The discussion in this paragraph is drawn from Braun and Chyba, "Proliferation Rings." For a somewhat skeptical view, see Alexander H. Montgomery, "Ringing in Proliferation: How to Dismantle an Atomic Bomb Network," *International Security* 30 (Fall 2005): 153–87.

16. The NPT was signed on July 1, 1968, and entered into force on March 5, 1970. Treaty on the Non-Proliferation of Nuclear Weapons available online at www.state.gov/www/global/arms/treaties/npt1.html. India, Israel, and Pakistan have never joined the NPT. North Korea announced its withdrawal from the NPT in January 2003. See "North Korea Announces Withdrawal from NPT, January 10: Statement and Reaction," *Disarmament Documentation* (www.acronym.org.uk/docs/0301/doc02.htm).

17. For a discussion of latent proliferation in the context of Iran, see George Perkovich, "Dealing with Iran's Nuclear Challenge" (Washington: Carnegie Endowment for International Peace, April 28, 2003) (www.ceip.org/files/projects/npp/pdf/Iran/iranianuclearchallenge.pdf). In January 2004, Iran's president Mohammad Khatami stated publicly that his country's nuclear program was peaceful and that Iran was "vehemently" opposed to the production of nuclear arms. See "Iran Denies Receiving Nuclear Material from North Korea," Agence France-Presse, Davos, Switzerland, January 21, 2004 (www.spacewar.com/2004/040121200135.i5cph0v8.html).

18. In October 2005, North Korea indicated it was ready to rejoin the treaty provided that some of its demands were met (www.nti.org/d_newswire/issues/2005_10_21.html# 9E3CE6E2).

19. For an account of accusations and denials regarding the Iranian program, see Braun and Chyba, "Proliferation Rings," pp. 17–20.

20. For a history of the Indian program tracing its roots to domestic politics, see George Perkovich, *India's Nuclear Bomb: The Impact on Global Proliferation* (University of California Press, 1999). For a sympathetic account of this history, see Sumit Ganguly, "India's Pathway to Pokhran II: The Prospects and Sources of New Delhi's Nuclear Weapons Program," *International Security* 23, no. 4 (1999): 148–77. The Pakistani program is described in Samina Ahmed, "Pakistan's Nuclear Weapons Program: Turning Points and Nuclear Choices," *International Security* 23, no. 4 (1999): 178–204.

21. For a summary of the Israeli program, see Cirincione and others, *Deadly Arsenals*, pp. 259–75. For the program's history, see Avner Cohen, *Israel and the Bomb* (Columbia University Press, 1998).

22. For a discussion of the North Korean claim, see Paul Kerr, "Examining North Korea's Nuclear Claims," *Arms Control Today* 35 (March 2005). For a summary of the North Korean program, see Cirincione and others, *Deadly Arsenals*, pp. 279–91. A technical account of the North Korean plutonium program is available in David Albright and Kevin O'Neill, eds., *Solving the North Korean Nuclear Puzzle* (Washington: Institute for Science and International Security Press, 2000).

23. The Libyan and Iraqi nuclear weapons programs are reviewed by Cirincione and others, *Deadly Arsenals*, pp. 317–61. See also Bruce Jentleson and Christopher Whytock, "Who 'Won' Libya? The Force-Diplomacy Debate and Its Implications for Theory and Policy," *International Security* 30 (Winter 2005/06): 47–86.

24. President Kennedy's comments are often paraphrased and sometimes recalled incorrectly. In response to a question at a news conference on March 21, 1963, Kennedy said: "Personally I am haunted by the feeling that by 1970, unless we are successful, there may be 10 nuclear powers instead of four, and by 1975, 15 or 20. With all of the history of war, and the human race history, unfortunately, has been a good deal more than peace, with nuclear weapons distributed all through the world, and available, and the strong reluctance of any people to accept defeat, I see the possibility in the 1970s of the President of the United States having to face a world in which 15 or 20 or 25 nations may have these weapons. I regard that as the greatest possible danger and hazard." See President John F. Kennedy, News Conference 52, March 21, 1963, John F. Kennedy Library and Museum, Boston.

25. The phrase is from Albert Wohlstetter, *Moving toward Life in a Nuclear Armed Crowd?* ACDA/PAB-263 (Los Angeles: Pan Heuristics Division of Science Applications, December 1975), rev. April 1976. A subsequent version, titled "Life in a Nuclear Armed Crowd," appears in Albert Wohlstetter and others, *Swords from Plowshares* (University of Chicago Press, 1979), chap. 6, pp. 126–50.

26. For a discussion of the prospects for a variety of nations continuing to adhere to the nuclear nonproliferation regime, see Kurt M. Campbell, Robert J. Einhorn, and Mitchell B. Reiss, *The Nuclear Tipping Point: Why States Reconsider Their Nuclear Choices* (Brookings, 2004). See also Tanya Ogilvie-White, "Is There a Theory of Nuclear Proliferation? An Analysis of the Contemporary Debate," *Nonproliferation Review* 4 (Fall 1996): 43–60.

27. There is a long-standing scholarly debate over whether, and if so why, nuclear weapons proliferation to more and more countries is dangerous. Here we note that preventing nuclear proliferation has been a cornerstone of U.S. international security policy for decades. For the scholarly debate, see Scott D. Sagan and Kenneth N. Waltz, *The Spread of Nuclear Weapons: A Debate Renewed* (New York: W. W. Norton, 2003).

28. See Felicity Barringer, "Traces of Enriched Uranium Are Reportedly Found in Iran," *New York Times*, August 27, 2003.

29. In his first address after the attack on parliament in December 2001, as the country prepared for troop mobilization, India's prime minister Vajpayee declared: "Now the fight against terrorism has reached its last phase. We will fight a decisive battle to the end." See "War against Terrorism Will Be Fought Decisively: PM," *indiainfo.com*, December 13, 2001 (newsarchives.indiainfo.com/spotlight/parliament/13pm4.html). A few days later, Pakistan's foreign minister countered: "India should know that Pakistan is in a position to make an effective defence of its territory. Our forces are absolutely well-prepared to counter any aggressive mood." "India-Pakistan Tensions Mount," Associated Press, December 26, 2001.

30. This is known to political scientists as the "stability/instability paradox." For a nuanced view of the limitations of the applicability of this paradox to the India/Pakistan conflict, see S. Paul Kapur, "India and Pakistan's Unstable Peace: Why Nuclear South Asia Is Not Like Cold War Europe," *International Security* 30 (Fall 2005): 127–52.

31. Kashmir has been a source of conflict between India and Pakistan since partition in 1947 and has played a part in four wars since then. A ceasefire between the two countries has been in effect since November 2003, surviving occasional cross-border sniping, a change of government in India, and the terrorist attacks on New Delhi in October 2005.

32. Zia Mian, R. Rajamaran, and M. V. Ramana, "Early Warning in South Asia: Constraints and Implications," *Science and Global Security* 11, no. 2–3 (2003): 109–50. Currently, neither India nor Pakistan has its nuclear weapons mounted on missiles held in a state of high alert.

33. White House, National Security Strategy of the United States of America, September 17, 2002 (www.whitehouse.gov/nsc/nss.html). The document alternates between affirmations of deterrence and assertions of its limitations. See also Robert Jervis, "Confrontation between Iraq and the U.S.: Implications for the Theory and Practice of Deterrence," *European Journal of International Relations* 9, no. 2 (2003): 315–37.

34. White House, National Security Strategy of the United States of America, March 2006 (www.whitehouse.gov/nsc/nss/2006/nss2006.pdf), p. 23.

35. Francis J. Gavin, "Blasts from the Past: Proliferation Lessons from the 1960s," *International Security* 29 (Winter 2004/5): 100–35.

36. The United States and the Russian Federation signed the Moscow Treaty in May 2002, which commits them to reducing their operationally deployed strategic nuclear weapons to between 1,700 and 2,200 by the end of 2012. The treaty does not include non-strategic weapons or reserve strategic nuclear weapons. The Moscow Treaty was ratified by the U.S. Senate in March 2003, with some reporting conditions attached. For a summary of the treaty, see Committee on International Security and Arms Control, *Monitoring Nuclear Weapons*, pp. 26–27. In May 2004 President Bush approved a plan to cut the U.S. nuclear stockpile (that is, all warheads, including reserves) "almost in half" by 2012. See Linton F. Brooks, administrator of the National Nuclear Security Administration,

"A New Triumph of Sanity," remarks delivered to the Carnegie Endowment for International Peace Nonproliferation Conference, Washington, June 21, 2004 (www.nnsa. doe.gov/docs/speeches/2004/speech_%20Carnegie_Nuclear%20_Policy_(6-04).pdf).

37. See, for example, former senator Sam Nunn, cochairman of the Nuclear Threat Initiative, "U.S. Nuclear Weapons Policies and Programs," remarks delivered to the Carnegie Endowment for International Peace Nonproliferation Conference, Washington, June 21, 2004 (www.nti.org/c_press/statement_nunnceip_062104.pdf).

38. See Pavel Podvig, "History and the Current Status of the Russian Early-Warning System," *Science and Global Security* 10 (2002): 21–60.

39. Keir A. Lieber and Daryl G. Press, "The Rise of U.S. Nuclear Primacy," *Foreign Affairs* 85 (March/April 2006): 42–55.

40. Vitaly Shlykov, quoted in Fred Weir, "In Moscow, Buzz over Arms Race II," *Christian Science Monitor*, April 24, 2006.

41. President Vladimir Putin, Annual Address to the Federal Assembly, May 10, 2006 (www.kremlin.ru/eng/speeches/2006/05/10/1823_type70029_105566.shtml).

42. For critical discussions of China as the next U.S. peer competitor, see Thomas J. Christensen, "Posing Problems without Catching Up," *International Security* 25 (Spring 2001): 5–40; Alastair Iain Johnston, "Is China a Status Quo Power?" *International Security* 27 (Spring 2003): 5–56; and Aaron L. Friedberg, "The Future of U.S.-China Relations: Is Conflict Inevitable?" *International Security* 30 (Fall 2005): 7–45.

43. Mathew Shand and Fred Gale, *China: A Study of Dynamic Growth*, Report WRS-04-08, USDA/ERS (Washington: U.S. Department of Agriculture, October 2004) (www.ers.usda.gov/publications/wrs0408/); Robert Wang, "China's Economic Growth: Source of Disorder?" *Foreign Service Journal* 82 (May 2005): 18–23; Melinda Liu, "China Slows Down: Falling Prices, Profits and Oil Demand Signal That the Breakneck Boom Is Shifting to Safer Speed," *Newsweek International*, August 22, 2005 (msnbc.com/id/8940949/site/newsweek/page/2/).

44. Were U.S. economic growth to average 2 percent, China, with persistent 8 percent growth, would pull even in about 35 years; were U.S. economic growth to stop altogether, China with continuing 8 percent growth would pull even in about a quarter century. Data for U.S. GDP are from World Bank, *United States at a Glance* (Washington, September 14, 2004) (www.worldbank.org/data).

45. Shand and Gale, *China: A Study of Dynamic Growth*.

46. Christensen, "Posing Problems"; Harold Brown, Joseph W. Prueher, and Adam Segal, eds., *Chinese Military Power: Report of an Independent Task Force Sponsored by the Council on Foreign Relations Maurice R. Greenberg Center for Geoeconomic Studies* (New York: Council on Foreign Relations Press, 2003).

47. See, for example, Peter Harmsen, "China's Shenzhou Safely Places Two Astronauts in Orbit," *SpaceDaily*, October 12, 2005 (www.spacedaily.com/news/china-05zzzzzzzzl. html).

48. Office of the Secretary of Defense, *Annual Report to Congress: The Military Power of the People's Republic of China, 2005* (Government Printing Office, July 2005), esp. p. 13: "The pace and scope of China's military build-up are, already, such as to put regional military balances at risk. Current trends in China's military modernization could provide China with a force capable of prosecuting a range of military operations in Asia—well

beyond Taiwan—potentially posing a credible threat to modern militaries operating in the region." For similar views, see National Security Strategy of the United States of America, September 2002: "In pursuing advanced military capabilities that can threaten its neighbors in the Asia-Pacific region, China is following an outdated path that, in the end, will hamper its own pursuit of national greatness." For a reply, see "The Pentagon Eyes China's Military: Back to Threat-Based Planning," *IISS Strategic Comments* 11, issue 5 (July 2005).

49. See quoted remarks of Chinese officials in Hui Zhang, "Action/Reaction: U.S. Space Weaponization and China," *Arms Control Today* 35 (December 2005): 6–11.

50. See Brown, Prueher, and Segal, *Chinese Military Power*, pp. 51–53.

51. See Robert S. Norris and Hans M. Kristensen, "NRDC Nuclear Notebook: U.S. Nuclear Forces, 2005," *Bulletin of the Atomic Scientists* 61 (January/February 2005): 73–75 (www.thebulletin.org/article_nn.php?art_ofn=jf05norris).

52. In a letter to President Clinton two days after India's nuclear tests on May 11, 1998, Prime Minister Vajpayee wrote: "I have been deeply concerned at the deteriorating security environment, specially the nuclear environment, faced by India for some years past. We have an overt nuclear weapon state on our borders, a state which committed armed aggression against India in 1962. Although our relations with that country have improved in the last decade or so, an atmosphere of distress persists mainly due to the unresolved border problem. To add to the distress that country has materially helped another neighbour of ours to become a covert nuclear weapons state" (www.indian embassy.org/indusrel/pmletter.htm).

53. White House, Office of the Press Secretary, *Joint Statement between President George W. Bush and Prime Minister Manmohan Singh*, July 18, 2005 (www.white-house.gov/news/releases/2005/07/20050718-6.html).

54. William Clinton, *President's Radio Address*, May 25, 1998.

55. Researchers at both the Cato Institute and the Carnegie Endowment have advocated a closer U.S.-India partnership and U.S. acceptance of India's nuclear status. See Victor M. Gobarev, *India as a World Power: Changing Washington's Myopic Policy* (Washington: Cato Institute, 2000); and Ashley Tellis, *India as a New Global Power* (Washington: Carnegie Endowment for International Peace, 2005).

56. Atal Behari Vajpayee, *India, USA and the World: Let Us Work Together to Solve the Political-Economic Y2K Problem* (Asia Society, September 28, 1998) (www.asiasociety.org/speeches/vajpayee.html).

57. Tellis, *India as a New Global Power*.

58. Purchasing power parity attempts to take into account the relative purchasing power of different countries' currencies for the same goods and services. Figures from Central Intelligence Agency, *Rank Order—Purchasing Power Parity*, last updated January 10, 2006 (www.cia.gov/cia/publications/factbook/rankorder/2001rank.html).

59. G. Srinivasan, "ESCAP Pegs India's Growth Rate at 7.5 pc," *Hindu Business Line*, April 27, 2005; and Dominic Wilson and Roopa Purushothaman, *Dreaming with the BRICs: The Path to 2050* (Goldman Sachs, October 2003) (www.gs.com/insight/research/reports/report6.html).

60. Quoted in "U.S. Military Wants India to Undertake Low-end Operations in Asia," *Hindu*, July 4, 2003.

61. U.S. Embassy, New Delhi, *New Framework for the U.S.-India Defense Relationship*, June 28, 2005 (newdelhi.usembassy.gov/ipr062805.html).

62. NASA press release 06-219, "NASA Agrees to Cooperate with India on Lunar Mission," May 9, 2006.

63. Embassy of India, *India-U.S. Economic Relations*, 2004 (www.indianembassy.org/ Economy/economy.htm).

64. Ian Roxborough, "Globalization, Unreason and the Dilemmas of American Military Strategy," *International Sociology* 17 (September 2002): 339–59.

65. For a review and the historical context, see MacGregor Knox and Williamson Murray, eds., *The Dynamics of Military Revolution, 1300–2050* (Cambridge University Press, 2001). The U.S. victories in initial combat operations did not, of course, speak to American ability to manage the Iraqi occupation.

66. See, for example, Charles Dunlap, "Joint Vision 2010: A Red Team Assessment," *Joint Force Quarterly* (Autumn/Winter 1997/98): 47–49; Lloyd J. Matthews, "Challenging the United States Symmetrically and Asymmetrically: Can America Be Defeated?" U.S. Army War College Strategic Studies Institute, July 1998 (www.strategicstudiesinstitute.army.mil/pdffiles/PUB230.pdf).

67. Quoted by Patrick J. Garrity, *Why the Gulf War Still Matters: Foreign Perspectives on the War and the Future of International Security*, Report 16 (Center for National Security Studies, July 1993), p. xiv.

68. *Report to Congress on An Assessment of the Impact of Repeal of the Prohibition on Low Yield Warhead Development on the Ability of the United States to Achieve its Nonproliferation Objectives*, jointly submitted by the secretary of state, the secretary of defense, and the secretary of energy, March 2004, p. 4.

69. The Nuclear Posture Review is a classified document, but substantial portions were leaked. These are available at www.globalsecurity.org/wmd/library/policy/dod/ npr.htm.

70. For example, the leaked Nuclear Posture Review reads in part: "With a more effective earth penetrator, many buried targets could be attacked using a weapon with a much lower yield than would be required with a surface burst weapon. This lower yield would achieve the same damage while producing less fallout (by a factor of ten to twenty) than would the much larger yield surface burst. For defeat of very deep or larger underground facilities, penetrating weapons with large yields would be needed to collapse the facility."

71. Ellen L. Frost, "Globalization and National Security: A Strategic Agenda," in *The Global Century: Globalization and National Security*, edited by Richard L. Kugler and Ellen L. Frost (National Defense University, 2001), pp. 35–74 (www.ndu.edu/inss/books/ Books_2001/Global%20Century%20-%20June%202001/C2Frost.pdf).

72. The report adds: "Most important, the phenomenon of accelerated global integration is largely irresistible." *Final Report of the Defense Science Board Task Force on Globalization and Security*, December 1999 (www.acq.osd.mil/dsb/reports/globalization.pdf), p. 5. The Defense Science Board is a federal advisory committee established to provide independent advice to the secretary of defense.

73. In an August 1948 resolution, the United Nations Commission for Conventional Armaments defined WMD as "atomic explosive weapons, radioactive material weapons, lethal chemical and biological weapons, and any weapons developed in the future which have characteristics comparable in destructive effect to those of the atomic bomb or

other weapons mentioned above." See United Nations Security Council, Commission for Conventional Armaments, "Resolution Adopted by the Commission at its Thirteenth Meeting, 12 August 1948, and a Second Progress Report of the Commission," S/C.3/32/Rev.1 (August 12, 1948), p. 2. We choose not to use the term WMD here, first, because radiological and chemical weapons are poorly described as "weapons of mass destruction" since they are unlikely to achieve casualties greater than those achieved by conventional explosives, and, second, the term "WMD" lends itself to intellectual confusion as it tends to blur the very important differences among nuclear, biological, and other weapons. For a discussion of these points, see Christopher F. Chyba, "Toward Biological Security," *Foreign Affairs* 81 (May/June 2002): 122–36.

74. Christopher F. Chyba and Alex L. Greninger, "Biotechnology and Bioterrorism: An Unprecedented World," *Survival* 46 (Summer 2004): 143–62; and National Research Council, *Globalization, Biosecurity, and the Future of the Life Sciences* (Washington: National Academies Press, 2006) (darwin.nap.edu/books/0309100321/html/).

75. See Braun and Chyba, "Proliferation Rings." The role of tacit knowledge in nuclear weapons construction must also be considered, however. See Donald MacKenzie and Graham Spinardi, "Tacit Knowledge, Weapons Design, and the Uninvention of Nuclear Weapons," *American Journal of Sociology* 101 (July 1995): 44–99. The importance of tacit knowledge is especially argued by Montgomery, in "Ringing in Proliferation."

76. William Miller, "Deterrence, Intervention, and Weapons of Mass Destruction," in *The Global Century*, edited by Kugler and Frost, pp. 299–313 (www.ndu.edu/inss/books/Books_2001/Global%20Century%20-%20June%202001/C14Mille.pdf).

77. Roxborough, "Globalization, Unreason and the Dilemmas of American Military Strategy."

78. For the argument that deterrence is unlikely to be effective against at least certain biological terrorist attacks, see Chyba, "Biological Terrorism and Public Health," and "Toward Biological Security." For a discussion of the circumstances under which terrorism can be deterred, see Robert Trager and Dissislava Zagorcheva, "Deterring Terrorism: It Can Be Done," *International Security* 30 (Winter 2005/06): 87–123.

79. The putative difficulty in deterring leaders of so-called rogue states or terrorist groups is a key aspect of the 2002 National Security Strategy.

80. Chyba, *Biological Terrorism, Emerging Diseases, and National Security,* and "Biological Terrorism and Public Health."

81. See, for example, John Hendren, "Missile-Defense Test Failure Adds to Program Delays," *Los Angeles Times*, February 15, 2005; and U.S. Government Accountability Office, "Missile Defense Agency Fields Initial Capability but Falls Short of Original Goals," GAO Report GAO-06-327, March 15, 2006.

82. Treaty on the Non-Proliferation of Nuclear Weapons (www.state.gov/t/np/trty/16281.htm).

83. Estimates for the number of Russian tactical warheads are especially uncertain. Much of the basic factual information in this section is taken from Cirincione and others, *Deadly Arsenals*, pp. 121–62. See also the regularly updated Nuclear Threat Initiative, "Country Profiles," www.nti.org/e_research/profiles/index.html.

84. Substantial progress has been made, but a great deal still needs to be done. See Bunn and Wier, *Securing the Bomb*.

85. The estimate of 150–210 sites counts each separate bunker at a facility as an individual site. These data are from ibid., pp. 51–56.

86. Ibid., pp. 45–51.

87. Philipp C. Bleek, "Russia Adopts New Security Concept; Appears to Lower Nuclear Threshold," *Arms Control Today* 30 (January/February 2000).

88. Kokoshin said: "Under the current circumstances, when there is no opportunity to build substantial general-purpose force at all azimuths, the nuclear shield becomes even more important to prevent the aggression." Quoted in Yuri Fedorov, "Russia's Doctrine on the Use of Nuclear Weapons," Pugwash Meeting 279, November 2002, *Pugwash Online* (www.pugwash.org/reports/nw/federov.htm).

89. Quoted in Bleek, "Russia Adopts New Security Concept."

90. National Security Concept of the Russian Federation. Full English translation from *Rossiiskaya Gazeta*, January 18, 2000 (www.fas.org/nuke/guide/russia/doctrine/gazeta012400.htm).

91. "Military Doctrine of the Russian Federation," *Nezavisimaya Gazeta*, April 22, 2000, p. 5. English translation quoted in Fedorov, "Russia's Doctrine on the Use of Nuclear Weapons."

92. For details, see Cirincione and others, *Deadly Arsenals*, pp. 197–201, and references therein; Nuclear Threat Initiative, "Country Profiles"; and Rebecca Johnson, "End of a Nuclear Weapons Era: Can Britain Make History," *Arms Control Today* 36 (April 2006).

93. Strategic Defence Review, chap. 4: "Deterrence and Disarmament," pars. 62–68 (www.fas.org/nuke/guide/uk/doctrine/sdr98/chapt04.htm).

94. Strategic Defence Review, Factsheet 22: "Nuclear Deterrent" (www.fas.org/nuke/guide/uk/doctrine/sdr98/nuclear.htm).

95. Strategic Defence Review, chap. 4, par. 61 (www.fas.org/nuke/guide/uk/doctrine/sdr98/chapt04.htm).

96. Geoff Hoon quoted and paraphrased in "U.K. 'Prepared to Use Nuclear Weapons,'" *BBC News*, March 20, 2002 (news.bbc.co.uk/1/hi/uk_politics/1883258.stm).

97. Strategic Defence Review, Factsheet 22.

98. For details, see Cirincione and others, *Deadly Arsenals*, pp. 189–95, and references therein; see also Nuclear Threat Initiative, "Country Profiles."

99. President Jacques Chirac, speech at the Institut des Hautes Etudes de Défense Nationale, June 8, 2001 (www.elysee.fr).

100. Ministère de la Défense, *Livre Blanc sur la Défense* (Paris: Service d'Information et de Relations Publiques des Armées, February 1994).

101. President Jacques Chirac, speech, June 8, 2001, translation by Chyba.

102. See David S. Yost, "France's Evolving Nuclear Strategy," *Survival* 47 (Autumn 2005): 117–46.

103. President Jacques Chirac, discours lors de sa visite à la Marine Nationale, Toulon, November 8, 2001. Quoted in ibid.

104. Henri Bentégeat, interview in *Jane's Defence Weekly*, June 4, 2003.

105. President Jacques Chirac, quoted in Ariane Bernard, "Chirac Hints at Nuclear Reply to State-Supported Terrorism," *New York Times*, January 20, 2005; and in Oliver Meier, "Chirac Outlines Expanded Nuclear Doctrine," *Arms Control Today* 36 (March 2006).

106. For details, see Cirincione and others, *Deadly Arsenals*, pp. 163–81, and references therein; see also Nuclear Threat Initiative, "Country Profiles."

107. Alastair Iain Johnston, "Prospects for Chinese Nuclear Force Modernization: Limited Deterrence versus Multilateral Arms Control," *China Quarterly* 146 (June 1996): 552–53.

108. "The Issue of Nuclear Weapons," in *China's National Defense*, Beijing, July 1998 (russia.shaps.hawaii.edu/security/china-defense-july1998.html).

109. Ibid.

110. For more on these points, see Center for Nonproliferation Studies, "China's Nuclear Doctrine" (cns.miis.edu/research/china/coxrep/doctrine.htm).

111. *China's Endeavors for Arms Control, Disarmament and Non-proliferation*, Beijing, September 2005.

112. Cited in Joseph Kahn and David Lague, "Chinese General Threatens Use of A-Bombs if U.S. Intrudes," *New York Times*, July 15, 2005.

113. "China Plays Down Nuclear Threat," *BBC News*, World Edition, July 16, 2005 (news.bbc.co.uk/2/hi/asia-pacific/4688471.stm).

114. Quotations from Pan Zhenqiang, "China Insistence on No-First-Use of Nuclear Weapons," *China Security* 1 (Autumn 2005): 5–9. General Pan is former director of the Institute for Strategic Studies of the National Defense University of the People's Liberation Army. Pan provides five reasons why China has chosen a no-first-use policy: (1) the only purpose of nuclear weapons is retaliation to nuclear attack, pending complete nuclear disarmament; (2) changing the no-first-use policy would threaten the strategic stability between China and the United States; (3) changing the no-first-use policy would deliver a "crushing blow" to international arms control and efforts to maintain peace and stability; (4) such a change would tarnish China's international image; and (5) such a change would threaten rather than stabilize cross-strait relations. For supporting views, see also the articles by Shen Dingli and Sun Xiangli in the same issue of *China Security*.

115. "Since the first day when it came into possession of nuclear weapons, the Chinese government has solemnly declared that it would not be the first to use such weapons at any time and in any circumstance." See *China's Endeavors for Arms Control*, sec. III.

116. For more details, see Cirincione and others, *Deadly Arsenals*, pp. 221–37, and references therein; see also Nuclear Threat Initiative, "Country Profiles."

117. See C. Raja Mohan, "No First Use of Nuclear Weapons," Pugwash Meeting 279, November 2002 (www.pugwash.org/reports/nw/rajamohan.htm).

118. *Draft Report of National Security Advisory Board on Indian Nuclear Doctrine*, August 17, 1999 (www.indianembassy.org/policy/CTBT/nuclear_doctrine_aug_17_1999.html), secs. 2.1, 2.3, and 2.4.

119. C. Raja Mohan, "Nuclear Command Authority Comes into Being," *Hindu*, January 5, 2003 (www.hinduonnet.com/2003/01/05/stories/2003010504810100.htm). For Indian views on India's options with respect to "weapons of mass destruction," see also Raja Menon, *A Nuclear Strategy for India* (New Delhi: SAGE, 2000); Raja Menon, ed., *Weapons of Mass Destruction: Options for India* (New Delhi: SAGE, 2004); and Delhi Policy Group, *Nuclear Weapons and Security* (New Delhi: Bibliophile South Asia, 2005).

120. Quoted in Cotta-Ramusino and Martellini, *Nuclear Safety, Nuclear Stability, and Nuclear Strategy in Pakistan*.

121. For more details, see Cirincione and others, *Deadly Arsenals*, pp. 239–58, and references therein; see also Nuclear Threat Initiative, "Country Profiles."

122. President General Pervez Musharraf, quoted in Rana Qaisar, "Pakistan Army Gets Hatf-V Missiles," *Lahore Daily Times*, January 9, 2003.

123. For a comprehensive review of what is known or inferred about Pakistan's nuclear doctrine, see Rifaat Hussain, "Nuclear Doctrines in South Asia," SASSU Research Report 4 (December 2005) (www.sassu.org.uk/publications/R_Hussain.pdf).

124. Abdul Sattar, speaking in Islamabad in Novermber 1999, quoted in Rifaat Hussain, "Nuclear Doctrines in South Asia," p. 13.

125. See, for example, Stephen P. Cohen, "India, Pakistan and Kashmir," *Journal of Strategic Studies* 25 (December 2002): 57.

126. General Khalid Kidwai, quoted by Cotta-Ramusino and Martellini, *Nuclear Safety, Nuclear Stability, and Nuclear Strategy in Pakistan*.

127. For histories of the Israeli nuclear weapons program, see Cohen, *Israel and the Bomb*; Seymour M. Hersh, *The Samson Option: Israel's Nuclear Arsenal and American Foreign Policy* (New York: Random House, 1991).

128. For these claims, see Cirincione and others, *Deadly Arsenals*, pp. 259–75. See also Warner D. Farr, "The Third Temple's Holy of Holies: Israel's Nuclear Weapons," Counterproliferation Paper 2 (U.S. Air Force Counterproliferation Center, September 1999); Nuclear Threat Initiative, "Country Profiles"; and remarks by C. F. Chyba in *The Comprehensive Test Ban Treaty: Next Steps*, CISAC-LAWS Roundtable Discussion (Stanford University, July 19, 2000), pp. 59–62.

129. Israel "must be in a position to threaten another Hiroshima to prevent another Holocaust." See Avner Cohen and Marvin Miller, *Nuclear Shadows in the Middle East: Prospects for Arms Control in the Wake of the Gulf Crisis* (Cambridge, Mass.: MIT Press, 1990), p. 18; see also Cirincione and others, *Deadly Arsenals*, pp. 268–69.

130. Quoted in Gerald Steinberg, "Middle East Peace and the NPT Extension Decision," *Nonproliferation Review* 4 (Fall 1996): 17–29.

131. Shimon Peres, quoted in "Before Meeting with King, Peres Claims Israel's Nuclear Arsenal Was Built for Peace," *Jordan Times*, July 14, 1998.

132. Suggested by Louis Rene Beres, "Israel's Bomb in the Basement: A Revisiting of 'Deliberate Ambiguity' vs. 'Disclosure,'" in *Between War and Peace: Dilemmas of Israeli Security*, edited by Efraim Karsh (London: Frank Cass, 1996), pp. 113–33.

133. See the discussion in Farr, "The Third Temple's Holy of Holies."

134. See Nuclear Threat Initiative, "Country Profiles."

135. Anthony Faiola and Philip P. Pan, "N. Korea Declaration Draws World Concern," *Washington Post*, February 11, 2005.

136. Braun and Chyba, "Proliferation Rings," p. 11; and "Joint Statement of the Fourth Round of the Six-Party Talks," Beijing, September 19, 2005 (www.state.gov/r/pa/prs/ps/2005/53490.htm).

137. Belarus, Kazakhstan, and Ukraine were left with nuclear weapons deployed on their territories after the breakup of the Soviet Union; these countries gave up their weapons and ratified or acceded to the NPT by 1993, 1994, and 1994, respectively. South Africa acceded to the NPT in 1991 and by 1994 had destroyed the six nuclear devices it had manufactured beginning in the late 1970s. See Cirincione and others, *Deadly Arsenals*, pp. 407ff.

138. See Sir Basil Henry Liddell Hart, *Strategy,* 2nd ed. rev. (London: Faber & Faber, 1967), pp. 319–21. See also *Department of Defense Dictionary of Military and Associated Terms,* Joint Publication 1-02, April 12, 2001 (as amended through 30 November 2004) (www.asafm.army.mil/pubs/jp1-02/jp1-02.pdf).

139. For a discussion of the role of the United States in establishing a norm of the non-use of nuclear weapons, see, for example, Nina Tannenwald, "The Nuclear Taboo: The United States and the Normative Basis of Nuclear Non-Use," *International Organization* 53 (Summer 1999): 433–68.

two
Deterrence, Preventive War, and Preemption

David Holloway

The Bush administration has made important changes in U.S. national security strategy and nuclear weapons policy. It withdrew from the Anti-Ballistic Missile (ABM) Treaty in December 2001, and in October 2004 it began to deploy a national missile defense system.[1] It has outlined possible new missions for nuclear weapons and taken steps to enhance U.S. readiness to resume nuclear testing. Besides these specific steps, the administration has issued a number of statements that appear to mark a significant shift in U.S. thinking about nuclear weapons.

The first such statement was the Nuclear Posture Review, which Secretary of Defense Donald H. Rumsfeld sent to Congress on December 31, 2001, in response to a long-standing congressional mandate. The review itself is classified, but detailed excerpts have been leaked to the public, making it possible to identify some of its main points.[2] The review focused on the need for a "broader array of capability . . . to dissuade states from undertaking political, military, or technical courses of action that would threaten U.S. and allied security."[3] New capabilities must be developed, it argued, to destroy hard and deeply buried targets, find and attack mobile and relocatable targets, defeat chemical or biological agents, and improve accuracy and limit collateral damage. The review also identified a number of contingencies, which, it said, the Department of Defense needed to take into account in setting requirements for nuclear weapons. It named seven countries that could, in certain contingencies, be targets for nuclear strikes by the United States: North Korea, Iraq, Iran, Syria, Libya, China, and Russia.[4]

Another statement, the National Security Strategy issued by President George W. Bush in September 2002, focused on the threat from nuclear, chemical, and biological weapons in the hands of terrorists and "rogue states," including states that support terrorists. In the cold war, it asserted, "deterrence was an effective defense. But deterrence based only upon the threat of retaliation is less likely to work against leaders of rogue states more willing to take risks, gambling with the lives of their people, and the wealth of their nations."[5] The 2002 National Security Strategy gave priority to preemption in dealing with rogue states and terrorists: "The greater the threat, the greater is the risk of inaction—and the more compelling the case for taking anticipatory action to defend ourselves, even if uncertainty remains as to the time and place of the enemy's attack."[6] The document stressed U.S. willingness to act on its own: "We will not hesitate to act alone, if necessary, to exercise our right of self-defense by acting preemptively against . . . terrorists, to prevent them from doing harm against our people and our country."[7]

The 2002 National Security Strategy also expressed the determination not to allow any other state to surpass or equal the military might of the United States: "Our forces will be strong enough to dissuade potential adversaries from pursuing a military build-up in hopes of surpassing, or equaling, the power of the United States."[8] The 2001 Nuclear Posture Review made reference to the same goal: "Systems capable of striking a wide range of targets throughout an adversary's territory may dissuade a potential adversary from pursuing threatening capabilities."[9] These documents put new emphasis on the concept of "dissuasion," the idea that the United States should maintain a military dominance so great that other states will refrain from even trying to catch up. U.S. policy during the cold war did not espouse this concept. Washington was certainly not happy when the Soviet Union built up its strategic nuclear forces, but from the late 1960s on it proclaimed its commitment to the principles of parity and equality in managing its relations with the Soviet Union.[10]

A third document, the National Strategy to Combat Weapons of Mass Destruction (NS-WMD), issued in December 2002, outlined a series of steps to strengthen nuclear nonproliferation, enhance counterproliferation, and improve "consequence management" measures in the event of an attack with biological, chemical, or nuclear weapons.[11] This report focused on terrorists seeking to acquire such weapons and on nations "that have supported and continue to support terrorism, already possess WMD and are seeking greater capabilities, as tools of coercion and intimidation."[12] The "counterproliferation efforts" it outlined included the possible preemptive use of military force. The report echoed earlier statements by the president when it asserted: "We will not permit the world's most dangerous regimes and terrorists to threaten us with the world's most destructive weapons."[13]

These statements are designed to provide guidance for U.S. nuclear policy. The administration has made other significant statements about nuclear policy (including a National Strategy for Combating Terrorism) and has proposed new measures—notably UN Security Council Resolution 1540 and the Proliferation Security Initiative—to deal with nuclear proliferation. Those are discussed elsewhere in this book. This chapter concentrates on the shift from deterrence to preemption in U.S. national security strategy. The administration reaffirmed that shift in March 2006 in a new version of the National Security Strategy, which asserted that "the place of preemption in our national security strategy remains the same."[14]

Preventive War and Preemption in the Cold War

Immediately after Hiroshima, the physicist Robert Oppenheimer claimed that nuclear weapons would give the advantage to the aggressor and thus encourage surprise attacks.[15] That was why he, along with many others, believed that international control of atomic energy—or even some form of world government—was essential if large-scale nuclear war was to be avoided. The international system that had given rise to World War I and World War II could not, in this view, cope with nuclear weapons.[16] Oppenheimer was the principal intellectual force behind the U.S. government's Acheson–Lilienthal Report, which proposed a plan for bringing atomic energy under international control.[17]

In 1946 the United States and the Soviet Union, along with a number of other countries, began negotiations, under the auspices of the United Nations, on the international control of atomic energy. The Baruch Plan put forward by the United States was a modification of the Acheson–Lilienthal Report. It followed the report in proposing that all "dangerous" nuclear activities (that is, those capable of leading to the making of nuclear bombs) be controlled by an international agency under the jurisdiction of the UN Security Council.[18] The two new elements in the Baruch Plan were, first, that the permanent members of the Security Council would have to give up the right of veto in this area and, second, that any state that broke the agreement would be liable to punishment. In addition, the Soviet Union would have had to agree to an inspection system that could operate in the Soviet Union or the United States without veto before the United States gave up its nuclear weapons.[19] Joseph Stalin was determined, however, to match the United States by developing a bomb of his own, and the Soviet Union rejected the Baruch Plan in 1946. It tested its first atomic bomb in August 1949, several years before the Central Intelligence Agency predicted it would do so.[20]

The United States had to face a nuclear-armed Soviet Union sooner than expected. What was it to do? The talks on international control had failed. One option was a war to prevent the Soviet Union from building up a large nuclear force. Some political figures—including Winston Churchill and Bertrand Russell—had advocated a preventive war against the Soviet Union while the United States still had a monopoly on nuclear weapons. That option did not disappear with the Soviet atomic bomb test, because the United States still had enormous superiority in nuclear weapons, especially in the means to deliver them to target. In the early 1950s—and certainly in 1952–55—U.S. military planners thought they had enough weapons to defeat the Soviet Union quickly and to destroy its military power. The Soviet Union, on the other hand, could not deliver nuclear strikes against the United States, though it did have some capability to strike U.S. bases and allies in Western Europe. Preventive war seemed to some senior U.S. military officers to be a realistic option.[21]

President Dwight D. Eisenhower raised the possibility of preventive war in a memorandum to his secretary of state, John Foster Dulles. Fearing that an intense and costly arms race could lead either to war or to some form of dictatorship in the United States, he wondered whether it might not be right for the United States "to *initiate* war at the most propitious moment."[22] Eisenhower seems to have been thinking out loud in this memorandum—something he often did—and does not appear ever to have considered preventive war to be a serious option. He rejected it outright in a press conference in 1954:

A preventive war, to my mind, is an impossibility today. How could you have one if one of its features would be several cities lying in ruins, several cities where many, many thousands of people would be dead and injured and mangled, the transportation systems destroyed, sanitation instruments and systems all gone? That isn't preventive war; that *is* war.

I don't believe there is such a thing; and, frankly, I wouldn't even listen to anyone seriously that came in and talked about such a thing.[23]

When a reporter shrewdly asked him whether he opposed preventive war for military reasons alone, he replied: "There are all sorts of reasons, moral and political and everything else, against this theory, but it is so completely unthinkable in today's conditions that I thought it is no use to go any further."[24] These statements indicate that deterrence was, in some sense, a choice of the United States.

Discussions of the 1950s drew a clear distinction in principle between *preventive war* and *preemption*.[25] Preventive war is war initiated by one side at a time of greatest advantage to itself, in order to prevent the emergence of a particular threat or to forestall war at a less advantageous time. A preemptive strike is undertaken when one side believes that war is imminent, that the enemy is about to attack, and strikes first in order to lessen the damage that an enemy first strike could do. Preventive war ceased to be a serious option for the United States once the Soviet Union began to acquire the capacity to retaliate against the United States. But the United States and the Soviet Union developed military strategies of nuclear preemption in the 1950s, in the belief that, if war were inevitable, it would be best to strike first in order to destroy as many of the enemy's forces as possible before it could launch its attack.[26] The incentives for preemption differed in the two cases. If the United States struck first, it had a good chance of destroying all or most of the Soviet strategic nuclear forces, thereby reducing the damage to the United States.[27] If the Soviet Union struck first, it could blunt an American nuclear strike by attacking U.S. air bases in Europe, North Africa, and Asia; if it did not strike first, it ran the risk of losing all or most of its strategic nuclear forces before they got off the ground.

This is not to suggest that preemption would have been a simple strategy to implement. It offered the advantages that would follow from striking the first blow, but it also ran the risk, in the event of faulty intelligence, of starting an unnecessary catastrophic war. Reliable warning of an impending attack is crucial for a strategy of preemption, but the activities that would provide the best evidence—enemy preparations for war, for example—might also reduce the effectiveness of a first strike. As the Soviet Union acquired large strategic nuclear forces in the 1960s, and with them the capacity to retaliate in the event of a first strike by the United States, the incentives for preemption were reduced on both sides. The United States could not hope to escape retaliation even if it struck first, while the Soviet Union did not have to strike first in order to avoid having most of its strategic forces destroyed.

Further insight into American thinking about preventive war comes from U.S. policy toward China in the 1960s. Some members of the Kennedy administration, including the president, were extremely worried about the prospect of China's acquiring nuclear weapons. According to McGeorge Bundy, President John F. Kennedy's national security adviser, Kennedy thought in January 1963 that the possibility that China would get nuclear weapons was "probably the most serious problem facing the world today." Kennedy was "of a mind," according to Bundy, "that nuclear weapons in the hands of the Chinese Communists would so upset the world political scene it would be intolerable to the United States and to the West."[28] There was discussion in the Kennedy and Johnson administrations of preventive military action against China in order to "strangle the baby in the cradle."[29]

In July 1963 Kennedy authorized W. Averell Harriman, who was heading the U.S. delegation at the negotiations in Moscow on the Limited Test Ban Treaty, to raise with Nikita Khrushchev the question of Chinese nuclear weapons. As soon as Harriman mentioned the prospect of China's becoming a nuclear power, Khrushchev dismissed the issue, saying (according to the U.S. minutes of the meeting):

> USSR had common basic concepts with China. *If sometimes irresponsible or militant statements were made, that was only natural because whenever someone lacked means he was one who shouted loudest. On the other hand, when one possessed means he was more restrained because he knew that his adversary was aware of what he had for defense and even for attack.* (Gromyko interjected that attack should be understood as retaliation, and Khrushchev agreed he had meant attack in return for aggression.)[30] (Emphasis added)

In the event, of course, the United States did not launch a preventive strike against China. China tested its first atomic bomb in October 1964 and eventually established forces designed to provide a retaliatory capability against both the Soviet Union and the United States. Khrushchev's prediction proved to be correct in this case. In time China signed a series of arms control agreements, including the Nuclear Non-Proliferation Treaty (NPT).[31]

Deterrence in the Cold War

The first formulations of nuclear deterrence in the United States were a response to Oppenheimer's claim that the atomic bomb would make war more likely. The economist Jacob Viner and political scientist Bernard Brodie argued that an aggressor fearing retaliation in kind would not attack. Nuclear weapons, rather than encouraging war, could help to deter it and thus make peace more secure.[32] When Eisenhower ruled out preventive war, he made the judgment that deterrence would work. He believed the United States could live with a nuclear Soviet Union and deter Soviet aggression with the help of nuclear weapons. This belief rested on his view of the Soviet leaders. He did not like them, of course, but thought that they wanted to hold on to their power and were therefore not eager for war. He did not regard them as "early Christian martyrs" who wished to die for their cause.[33] In his mind, they understood that a nuclear war would be so destructive as to make victory in such a war essentially meaningless. The United States therefore had to be ready for competition with the Soviet Union "over the long pull."[34]

The basic idea of nuclear deterrence—that the enemy will be deterred from launching a nuclear strike by the threat of retaliation in kind—is a simple one, but it was not easy to translate into practice during the cold war. The United States adopted many variants of the policy of nuclear deterrence—"massive retaliation," "flexible response," "limited strategic options," "countervailing strategy," and so on—in the effort to maintain the credibility of its deterrent threats.[35] The threat to retaliate in the event of a strike against one's homeland is relatively straightforward, but the policy of extended deterrence in Europe, where the North Atlantic Treaty Organization (NATO) faced the superior conventional forces of the Warsaw Pact, posed a serious problem of credibility. How could the threat to use nuclear weapons in response to a conventional attack by the Warsaw Pact be made credible, when the use of nuclear weapons by NATO would be likely, in turn, to meet a nuclear response from the Soviet Union? Many Europeans were fearful that the United States *would not* be willing to risk a Soviet nuclear strike against an American city in order to defend Western Europe; and many were equally fearful that the Americans *would* be willing to use nuclear weapons, thereby causing death and destruction in Central Europe. The problem of extended deterrence was the source of much anxiety and debate in the Atlantic Alliance from the 1940s to the 1980s. What forces and what doctrine were needed to deter the Soviet Union in Europe? And what forces and what doctrine were needed to reassure U.S. allies? The problem of extended deterrence for Europe provided much of the driving force behind the development of deterrence theory in the United States.

Although deterrence was the primary purpose of nuclear policy, the United States engaged in constant planning for nuclear war with the aim of prevailing if such a conflict did take place. The purpose of war planning was not only to ensure that the United States would be able to inflict unacceptable damage on the Soviet Union in a retaliatory strike. Nuclear strikes were planned against a range of different targets and designed to destroy the enemy's forces as well as the military and economic infrastructure that would enable it to wage war.[36] For many analysts, these war plans contradicted the emphasis on deterrence, because their ultimate goal was to find a way to be able to prevail in a nuclear war, and the drive to achieve this goal would, it was feared, either destabilize the deterrent relationship or result in an arms race as the Soviet Union responded. For others, the deterrent power of U.S. forces was enhanced by such plans and the preparations they entailed, because only if the Soviet leaders understood that they could not win a nuclear war would they be deterred from aggression.[37] The arguments between these two schools of thought continued in the United States throughout the cold war. The accumulation of nuclear weapons by the United States and the Soviet Union made it clear to everyone in these debates, however, that the side that "prevailed" in a nuclear war could not avoid itself suffering destruction on an immense scale.

It would be wrong to idealize, in retrospect, the stability of the U.S.-Soviet strategic nuclear balance. The risk of war never vanished entirely, and anxiety about the danger of war was sometimes acute, not only in the late 1950s and early 1960s, during the Berlin and Cuban crises, but in the early 1980s too—during the political crisis surrounding medium-range missiles in Europe.[38] In the most dangerous crisis of all, the United States came close to attacking Soviet forces and invading Cuba in order to prevent the deployment of Soviet missiles on the island. After intensive discussion, President Kennedy decided to impose a naval blockade rather than resort to an air strike as the first option. But if Khrushchev had not agreed to withdraw the missiles from Cuba in return for an American commitment not to invade the island, it is possible that Kennedy would have launched air strikes against Soviet missile installations in Cuba and mounted an invasion of the island.[39] Fortunately, we do not know what the consequences would have been, but those actions could have led, as both Kennedy and Khrushchev feared, to nuclear war.

The United States and the Soviet Union developed and deployed their nuclear forces in conditions of intense political rivalry, but political leaders in both countries understood, from the mid-1950s on, that all-out war would be a mutual catastrophe.[40] Especially after the Cuban missile crisis, which had brought the world close to nuclear war, the United States sought to stabilize its nuclear relationship with the Soviet Union and thereby reduce the risk of war. Arms control became one of the primary mechanisms for pursuing that goal. Difficult and frustrating though it was, the arms control process created a fabric of treaties and agreements that provided the context for managing relations among the nuclear powers and slowing the spread of nuclear weapons. Bilateral negotiations between the two superpowers produced a number of treaties, the most important being the Anti-Ballistic Missile (ABM) Treaty of 1972 and the various agreements reached in the Strategic Arms Limitation Talks (SALT) and Strategic Arms Reduction Treaty (START) negotiations. Multilateral negotiations, in which the United States and the Soviet Union inevitably played important roles, resulted in important agreements such as the Limited Test Ban Treaty of 1963 and the Nuclear Non-Proliferation Treaty of 1968.[41]

By the mid-1960s the United States was locked into a relationship of mutual deterrence with the Soviet Union. Yet mutual vulnerability to devastating nuclear strikes did not appeal to everyone as the basis for security. One potential alternative to deterrence was defense against nuclear attack. The United States and the Soviet Union devoted considerable effort to the creation of such defenses. Both deployed air defenses in the 1940s and 1950s and, on a more limited scale, ballistic missile defenses in the following decade. The 1972 ABM Treaty, however, severely limited the deployment of ballistic missile defenses on both sides. Each side came to the realization that such defenses would be immensely costly as well as ineffective against an opponent who could adopt countermeasures in order to penetrate or overcome the defense. Complete defense against ballistic missile attack proved to be impossible during the cold war; missile defense could not provide an alternative to reliance on deterrence. Nevertheless, the desire to escape from deterrence remained powerful. Part of the popular appeal of President Ronald Reagan's Strategic Defense Initiative stemmed from the promise—illusory though it was—to offer an escape from the relationship of mutual deterrence with the Soviet Union.

During the cold war, the United States had several options to choose from in facing the challenge of nuclear weapons: disarmament, preventive war, defenses, and deterrence, as well as the incorporation of nuclear weapons into military strategy. The early attempt at disarmament through international control of atomic energy failed. Presidents Harry S. Truman and Dwight Eisenhower both rejected the option of preventive war against the Soviet Union, while later administrations decided not to use military force to prevent China from building the bomb. The ABM Treaty severely constrained ballistic missile defenses when it was realized that such defenses would be costly, ineffective, and potentially destabilizing. The preventive war option disappeared as the Soviet Union and China built up their strategic nuclear forces. The growth of nuclear stockpiles created a situation in which nuclear war would be catastrophic for all the countries involved, thereby making the search for an effective military strategy with nuclear weapons increasingly futile. Once these other options were foreclosed, the United States inevitably became involved in managing relationships of mutual deterrence with the Soviet Union and China. Arms control was an important part of that policy.

Given the destructive power of nuclear weapons and the impossibility of effective defense against ballistic missiles, deterrence is probably the only possible policy option when each side in a hostile relationship has substantial nuclear forces. There is, however, a period in the establishment of deterrent relationships when one side may have the option of taking action to prevent the other side from going nuclear. American presidents at least considered that possibility in relation to both the Soviet Union and China; and Kennedy came close to taking such action in order to prevent the deployment of Soviet missiles on Cuba.[42] But the preventive use of force in these cases was fraught with risk and would have been very difficult to carry out. Before 2003 the only case in which a state took military action to prevent another state from acquiring nuclear weapons was the Israeli attack on the Iraqi Osirak reactor in 1981.

The Spread of Nuclear Weapons

In 1946 the U.S. Congress adopted the Atomic Energy Act, which prohibited the United States from giving nuclear weapons, information on how to build them, or information on the "technical uses of atomic energy" to any other country.[43] This did not prevent other countries from building the bomb. In 1949 the Soviet Union detonated a copy of the first American plutonium design. Britain, which had been a junior partner in the Manhattan Project, tested its own version of the American plutonium design in 1952. France tested its first explosive device in 1960, and in 1964 China, which had received considerable help from the Soviet Union, followed suit.

In December 1953 President Eisenhower made a major change in U.S. policy. In his "Atoms for Peace" speech to the UN General Assembly he promised to encourage the development and spread of atomic energy for peaceful purposes.[44] Scientists and engineers—but apparently not the president—understood that a peaceful nuclear program could provide industrial infrastructure, as well as technical education and experience, that would be useful in making nuclear weapons. Eisenhower, however, hoped that cooperation in the peaceful uses of atomic energy would help to dampen the nuclear arms race.[45] The U.S. Atomic Energy Act was amended to allow the United States to give assistance to peaceful programs, and the Atoms for Peace plan was put into effect. The Soviet Union, which had responded to the initial proposal with skepticism bordering on incredulity, started its own program to help socialist countries develop nuclear power for peaceful purposes.[46] The International Atomic Energy Agency (IAEA) was established in 1957 to monitor peaceful nuclear programs and to ensure that they were not converted to the making of weapons.

In the mid-1960s the United States and the Soviet Union came to understand that they had a common interest in preventing more states from acquiring nuclear weapons. The Chinese test focused Washington's attention on the issue; Moscow was especially concerned that West Germany might acquire nuclear weapons.[47] In 1968 the two countries signed the Nuclear Non-Proliferation Treaty along with Britain (and many other countries), but France and China did not. The treaty committed the five existing nuclear weapons states to pursue nuclear disarmament, while the other signatories promised not to acquire nuclear weapons. Since 1968, 189 states have signed the treaty. India, Israel, and Pakistan, which possess nuclear weapons but are not recognized in the treaty as "nuclear weapons states," are the only relevant states not to have signed. North Korea withdrew from the treaty in 2003.

The NPT has been the cornerstone of the nuclear nonproliferation regime, providing a framework in which individual states could decide not to acquire nuclear weapons, in the expectation that other states would also forgo those weapons and that the nuclear weapons states would work toward disarmament. By one estimate, in the 1960s twenty-three states had nuclear weapons, were doing weapons-related research, or were discussing the pursuit of nuclear weapons; in 2005 only ten states fell into those categories.[48] Four states have given up nuclear weapons they already possessed: in 1991–92 South Africa dismantled the small number of weapons it had built, and in 1993–94 Belarus, Kazakhstan, and Ukraine transferred to Russia the Soviet nuclear warheads that had been left on their territory when the Soviet Union ceased to exist. To that extent the treaty has been a success. As explained in chapter 1, there are today eight nuclear weapons states: the five named in the treaty, as well as India, Israel, and Pakistan; North Korea may also have nuclear weapons. This is a smaller number than most analysts forecast four decades ago; it is also eight or nine more states than the advocates of international control hoped for in the immediate years after World War II.

Whatever success it may have had in the past, the nonproliferation regime faces grave challenges today. The NPT can be understood as a set of bargains, and each of these is under strain. The central bargain is that non-nuclear states agree to forgo nuclear weapons as long as the nuclear weapons states work for disarmament. The non-nuclear weapons states have severely criticized the nuclear weapons states for failing to live up to their commitments under the treaty. This has raised the prospect that the consensus underlying the treaty will be weakened unless the nuclear weapons states redouble their efforts to meet their commitment under Article VI of the treaty to pursue nuclear disarmament. This is an important issue. It will be easier to strengthen the existing regime if there is agreement that the system is working or has a chance of working. The consensus on nonproliferation did not come into existence at a stroke when the NPT was signed. It took many years to achieve the almost universal acceptance of the treaty. It will surely complicate the effort to stop the spread of nuclear weapons if the norm of nonproliferation is undermined by the failure of the nuclear weapons states to do all they can to carry out their obligations under Article VI. The failure of the NPT Review Conference of May 2005 to reach agreement on substantive steps to strengthen the nonproliferation regime is highly regrettable.[49]

The second bargain in the treaty is that non-nuclear weapons states agree to forgo nuclear weapons in return for help in developing nuclear energy for peaceful purposes. It has become clear in recent years, however, that the relationship between nuclear weapons development and peaceful nuclear programs needs to be rethought. Under the current regime, it is possible for states to get to the brink of a nuclear weapons capability without violating the NPT. A number of states—Japan is one—could move quickly to develop a substantial nuclear force.[50] This makes it difficult to monitor nuclear activities and to determine with certainty when clandestine nuclear weapons development is taking place. A new approach is needed to strengthen the barriers between peaceful nuclear programs and nuclear weapons development. In 1997 the IAEA introduced the Additional Protocol, which supplements safeguards agreements between the IAEA and its member states in order to strengthen NPT verification. By March 2006, seventy-five countries had such agreements in force and a further thirty-three had signed the Additional Protocol but had not yet taken the additional steps necessary to bring it into force.[51] And in a move that recalls the Acheson-Lilienthal Report, which recommended that "dangerous activities" be controlled by an international agency, an international committee of experts has proposed to the IAEA that elements of the nuclear fuel cycle be put under international control.[52] If progress could be made in strengthening safeguards and internationalizing the fuel cycle, that would enhance the barriers between nuclear power programs and nuclear weapons development, thereby strengthening the non-proliferation regime.

The third bargain in the treaty is that non-nuclear weapons states agree to forgo nuclear weapons as long as other non-nuclear weapons states agree not to acquire nuclear weapons. This bargain too is under strain. If non-nuclear states were to conclude that the nonproliferation regime was unraveling, they might decide to acquire nuclear weapons of their own, for their own security. In February 2003, George Tenet, then head of the Central Intelligence Agency, warned:

> We have entered a *new world of proliferation*. In the vanguard of this new world are knowledgeable non-state purveyors of WMD materials and technology.... This is taking place side by side with the continuing weakening of the international nonproliferation consensus. Control regimes, like the Non-Proliferation Treaty, are being battered by developments such as North Korea's withdrawal from the NPT and its open repudiation of other agreements.[53]

Tenet argued that North Korea's nuclear program, combined with the weakening of international controls, would encourage other states to follow suit. Many observers believe that North Korean nuclear weapons could provoke South Korea, Japan, and perhaps Taiwan into making nuclear weapons of their own. Similarly, Iranian nuclear weapons might stimulate Saudi Arabia, Egypt, and Syria to build nuclear weapons. Many states in the world have the capacity to build nuclear weapons. If those states concluded that nuclear weapons were necessary for their security, the number of nuclear weapons states could increase rapidly. In Tenet's words, "the 'domino theory' of the 21st century may well be nuclear."[54]

To date, three nuclear weapons states have not signed the NPT and under its terms are not permitted to do so unless they give up their nuclear weapons. India and Pakistan have conducted nuclear weapons tests; Israel may have done so too but has never officially acknowledged that it has nuclear weapons.[55] The United States tried to dissuade India and Pakistan from testing nuclear weapons, and the Clinton administration imposed sanctions on the two countries when they nevertheless conducted tests in May 1998. In an effort to persuade India to give up its nuclear ambitions, the Clinton administration initiated a strategic dialogue with India. The ironic result is that the United States now wants to recognize India as a nuclear weapons state.[56] In July 2005 President Bush called India "a responsible state with advanced nuclear technology" and declared that it should acquire the same benefits and advantages as other such states, that is, the five nuclear weapons states named in the NPT.[57] In March 2006 the two countries agreed to civil nuclear cooperation and to the placing of some Indian nuclear facilities under IAEA safeguards.

The U.S. nuclear relationship with Pakistan is more complicated. Pakistan is an important ally of the United States in the struggle against the Taliban and al Qaeda, even though it has strong Islamist groups that may at some point present a threat to the country's political stability. Pakistan is the home of A. Q. Khan's institute, which has exported nuclear technologies to states with clandestine nuclear programs. The United States has tried to make Pakistan stop this dangerous trade and to maintain strict control over its nuclear weapons.[58] Pakistan would like to have the kind of agreement with the United States that India has concluded, but President Bush has rejected that idea. In the case of Israel, the United States has turned a blind eye to its possession of nuclear weapons—a policy made easier by Israel's refusal to make any statements about its nuclear weapons status.

In addition, several states that signed the NPT nonetheless organized clandestine nuclear weapons programs. Iraq, North Korea, Libya, and probably Iran fall into this category. The history of their nuclear programs has exposed serious weaknesses in the nonproliferation regime. First, it can be difficult to monitor what states are actually doing. For example, discoveries made in 1991, after the Gulf War, showed that the Iraqi nuclear program was more advanced than had been thought and prompted the IAEA to strengthen the safeguards regime by means of the Additional Protocol. Second, the treaty itself has structural flaws. A state can withdraw from the treaty, for example, after giving three months' notice, provided the UN Security Council, to which notice has to be given, takes no action to prevent withdrawal, and the other parties, who also have to be notified, do not persuade it to stay. Or, to take another example, a state can move to the brink of nuclear weapons capability, thereby giving itself the option to develop nuclear weapons quickly if it should decide to do so, without violating the treaty. Third, the international community lacks agreed mechanisms for effectively enforcing the commitments made by the signatories to the NPT. The crises over the North Korean and Iranian nuclear programs have shown the need for a more transparent regime, for clearer and stronger barriers between the peaceful and the military uses of nuclear technology, and for more effective mechanisms for ensuring compliance with the treaty.

There is also a growing danger that nonstate actors might acquire either nuclear weapons or the nuclear materials from which to make a bomb. This presents an urgent and complex problem for the nonproliferation regime, which, after all, was created to prevent the spread of nuclear weapons to *states*. This problem has existed for years, but recent developments have made it more serious. The breakup of the Soviet Union and the consequent deterioration in security in its nuclear complex increased the risk that terrorists would be able to get their hands on nuclear weapons or nuclear materials. The attacks of September 11, 2001, showed that terrorist groups were now willing to inflict mass casualties, and subsequent evidence of al Qaeda's nuclear ambitions suggests that its members hope to be able to kill on a still larger scale.[59] The combination of these two factors—increased supply and increased demand—has made the nuclear threat from terrorist groups much more salient than before.

Deterrence and Preventive Force in the Bush Administration's Policy

In responding to this new situation, the Bush administration moved preemption to the fore of its thinking, in place of deterrence. The 2002 National Security Strategy argued that the "grim strategy of mutual assured destruction" should not be applied either to "rogue states" or to terrorists seeking weapons of mass destruction:

> None of these contemporary threats rival the sheer destructive power that was arrayed against us by the Soviet Union. However, the nature and motivations of these new adversaries, their determination to obtain destructive powers hitherto available only to the world's strongest states, and the greater likelihood that they will use weapons of mass destruction against us, make today's security environment more complex and dangerous.[60]

The 2002 National Security Strategy called for "preemption" not only against terrorists but also against "rogue states," which "are determined to acquire weapons of mass destruction" and show "no regard for international law, and callously violate international treaties. . . . We must be prepared to stop rogue states and their terrorist clients before they are able to threaten or use weapons of mass destruction."[61] The doctrine did not distinguish between rogue states such as Iraq, Iran, and North Korea—members of President Bush's "axis of evil"—and terrorist groups or networks such as al Qaeda.[62]

What the Bush administration means by preemption is something akin to what was meant by "preventive war" in the debates of the 1950s. As the following quotation indicates, the 2002 National Security Strategy recognizes that it is stretching the original meaning of preemption to meet a new situation:[63]

> We must adapt the concept of *imminent threat* to the capabilities and objectives of today's adversaries. . . . The greater the threat, the greater is the risk of inaction—and the more compelling the case for taking anticipatory action to defend ourselves, even if uncertainty remains as to the time and place of the enemy's attack. . . . The U.S. will not use force in all cases to preempt *emerging threats*, nor should nations use preemption as a pretext for aggression. Yet in an age where the enemies of civilization openly and actively seek the world's most destructive technologies, the U.S. cannot remain idle while dangers gather. (Emphasis added)

In this expanded meaning, preemption applies not only to *imminent* but also to *emergent* threats. War against emergent threats has traditionally been described as "preventive war," which is prohibited by international law. Preemption, on the other hand, is permissible under certain conditions: if the threat is imminent, if no other means are available to deal with it, and if the preemptive action is proportionate to the threat.[64] The Bush administration argues that the concept of preemption must be stretched to include emergent threats of the kind that the United States now faces, and that preemption defined in this way is part of the country's right of self-defense.

In the administration's view, certain states—rogue states—must not be allowed to acquire nuclear weapons. This is not a new claim for an American administration. "Preventive war" thinking was an important part of U.S. policy during the cold war, and in 1994 the Clinton administration almost went to war with North Korea in order to prevent it from developing a nuclear force, which would have presented "intolerable risks." Severe economic restrictions were to be imposed on North Korea, but it was feared that those sanctions would provoke an attack by North Korea on South Korea. President Clinton had three deployment options, each of which aimed to make U.S. forces in and around Korea "ready to defeat a North Korean attack, if that became the only way we could block the North Koreans from getting a nuclear arsenal."[65] War was avoided only because former president Jimmy Carter obtained Kim Il Sung's agreement to freeze North Korean nuclear activities at Yongbyon and to engage in negotiations about the North Korean nuclear program.

The term "rogue state" became current in the 1990s to denote states that the United States regarded as flouting international law and posing a threat to international peace and security. The Bush administration's use of the term points to a subtle but important shift in Washington's approach to nuclear proliferation. The Clinton administration, like previous administrations, stressed the threat that would come from the spread of nuclear weapons. The Bush administration, by contrast, has emphasized the threat from "outlaw regimes that seek and possess nuclear, chemical, and biological weapons." In other words, the threat arises not so much from the weapons themselves as from the character of the states that possess them or are trying to acquire them. The distinction is not absolute, because U.S. administrations have always differentiated among governments and regimes in this manner, but the shift in emphasis is clear, as signaled by the Bush administration's acceptance of India in 2005 as a "responsible" nuclear weapons state. The president's second Inaugural Address echoed this concern about the character of states, the type of regime they have, in assessing threats to national security: "The survival of liberty in our land increasingly depends on the success of liberty in other lands."[66] Precisely because the Bush administration believes that U.S. national security depends heavily on the character of the states that make up the international system, it sees regime change and the spread of democracy as important instruments for making the world a safer place. This assessment extends to judgments about nuclear threats.

As mentioned above, the Bush administration claims that the United States has the right to use military force to prevent rogue states from acquiring nuclear weapons. Moreover, it claims it does not have to wait until those states begin to make preparations to attack the United States or its allies—circumstances that would fit the traditional definition of preemption. It claims the right to prevent those states from acquiring the weapons in the first place. This is clear from Bush's March 17, 2003, address to the nation, on the eve of the war against Iraq:

> We are now acting because the risks of inaction would be far greater. In one year, or five years, the power of Iraq to inflict harm on all free nations would be multiplied many times over. With these capabilities, Saddam Hussein and his terrorist allies could choose the moment of deadly conflict when they are strongest. We choose to meet that threat now, where it arises, before it can appear suddenly in our skies and cities.[67]

This reads like a classic definition of preventive war.

The war against Iraq was a preventive war rather than a preemptive action, in the traditional meaning of those terms. Two of the criteria for distinguishing between preventive and preemptive action are especially relevant here. First, Iraq did not pose an imminent threat to the United States or its allies; there was no evidence that Iraq was about to attack. Even in the prewar intelligence assessments, Iraq was said to be years away from having nuclear weapons, unless it managed to acquire fissile material from another source; and even then it would have taken months to make nuclear weapons.[68] We now know that the prewar assessments were mistaken, that they greatly overstated Iraqi progress in the development of nuclear weapons (as well as the stockpiles of chemical and biological weapons held by Iraq). Second, the United States did not take military action as a last resort: the UN Inspection Commission (UNMOVIC) was still working in Iraq and had to be withdrawn to allow military operations to begin. Most members of the Security Council wanted the commission to continue its work and opposed the use of force before the commission had completed its mission.

The Legality and Legitimacy of Preventive Force

The Bush administration claims that it has the right not only to use force to prevent certain states from acquiring nuclear weapons but also to do so unilaterally if need be, without the sanction of the UN Security Council. In 2003 it sought the explicit approval of the UN Security Council for military action against Iraq, but when that approval was not forthcoming, it took military action against Iraq in coalition with a number of other states, claiming that previous Security Council resolutions gave it the authority to do so.[69] That decision sparked enormous controversy in the United States and around the world about the legality and the legitimacy of the war against Iraq.

The Bush administration has argued that in the face of terrorist threats or threats from rogue states it would be suicidal to wait until the threat materializes. States must have the right to take preventive action, unilaterally if need be, in order to deal with emergent, and not only imminent, threats. Preventive force might range from air strikes against particular installations (as in the case of the Israeli strike against the Iraqi Osirak reactor) to a war designed to replace a political regime (as in the U.S. war on Iraq). Critics of the administration have countered that, except in the case of self-defense in response to an actual or imminent attack, explicit authorization by the UN Security Council is required to make the use of force legitimate. The Security Council has the authority, under Chapter VII of the UN Charter, to decide on military action, including the use of preventive force, against a state when it deems this "necessary to maintain or restore international peace and security." No state should use preventive force without Security Council authorization.[70]

Two issues merit consideration here: the need for preventive force and the authorization of such force. On the first point, a number of states believe that the security threats they now face require preventive action, including possibly the use of force. The UN High-Level Panel on Threats, Challenges and Change noted in December 2004: "In the world of the twenty-first century, the international community does have to be concerned about nightmare scenarios combining terrorists, weapons of mass destruction and irresponsible States, and much more besides, which may conceivably justify the use of force, not just reactively but preventively and before a latent threat becomes imminent."[71] Several governments have indicated that they are ready to take preventive military action if faced with threats of this kind.[72]

There is much less agreement on the second point, with the Bush administration arguing for the right of unilateral action, and its critics, including the UN High-Level Panel, reserving to the UN Security Council the right to authorize preventive force. The administration's stance would make it acceptable *in principle* for any state to undertake preventive military action against what it regarded as a future threat, thereby relaxing whatever moral and legal restraints exist on the use of force and devaluing the role of diplomacy in dealing with such threats.[73] The UN High-Level Panel has countered that "in a world full of perceived potential threats, the risk to the global order and the norm of non-intervention on which it continues to be based is simply too great for the legality of unilateral preventive action, as distinct from collectively endorsed action, to be accepted. Allowing one to so act is to allow all."[74] From the point of view of world order, this is certainly the desirable position. The question is, will individual states find it acceptable if the UN Security Council proves to be unresponsive to their security needs? According to the High-Level Panel, if the Security Council were to refuse to authorize preventive military action in a particular case, there would still (by definition) be time to pursue other strategies for dealing with the threat and to reconsider the military option. That is true, but would states—especially the most powerful states—be willing to let the Security Council prevent them from acting if they believed their vital national security interests were at stake? The report of the High-Level Panel appears to recognize this problem, because the provision for reconsidering the military option, after the Security Council has refused to authorize it, fails to specify who is supposed to reconsider the issue:

it could be either the Security Council or the individual state, alone or in partnership with one or more other states, as in the U.S. invasion of Iraq.[75]

In the 1990s an analogous situation arose with respect to humanitarian intervention. NATO decided in 1999 that it could not stand by in the face of a possible humanitarian disaster in Kosovo and launched a military attack on Serbia in defense of the Kosovar Albanians. The UN Security Council did not authorize NATO's operation, and some major powers—notably Russia—were opposed to it. Nevertheless, the Independent International Commission on Kosovo, an unofficial committee set up in 1999 at the initiative of Sweden's prime minister, concluded, in a widely quoted judgment, that NATO's operation was "illegal but legitimate."[76] It was illegal "because it did not receive prior approval from the United Nations Security Council. . . . [It] was justified because all diplomatic avenues had been exhausted and because the intervention had the effect of liberating the majority population of Kosovo from a long period of oppression under Serbian rule."[77] Legitimacy is greatest when it coincides with legality. The chief legitimacy available for the exercise of military power today is the sanction provided by the UN Security Council. But the implication of the report on Kosovo is that the degree of legitimacy in preventive military intervention not sanctioned by the Security Council will be determined by such factors as the seriousness of the threat it is designed to prevent, the degree to which the action is multilateral, the "disinterestedness" of the states taking part, and the extent to which the force used is necessary and proportionate. In other words, it may be possible to generate some kind of legitimacy for collective preventive military action even if there is no mandate from the UN Security Council. The Bush administration's emphasis on the fact that it is fighting as part of a coalition can be seen as an effort to enhance the legitimacy of the war in Iraq.

The Kosovo intervention sparked widespread discussion about the circumstances under which the international community would be justified in intervening forcibly in a sovereign state for humanitarian reasons. The International Commission on Intervention and State Sovereignty, which was established by the Canadian government in 2000, argued in its 2001 report, *The Responsibility to Protect*, that changes in international law had altered the meaning of sovereignty from control over territory to state responsibility, including responsibility to the international community as well as the state's own citizens.[78] This doctrine implies that states enjoy sovereignty only to the extent to which they conduct themselves responsibly and are therefore liable to intervention if, for example, they violate in an egregious manner the human rights of their citizens. This doctrine does not provide a clear basis for legitimate intervention apart from a mandate from the UN Security Council.[79] But the Security Council is a cumbersome body, and the veto possessed by the permanent members often makes collective action impossible. The discussion of legality and legitimacy in recent years is symptomatic of the search for sources of legitimate authority, other than Security Council sanction, for collective military action to prevent humanitarian catastrophes.[80]

The spread of nuclear weapons and nuclear technology raises a similar question: under what circumstances is it legitimate to use military force to prevent a state from acquiring nuclear weapons? The Bush administration removed sanctions imposed on India and Pakistan despite their tests of nuclear weapons in 1998, and it has recognized India as a "responsible" nuclear weapons state; moreover, it shows no signs of putting pressure on Israel to give up its nuclear weapons. On the other hand, President Bush has said: "The United States of America will not permit the world's most dangerous regimes to threaten us with the world's most destructive weapons."[81] Hence the Bush administration has moved toward a doctrine of "responsibility" in its approach to nuclear weapons, assessing the threat in terms of the character of the state that has the weapons: is it responsible, or is it a rogue state? This raises a number of fundamental questions. What kinds of danger must regimes pose, and what kinds of irresponsibility must they demonstrate, in order to become liable to military intervention to prevent them from acquiring nuclear weapons? What are the relevant criteria for judging when force may be used to punish proliferant states? Is the key distinction whether or not they have signed the Non-Proliferation Treaty? In that case, why were sanctions imposed on India and Pakistan? And what significance does withdrawal from the treaty have? Perhaps the most important question of all is: who has the authority to answer these questions? The United States? The UN Security Council? Some other international body, state, or collection of states? As the debate over the war in Iraq has shown, these are extremely contentious issues to which there are at present no agreed answers.[82]

Deterrence and Dissuasion in Dealing with Nuclear Threats

The Bush administration clearly sees a much smaller role for deterrence now than during the cold war. This does not mean, however, that deterrence has been—or should be—abandoned as an instrument of policy. Secretary of State Colin Powell explained the relationship between deterrence and preemption as follows:

You will find that . . . we have not abandoned deterrence. We still have thousands of nuclear weapons. We still have a magnificent nuclear force that can deter. We haven't abandoned these time-honored methods of using our national power. But . . . there is a new threat out there now. There is a threat that doesn't respond the way older threats did to deterrence. . . . These are terrorists. These are people that are willing to ignore what's going to happen to them. They are suicidal. They believe in evil concepts. And they're going to come at us. And so, the doctrine of preemption, or an element of preemption in our strategy is appropriate. It's not a new doctrine. It's been around for as long as warfare has been around. I can give you example after example in our own history of preemptive actions. . . . When you have this kind of new threat, this kind of new enemy, then this doctrine of preemption should rise a little higher in your consideration, because this kind of enemy will not be deterred or contained the way, perhaps, the Soviet Union might have been and was contained and deterred in the past.[83]

What, then, is the role of nuclear deterrence in U.S. policy? Three factors need to be considered in answering this question: relations with Russia and China, the so-called "rogue states" that are seeking to acquire nuclear weapons, and terrorist groups.

The primary purpose of U.S. nuclear policy during the cold war was to deter aggression by the Soviet Union or China. That became a much less important mission after the collapse of the Soviet Union, even though Russia continues to possess thousands of nuclear weapons. The United States and Russia have made significant reductions in their nuclear forces, though between them they still have about 95 percent of all the nuclear weapons in the world.[84] On May 24, 2002, Presidents George W. Bush and V. V. Putin signed the Moscow Treaty on Strategic Offensive Reductions (SORT) in which the two countries agreed to reduce their strategic nuclear forces to no more than 1,700–2,200 warheads each by the end of 2012. The treaty contains only four pages of text and places no limit on nondeployed warheads; nor does it have inspection provisions, although those of the START I Treaty remain in effect.[85] The Moscow Treaty will not lead to quicker or deeper reductions than would have been provided by START II and the proposals for START III if these had been ratified and implemented rather than put aside. But the very simplicity of the Moscow Treaty has been taken as a sign that the two "countries are no longer mortal enemies. . . . Our agreements need not be based on mutual suspicion or an adversarial relationship."[86] When they signed the Moscow Treaty, Bush and Putin declared that "the era in which the United States and Russia saw each other as an enemy or strategic threat has ended."[87]

Deterrence is nevertheless a residual element in U.S.-Russian relations. According to the 2001 Nuclear Posture Review, "Russia's nuclear forces . . . remain a concern," and if U.S. relations with Russia were to deteriorate, the U.S. might have to revise its nuclear force levels and posture.[88] For its part, the Russian government will clearly take steps to ensure that Russian strategic forces can penetrate whatever missile defense system the United States deploys.[89] These policies display a desire to hedge against a worsening of the relationship and a determination to ensure that forces required for deterrence are in place in case they should be needed. But even in this context the Moscow Treaty's target of 1,700–2,200 strategic warheads by 2012 seems far too high. The noted analysts Sidney Drell and James Goodby have recently made a strong case for much smaller U.S. strategic forces.[90] Reduction of U.S. and Russian forces to the lowest possible level would signal the intention of the two countries to meet their obligations under Article VI of the NPT. This would make it possible to reduce stockpiles of weapons and materials, thereby lessening the chance of theft by terrorists. It would also go further toward dismantling a once extremely dangerous nuclear relationship, thus offering a signpost to a safer world.

Deterrence continues to play a role in U.S.-Chinese relations as well. Although the United States and China cooperate in many areas, there has been no post–cold war transformation of the kind that has taken place in the U.S.-Russian relationship. As the Nuclear Posture Review makes clear, U.S. requirements for nuclear forces take into account the fact that China and the United States could become involved in "a military confrontation over the status of Taiwan."[91] The United States has an interest in deterring China from taking any steps that might precipitate such a confrontation, or from escalating if a confrontation should occur. China, for its part, has maintained a very small intercontinental force over the years. It was opposed to U.S. withdrawal from the ABM Treaty, and since the capacity to retaliate with nuclear weapons in the event of a nuclear attack is a principle of Chinese strategic doctrine, China is likely to undertake the steps it considers necessary in order to retain such a capability.[92]

What role does deterrence play in relations with states such as North Korea or Iran? The 2002 National Security Strategy claims that deterrence is not an appropriate strategy for dealing with rogue states, because their leaders are "more willing" than the leaders of the Soviet Union were "to take risks, gambling with the lives of their people, and the wealth of their nations." In other words, leaders such as Saddam Hussein or Kim Jong Il could not be deterred from using nuclear weapons, if they had them, or from giving them to terrorist groups. This argument confuses the rationality required for nuclear deterrence to be effective with the ruthlessness of the opponent. Saddam Hussein, for example, was a despicable and cruel despot, but there is little evidence to suggest that he did not understand the consequences of using any weapon of potential mass destruction—especially nuclear weapons—against the United States or one of its allies.[93]

For deterrence to work, the deterrer must know what the person being deterred holds dear—power or personal wealth, for example. If a leader is not concerned about the well-being of his population, that may indicate that he is callous, not that he is irrational. There is no evidence, for example, that Saddam Hussein was less "rational" than Stalin or Mao, or that he was unaware of the enormous imbalance of nuclear firepower in relation to the United States that would still have existed if Iraq had acquired one or two nuclear weapons. The evidence in fact points the other way: during the First Gulf War Saddam did not use the biological and chemical weapons he had in his arsenal against coalition forces or against Israel. The same arguments would apply to the provision of nuclear weapons by a rogue state to a terrorist group. If such a group were to use a weapon received from such a state—or indeed any state—that would be tantamount to the "proxy" use of a weapon and thus be liable to retaliation. In arguing that the leaders of states like North Korea or Iran cannot be deterred, the administration underestimates the potential of deterrence as a policy. This does not mean that deterrence is a foolproof policy, any more than it was during the cold war, but it remains one of the instruments available to the United States in dealing with nuclear threats.

Deterrence is much less likely to be an effective strategy for dealing with nuclear threats from terrorist groups. Some groups use terrorism as a means to attain particular political goals. Such groups should in principle be deterrable, because something they value can be put at risk. But they may be shadowy groups with no "return address" against which to retaliate, or they may completely miscalculate the consequences of their actions in ways that make deterrent threats ineffective. Besides, it is a standard terrorist tactic to provoke the authorities into drastic action, in the hope that such action will expose the authorities' "true character" and undermine their popular support; in that case, harsh retaliation may be exactly what the terrorists want to see happen, and the threat of such retaliation will then not serve as a deterrent.

Other groups may have a purely apocalyptic vision and thus be willing to act regardless of the consequences; they may have a cult of martyrdom and in this respect differ from the Soviet leaders whom Eisenhower regarded as *not* being "early Christian martyrs."

The nuclear threat from terrorist groups has become much more salient in recent years, as the danger that such groups might get their hands on nuclear weapons or nuclear materials has grown. Terrorist groups might be able to steal weapons or materials from the enormous inventories in the nuclear weapons states, especially perhaps from inadequately safeguarded installations of the former Soviet nuclear weapons complex. Private networks such as that headed by A. Q. Khan might be willing to provide technology or materials illicitly to whoever is willing to pay. There is also the possibility that a rogue state might help terrorists, though a state that has created its nuclear program at great risk and with great effort might not be the most likely source of nuclear weapons or nuclear materials. Nevertheless, it is a matter of the utmost urgency to prevent nuclear weapons or nuclear materials from falling into the hands of terrorist groups. That would be the most effective means of denying to terrorist groups the possibility of making use of nuclear weapons or nuclear materials. Nuclear weapons and nuclear materials need to be secured and safeguarded. But deterrence has a role to play too. Terrorist groups would find it difficult to obtain or to build nuclear weapons without the help of a state, which means that such states may well be held accountable—and thus deterred—if terrorist groups do plan to detonate a nuclear weapon.[94]

Even though its role has declined greatly with the end of the cold war and might be reduced even further, deterrence has a residual role in U.S. policy toward Russia. It is also still a factor in U.S. relations with China. It has a potentially greater role than the Bush administration has acknowledged in relations with aspirant nuclear states such as North Korea and Iran. And even though its role in countering the threat of nuclear terrorism is probably quite small, it may nevertheless contribute to the effort to prevent nuclear weapons and nuclear materials from falling into terrorist hands.

Of the policy options during the cold war (disarmament, preventive war, defenses, deterrence, and the incorporation of nuclear weapons into U.S. military strategy), deterrence was the central organizing response to the nuclear threat from the Soviet Union and China. Since the other nuclear powers were allies, the United States did not think they needed to be deterred. The Bush administration has reshuffled the different ways of dealing with the nuclear threat. It still does not regard disarmament as a realistic option. It has, however, given a new priority to defenses against ballistic missiles, withdrawing from the ABM Treaty and beginning construction of a missile defense system. Deterrence remains a policy goal but is no longer the organizing principle for dealing with nuclear threats. Instead, preventive force occupies the central position in the administration's strategy for eliminating the danger of a nuclear attack on the United States and its allies. The National Strategy for Combating Terrorism, published by the White House in February 2003, states: "We cannot wait for terrorists to attack and then respond. The United States and its partners will disrupt and degrade the ability of terrorists to act, and compel supporters of terrorism to cease and desist. Preventing terrorist groups from gaining access to technology, particularly that which supports WMD will be one of our highest priorities."[95] That approach was apparent in the administration's justification for the attack upon Iraq. It was also an element in the U.S. rationale for attacking Afghanistan and the al Qaeda terrorists who had ensconced themselves in that country.

The Bush administration has also introduced a new concept into the array of policy instruments for stopping the spread of nuclear weapons to nation-states. As noted in the introduction to this chapter, the Nuclear Policy Review and the National Security Strategy both emphasize the importance of *dissuasion*, which they define as an effort to ensure that the United States is strong enough in military terms to dissuade potential adversaries from taking courses of action that could threaten U.S. and allied interests. Dissuasion is a very broad concept, and recent discussions have not made it more specific or clarified its implications for force planning. According to one analyst, "Dissuasion aims at urging potential geopolitical rivals not to become real rivals by making clear that any sustained malevolent conduct will be checkmated by the United States. It involves military pressure applied with a velvet glove, not crude threats of war and destruction."[96] This implies that the United States should use its military dominance to convince other states that they should not try to match U.S. military power or take military actions that would threaten the United States or its allies. Such a strategy could lead the United States to resist reductions in strategic nuclear forces on the grounds, for example, that reductions would encourage China to build up its forces in the hope of matching those of the United States. The goal of dissuasion might also be used as a rationale for the development of new types of nuclear weapons, on the grounds that the capability to destroy hard and deeply buried targets, for example, would dissuade other states from trying to develop nuclear (or chemical or biological) weapons in underground facilities or from storing them there (see chapter 7).

   The implications of a policy of dissuasion remain a matter of debate. At the most general level, it looks like merely a justification for U.S. military superiority. But the very preponderance of U.S. military power could have perverse effects from the point of view of U.S. interests. Its military power, especially when allied to a doctrine that claims the right of unilateral military intervention, might make other states feel insecure and thus induce them to seek ways of countering U.S. power. One way to do that would be to develop nuclear weapons (or chemical or biological weapons), which many people see as "equalizers," a means whereby weaker states can balance the military might of more powerful states. Dissuasion might thus prove to be a counterproductive strategy. It is important, in defining the practical steps that follow from adopting a policy of dissuasion, not to let that policy inhibit moves to reduce the salience of nuclear weapons in international politics, a goal that is after all very much in the interest of the United States.

Assessing the Administration's Policy

Notwithstanding the dominant military position of the United States, the conditions under which it can initiate preventive war, or even launch preventive strikes, are very restricted. Past experience suggests, as Drell and Goodby point out, that preventive military action against nascent nuclear programs can be useful under three conditions.[97] The first is when the state attacked has little hope of successful retaliation against the homelands of the attacking powers. That was true of Iraq in 1991 and 2003, and of North Korea in 1994 (though North Korea could retaliate against a U.S. ally, South Korea). The second is when most of the international community views the proliferant state as a threat to international peace and security. This has certainly been true of North Korea and Iraq. The third is when peaceful means of blocking nuclear weapons programs have failed or are judged unlikely to work. This justification was true of Iraq in 1991, but not in 2003.

   Iraq in 2003 met two of these conditions. First, it was in no position to retaliate against the United States or its allies. It had been weakened economically and militarily by defeat in the Gulf War and by years of sanctions, and its nuclear, biological, and chemical weapons programs had been dismantled in the 1990s by authority of the United Nations. Second, Iraq had no allies, and the UN Security Council had earlier agreed that Iraq should not be allowed to possess nuclear (or chemical or biological) weapons. However, the members of the Security Council disagreed on one key question: the use of force. In March 2003 most of the members wanted the inspections to continue and the decision about the use of force deferred. The unwillingness of the United States and Britain to do so led to the highly controversial decision to go to war.[98] The United States and its allies had no difficulty in winning a quick military victory and deposing Saddam Hussein.

The desire to prevent Iraq from acquiring nuclear weapons was one of the motives, and certainly the main justification, for the war.[99] The weapons programs that provided the primary *casus belli* turned out not to exist, however. The reasons for this intelligence failure have been the subject of extensive discussion. The important point to note here is that this was not an isolated failure in the history of nuclear intelligence. There are other recent examples to note. The IAEA was surprised to discover, after the First Gulf War, how much progress Iraq's nuclear program had made. In 2003 American and British intelligence services were surprised by the amount of equipment Libya had accumulated before it decided to dismantle its nuclear program. And a great deal of uncertainty still appears to surround key elements of the North Korean nuclear program (for example, what uranium-enrichment program it has, and where it is based).[100] Under current conditions, it can be extremely difficult for international organizations or foreign governments to know precisely the state of a country's nuclear program if that country wants to keep the matter secret or ambiguous. This creates many difficulties for the nonproliferation regime. It also presents serious problems for a state wishing to undertake preventive military action: political problems in justifying an attack, and military problems in identifying targets. Because of the intelligence failure in Iraq, future governments may find it harder to make the political case for the use of preventive force on the basis of intelligence information.

More important, the difficult occupation that the United States and its allies in Iraq find themselves engaged in has considerably dimmed the attractiveness of preventive military action. This has proved to be a much more complex operation than the Bush doctrine implied in its argument for preventive force or than the administration acknowledged when it made the case for war. The overthrow of Saddam Hussein's regime did not lead, as the administration had anticipated, to the quick and peaceful installation of a democratic government that could serve as a beacon of hope for the rest of the Middle East. The United States and its allies have confronted political rivalries and armed insurgency in Iraq, and it is by no means clear what the outcome will be. Even if a stable democratic government is eventually established, the cost to the United States (not to mention Iraq) will be very high, with the result that similar exercises in regime change will not be lightly undertaken in the future. Meanwhile, the requirement for a large contingent of U.S. forces in Iraq lessens the administration's capacity to engage in preventive military action elsewhere.

North Korea would be a more difficult case than Iraq. It too lacks allies, but it does have the capacity to strike in a devastating fashion at the capital of South Korea, an ally of the United States. An American military strike against North Korea could well elicit an attack on Seoul leading to tens if not hundreds of thousands of South Korean casualties. That makes resort to preventive force much more problematic in North Korea than in Iraq, especially if South Korea, which would bear the brunt of any North Korean retaliation, were opposed to such action. The Bush administration has been forced in this instance to count on diplomacy. It has been relying on multilateral negotiations—the six-party talks involving China, Japan, Russia, and South Korea, as well as North Korea and the United States—to bring pressure on North Korea to desist from the development of nuclear weapons.

Iran, the third state in President Bush's axis of evil, is very different from Saddam's Iraq or North Korea. It has a lively civil society, even if that society lacks the democratic mechanisms to enable it to shape politics. Different political viewpoints contend with one another in a political system that nevertheless remains under the ultimate control of religious leaders. There have been disagreements in the international community about the proper approach to Iran. The United States has pursued a policy of isolation, whereas the European states, including Russia, have argued for engagement as a way of drawing a revolutionary state back into the international community. Three members of the European Union—Britain, France, and Germany— have conducted intense negotiations with Iran in order to find a way of ensuring that Iran's nuclear program does not provide the basis for the development and production of nuclear weapons. Whether those negotiations will succeed is very much open to question, especially after the election of the conservative Mahmoud Ahmadinejad as president of Iran. The threat of military force by the United States, or by Israel, against Iran hovers in the background of the negotiations. An operation of the kind undertaken in Iraq is hardly conceivable, in view of the resistance it would provoke in Iran. Military action of some kind against Iranian nuclear installations would be much more feasible, although it is not clear how long such action could delay the Iranian program; moreover, the political costs in the Middle East might far outweigh the benefits to be gained from the use of preventive force.

The one recent success in reversing a nuclear program is Libya, which announced in December 2003 that it would disclose and dismantle all its nuclear, chemical, biological, and missile programs. For thirty years, Libya had been something of a pariah state—though it was not a member of the axis of evil—because of its support for, and involvement in, terrorist activities. Although it had signed the Nuclear Non-Proliferation Treaty in 1968 and ratified it in 1975, and had concluded a safeguards agreement with the IAEA in 1980, it nevertheless started a nuclear weapons program in the 1970s and intensified its effort in the mid-1990s. It imported nuclear technologies, small quantities of fissile material, and the design for a fission bomb. Even as it was illicitly importing centrifuges for uranium enrichment and pursuing the goal of a nuclear weapon, Libya began to make contact with the United States and Britain, perhaps as early as 1999. The economy was suffering as a result of sanctions, and the nuclear and other clandestine weapons programs were costly and proceeding very slowly. The Libyan leader, Colonel Muammar al-Qadhafi, was apparently eager to have the long-standing sanctions removed and to be accepted as a legitimate member of the international community. The heightened fear of a U.S. invasion after 9/11 may also have encouraged the change in policy: Qadhafi may well have feared that Libya would suffer the same fate as Iraq. The interception of a ship carrying centrifuge parts to Libya in October 2003 seems to have precipitated the final decision to abandon the nuclear weapons program and to dismantle it under IAEA supervision. Libya had not come close to producing a bomb, but its change of policy revealed a great deal of information about the illegal underworld of nuclear smuggling. President Bush announced: "Libya has begun the process of rejoining the community of nations."[101]

The most important criticism that can be made of the Bush doctrine—and it is a fundamental one—is that it does not do what it claims to do: it does not provide an effective way of dealing with nuclear threats to the United States. Preventive force—or preemption, in the sense in which the administration uses the term—does not provide a solution for the problem of nuclear proliferation to states or nonstate actors. The conditions under which preventive military action can be undertaken are severely constrained in both military and political terms. This does not mean that preventive force might not have an important role. It remains what it always has been: an option available to states in the most dangerous and critical circumstances. Its use is complicated, however, and the Bush doctrine, in assigning a central role to preventive force and asserting U.S. willingness to act alone, now looks like a misguided and flawed attempt to rethink national security strategy in the post-9/11 world.

Conclusion

The Bush doctrine combines a profound sense of vulnerability and threat with a strong consciousness of the immense military power at the disposal of the United States. It has antecedents in U.S. thinking about nuclear weapons, as well as in older traditions of thought about America's place in the world.[102] It can, nevertheless, be understood most immediately as a response to the changing nature of nuclear threats to the United States, and more particularly as a reaction to 9/11, which dramatized so powerfully the new character of threats to U.S. national security. It also reflects changes in the balance of power in the world and especially the unprecedented military dominance the United States has enjoyed since the end of the cold war. Preventive war against Iraq in 2003 was very different from that envisaged against the Soviet Union in the 1950s, when the United States would have had to use nuclear weapons, causing huge casualties in the Soviet Union and Europe. The United States did not have to use nuclear weapons against Iraq because it enjoyed overwhelming conventional superiority. Besides, conventional forces can now perform missions that they could not perform in the 1950s and 1960s, thanks to greatly improved intelligence collection and targeting capabilities. From a military point of view, preventive war is much more feasible for the United States now than it was during the cold war.

The Bush national security doctrine is the first full-fledged attempt by the United States to devise a strategy for the post–cold war world. It aims to prevent nuclear weapons from falling into the hands of terrorist groups or of states that the United States regards as irresponsible. The doctrine assigns to preventive force a key role in achieving the latter goal, moving deterrence from the central position it occupied during the cold war. The doctrine declares that the United States will act unilaterally if need be, without the support and consent of the rest of the world. It also seeks to ensure that no other state will even think it worthwhile to challenge American military dominance.

The Bush administration has presented the war on Iraq as an example of the kind of preventive action that the national security strategy outlined; indeed, the doctrine reads as though it was written to justify that particular war. It was not, however, the invasion of Iraq that prevented Saddam Hussein from acquiring nuclear weapons; UN inspectors had already shut down his nuclear program in the 1990s, after the First Gulf War. Moreover, the difficult experience of occupation in Iraq makes it unlikely that the United States will undertake another such war to prevent a state from acquiring nuclear weapons. This does not mean that the United States will never use preventive force for that purpose. But the circumstances under which military force can be used successfully are constrained, as the crises in North Korea and Iran show.

In spite of its continuing commitment to preemption, the Bush administration appears now to be more aware of the difficulties of such a strategy. The emphasis on diplomacy in dealing with North Korea and Iran indicates less readiness on the part of the United States to resort to force and more willingness to work with other governments—though it is too early to predict how those crises will turn out. The Bush doctrine is right to stress the importance of prevention in dealing with nuclear threats to U.S. national security and stopping the spread of nuclear weapons, but it is wrong to tie prevention so closely to the use of military force. Prevention needs to be conceived more broadly, and the use of force integrated more closely with other instruments of policy. What is the role of force in dealing with nuclear threats? How can it be used to support other methods, in particular diplomacy? When is it appropriate to use force, and by whose authority?

The United States needs to reconsider other issues as well when it moves, as it inevitably must, to formulating a new strategy for dealing with the challenge of nuclear weapons. The first is the tension between the principle of *dissuasion,* which implies that large nuclear forces should be maintained and new types of nuclear weapons developed, and the commitment of the United States, under Article VI of the Non-Proliferation Treaty, to pursue nuclear disarmament. American military preponderance, unless it is carefully managed and used, may encourage the nuclear ambitions of other states. Second, the administration's interest in developing new nuclear weapons (which is analyzed in chapter 7) runs counter to the goal of reducing the salience of nuclear weapons in international politics. Third, the Bush administration has welcomed India into the "nuclear club" and refrained from putting pressure on Israel but is doing its utmost to keep other countries from acquiring nuclear weapons and joining that club. There is some danger that recognition of India's nuclear weapons status—which is good insofar as it resolves an anomalous situation—may encourage other states to think that they can attain the same status if they proceed with nuclear weapons development. Fourth, the connection between regime change and nuclear weapons is not clear: the administration insisted on regime change in Iraq as a way of dealing with the nuclear issue. But in Libya, which it portrays as a major success, it adopted a different approach, helping the regime to survive in return for its decision to give up its nuclear ambitions. Something similar might conceivably happen in North Korea.

It is hard to disagree with the administration's contention that the existing nonproliferation regime is inadequate, but the Nuclear Non-Proliferation Treaty, for all its weaknesses, enjoys the overwhelming support of the international community, and this is a fact of some importance. None of the signatory states that have organized clandestine nuclear weapons programs—Iraq, North Korea, Libya, and probably Iran—has had explicit encouragement or support from other governments for those programs. It is true that they have been able to import nuclear technology from abroad for ostensibly peaceful purposes, and to acquire other technologies illicitly. But the international community has been decidedly opposed to their efforts to acquire nuclear weapons, and that surely provides a basis on which to erect stronger controls. It makes more sense to build on the existing regime than to undermine it or push it to the sidelines. The fact that there is a widespread understanding of the destructiveness of nuclear weapons, and almost universal agreement that they should not spread further, provides the basis for a stronger nonproliferation regime. Constructing such a regime will not be easy, but doing so is very much in the interest not only of the United States but also of the other states that have signed the Non-Proliferation Treaty. Furthermore, the United States is better placed than any other country to provide the leadership needed to carry out this vitally important task. In accepting the challenge, the United States—and other countries too—must look much more carefully at the role of preventive force, at the conditions for the legitimate use of such force, and at the utility of international norms, regimes, and institutions, than the Bush national security strategy has done.

Notes

1. Announcement of Withdrawal from the ABM Treaty, December 13 (www. state.gov/t/ac/rls/fs/2001/6848.htm). See also 2001 Department of Defense, Missile Defense Agency Fact Sheet, Block 2004 (www.mda.mil/mdalink/html/factsheet.html).

2. U.S. Department of Defense, *Nuclear Posture Review [Excerpts]*, submitted to Congress, December 31, 2001 (www.globalsecurity.org/wmd/library/policy/dod/npr. htm [January 30, 2003]).

3. Secretary Rumsfeld, Foreword to ibid., p. 1.

4. Ibid., p. 3.

5. White House, National Security Strategy of the United States of America, September 17, 2002 (www.whitehouse.gov/nsc/nss.html), p. 15.

6. Ibid.

7. Ibid., p. 6.

8. Ibid., p. 30.

9. *Nuclear Posture Review [Excerpts]*, p. 2.

10. The most poignant statement of this came from Henry Kissinger when he was facing domestic opposition to the negotiation of a second SALT agreement: "And one of the questions we have to ask ourselves as a country is what in the name of God is strategic superiority? What is the significance of it, politically, militarily, operationally, at these levels of numbers? What do you do with it?" Quoted in Lawrence Freedman, *The Evolution of Nuclear Strategy*, 3rd ed. (London: Palgrave Macmillan, 2003), p. 346.

11. We have mostly avoided the term "weapons of mass destruction" because it lumps together weapons that are very different in the amount of destruction they cause, the consequences of their use, and in the countermeasures that can be employed to deal with them.

12. See White House, National Strategy to Combat Weapons of Mass Destruction, December 2002 (www.whitehouse.gov/news/releases/2002/12/WMDStrategy.pdf), p. 1.

13. Ibid. Broadly speaking, nonproliferation describes what the State Department does in this area and counterproliferation describes what the Defense Department does. In the National Strategy to Combat Weapons of Mass Destruction, the section on counterproliferation has subheadings on interdiction, deterrence, and defense and mitigation; the subheadings in the section on nonproliferation are active diplomacy, multilateral regimes, cooperative threat reduction, controls on nuclear materials, export controls, and nonproliferation sanctions.

14. White House, National Security Strategy of the United States of America, March 2006 (www.whitehouse.gov/nse/nss/2006/nss206.pdf), p. 23.

15. Oppenheimer called atomic weapons "weapons of aggression, of surprise, and of terror. . . . It is a weapon for aggressors, and the elements of surprise and of terror are as intrinsic to it as are the fissionable nuclei." Robert Oppenheimer, "Atomic Weapons and the Crisis in Science," *Saturday Review of Literature*, November 24, 1945, p. 10. Quoted by Bernard Brodie, "The Implications for Military Policy," in *The Absolute Weapon*, edited by Brodie (New York: Harcourt, Brace, 1946), p. 73. Oppenheimer had said something similar in his farewell address at Los Alamos earlier in the month. See Alice Kimball Smith and Charles Weiner, eds., *Robert Oppenheimer: Letters and Recollections* (Stanford University Press, 1995), p. 318.

16. Lawrence S. Wittner, *One World or None: A History of the World Disarmament Movement through 1953* (Stanford University Press, 1993), pp. 59–71.

17. U.S. Department of State, *A Report on the International Control of Atomic Energy* (1946). On the preparation of this report, see McGeorge Bundy, *Danger and Survival* (New York: Random House, 1988), pp. 157–60.

18. The report defined as dangerous any activity that offered a solution to one of the three major problems in making atomic weapons: the supply of raw materials, the production of fissionable materials, and the use of these materials to make such weapons.

19. Bundy, *Danger and Survival*, pp. 160–84.

20. David Holloway, *Stalin and the Bomb* (Yale University Press, 1994), pp. 161–66, 213–18.

21. Marc Trachtenberg, "A 'Wasting Asset': American Strategy and the Shifting Nuclear Balance, 1949–1954," in Trachtenberg, *History and Strategy* (Princeton University Press, 1991), pp. 100–52. On Churchill, see p. 105; on Russell, see p. 103. For military thinking in the early Eisenhower years, see pp. 132ff.

22. Bundy, *Danger and Survival*, p. 249.

23. Ibid., p. 250.

24. Ibid., p. 251.

25. Edward Luttwak, *A Dictionary of Modern War* (London: Allen Lane, 1972), p. 156; Wolfram F. Hanreider and Larry V. Buel, *Words and Arms: A Dictionary of Security and Defense Terms* (Boulder, Colo.: Westview Press, 1979), pp. 97, 98.

26. On preemption in U.S. war planning, see Scott D. Sagan, "SIOP-62: The Nuclear War Plan Briefing to President Kennedy," *International Security* 12 (Summer 1987): 28–32, 50; for Soviet strategy, see *Sovremennaia voina* (Modern war) (Moscow: General Staff Academy, 1960), pp. 50ff.

27. In the spring and summer of 1961, as photographic evidence became available about the backward state of Soviet strategic forces, it became clear that the United States was in a position to mount something like a "surgical" strike against them. Calculations in the Pentagon showed that, even in the best case, 2 million or 3 million Americans (and tens of millions of Europeans) would die if the Soviet Union retaliated. Fred Kaplan, *The Wizards of Armageddon* (Stanford University Press, 1991), pp. 294–302.

28. From a memorandum for the record by John A. McCone, director of Central Intelligence, following a meeting with Bundy on January 11, 1963. *Foreign Relations of the United States*, [hereafter *FRUS*], *1961–1963*, vol. 22, *North East Asia* (Government Printing Office, 1996), p. 339.

29. This whole episode is dealt with in William Burr and Jeffrey T. Richelson, "Whether to 'Strangle the Baby in the Cradle,'" *International Security* 26 (Winter 2000/2001), pp. 54–99.

30. *FRUS, 1961–1963*, vol. 7, *Arms Control and Disarmament* (GPO, 1995), p. 860. A note on the translation here: the Russian word for "means" (*sredstva*) often means "weapons," as it clearly does in this context.

31. Michael D. Swaine and Alastair Iain Johnston, "China and Arms Control Institutions," in *China Joins the World: Progress and Prospects*, edited by Elizabeth Economy and Michel Oksenberg (New York: Council on Foreign Relations Press, 1999), pp. 90–135.

32. Brodie, "Implications for Military Policy," p. 73; Jacob Viner, "The Implications of the Atomic Bomb for International Relations," in Viner, *International Economics* (New York: Free Press, 1951), pp. 301–02. This is the text of a lecture given by Viner on November 16, 1945, to the American Philosophical Society.

33. Quoted by Robert R. Bowie, in "Bowie's Commentary," in *American Cold War Strategy: Interpreting NSC 68*, edited by Ernest R. May (Boston: St. Martin's Press, 1993), p. 112.

34. The phrase comes from National Security Council, *Basic National Security Policy*, NSC 162/2 (October 30, 1953). See *FRUS, 1952–54*, vol. 2, *National Security Policy* (GPO, 1984), p. 591. If Eisenhower had had a different view of the Soviet leaders—if he had believed that they were indeed "early Christian martyrs" and willing not to count the cost in their pursuit of communism—he might have regarded preventive war as a more plausible option for the United States.

35. Freedman, *The Evolution*, chaps. 6, 16, 25, and 26.

36. David Alan Rosenberg, "The Origins of Overkill: Nuclear Weapons and American Strategy, 1945–1960," *International Security* 8 (Spring 1983): 3–71.

37. Freedman, *The Evolution*, pp. 342–77.

38. The tensions of the early 1980s are discussed in detail in Benjamin B. Fischer, *A Cold War Conundrum* (Central Intelligence Agency, 1997) (www.cia.gov/csi/monograph/coldwar/source.htm). Fischer concludes that there was a genuine "war scare" in Moscow in late 1983, in the sense that the Soviet leaders were fearful that the United States might indeed launch a nuclear attack against the Soviet Union.

39. For a discussion of this point, see Barton J. Bernstein, "Reconsidering the Missile Crisis: Dealing with the Problems of the American Jupiters in Turkey," in *The Cuban Missile Crisis Revisited*, edited by James A. Nathan (New York: St. Martin's Press, 1992), pp. 100–01.

40. After his return from the Geneva summit in July 1955, Eisenhower stated: "There seems to be a growing realization by all that nuclear warfare, pursued to the ultimate, could be practically race suicide." *Public Papers of the Presidents of the United States: Dwight D. Eisenhower, 1955* (GPO, 1960), p. 175. In April 1956, Khrushchev told Harold Stassen, Eisenhower's special assistant on disarmament, "Nearly everyone knew that war was unacceptable and that co-existence was elementary." *FRUS 1955–1957*, vol. 20, *Regulation of Armaments and Atomic Energy* (GPO, 1990), p. 380.

41. George Bunn, *Arms Control by Committee* (Stanford University Press, 1992), provides an analysis of the arms control process, its failures, and its achievements.

42. In 1969 the Soviet Union dropped hints that it was planning to strike Chinese nuclear installations, but that it seriously intended to do so is not clear. It viewed Chinese manpower and prolonged wars along the border as a greater threat than Chinese nuclear weapons. See David Holloway, "Assessing Chinese Nuclear Policy," in *Tracking the Dragon. National Intelligence Estimates on China during the Era of Mao, 1948–1976*, edited by Christian Ostermann (Washington: Wilson Center Press, forthcoming).

43. Bunn, *Arms Control by Committee*, chap. 4.

44. For the text of the speech given to the UN General Assembly on December 8, 1953, see www.eisenhower.utexas.edu/atoms.htm.

45. State Department experts of the time believe that Eisenhower was not advised of the connection between peaceful and weapons uses of nuclear energy because his advisers just before the speech was given were the secretary of state and the chairman of the Atomic Energy Commission, neither of whom had technical backgrounds or were aware of the connection. U.S. Atomic Energy Agency historians are in agreement. See Kenneth Thompson, ed., *Gerard Smith on Arms Control* (Lanham, Md.: University Press of America, 1987), p. 117; Phillip Farley, "Nuclear Nonproliferation," in *Gerard C. Smith: A Career in Progress*, edited by Henry Owen and John T. Smith (Lanham, Md.: University Press of America, 1989), pp. 87–102; Bunn, *Arms Control by Committee*, p. 84; and Richard Hewlett and Jack M. Holl, *Atoms for Peace and War: Eisenhower and the Atomic Energy Commission* (University of California Press, 1989), p. 210. However, after the Soviet and British weapons tests and after the initiation of national nuclear programs in Belgium, Canada, France, and Italy, existing U.S. legislation prohibiting any assistance was probably futile. See Bunn, *Arms Control by Committee*, p. 84. Leonard Spector says

that Eisenhower responded to the reality that other states could acquire nuclear weapons without help from the United States. See Spector, *A Historical and Technical Introduction to the Proliferation of Nuclear Weapons* (Washington: Carnegie Endowment for International Peace, 1992), p. 9.

46. See Bunn, *Arms Control by Committee*, chap. 5; Holloway, *Stalin and the Bomb*, pp. 349–50.

47. Francis J. Gavin, "Blasts from the Past: Proliferation Lessons from the 1960s," *International Security* 29 (Winter 2004/5): 101; R. M. Timerbaev, *Rossiia i iadernoe neraspros-tranenie* (Russia and nuclear Nonproliferation) (Moscow: Nauka, 1999), pp. 207–08.

48. Joseph Cirincione, Jon B. Wolfsthal, and Miriam Rajkumar, *Deadly Arsenals: Nuclear, Biological, and Chemical Threats*, 2nd ed. (Washington: Carnegie Endowment for International Peace, 2005), p. 20.

49. Wade Boese, "Nuclear Nonproliferation Treaty Meeting Sputters," *Arms Control Today* 35 (July/August 2005) (www.armscontrol.org/act/2005_07/NPT.asp).

50. Cirincione and others, *Deadly Arsenals*, p. 55, give a list of thirty states that "have the potential ability to develop nuclear weapons, but have chosen not to do so." Not all of those states could move as quickly as Japan to make nuclear weapons.

51. "Strengthened Safeguards: Status of Additional Protocols" (www.iaea.org/Our-Work/SV/Safeguards/sg_protocol.html).

52. "Expert Group Meeting on Control of Nuclear Fuel Cycle," September 10, 2004 (www.iaea.org/OurWork/SV/Safeguards/sg_protocol.html for).

53. *DCI's Worldwide Threat Briefing*, February 11, 2003, n.p. (www.cia.gov/cia/public_affairs/speeches/2003/dci_speech_02112003.html).

54. Ibid.

55. There has been speculation that an event over the South Atlantic in September 1979 was an Israeli nuclear test. See, for example, Central Intelligence Agency, *The 22 September 1979 Event*, Interagency Intelligence Memorandum (December 1979). My thanks to Ted Postol for giving me a copy of this.

56. On this dialogue, see especially Strobe Talbott, *Engaging India: Diplomacy, Democracy, and the Bomb* (Brookings, 2004). Talbott, who was the chief American interlocutor in this dialogue, is well aware of the irony.

57. Indo–U.S. Joint Statement, July 18, 2005 (www.dae.gov.in/jtstmt.htm).

58. For a discussion of U.S. policy toward Pakistan, see Touqir Hussain, *U.S.–Pakistan Engagement: The War on Terrorism and Beyond*, Special Report 145 (Washington: United States Institute of Peace, 2005).

59. On al Qaeda's interest in nuclear weapons see, for example, David Albright, Kathryn Beuhler, and Holly Higgins, "Bin Laden and the Bomb," *Bulletin of the Atomic Scientists* 58 (January/February 2002): 23–24.

60. National Security Strategy (September 2002), p. 13.

61. Ibid., p. 14.

62. President Bush referred to the "axis of evil" in his State of the Union address on January 29, 2002 (www.whitehouse.gov/news/releases/2002/01/20020129-11.html).

63. Both of these passages come from National Security Strategy (September 2002), p. 15.

64. There is an enormous literature on international law pertaining to the use of

armed force by states, specifically regarding the war on Iraq. See, for example, Thomas Graham Jr., "National Self-Defense, International Law, and Weapons of Mass Destruction," *Chicago Journal of International Law* 4 (Spring 2003): 1–17; Abraham D. Sofaer, "On the Necessity of Pre-emption," *European Journal of International Law* 14 (2003): 209–26; and Allen S. Weiner, "The Use of Force and Contemporary Security Threats: Old Medicine for New Ills?" Unpublished ms. on file with the author.

65. Ashton B. Carter and William J. Perry, *Preventive Defense* (Brookings, 1999), pp. 126, 131.

66. President Bush, second inaugural address (www.whitehouse.gov/news/releases/2005/01/20050120-1.html).

67. Remarks by the president in Address to the Nation, March 17, 2003 (www.whitehouse.gov/news/releases/2003/03/20030317-7.html).

68. For "key judgments" from the October 2002 National Intelligence Estimate on Iraq's programs for weapons of mass destruction, see www.fas.org/irp/cia/product/iraq-wmd.html.

69. Of particular relevance is the British attorney-general's memorandum of March 7, 2003, to Prime Minister Tony Blair on the legality of the Iraq War (www.globalpolicy.org/security/issues/iraq/document/2003/0307advice.htm).

70. Graham, "National Self-Defense," pp. 12–14.

71. United Nations, *A More Secure World: Our Shared Responsibility*, Report of the High-Level Panel on Threats, Challenges, and Change (New York, 2004), p. 64.

72. The Russian minister of defense, Sergei Ivanov, said on October 2, 2003, that Russia "can no longer completely rule out the preventive use of force if demanded by the interests of Russia or its alliance commitments." Vladimir Mukhin, "Preventivnyi udar ot Ivanova," (A preventive strike by Ivanov) *Nezavisimaya Gazeta*, October 3, 2003, p. 1. President Putin said on November 3, 2003: "If the principle of preventive use of force is established in international practice, then Russia will have the right to act in a similar way to protect its national interests." Interview with Italian news media, Johnson's Russia List 11-5-03 (www.cdi.org/russia/johnson/7401-16.cfm). The Israeli minister of defense warned in December 2003 that Israel might take military action to destroy Iran's nuclear capabilities. Conal Urquhart, "Israel Warns Iran on N-weapons," *Manchester Guardian*, December 22, 2003 (www.guardian.co.uk/iran/story/0,12858,1111570,00.html). India's external affairs minister Yashwant Singh, in an Agence France-Presse interview on April 2, 2003, asserted India's right to take "pre-emptive" military action against Pakistan, along the lines of the coalition war against Iraq. He stated: "We derive some satisfaction . . . because I think all those people in the international community . . . realize that India has a much better case to go for pre-emptive action against Pakistan than the U.S. has in Iraq." Rahul Roy-Chaudhuri, *Nuclear Doctrine, Declaratory Policy, and Escalation Control* (Washington: Henry L. Stimson Center, April 2004), n.p. (www.stimson.org/southasia/pubs.cfm?ID=105).

73. The fact that other countries have at least rhetorically adopted the preventive posture points to the dangers. But perhaps it also implies some convergence on the need to change the law.

74. United Nations, *A More Secure World*, p. 63.

75. Ibid.

76. Independent International Commission on Kosovo, *The Kosovo Report* (Oxford University Press, 2000), Executive Summary, n.p. (www.reliefweb.int/library/documents/thekosovoreport.htm).

77. Ibid.

78. International Commission on Intervention and State Sovereignty, *The Responsibility to Protect* (Ottawa: International Development Research Center, 2001), p. 13.

79. At their summit meeting at the United Nations in New York in September 2005, the heads of state and government declared: "We are prepared to take collective action, in a timely and decisive manner, through the Security Council, in accordance with the UN Charter, including Chapter VII, on a case-by-case basis in cooperation with the relevant regional organizations as appropriate, should peaceful means be inadequate and national authorities manifestly failing to protect their populations from genocide, war crimes, ethnic cleansing and crimes against humanity." *Draft Outcome Document*, September 13, 2005, p. 27 (www.responsibilitytoprotect.org).

80. As Gerhard Casper has pointed out, the term "legitimacy" is used in different ways in the discussion of collective action by states. In its restrictive sense, legitimacy denotes the degree to which an unlawful action (that is, without UN Security Council sanction) meets the criteria that would normally be applied in making a lawful decision ("seriousness of threat," "proportionality," and so on). In its expansive and empowering sense, legitimacy is determined by "normative considerations that go beyond the legal status quo." Gerhard Casper, "Law, Legitimacy and Preventive Force," paper presented at a conference on the preventive use of force, Stanford University, May 26, 2005. I am grateful to Gerhard Casper for discussions on these issues.

81. State of the Union Address, January 29, 2002 (www.whitehouse.gov/news/releases/2002/01/20020129-11.html).

82. For a helpful guide to those issues, see George P. Shultz and Coit D. Blacker, cochairs, "Preventive Force: Issues for Discussion," prepared by the Stanford University Group on Preventive Force (Stanford University, 2005). I was a member of the group and benefited greatly from its discussions.

83. Secretary of State Colin Powell, statement to the Senate Foreign Relations Committee, September 26, 2002 (www.state.gov/secretary/former/powell/remarks/2002/13765.htm).

84. Cirincione and others, *Deadly Arsenals*, p. 8.

85. For the text of the treaty and accompanying documents, see www.state.gov/t/ac/trt/18016.htm.

86. James Dao, "U.S.-Russia Atomic Arms Pact Wins Senate Panel's Backing," *New York Times*, February 6, 2003, p. A-10.

87. Joint Declaration on the New Strategic Relationship, May 24, 2002 (www.state.gov/t/ac/trt/18016.htm#13).

88. *Nuclear Posture Review [Excerpts]*, p. 17.

89. President V. V. Putin said on February 18, 2004: "I have already spoken about our nuclear deterrent force, about how we can be sure about it for some decades ahead, and about how we are able to resolve any tasks, including penetrating missile defense systems, should such systems be created. . . . We have also said repeatedly that as other countries increase the number and quality of their arms and military potential, then Russia

will also need to ensure it has new-generation arms and technology. In this respect, I am pleased to inform you that successfully concluded experiments during these exercises enable us to confirm that the Russian Armed Forces, the Strategic Missile Forces, will receive new hypersound-speed, high-precision new weapons systems that can hit targets at intercontinental distance and can adjust their altitude and course as they travel. . . . This gives us grounds to affirm that with the powerful means we have at our disposal for conducting armed warfare, and I refer here to the new arms I just described and to other new technology that we have, Russia can reliably ensure its strategic stability in the long-term perspective" (www.acronym.org.uk/docs/0402/doc30.htm). See also *Aktual'nye zadachi razvitiia vooruzhennykh sil Rossiskoi Federatsii* (Current tasks in the development of the armed forces of the Russian Federation) (Moscow: Ministry of Defense, 2003), p. 42.

90. Sidney D. Drell and James E. Goodby, *What Are Nuclear Weapons For? Recommendations for Restructuring U.S. Strategic Nuclear Forces* (Washington: Arms Control Association, 2005), pp. 15–16. Drell and Goodby propose 500 warheads in an operationally deployed force and 500 in a ready responsive force on each side, with the operationally deployed force phased out over time.

91. *Nuclear Posture Review [Excerpts]*, p. 16.

92. Since it first tested the bomb, China has adhered to a no-first-use policy. In July 2005, however, a senior Chinese officer told American journalists that if the United States were to use conventional military force in a confrontation over Taiwan, China would have to respond with nuclear weapons. This was no doubt intended as a warning that a Sino-American war over Taiwan could not remain limited, and that China would not necessarily refrain from the use of nuclear weapons while the United States exploited its conventional superiority. See "Top Chinese General Warns U.S. over Attack," *Financial Times*, July 15, 2005.

93. He used chemical weapons against Iran and against Iraqi villages, but there was no danger that the United States would retaliate.

94. For a discussion of deterrence in relation to terrorism, see Klaus-Dieter Schwarz, *Die Zukunft der Abschreckung* (The Future of Deterrence) (Berlin: Stiftung Wissenschaft und Politik, June 2005), pp. 24–28.

95. See National Strategy for Combating Terrorism (White House, 2003), p. 15 (www.whitehouse.gov/news/releases/2003/02/20030214-7.html).

96. Richard L. Kugler, "Dissuasion as a Strategic Concept," *Strategic Forum* 196 (December 2002): 2. See also M. Elaine Bunn, "Force Posture and Dissuasion"; and Scott Sagan, "Dissuasion and the NPT Regime: Complementary and Contradictory Strategies," both of which are in *Strategic Insights* 3, no. 10 (October 2004) (www.ccc.nps.navy.mil/si/archiveDate.asp#vol3).

97. Sidney D. Drell and James E. Goodby, *The Gravest Danger: Nuclear Weapons* (Stanford, Calif.: Hoover Institution Press, 2003), pp. 38–44.

98. Hans Blix, *Disarming Iraq* (New York: Pantheon Books, 2004), pp. 218, 252–53.

99. Ibid., pp. 266–67.

100. On Iraq in 1991–92, see ibid., pp. 23–24; on Libya, see Sharon A. Squassoni and Andrew Feickert, "Disarming Libya: Weapons of Mass Destruction," Congressional Research Service Report (April 22, 2004) (www.fpc.state.gov); and on North Korea, see

Nuclear Threat Initiative, Country Profile on North Korea (www.nti.org/e_research/profiles/NK/Nuclear/44_74.html).

101. The preceding paragraph is based on Nuclear Threat Initiative, Country Profile on Libya (www.nti.org/e_research/profiles/Libya/index.html).

102. For quite different views of the elements of continuity and change, see John Lewis Gaddis, *Surprise, Security, and the American Experience* (Harvard University Press, 2004); and Melvyn P. Leffler, "9/11 and American Foreign Policy," *Diplomatic History* 29 (June 2005): 395–413.

three

The Nuclear Nonproliferation Regime and Its History

George Bunn

"The proliferation of nuclear weapons poses the greatest threat to our national security," said President George W. Bush in his National Security Strategy of 2006. To deal with this continuing threat, the United States over the past half-century has helped build an international "nonproliferation regime." This chapter describes the regime and its history. The regime consists of international agreements and cooperative national actions to prevent the spread of nuclear weapons to additional countries or to terrorists.

The initiating agreement for the regime was the Treaty on the Non-Proliferation of Nuclear Weapons (or Non-Proliferation Treaty, NPT) of 1968. The NPT had been preceded by a U.S. effort that stimulated the spread of nuclear knowledge and nuclear reactors: President Dwight D. Eisenhower's 1953 proposal for an Atoms for Peace program. This was based on early optimism concerning both the benefits of atomic energy for peaceful purposes and the possibilities for preventing its diversion to weapons. The U.S. program, and similar but smaller French and Soviet programs, helped to spread research reactors with weapons-usable, highly enriched uranium around the world and taught many about the science of nuclear reactions. These reactors, and the education that went with them, contributed to nuclear weapon proliferation in Iraq, Iran, and North Korea.[1]

Atoms for Peace also gave rise to the International Atomic Energy Agency (IAEA), established in 1957, whose mission is to promote and control the peaceful uses of atomic energy. This agency has become the key international inspection agency for today's nuclear nonproliferation regime. The NPT prohibits member nations that do not have nuclear weapons from acquiring them and calls for inspections by the IAEA to ensure that the plutonium or highly enriched uranium acquired to run research or power reactors (or for any other purpose) is not used to make nuclear weapons.[2] The nuclear nonproliferation regime now includes many bilateral and multilateral agreements, as well as both cooperative and unilateral efforts.

In defining these efforts, the U.S government distinguishes between "nonproliferation" and "counterproliferation." As defined by the Joint Chiefs of Staff, counterproliferation means: "Those actions . . . taken to defeat the threat and/or use of weapons of mass destruction against the United States, our military forces, friends and allies."[3] The term can include many actions to prevent the spread of nuclear weapons and even to retrieve, sometimes by threats of force, nuclear weapon components or technology acquired by rogue states or by terrorists. Two examples of counterproliferation, in the view of the George W. Bush administration, are the invasion of Iraq in 2003 to prevent its acquisition of nuclear and other weapons of mass destruction (the justification given by the United States to the UN Security Council in 2003), and the 2004 apprehension of uranium-enrichment technology aboard a German ship destined for Libya.

Elements of the Nonproliferation Regime

The nonproliferation regime's original purpose was to prevent the proliferation of nuclear weapons beyond the five countries that had them when the NPT was signed in 1968: China, France, the Soviet Union, the United Kingdom, and the United States. These were also the "P-5," the permanent five members of the UN Security Council, the only members having a veto on Security Council decisions, and the only countries permitted to have nuclear weapons among those that joined the treaty.[4] The idea for such a treaty was supported unanimously in a 1961 resolution of the UN General Assembly. Not surprisingly, since it arose in the midst of the cold war, the idea initially met with some debate.

The Nuclear Non-Proliferation Treaty

In 1959, with the support of the United States, the General Assembly adopted a resolution proposed by Ireland that called for a treaty prohibiting countries not yet having nuclear weapons from acquiring them. It included language concerning inspection, as demanded by the United States, but no provisions to prohibit deployment of U.S. nuclear weapons in foreign countries or with foreign participation, as demanded by the Soviet Union (such as deployments in Germany with, and under the control of, U.S. forces, or deployments on naval vessels that were to make up a proposed "multilateral force" operated jointly with West Europeans). The resolution did not receive unanimous support, even among the P-5: the Soviet Union and France both abstained.

After further negotiations at the beginning of the Kennedy administration in 1961, the General Assembly unanimously agreed to a revised Irish resolution. Even India and Pakistan voted for the resolution.[5] Without really resolving the earlier disputes, this resolution called for a nonproliferation treaty under which nuclear powers "would undertake to refrain from relinquishing control of nuclear weapons and from transmitting the information for their manufacture to States not possessing such weapons." It imposed a complementary obligation on countries not having nuclear weapons: they were not to receive or manufacture such weapons.[6] This resolution sounded an "international call" for the NPT. However, it took until 1968 to negotiate the treaty because the United States and its allies disagreed with the Soviet Union and its allies on several major points. After those differences were resolved, the Soviet Union and the United States, working together, worked with the nonaligned members at the negotiating conference to produce a final treaty draft. It was accepted eventually by almost every country in the world—but not by Israel, India, Pakistan, and, most recently, North Korea.[7] North Korea joined the NPT at Soviet insistence in the 1980s in order to continue receiving Soviet aid pursuant to the Soviet Atoms for Peace program. It gave notice of withdrawal in 1993, rescinded its withdrawal on the next-to-the-last day of the notice period, and then withdrew again in 2003. The validity of its withdrawal has been contested.[8]

As just mentioned, U.S.-Soviet differences over issues such as whether the NPT should prohibit the United States from deploying nuclear weapons outside its territory took several years to resolve. The language eventually agreed upon did not prohibit the United States from deploying U.S. weapons in allied countries such as Germany provided that American servicemen retained control of the weapons. While the Soviet Union disliked this conclusion, it did not publicly challenge it after the NPT was signed.[9]

The verification provisions proved to be the next large obstacle. They had Soviet support—provided no inspections were required in the Soviet Union. The sticking point was that they did require inspections of peaceful nuclear facilities in NPT countries that did not have nuclear weapons. These inspections were to be conducted by the IAEA to ensure that the nuclear facilities of such members were not used to make nuclear material for use in weapons. Here the parties at odds over the relevant language of the NPT were primarily the Soviet Union and some NATO allies of the United States that are now members of the European Union. These allies had earlier created Euratom, their own multilateral agency, with its own inspectors, for monitoring their peaceful nuclear facilities. They were not about to accept inspectors from the multinational IAEA, which included nationals of the Soviet Union or of Soviet-allied states.[10] For its part, the Soviet Union belonged to the IAEA but was not, of course, a member of Euratom and did not trust Euratom's inspectors to assure it that NATO members such as West Germany were not making nuclear weapons. At the same time, the Soviet Union did not want IAEA inspectors looking at its own reactors, even those for generating electric power. It took years to reach a compromise on these opposing views on IAEA verification of the NPT's provisions.[11]

As finally adopted, the NPT secures the promise that non-nuclear members will not acquire nuclear weapons "from any transferor whatsoever" and will not seek or receive assistance in making them. This promise was as important to non-nuclear weapon neighbors or rivals as it was to the Soviet Union or the United States. It constituted a commitment to neighbors and rivals to the effect that "we won't get the bomb if you don't."[12] To verify that this promise was being kept, non-nuclear weapon members accepted a requirement for inspection of their peaceful nuclear operations such as research and power reactors to ensure that the nuclear material and technology used by these reactors were not also used to make nuclear weapons.[13]

The NPT promises members who agree not to acquire nuclear weapons "the fullest possible exchange of equipment, materials and scientific and technological information on the peaceful uses of nuclear energy." As the NPT states, this agreement should not be interpreted "as affecting the inalienable right" of all its members to produce and use "nuclear energy for peaceful purposes," though conforming with the provisions against seeking or receiving assistance in making weapons. It also promises that the parties will "pursue negotiations in good faith on effective measures relating to the cessation of the nuclear arms race at an early date and to nuclear disarmament, and on a treaty on general and complete disarmament under strict and effective international control."[14] To countries not aligned with the United States or Russia, this obligation has become one of the most important provisions of the treaty. Without further progress toward nuclear weapon disarmament (if not "general and complete disarmament"), these countries see the NPT as perpetuating an unequal world in which some countries have nuclear weapons and some do not.

Inspection Agreements

From the point of view of the United States, the next most important element of the NPT is the agreement to accept inspections by the IAEA, to see that the treaty is being observed. In the wording of the treaty, each of its members not having nuclear weapons must "accept safeguards, as set forth in an agreement to be negotiated and concluded with the International Atomic Energy Agency" pursuant to the agency's "safeguards system."[15] To this day, some non-nuclear weapon members have not signed an IAEA safeguards agreement, despite repeated notices of their deficiency from the IAEA.[16]

Negotiating a "safeguards system" to meet the standards of the 1968 treaty took until 1971.[17] By the early 1990s, after IAEA inspectors had failed to detect Iraqi efforts to build nuclear weapons before the 1991 Gulf War, the IAEA and many NPT parties pressed for a much stronger system than that established in 1971. The proposed new IAEA standards for improved NPT safeguards are included in an Additional Protocol that NPT parties are expected to accept.[18] To encourage its adoption by non-nuclear weapon members, the P-5 (the five nuclear weapon states permitted by the NPT) negotiated Additional Protocols with the IAEA for themselves. These required, often for the first time, inspections of peaceful nuclear activities on P-5 territories. As of May 2006, new Additional Protocol inspection agreements were in force in only 75 of the 188 NPT member countries: 72 without nuclear weapons and 3 of the P-5 nuclear weapon members (Britain, France, and Russia).[19] In 2004 the U.S. Senate consented to U.S. ratification of an Additional Protocol designed to cover peaceful nuclear activities in the United States. However, the necessary U.S. regulatory and administrative changes had not been adopted by May 2006. Thus the Additional Protocol was not yet in force for the United States.

At the Gleneagles G-8 (Group of Eight) summit meeting of July 2005, the United States agreed with the other seven members that the protocol should "become the universally accepted norm for verifying compliance with NPT safeguards obligations. The Additional Protocol must become an essential new standard in the field of nuclear supply arrangements. We will continue to work together to strengthen NSG [Nuclear Supplier's Group] guidelines accordingly."[20]

The Additional Protocol expands the IAEA's inspection authority considerably. Its general objective for NPT members without nuclear weapons is to ensure that their declaration to the IAEA about their nuclear activities is not only correct but a complete list of those activities. Iran's nondisclosure to the IAEA until recent years of its secret uranium-enrichment facilities clearly would violate its Additional Protocol. As of 2006, however, Iran had not yet ratified such a protocol, although it had signed one.

The protocol provides broader access to various nuclear-related sites within the territory of a non-nuclear weapon NPT member than possible before, when inspectors could only examine agreed "strategic points" having nuclear material (such as a nuclear reactor with nuclear fuel) at a "declared" site. Under the protocol, they can look at any location on the site, not just the strategic point. To go beyond such a point before the protocol was adopted, inspectors had to ask for a "special inspection," and if the country to be inspected resisted, they had to ask the IAEA Board of Governors to approve their request. It was in response to the IAEA demand for a special inspection in North Korea in 1992–93 (at two locations not far from the regularly inspected plutonium-separation facility) that the country issued a first notice of withdrawal from the NPT.[21]

Under the protocol, non-nuclear weapon NPT members must declare many more sites than under the earlier IAEA agreement. They must declare, and permit inspections at, locations that do not have nuclear material but do have nuclear-related activities. Iran's uranium-enrichment equipment, for example, is not located at the site of the research reactors that were regularly inspected. The centrifuge enrichment facilities, not yet in operation, had not been declared by Iran. Later, when IAEA inspectors were permitted to inspect them, they found small particles of enriched uranium in them, suggesting that they had been operated. Iran insisted that what it had purchased were second-hand centrifuge components and that the small particles of enriched uranium in them must have come from the country that had owned them first, an argument that the IAEA did not reject after the particles were analyzed at an IAEA laboratory in Austria. Iran did admit that it had experimented with the enrichment of uranium at other undeclared facilities without reporting this fact to the IAEA. It then permitted the IAEA to inspect those facilities, but later refused the inspectors access to them. These episodes clearly show the need for access to nuclear-related facilities even if they are said not to contain enriched uranium or separated plutonium.[22]

Under the protocol, non-nuclear weapon NPT members must also facilitate access to locations beyond those listed in their expanded declarations of sites for inspection if inspectors indicate a special need based on specific information or a need to implement specific technical measures such as "environmental monitoring." This means taking samples for lab testing—such as samples of dust or other deposits on roofs, or leaves of trees outside buildings in the inspected areas; similar deposits on desks, floors, and walls inside such buildings; and water in streams, lakes, or other bodies of water in the area.[23] The resulting information can show whether relevant nuclear activity has taken place recently in the area. To enhance inspection, the IAEA also uses satellite photography purchased commercially or obtained from governments and sometimes relies on other forms of intelligence about nuclear activities provided by its members.

Nuclear Weapon–Free Zones

The nonproliferation regime includes treaties providing for "nuclear weapon–free zones" in several regions of the world where no country has nuclear weapons. These cover Africa, Latin America, Southeast Asia, the South Pacific, and Mongolia.[24] A new zone for Central Asia has been the subject of treaty negotiations for several years. A treaty along these lines for the Middle East, where Israel has nuclear weapons, has been under debate for many years, but Israel has not been willing to give up its weapons until its disputes with the Palestinians and nearby Muslim countries are resolved and peace has reigned for two years.[25]

Nuclear Security

The IAEA has adopted the term "nuclear security" to describe the "prevention and detection of, and response to, theft, sabotage, unauthorized access, illegal transfer or other malicious acts involving nuclear material, other radioactive substances or their associated activities."[26] Nuclear security includes what has long been called "physical protection" of nuclear material from theft and sabotage. "Nuclear security" efforts encompass voluntary actions to better protect nuclear materials, nation-to-nation assistance such as the U.S. Nunn-Lugar Cooperative Threat Reduction program, and international agreements such as the Convention on Physical Protection of Nuclear Material of 1980. Since September 11, 2001, nuclear security has become an increasingly important activity of both the IAEA and many states. In 2005 the International Convention for the Suppression of Acts of Nuclear Terrorism was added to the nonproliferation regime. It is the first antiterrorism treaty approved by the UN General Assembly since the terrorist attacks of 9/11. The initial draft was proposed by Russia in 1997, but it saw many changes before being approved by the General Assembly on April 13, 2005.[27]

This new treaty requires its members to adopt criminal laws to prohibit the unlawful use or possession of a nuclear explosive or radioactive device with intent to cause death, serious bodily injury, or substantial damage to property or to the environment. They must also adopt laws, regulations, or other measures to ensure that such terrorist acts are not made justifiable by considerations of a political, ideological, racial, ethnic, or religious nature.[28] The United States supported adoption of this treaty, which, as one expert sees it, will

> dovetail with the Bush administration's evolving neomultilateralism, characterized by international cooperation among sovereign states, manifested by parallel or joint action towards common goals on a domestic or international level, accompanied by corresponding developments in treaty-based and UN-based international law. Consistent with past expressions of Bush policy, such as promotion of the Proliferation Security Initiative [described later in the chapter], the Nuclear Terrorism Convention does not emphasize the role of international bureaucracies [such as the IAEA].[29]

Although the NPT requires its non-weapon members to account to the IAEA for nuclear material, it does not provide for nuclear security, except insofar as the member's need to keep material "safeguarded"—accounted for—to meet NPT "safeguards" requirements results in greater protection for the material than would otherwise be the case. The first treaty added to the nonproliferation regime to improve nuclear security was the Convention on Physical Protection of Nuclear Material of 1980. But its security requirements apply only to international shipments of nuclear material used for peaceful purposes between parties to the treaty—to prevent theft or sabotage along the way, whether shipments are by train, truck, aircraft, or ship.[30] Attempts to expand the terms, to apply to nuclear material at reactors within each member country, eventually succeeded in gaining an amendment to the treaty, in 2005.[31] In addition, Security Council resolution 1540 of 2004 (discussed in a later section) contains general requirements for the physical protection of nuclear material within all countries around the world, not just those that have joined the Convention on Physical Protection.

Nuclear security is also the subject of the Nunn-Lugar Cooperative Threat Reduction plan supported by the United States. This was initially intended to help Russia, as well as Belarus, Kazakhstan, and Ukraine (former Soviet republics that inherited Soviet nuclear facilities and weapons), improve the security surrounding nuclear weapons, weapon-usable nuclear materials, and related nuclear facilities. It has been expanded by the IAEA, the United States, and the other G-8 countries to include, for example, assistance to less-industrialized countries around the world to strengthen the physical protection of research reactors with weapon-usable highly enriched uranium from thieves and terrorists.

The nuclear security role of the IAEA itself has expanded greatly since September 11, 2001. The agency is now charged with "facilitating the development of, and adherence to, legally binding and non-binding international instruments, developing guidelines and recommendations acceptable to the international community" and providing various advisory and training services. The "international instruments" include not only the NPT, the Physical Protection Convention, and UN Security Council Resolution 1540 but also various multilateral and national initiatives designed to improve nuclear security.[32]

Prohibitions on Nuclear Testing

The 1963 Limited Test Ban Treaty prohibits nuclear tests everywhere but underground, while 1974 and 1976 treaties prohibit even underground weapon tests if their explosive yield exceeds 150 kilotons.[33] The 1996 Comprehensive Test Ban Treaty (CTBT), not yet in force, would ban nuclear tests everywhere, including all those underground. These treaties are intended to inhibit countries having nuclear weapons from testing those weapons to see if and how they work. By discouraging the testing usually thought necessary to develop nuclear weapons, they contribute to nonproliferation. The last such tests were carried out by India and Pakistan in 1998. In 1999 the U.S. Senate failed to reach the two-thirds vote required for U.S. consent to CTBT ratification. Although this question can be presented to the Senate again, the Bush administration is opposed to letting the CTBT come into force for the United States; and without the United States, China, India, and a few other countries that have failed to join, the treaty cannot come into effect for any country.[34]

In 2002 an expert committee of the U.S. National Academy of Sciences concluded "that the United States has the technical capabilities to maintain confidence in the safety and reliability of its existing nuclear weapon stockpile under the CTBT, provided adequate resources are made available to the Department of Energy's nuclear weapon complex and are properly focused on this task."[35] The committee said another key question was what impact foreign testing would have on U.S. security without a CTBT, compared with the impact with a treaty if that treaty was violated clandestinely by other countries. The committee concluded that a no-CTBT world "could be a more dangerous world than today's, for the United States and others" in that even more countries would likely acquire nuclear weapons than have them today. If more countries had nuclear weapons, the committee concluded, the world could expect the following results:

> The directions from which nuclear attack on the United States and its allies would have become conceivable—and the means by which such attack might be carried out (meaning not only intercontinental ballistic missiles [ICBM] but also, among others, ship-based cruise missiles, civilian as well as military aircraft, and truck bombs following smuggling of the weapons across U.S. borders)—would have multiplied alarmingly. . . . [The] worst-case scenario under a no-CTBT regime poses far bigger threats to U.S. security—sophisticated nuclear weapons in the hands of many more adversaries—than the worst-case scenario of clandestine testing in a CTBT regime, within the constraints posed by the monitoring system.[36]

As things stood in late 2005, three of the forty-four states required to join before the CTBT goes into effect had not yet even signed—these were India, Pakistan, and North Korea. Of the forty-one that had signed, only thirty-two had ratified the treaty, and these included only three of the P-5: France, Russia, and the United Kingdom—but not China or the United States.[37] Should China and the United States ratify, international opinion in support of the CTBT, expressed in UN General Assembly resolutions, for example, might help persuade most of the others that have signed the treaty to ratify it. Indeed, in 2004 the UN General Assembly adopted a resolution supporting the CTBT with only the United States dissenting. Of the forty-four states required to join in order for the treaty to go into effect, only India, Pakistan, and North Korea would then remain outside the treaty.[38]

Is there now a moratorium on testing? As a general rule, when a treaty prohibiting particular conduct is signed, the signers are expected to observe its prohibitions even before ratification, at least until it is obvious that the treaty will not go into effect.[39] The signers of the CTBT observed such a moratorium. India and Pakistan, which did not sign, conducted tests after the initial CTBT signing by others, but they have not tested since. Nor has any other country. In a mid-2005 joint statement with President Bush, India's prime minister Manmohan Singh agreed to continue India's moratorium on testing.[40] The Bush administration called for a moratorium on nuclear testing at an international conference in 2006.[41] Continuing the moratorium on testing seems essential to preventing testing by other nations having nuclear weapons.

For most of the more than 180 countries not having nuclear weapons, the CTBT could contribute to nonproliferation by reducing the discrimination inherent in the NPT between those that are permitted to have nuclear weapons and those that are not. The preamble of the NPT refers to a promise the P-5 made in the 1960s "to seek to achieve the discontinuance of all test explosions of nuclear weapons for all time."[42] The CTBT's negotiation was completed in 1996 in large part because the P-5 had promised the non-nuclear weapon NPT countries that if they would agree to extend the NPT in 1995, when it would otherwise have expired, the P-5 would agree to complete negotiation of the CTBT no later than 1996. Many non-nuclear weapon countries saw this as part of the P-5's NPT obligation to negotiate "effective measures relating to the cessation of the nuclear arms race."[43] Without that promise, non-nuclear weapon members might well have let the NPT expire in 1995 when their votes were necessary to extend the life of the treaty.[44]

In repayment for these votes, the United States, during the Clinton administration, became a leader in the negotiation of the CTBT. But President Clinton was unable to persuade the U.S. Senate to vote for ratification of the treaty, and the Bush administration now opposes the treaty. Many attending the 2005 NPT Review Conference expressed frustration at the Bush administration's opposition. Indeed, a group of states friendly to the United States known as the G-10 (Australia, Austria, Canada, Denmark, Hungary, Ireland, the Netherlands, New Zealand, Norway, and Sweden) called upon all recalcitrant states, including the United States, to "ratify the Treaty without delay."[45]

Will the United States resume nuclear weapon tests? In its 2001 Nuclear Posture Review (NPR), the U.S. Defense Department said that the United States "supports the continued observance of the testing moratorium" (resulting from the CTBT's negotiation) but may not be able to do so "for the indefinite future."[46] In 2005 the Bush administration proposed some nuclear weapon improvements, which, if pursued, might lead to a demand by the weapons developers for testing (see chapter 7).

Proliferation Security Initiative (PSI)

The attack of September 11, 2001, and growing U.S. fear that terrorists would acquire nuclear weapons have added a new dimension to the nonproliferation regime: nontreaty cooperation in an attempt to detect and prevent illicit trading of nuclear materials and technology.[47] One such effort is called the Proliferation Security Initiative (PSI). It is a U.S.-led informal "arrangement" among fifteen or so core members—allies and friends of the United States—that have agreed to cooperate in attempting to intercept illegal shipments of weapon-usable materials and equipment by sea, air, truck, or train across both national land boundaries and international waters.[48] Other countries have cooperated in specific actions when asked to do so.

The PSI's purpose is to prevent or deter illicit trading related to nuclear, chemical, and biological weapons among nonstate individuals and companies as well as among nation-states (see chapter 5). The PSI's leading proponent within the U.S. government called it a "counterproliferation arrangement."[49] Counterproliferation, as mentioned earlier, has been defined by the Joint Chiefs of Staff as including "actions taken to defeat the threat and/or use of weapons of mass destruction against the United States, our military forces, friends and allies." The PSI is one of the tools that the Bush administration uses to implement that broad purpose.

UN Security Council Resolution 1540

Another recent addition to the regime is UN Security Council Resolution 1540, adopted in April 2004 after months of negotiation. Although not a treaty, it acts somewhat like an "amendment" to the NPT to (1) deal with "nonstate actors" such as terrorists and (2) require nation-states to adopt national criminal laws and physical security measures to protect their nuclear material, equipment, and technology from theft and sabotage. Resolution 1540 was proposed by President Bush in 2003 because, among other reasons, the NPT did not deal adequately with terrorists.[50]

Amending the NPT to deal with terrorists would have been difficult—it would have required the agreement of many more countries than were necessary for the adoption of Resolution 1540 by the UN Security Council.[51] Moreover, an amendment would not have applied to NPT non-members Israel, India, Pakistan, and North Korea. Thus the Bush administration's effort has produced international rules applicable even to non-NPT members to help prevent terrorists and thieves from acquiring nuclear weapons. One of the resolution's new requirements for all nations is that they must adopt national laws and regulations prohibiting the theft of nuclear material and technology within their territories. They must also adopt security measures such as fences, walls, and locks to protect their nuclear material and technology from terrorists and thieves (see chapter 5).[52]

How Resolution 1540 will be enforced against states that have taken little or no action to comply with its terms is unclear. States have already been inconsistent in their response to its initial requirement, that every national government submit a report on what it has done to comply with the resolution—for example, what relevant statutes and regulations the government had in place before the resolution and which ones it adopted pursuant to the resolution. Some states reported that they had no laws and regulations pertaining to issues on which the resolution required action, whereas others had covered all the required subjects and had many relevant laws and regulations in place. Still others failed to file a report. An implementing committee consisting of representatives of the current members of the Security Council has been created to review the submissions. What the council will do to further implement the resolution remains to be seen.

Negative Security Assurances

The nonproliferation regime also includes "no-first-use" nontreaty promises by the P-5 in which they agree not to use nuclear weapons against any of the NPT parties not having nuclear weapons—with an exception or two stated by each P-5 member apart from China. (The U.S. exception permits the United States to use nuclear weapons first against a non-nuclear weapon NPT member if that member attacks another non-nuclear weapon NPT member while the attacking member is allied with a nuclear weapon state.)[53] These declarations are called "negative security assurances." They were made jointly by the P-5 in 1995 before the UN Security Council as part of the consideration paid to non-nuclear weapon NPT parties to persuade them to vote for the extension of the NPT when it was about to expire that year. These declarations were intended to help reassure non-nuclear weapon NPT parties that they did not need to acquire nuclear weapons themselves because the P-5 would not use nuclear weapons against them.[54] As explained in the next section, the United States has stated broad exceptions to this promise and called it only a "political," not a "legal," obligation. The current believability of its reassurance to non-nuclear weapon NPT parties is therefore unclear.

Positive Security Assurances

In addition, the P-5 countries have promised to seek UN Security Council protection for NPT members not having nuclear weapons in the event these members are threatened with nuclear attack by an enemy having nuclear weapons. These so-called positive security assurances promise that the P-5 will seek immediate UN Security Council orders providing for assistance to any non-nuclear weapon NPT member being threatened by another nation's nuclear weapons.[55] These assurances appear to have helped gain support for the NPT and later for its 1995 extension from NPT parties that did not have nuclear weapons themselves and were not allied with a country such as the United States that did have nuclear weapons. These assurances are not as strong as the alliance treaty promises of defense against attack given to military allies of the United States such as Germany, Italy, Japan, and South Korea. Some or all of these countries would probably have sought nuclear weapons if they had not had a military alliance with the United States.[56]

Multilateral Institutions and Conferences

The regime relies on international organizations and conferences to change and enforce its policies. The most important of these are the IAEA, which is responsible for inspection, and the UN Security Council, which has the authority to enforce IAEA inspection requests or to issue other orders requiring compliance with the NPT.[57] A Security Council order prohibiting the acquisition of nuclear weapons could be based on IAEA reports concerning NPT inspection results, reports by a separate inspector organization created by the council, or information provided by members of the council.

The UN General Assembly also plays an important role in that it debates and adopts resolutions every year concerning recommended practices or negotiations toward preventing the further proliferation of nuclear weapons, reducing the existing stockpiles of those weapons, and proceeding toward nuclear disarmament. A case in point is the negotiation of the NPT following the General Assembly's unanimous adoption in 1961 of a resolution calling for such a treaty.

NPT members also hold formal, treaty-prescribed review conferences every five years, along with preparatory committee gatherings ("PrepComs") almost every year, to identify issues, recommendations, and procedures for the future. NPT review conferences seek consensus on what NPT members are willing to do to strengthen the nonproliferation regime, to accept measures such as the Comprehensive Test Ban Treaty, or to seek future agreement on, for example, a treaty ending production of fissile material for nuclear weapons.

However, the 2005 NPT Review Conference failed to reach agreement on almost everything but the number of conference participants and its cost. It failed to reach a consensus for many reasons, particularly the entrenched and antagonistic positions of such countries as Iran and the United States. In the absence of a final report, Iran was able to avoid any serious discussion of a long IAEA investigation of whether it had complied with the NPT. A sticking point for the United States was opposition to any reference to past U.S. promises to negotiate nuclear-weapon-control agreements, promises made during the Clinton administration at the 1995 and 2000 NPT review conferences.[58]

The "political commitments" of the Clinton administration, as they were referred to by Bush administration representatives, included promises to negotiate and bring into force the CTBT, to continue a moratorium on nuclear weapon tests until the treaty was in force, to negotiate a Fissile Material Cut-off Treaty (FMCT, to halt production of fissile material for nuclear weapons) with effective verification, to continue the Anti-Ballistic Missile (ABM) Treaty from which the Bush administration later withdrew, and to negotiate "effective measures relating to nuclear disarmament" for non-strategic as well as strategic nuclear weapons.[59] The Bush representatives argued that since the terrorist attacks of September 11, 2001, terrorists had become the major threat to the world, that the CTBT and other multilateral treaties supported by other countries did not focus on that threat, and that UN Security Council Resolution 1540 and the Proliferation Security Initiative, both initiated by the Bush administration, were more relevant than arms control treaties.[60] The Bush representatives listed the administration's success in the final implementation of the Strategic Arms Reduction Treaty (START) and in the negotiation of the Moscow Treaty, which provides for further reductions of strategic missiles until the year 2012. The statement also noted that to date the United States had eliminated sixty-four heavy bombers, removed thirty-seven intercontinental ballistic missiles from their silos, dismantled many silos, and removed four ballistic missile submarines from strategic missile service.[61]

Many delegations, including the twenty-five members of the European Union (EU), disagreed with the U.S. position on these and other matters. In particular, the EU statement urged that (1) the CTBT be ratified by the United States, as well as by China and some others whose ratification was essential to bringing the treaty into force; and (2) an FMCT be negotiated at the Geneva Conference on Disarmament (the usual negotiating forum for multilateral arms control measures) where U.S. opposition to verification provisions for such a treaty has thus far blocked negotiations. While a U.S. report mentioned the unilateral and other nontreaty measures the United States had initiated, the EU statement emphasized the need for multilateralism and treaties.[62] The last national position statement presented at the conference was a sharp attack by Iran on the United States. The United States did not respond.[63]

Other governments can have a major effect on the nonproliferation regime even if they are not members of the NPT and do not participate in its conferences, as illustrated in recent U.S. negotiations with India. Not present at the 2005 NPT conference because it is not an NPT member, India has long wanted to join as a nuclear weapon state and thereby be recognized as a major world leader, like the P-5 members. It was willing to help NPT members persuade other countries not to acquire nuclear weapons so long as it did not have to give up its own nuclear weapons. However, amending the NPT to permit India to enter as a nuclear weapon state would be impossible since an amendment requires near consensus, and many non-nuclear weapon parties are opposed to giving such status to any country beyond the members of the P-5.

Less than a month after the 2005 NPT Review Conference ended in failure, President Bush and Prime Minister Singh of India issued a joint statement in Washington proposing U.S.-Indian agreement on issues related to nonproliferation that had been discussed at the conference. Their statement could be construed as giving India most of the benefits of joining the NPT as a nuclear weapon state. Yet under the language of the NPT, India could only join if it did so as a non-nuclear weapon state—which would mean giving up all its nuclear weapons and accepting IAEA safeguards on all its nuclear reactors and uranium-enrichment or plutonium-separation plants. Prime Minister Singh said India would accept IAEA safeguards on all its peaceful nuclear activities (as the P-5 have done, though not required by the NPT to do so) but would not accept them on its activities for making nuclear weapons (as none of the P-5 do). Thus without joining the NPT, India would accept many of the same obligations that nuclear weapon NPT parties accept, rather than those imposed on parties without such weapons. Indirectly, India would achieve what it sought long ago: to become the sixth NPT-permitted nuclear weapon state. It would do so without the necessity of joining or amending the NPT, and without the approval of the UN Security Council or UN General Assembly. It would take a step, with U.S. help, that would have been sharply criticized at the NPT Review Conference if the step had been publicly proposed before the conference ended.[64]

President Bush and Prime Minister Singh agreed to work with "friends and allies to adjust international regimes [including the nuclear nonproliferation regime] to enable full U.S. civil nuclear cooperation and trade with India, including expeditious consideration of fuel supplies for the safeguarded nuclear reactors at Tarapur."[65] Related benefits were planned for both sides. In India's case, if this agreement is accepted by Congress and the relevant statutory provisions are amended or waived, India should get nuclear assistance for peaceful purposes from the United States that is promised by NPT Article IV to non-nuclear weapon NPT parties, but it would not have to give up nuclear weapons as they did.[66]

The NPT would not have to be amended because India would not join the treaty. But U.S. atomic energy legislation would require major changes, because after India's test of 1974, Congress enacted strong statutory provisions to limit U.S. nuclear assistance to India (and Pakistan).[67] Following the 1974 test, members of Congress appeared intent on punishing India for seeking nuclear weapons using the training, nuclear technology, heavy water, and other resources that the United States had earlier provided to India for peaceful purposes. In 2005, however, President Bush promised Prime Minister Singh that he would seek the approval of Congress for assistance for peaceful purposes even though India continued to have nuclear weapons. Bush vowed to "work to achieve full civil nuclear energy cooperation with India as it realizes its goals of promoting nuclear power and achieving energy security."[68] This is a clear departure from Congress's approach in 1978[69]—and from the original intent of the NPT or of the Nuclear Suppliers Group.[70]

As already mentioned, the UN General Assembly also joins in the effort to prevent the spread of nuclear weapons. Indeed, it was responsible for the 1961 resolution that gave rise to the NPT negotiations. In contrast to the NPT Review Conference, the General Assembly does not act by consensus. Every year, its First Committee debates policy recommendations relating to nuclear nonproliferation and nuclear weapons reduction. Every year, the General Assembly can and does adopt resolutions recommending steps related to nonproliferation, nuclear weapons control, and nuclear arms reductions. During its 2005 meeting period, a Millennium World Summit of prime ministers and presidents was held to consider proposals on many subjects, one being appropriate language to deal with nuclear nonproliferation and related subjects such as nuclear weapon testing and nuclear disarmament. Despite a tentative agreement on nonproliferation and arms control language among drafting officials, the language was deleted from the final summit statement.[71]

As mentioned earlier, the UN Security Council also has the power to issue and enforce commands for compliance with the NPT. Some of the resolutions issued during and after the 1991 Gulf War had the effect of enforcing the NPT against Iraq, which in 1991 had been well on its way to making a nuclear weapon.

Export Control Organizations

Although the NPT does prohibit non-nuclear weapon parties from making nuclear explosives, the NPT-required inspections focus on publicly known nuclear reactors and other places where nuclear material is used or stored. NPT parties that export nuclear material, equipment, or technology are not required to report those exports to the IAEA or any other agency and do so only voluntarily.[72] If a country that wanted nuclear weapons secretly imported them or the materials to make them, it would in all likelihood not report that to the IAEA, as Iraq did not. If suppliers of nuclear materials, equipment, or technology were required to report such exports to the IAEA or to an export regulatory agency, the enforcement mechanisms for the NPT would clearly be strengthened.

One important organization created to provide international export controls is the Nuclear Suppliers Group, a voluntary association composed of forty-four suppliers of nuclear equipment, technology, and materials. It tries to achieve common export policies to inhibit the spread of technology and materials useful for making nuclear weapons.[73] Another voluntary group formed even earlier is the IAEA Zangger Committee. Its purpose is to interpret and define the language of the NPT dealing with nuclear material or other assistance that suppliers should avoid exporting to non-nuclear weapon states. Because the United States and some other suppliers wanted to go beyond simply interpreting the NPT (which is what the Zangger Committee does), they formed the NSG to list and describe those items of equipment and technology related to nuclear energy that should not be exported.[74] Compliance with its recommendations is voluntary, and some suppliers, Pakistan for example, are not members. The "proliferation ring" of Pakistani A. Q. Khan (described in chapter 4) helped spread nuclear equipment and technology for uranium enrichment to countries such as North Korea, Libya, and Iran.

Despite its voluntary nature, the NSG performs very useful functions. For example, it calls upon its members not to export uranium-enrichment or plutonium-separation technology or equipment to non-nuclear weapon countries unless the recipient facility is owned or operated by an organization formed by two or more national governments in which the inspectors from one country can watch operators from others to ensure that the plutonium or enriched uranium produced is not hidden away for use in making nuclear weapons.[75] Inspections would thus be continuous and not periodic, as they are under the IAEA.

A better way of dealing with the export of uranium-enrichment or plutonium-separation equipment and technology might be to have recipient facilities inspected continuously to ensure that they are not used to make nuclear weapons. Continuing inspections could take place with the help of resident inspectors from other countries. Adopted long ago by Euratom countries, this method has been recommended in recent years by the IAEA. A group of nuclear experts from twenty-six countries appointed by IAEA director general Mohamed ElBaradei has recommended that countries without nuclear weapons but wishing to build a uranium-enrichment plant do so multilaterally—in cooperation with other participating countries. To ensure that no nuclear weapons would be made from the enriched uranium produced by the enrichment plant, inspectors from other countries could provide continuous monitoring, with periodic inspections by the IAEA.[76]

A national enrichment plant being built by Brazil might satisfy this suggestion as it will be inspected not just by the IAEA but also by Argentina. Argentina and Brazil have a long-standing mutual monitoring agreement stemming from their settlement of earlier disputes and their termination of competitive programs seeking nuclear weapons. In a somewhat similar vein, Russia has proposed to provide a place on Russian territory for Iran to build an enrichment facility, to be operated by Iranians but monitored regularly by Russian inspectors and periodically by IAEA inspectors. A British-French-German trio that negotiated with Iran to restrain it from enriching uranium that could be used for nuclear weapons urged Iran to agree to the plan, but Iran rejected it.[77] The problem is that IAEA inspectors inspect periodically (not continuously) and the inspected reactor operators inevitably receive notice that the inspectors are coming. An enrichment plant can therefore switch from producing high-level uranium enrichment for weapons to low-level uranium enrichment for nuclear reactors fairly quickly when it learns that the inspectors are coming. What is needed is a group of reliable, competent, and resident inspectors who are not beholden to the country in which the reactor is located.

An alternative safeguard, proposed by President Bush in a speech on February 11, 2004, is that there be no exports of enrichment or reprocessing technology to states not already possessing such technologies, and that the supply of enriched uranium or separated plutonium be ensured at reasonable cost only to countries agreeing not to enrich or reprocess the material, subject to verification by the IAEA using Additional Protocol standards. The NSG took up these recommendations but was unable to reach a consensus on them.[78]

Counterproliferation

To reiterate, the Joint Chiefs of Staff define counterproliferation very broadly to include "those actions . . . taken to defeat the threat and/or use of weapons of mass destruction against the United States, our military forces, friends and allies." Before the U.S.-U.K. invasion of Iraq, the U.S. secretary of state argued before the UN Security Council that Iraq was trying to make nuclear and other unconventional weapons, as well as missiles, and that military action had to be taken to prevent Iraq from doing so.[79] Thus the 2003 U.S.-U.K. invasion of Iraq is a clear case of counterproliferation within the Joint Chiefs' definition. Another nontreaty example, this one implemented in considerable part by the State Department, is the Proliferation Security Initiative (PSI). Rather than rely on "cumbersome treaty-based bureaucracies" to prevent illicit trafficking in nuclear materials, then under secretary of state John Bolton argued, the United States should take initiatives to lead friends and allies in various voluntary and cooperative efforts to prevent such trafficking across borders and through international waters.[80] Bolton spoke of the successful PSI intervention to prevent Libya's attempts to acquire uranium-enrichment technology

In the Bush administration, counterproliferation includes efforts by the Defense, State, and Energy Departments to prevent the spread of nuclear weapons. Examples include the Nunn-Lugar Cooperative Threat Reduction Program. This is an important nontreaty effort by the U.S. government to prevent thieves, terrorists, and additional states from acquiring nuclear weapons. The program provides financial support for nuclear security efforts in Russia, in former Soviet republics, and now in other countries. The largest proportion of the U.S. appropriations for this and related programs go to the Defense Department, the next largest to the Energy Department, and the third largest to the State Department. The main aim of the programs is to provide financial assistance to help protect nuclear material (and nuclear weapons in the case of Russia) from theft or sabotage. The allies of the United States who form the Group of Eight (together with Russia and the United States) are cooperating in this effort. It is an extremely important program to prevent the acquisition of nuclear weapons by terrorists, thieves, or "rogue states."[81] As in the negotiation of the NPT and many other aspects of the regime over the years, the United States has been the most important leader of this effort.

Successes of the Nonproliferation Regime

The first and greatest success of both U.S. policy and the nonproliferation regime is that no nuclear weapons have been used in war since 1945. Second, such weapons appear to be in the hands of no more than eight or nine countries (members of the P-5, as well as Israel, India, Pakistan, and probably North Korea). As a result of the NPT and related efforts, many countries that had or were pursuing nuclear weapons—Belarus, Kazakhstan, South Africa, and Ukraine—gave them up. Others that had research programs geared toward learning how to make nuclear weapons joined the NPT and thereby promised not to make nuclear weapons and accepted inspections to ensure that they did not do so. These include Argentina, Australia, Brazil, Canada, Egypt, Germany, Indonesia, Italy, Japan, the Netherlands, Norway, Romania, South Korea, Spain, Sweden, Switzerland, Taiwan, Yugoslavia, and probably a number of others that have not revealed their early interest in nuclear weapons.[82] Given the tensions between neighbors and rivals in various regions, not to mention the tensions of the cold war, twenty-five to forty countries might now have nuclear weapons if there were no nuclear nonproliferation regime.[83]

The IAEA inspections that the NPT requires for its members that do not have nuclear weapons provide the basic standards for judging recent suspected nuclear programs in Iraq, Iran, and Libya, as they did in North Korea before that country announced its withdrawal from the NPT. The inspections are carried out by IAEA inspectors, pursuant to IAEA rules, with occasional guidance from the IAEA Board of Governors, and with enforcement when necessary by the UN Security Council—if the votes are there.[84]

The latest major improvement to the IAEA inspection system is the enhanced inspection authority given to the IAEA by the Additional Protocol. The members of the European Union joined the Additional Protocol together in June 2004. That same month, the G-8 proposed that acceptance of the Additional Protocol be a condition of supplying nuclear technology to any country.[85] That could be a major step toward strengthening the regime. However, as noted earlier, the NSG does not include some newer suppliers such as Pakistan and North Korea.

Another major achievement in the view of many NPT members is that the nations of the world having nuclear weapons appear to have stopped testing them. A resumption of testing by the United States might provide non-aligned states with a reasonable excuse to withdraw from the NPT. Furthermore, without the promise to end testing, NPT members without nuclear weapons would likely not have agreed to extend the NPT beyond 1995.[86] Accordingly, at a 2006 meeting of the UN Disarmament Commission, the United States called for "all states" to "maintain national moratoria on nuclear testing."[87]

In sum, the most important successes of the nonproliferation regime are that no more than nine countries now have nuclear weapons. So far as is known, no terrorists yet have nuclear weapons. But many nuclear experts believe that the actual use of nuclear weapons against the United States is much more likely to come from suicidal terrorists than from a hostile nation-state. The United States would find it difficult to track down and retaliate against such a group. "Deterrence" of a terrorist attack is thus not likely to work in the way that deterrence of a nation-state attack seems to work.[88]

Deficiencies or Failures of the Nonproliferation Regime

The regime continues to have unsettling deficiencies, including the one just mentioned. The NPT itself presents few barriers to the acquisition of nuclear materials or even nuclear weapons by terrorist groups. The first article of the NPT does prohibit the P-5 from transferring nuclear weapons to "any recipient whatsoever," obviously including a terrorist group. Also, the IAEA safeguard provisions require an accounting of weapon-usable nuclear material, the accounting checked periodically by IAEA inspectors. Otherwise, the treaty prohibits only the P-5 from providing nuclear weapons, or nuclear-weapon manufacturing assistance, to nation-states. It does not prohibit NPT members that are not P-5 members from helping terrorists make nuclear weapons. Moreover, it does not prohibit any party, whether it has nuclear weapons or not, from helping terrorists acquire nuclear weapons. The NPT was written in a day when no terrorists and few nations were thought likely to acquire the competence to make nuclear weapons in the foreseeable future. Because the NPT did not require security barriers against theft or sabotage of nuclear materials or nuclear weapons, the post-NPT "nuclear security" efforts have only gradually improved security.

Historically, the best-known failure of the nuclear nonproliferation regime (and U.S. policy) is that at least three countries in addition to the P-5 possess nuclear weapons: India, Israel, and Pakistan—and probably North Korea. Perhaps more troubling is the possible acquisition of nuclear weapons by terrorists, now considered by many to be a greater threat to the United States than the spread of nuclear weapons to more nation-states.

Latent Proliferation

Another major failure is that countries can come close to making nuclear weapons without violating their obligations to the NPT. This state of affairs is sometimes referred to as "latent proliferation": The problem stems in part from the fact that the education, experience, materials, and technology involved in making nuclear weapons can be drawn in large part from peaceful applications of nuclear energy. For example, Iran's efforts to build uranium-enrichment plants appear threatening because low-enriched uranium can be used to make nuclear reactor fuel to generate electricity, and highly enriched uranium can be used to make nuclear weapons. As some states point out, the NPT permits non-nuclear weapon NPT members to have uranium-enrichment or plutonium-separation technology that can produce fissile nuclear material useful for peaceful purposes as well as for nuclear weapons. The NPT clearly prohibits them from using this technology to make weapons, but once they have it, they have taken a major step toward making nuclear weapons.[89]

In the NPT negotiations of the 1960s, the proponents of the first draft, the Soviet Union and the United States, did not support the idea of letting non-nuclear weapon states of the NPT enrich uranium or separate plutonium. However, nonaligned countries demanded it as the price of their joining the NPT. As a result, the NPT gives its non-nuclear weapon members an "inalienable right . . . to develop, research, production and use of nuclear energy for peaceful purposes without discrimination," as long as they do not make nuclear weapons.[90] This permits the use of technologies beyond those necessary to own and operate a nuclear reactor—including, many argue, the right to enrich uranium or to separate plutonium. Both of these processes can be used to make fuel for nuclear reactors as well as nuclear explosives for weapons.[91]

Was it the intention of the NPT's drafters to permit non-nuclear weapon countries to get as close to bomb-building as enriching uranium or separating plutonium without significantly more checks than periodic inspections by IAEA inspectors? As one of the American negotiators of the NPT, I do not remember that we foresaw this as a necessary consequence of the language we finally accepted. Uranium enrichment is a most technologically difficult process developed by American scientists to fuel the first nuclear weapon used in war, the atomic bomb dropped on Hiroshima. At the time of the NPT negotiations in the 1960s, only the Americans, the British, and the Russians had the knowledge and technology to enrich uranium.

This technology can produce low-enriched uranium to fuel nuclear power reactors or highly enriched uranium for bombs. When burned in a nuclear power reactor, uranium produces plutonium, among other products. The plutonium can be separated out by "reprocessing" the "spent" fuel burned in the reactor and can then be used for either power reactors or bombs.

Do non-nuclear weapon countries such as Germany and the Netherlands violate the NPT because they have shares with Britain in a jointly controlled enrichment plant in the Netherlands (Urenco)? These countries have generally been considered compliant because regular observations—not just occasional visits by IAEA inspectors—are being carried out to see that bombs are not being built at the plant. Thus the two countries together with the United Kingdom check on plant operations, whose employees, directors, and managers come from the participating countries. In addition, the plant is subject to close inspection by the multilateral European nuclear control agency, Euratom. Its purpose is to see that the plants it monitors do not produce nuclear weapons. There are also occasional visits by IAEA inspectors. As a practical matter, the chances that the Urenco plant will produce highly enriched uranium for nuclear weapons seem slim.

At the same time, some experts argue that the NPT actually prohibits any non-nuclear weapon members, including Germany and the Netherlands, from separating plutonium and from enriching uranium.[92] This interpretation arises from an apparent conflict between two NPT provisions for non-proliferation (Articles I and II, introduced by the Soviet Union and the United States), on the one hand, and a provision for cooperation for peaceful uses insisted upon by the non-nuclear weapon states (Article IV), on the other hand. Article I says that NPT parties having nuclear weapons shall not "in any way assist, encourage or induce any non-nuclear-weapons State to manufacture or otherwise acquire nuclear weapons," while Article II says that NPT members not having nuclear weapons shall not "manufacture or otherwise acquire nuclear weapons . . . and [shall] not . . . seek or receive any assistance in the manufacture of nuclear weapons." Article IV says:

> Nothing in this Treaty shall be interpreted as affecting the inalienable right of all the Parties to this Treaty to develop research, production and use of nuclear energy for peaceful purposes without discrimination in conformity with Articles I and II . . . as well as to participate in the fullest possible exchange of information for . . . the further development of the applications of nuclear weapons for peaceful purposes.

Note, too, that Article III calls for the inspection of nuclear activities by the non-nuclear weapon NPT parties to ensure that all such activities are for peaceful purposes. Together, these four NPT articles state that nuclear weapon NPT parties may not assist any non-nuclear weapon country in making nuclear weapons by providing, without adequate checks, technology for peaceful uses or other assistance that can be used to make nuclear weapons. Furthermore, non-nuclear weapon NPT parties may not receive assistance for peaceful purposes that can also help them make nuclear weapons unless there are checks to prevent that from happening. The articles stipulate, of course, that non-nuclear weapon NPT parties may not make nuclear weapons. There is general agreement that these articles prohibit non-nuclear weapon NPT parties from enriching uranium or separating plutonium unless their nuclear activities are subject to IAEA inspection to prevent the enriched uranium or separated plutonium from being used to make bombs. But if IAEA inspections cannot be continuous in a given country and if inspectors do not happen to discover uranium enrichment to weapon-usable levels being carried out when they are not there, what action is required to serve the purposes of the NPT? Something more than periodic IAEA inspection is required for uranium-enrichment and plutonium-separation plants.

The added checks used for the European Urenco enrichment plant would seem to satisfy this requirement. The Urenco checks include cooperative ownership and management of the facilities with nationals of all four countries participating—among other reasons, to check on each other. In addition, Euratom provides continuous inspection and IAEA occasional inspections. This seems an adequate solution to the problem of preventing non-nuclear weapon countries from enriching uranium for bombs.

Various related proposals to deal with this problem have been suggested over the years. As already mentioned, the Nuclear Suppliers Group recommended that its members not export uranium-enrichment or plutonium-separation technology except in cases where it would be applied in an enrichment or separation facility owned and operated by more than one country. Mohamed ElBaradei, IAEA's director general, saw this as a nonbinding recommendation, "a gentlemen's agreement," that was "limited in its membership." Because the technology is spreading, ElBaradei added, it is essential to universalize the export control system and enact binding effective international controls on the trading and operation of this technology.[93] He also suggested a five-year moratorium on building new enrichment or reprocessing plants. Therefore ElBaradei is now prepared to accept (in addition to periodic IAEA inspections) continuous non-IAEA inspection by representatives of other nations at any separation or reprocessing plant used by non-nuclear weapon NPT members, to ensure that the plutonium or enriched uranium that it produces is not used to make nuclear weapons.

President Bush asked the NSG members "to refuse to sell enrichment and reprocessing equipment and technologies to any state that does not already possess full-scale, functioning enrichment and reprocessing plants." One purpose was to limit enrichment to the P-5 plus Germany, the Netherlands, Japan, and a few other countries that already had enrichment facilities.[94] In addition, of course, Israel, India, Pakistan, and North Korea, not members of the NPT or the NSG, already have enrichment or reprocessing technology, or both. Iran and Brazil, both NPT members, have long been pursuing uranium-enrichment facilities. So far, it has been very difficult to reach a consensus on President Bush's proposal, which would discriminate against countries such as Brazil, although its new enrichment plant is supposed to have continuing inspections by an Argentina-Brazil nuclear regulatory agency in addition to those by the IAEA. The Argentina-Brazil agency has been conducting inspections of nuclear facilities in both countries for some years.[95] ElBaradei's proposal would seem to accommodate this arrangement and reduce the discrimination. Would the existing suppliers agree to such a plan? The United States has not objected to it. Would other states such as Iran that want to enrich uranium accept it? Iran has refused to accept a Russian plan for cooperative enrichment of Iranian uranium in Russia, as noted earlier.

Today, many more people, companies, and countries than ever before are involved in transactions for the sale of nuclear equipment and materials that could be used either for peaceful or arms purposes.[96] This is one of the major changes placing the nuclear nonproliferation regime under increasing strain. In June 2004 the G-8 members, at President Bush's insistence, agreed to a one-year moratorium on their own export of enrichment or reprocessing technology to provide time to address the problem. This moratorium was extended in 2005.[97] One proposal on the table by then, put forth by the UN Secretary-General's High-Level Panel of distinguished leaders from many countries, was that the IAEA "act as guarantor for the supply of fissile material [usually, enriched uranium] to civilian nuclear users": "While that arrangement is being negotiated, states should, without surrendering the right under the [NPT] to construct such facilities, voluntarily institute a time-limited moratorium on the construction of any further enrichment or reprocessing facilities, with commitment to the moratorium matched by a guarantee of fissile materials by the current suppliers at market rates."[98]

Is such a solution likely to be effective when so many scientists, engineers, and middlemen in so many countries besides the G-8 have access to nuclear-related knowledge and technology?[99] This poses a great challenge to the nonproliferation regime, as discussed in chapter 4.

Inspections

The inspection system negotiated for the NPT in 1970–71 is itself a problem, although alleviated somewhat by the Additional Protocol standards. In February 2004, President Bush argued that "signing the Additional Protocol should be a condition for countries seeking equipment for their nuclear programs by next year."[100] The protocol greatly strengthens the regime's inspection requirements, but countries around the world, even the United States, have been slow to accept it.

Easy Withdrawal?

How easy is it to withdraw from the NPT—to be relieved of all its obligations? North Korea assumed it could withdraw on two occasions, in 1994 and 2003, and the UN Security Council did not act to prevent either action. All the NPT explicitly requires from the NPT party wanting to get out of the treaty is a ninety-day notice to the UN Security Council and the other parties plus a statement of the "extraordinary events, related to subject matter of this Treaty, [that] have jeopardized the supreme interests" of the withdrawing party.[101] Similar language had been negotiated with the Soviet Union for the Limited Test Ban Treaty in 1963, except that it did not require the withdrawing party to notify the Security Council of its intention or to give the reasons why. Such expanded terms of withdrawal from the NPT could raise more serious security problems than would withdrawal from the Limited Test Ban.

Under the NPT, then, the Security Council has authority to deal with threats to peace and has long been considered the enforcer of IAEA decisions on NPT compliance.[102] To the NPT negotiators, withdrawal from the treaty seemed likely to constitute a threat to the peace.[103] Indeed, during the NPT negotiating conference, the Soviet representative argued that a notice of withdrawal to the Security Council was essential because withdrawal could well suggest the pursuit of nuclear weapons by the withdrawing party and was "bound to be related to the powers of the Security Council."[104]

The UN Charter says that a threat to the peace is a necessary prerequisite for the use of force by the Security Council.[105] Could this body reject an NPT party's withdrawal if it would threaten the peace because the withdrawing party had already made, or was planning to make, nuclear weapons and with those weapons could well threaten neighboring or rival nations? The Security Council could authorize the use of force to prevent the making of nuclear weapons. And it could require the withdrawing party to observe the treaty, or it could take other action.[106]

NPT experience with Korea illustrates the complexity of this issue. In 1994 the Security Council debated whether sanctions should be imposed on North Korea for refusing to adhere to its NPT obligations after giving notice of its withdrawal from the NPT in 1993. But China would not agree, so the Security Council did not restrain North Korea from withdrawing from the NPT.

Subsequently, just as the United States was considering the use of force against a feared North Korean attack on South Korea, negotiations between North Korea's supreme leader and former President Jimmy Carter, followed by further negotiations at the ambassadorial level, led North Korea to rescind its 1993 notice of withdrawal on the last day before it would have become effective.[107] In further negotiations, in 1994, North Korea and the United States reached an "Agreed Framework" for possible nuclear inspections (see chapter 5).

In 2003, however, North Korea again notified the Security Council that it was withdrawing from the NPT. This time, it argued, it did not have to give more than a day's notice of withdrawal because all but one day of the required ninety-day notice period had elapsed before it had canceled its 1993 notice.[108] But the reasons it gave in 1993 did not seem relevant in 2003, and no facts were mentioned that would meet the requirements of the NPT withdrawal clause, namely, "extraordinary events, related to the subject matter of this Treaty, [that] have jeopardized the supreme interest of its country." Again the United States negotiated with China for a UN Security Council Resolution to restrain North Korea from withdrawing, and again China refused.

Hence withdrawal from the NPT can raise serious threats to international peace and security, and a Security Council resolution that authorizes the use of force to restrain a withdrawal may sometimes be justified, though P-5 support for such a resolution may be difficult to achieve.[109] The language of the NPT withdrawal provision suggests that even if the Security Council does not take action to prevent a withdrawal from the NPT, the withdrawal does not authorize removal of IAEA safeguards from nuclear facilities acquired while the withdrawing party was an NPT member.[110] This means that North Korea could not justifiably reject safeguards on the uranium or plutonium in the nuclear facilities it acquired while an NPT member. North Korea would probably not have been able to create all the facilities without information, help, or equipment from other countries, obtained when it was supposed to be observing NPT Article II, requiring it and other NPT members "not to seek or receive any assistance in the manufacture of nuclear weapons." Under the treaty's terms, all NPT members that were suppliers of nuclear material, technology, or assistance to North Korea had promised not to provide uranium or plutonium "or equipment or material especially designed or prepared for the processing, use or production" of enriched uranium or separated plutonium "for peaceful purposes" unless the uranium or plutonium were to be subject to IAEA safeguards. Only the P-5 nuclear weapon members had promised "not in any way to assist, encourage or induce any non-nuclear weapon state to manufacture or otherwise acquire nuclear weapons."[111]

The UN Security Council might be more likely to prevent such breaches if its members announced jointly, as a matter of principle, that a withdrawal from the NPT such as North Korea's withdrawal could well constitute a sufficient threat to the peace and thereby authorize the Security Council to call for the use of force to deal with the threat. This would establish a rule that withdrawal from the NPT suggested a possible threat to the peace justifying Security Council consideration and action. The twenty-five EU members have agreed with this view, which is clearly consistent with the meaning of the NPT withdrawal clause.[112] The withdrawal clause is less specific, but it does permit the Security Council to take action to prevent any threat to international peace and security that might result from a withdrawal (see chapter 5).

Terrorist Acquisition of Nuclear Weapons

Another failure of the NPT is that it did not safeguard against the acquisition of nuclear material or nuclear weapons by terrorists. It declared only that the P-5 would be prohibited from providing nuclear weapons to "any recipient whatsoever." Recent additions to the regime proposed by the Bush administration—UN Security Council Resolution 1540 and the Proliferation Security Initiative—would remedy this failing. Their contents were summarized earlier and are described in more detail in chapter 5.

U.S. Compliance with Its Nonproliferation Obligations

Over the years, the United States has probably contributed more than any other country to the nonproliferation regime and to its success. The heart of the regime today is still the NPT and the promises associated with it. However, a great many NPT members that do not have nuclear weapons believe their agreement to remain in the NPT is conditioned, first, upon nonacquisition of nuclear weapons by their non-nuclear weapon rivals and neighbors, and, second, upon P-5 compliance with NPT promises.

NPT Promise of Assistance to Peaceful Nuclear Programs

As mentioned earlier, the idea of P-5 assistance to peaceful nuclear programs arose from Eisenhower's Atoms for Peace plan. The obligation for such assistance is expressed in Article IV of the NPT, and its "inalienable right" clause. This suggests that Iran and other NPT members without nuclear weapons have the right to develop and use nuclear energy for peaceful purposes without discrimination so long as they do not make nuclear weapons.

Compliance with this "inalienable right" is discussed extensively at NPT review conferences every five years, and in other forums as well. The conference held in 2000 recognized that "this right constitutes one of the fundamental objectives of the Treaty."[113] The next conference, in 2005, was unable to reach a consensus on any of the central issues in regard to this right, a prime one being whether the right to peaceful uses continued for North Korea after it withdrew from and ignored the NPT, or whether attempts to prevent Iran from acquiring enrichment capacity were violations of its inalienable NPT right to develop and use nuclear energy without discrimination for peaceful uses. These issues were of serious concern to some NPT parties, particularly the nonaligned countries, but the conference apparently made no headway in resolving them. Indeed, the 2005 conference failed to reach agreement on any substantive proposals for strengthening the nuclear nonproliferation regime.

Positive Security Assurances

As already mentioned, positive security assurances are promises to defend non-nuclear weapon NPT members from attack so long as they refrain from acquiring nuclear weapons themselves. Countries formally allied with the United States have received treaty promises requiring the United States and other allies to join in their defense against a conventional as well as nuclear attack by another country. U.S. allies considered this a continuing obligation to them if they joined the NPT and refrained, as a result of joining, from acquiring their own nuclear weapons. The United States has military-alliance treaties of this kind with NATO countries plus Japan, Australia, and South Korea. In addition, it negotiated an alliance-like treaty with most of the countries of Latin America shortly after World War II (though most of these countries now classify themselves as nonaligned).[114] Clearly, something more than a treaty is required to create a military alliance. The current military alliances appear to have had a significant effect in reassuring countries such as Germany, Italy, Australia, South Korea, and Japan that they did not need to acquire nuclear weapons. But what happens if North Korea seems to threaten the use nuclear weapons against South Korea or Japan? How long would it be before South Korea and Japan sought nuclear weapons? Both are advanced in nuclear technology.

In their positive security assurances of 1995, the P-5 promised to "provide or support immediate assistance, in accordance with the Charter, to any non-nuclear-weapon State Party" to the NPT "that is a victim of an act of, or an object of a threat of, aggression in which nuclear weapons are used."[115] The United States now regards these positive security assurances as "politically," not "legally," binding.[116] How much nonaligned NPT members rely upon them in considering whether to acquire nuclear weapons is unclear. So far as is known, the assurances have never been tested by a request for assistance after the perceived threat of a nuclear attack against a nonaligned NPT member.[117]

Negative Security Assurances

Negative security assurances are a pledge by the United States to refrain from using nuclear weapons against any NPT member not having such weapons unless it attacks either the United States or a U.S. ally while the attacker is allied with a nuclear weapon state or is itself such a state. The pledge is much less than a "no-first-use-of-nuclear-weapons" promise. But it has been an important consideration given by the United States to non-nuclear weapon countries to persuade them to join the NPT and to continue as members. The United States has long contended that these assurances are not legally binding. By contrast, the International Court of Justice has said that they are legally binding promises not to use nuclear weapons against a non-nuclear weapon country.[118] The assurances were stated most recently in parallel declarations by the P-5 countries in 1995, before the UN Security Council. These declarations were part of the price the P-5 paid to persuade the NPT members not having nuclear weapons to extend the NPT indefinitely when it would otherwise have expired.[119] Many countries that have joined nuclear weapon–free zones—in Latin America, Africa, Southeast Asia, and the South Pacific—have been given a similar promise in annexes to the pertinent treaty governing such zones. These annexes have been signed by the United States and the four other P-5 members.[120]

The promises have never really been tested as a response to an actual attack. The Bush administration does not think these promises put a limit on U.S. power to use nuclear weapons.[121] During the Clinton administration, the United States modified the non-use promises, to the objection of some who had received them: One condition under which the United States might use nuclear weapons, for example, is to respond to a chemical or biological weapons attack against it (or an ally), even though the attacker might be one of the many non-nuclear weapon members of the NPT that had been given the non-use promise.[122]

The George W. Bush administration has gone a step further. In its 2001 Nuclear Posture Review, it sought to justify the use of "earth-penetrating" nuclear weapons to destroy underground enemy targets such as storage sites for biological weapons. This would not be a nuclear response to the use of biological weapons by an enemy, but a nuclear first use to prevent an enemy from retaining biological weapons, even though those weapons had not been used (see chapter 6). The administration does not consider the negative security assurances given by the United States in the past to be a barrier to such use. However, one could also argue that assurances given to non-nuclear weapon countries to get them to extend the NPT in 1995 would be violated, assuming of course that the country having the underground storage site had not first attacked the United States or a U.S. ally with nuclear weapons. According to a study of the current U.S. exceptions to its nuclear non-use promises, these exceptions have overtaken the promises.[123] At the same time, any use of nuclear weapons by the United States would have to be weighed against its "corrosive effect on a nearly universal [taboo] that has been cultivated through universal abstinence over 60 years."[124] In other words, there appears to be widespread acceptance of the no-first-use principle.

The P-5 Obligation to Negotiate to Stop the Nuclear Arms Race and to Take Steps toward Nuclear Disarmament

Perhaps the most widely discussed article of the NPT by nonaligned countries at various annual meetings and review conferences is Article VI. It is the one that calls on the P-5 to halt the nuclear arms race and work toward nuclear disarmament. The United States is criticized for its refusal to accept the CTBT; for its termination of the ABM Treaty, which brought an end to the START II Treaty; and for its decision to substitute the Moscow Treaty (SORT) of 2002 for START II. The Moscow Treaty calls for significant reductions in deployed strategic missiles, not their warheads. It permits the missiles to be redeployed with warheads in 2012, after the treaty expires.

As already mentioned, both the U.S. Senate and President Bush have refused to accept the CTBT. Such a treaty has been the goal of many earlier U.S. presidents, starting with President Eisenhower. In addition, the ABM Treaty, negotiated by the Nixon administration, was accepted by every administration since then until terminated by President George W. Bush. At the same time, the United States and Russia have informally agreed to major reciprocal reductions in the deployment of "tactical" nuclear weapons outside their national territories. The United States took the initiative under the first President Bush by announcing the withdrawal to U.S. territory of most nuclear weapons stationed abroad: its nonstrategic nuclear warheads on artillery and short-range missiles in Western Europe, its nuclear bombs for aircraft in several countries, and its nuclear weapons on American surface naval vessels. These withdrawals did not include strategic nuclear weapons on missiles in U.S. submarines and a few hundred aviation bombs deployed with U.S. forces in six NATO countries of Western Europe.[125] Eight days after the U.S. announcement, President Mikhail Gorbachev responded with unilateral steps that went even further.[126] Withdrawal measures such as these might be useful in reducing the threat of terrorists acquiring small and easily transportable nuclear weapons. Obviously, both Russia and the United States still have many nuclear weapons within their own territories, as do some other nuclear weapon countries. In Russia, their dismantlement and protection from thieves and terrorists is assisted by the Nunn-Lugar Cooperative Threat Reduction program.

The United States has also been criticized for its decision to invade Iraq in 2003, an act of counterproliferation (taken without UN Security Council authorization), to deal with nuclear and other unconventional weapons alleged to be there, rather than devoting more attention to North Korea's admitted pursuit of nuclear weapons. The Security Council has long been recognized as the ultimate enforcer of NPT-required IAEA inspections. In October 2002 the council authorized new inspections for nuclear and other unconventional weapons and for missiles in Iraq. Inspections begun in January 2003 had not yet been completed when the United States and its coalition partners launched their invasion in March. Impatient with the inspectors' failure to find any nonconventional weapons in Iraq in less than three months, and unable to obtain authorization for an invasion to enforce Iraq's nonproliferation obligations, the coalition decided to move ahead. The United States told the Security Council that the invasion was necessary to prevent Iraq from continuing its efforts to make nuclear and other nonconventional weapons. No nuclear weapons or efforts to make them (beyond those discovered earlier by international inspectors) were found.[127] Meanwhile, negotiations with North Korea over its nuclear weapons program received little attention until mid-2004. A second round of negotiations in 2005 merely produced an agreed statement of principles for future negotiations. Immediately after the announcement of this agreed statement, major differences between North Korea and the United States arose on what the language of the statement meant (see chapter 5).

Even moderate nonaligned NPT members have been critical of both the U.S. "preventive-war" invasion of Iraq and attitude toward reducing its own nuclear weapons. New Zealand, as the 2003 leader of the New Agenda Coalition of "centrist" nonaligned, non-nuclear weapon NPT members, most of whom are good friends of the United States, was also uneasy because "the number of nuclear weapons deployed or in storage, amounts to many thousands. Nuclear weapons continue to be part of security doctrines. There are disturbing references to new types of low-yield nuclear weapons and plans related to new battlefield uses for those weapons."[128] Another complaint is that the United States and India were the only two countries opposing a resolution sponsored by Japan calling, as the NPT does, for the eventual elimination of nuclear weapons. Even Britain voted for it.[129] The current U.S. policy of opposing limits on testing and acquisition of nuclear weapons for itself while supporting such limits on other countries is not popular around the world.

How Will Unpopular U.S. Actions Affect the NPT?

Perhaps the most pressing question is whether the U.S. withdrawal from the ABM Treaty and failure to agree to permanent commitments to reduce its nuclear warheads and missiles will give some non-nuclear weapon members an excuse to withdraw from the NPT. North Korea has already set a bad example in this regard, and others might follow, especially if they disagree with U.S. justification for "preemption" (preventive war) in the 2002 U.S. nuclear strategy documents discussed in this book. It also used this term in justifying its invasion of Iraq, which has been criticized even by friendly countries (see chapter 2).[130]

In the view of most NPT parties that do not have nuclear weapons, U.S. respect for its NPT obligation to limit, reduce, and ultimately eliminate nuclear weapons is essential to the health of the treaty. If non-nuclear weapon NPT members see North Korea (and perhaps Iran) pursuing nuclear weapons without restraint from the UN Security Council, and see the United States emphasizing the importance of its own nuclear weapons and its need to develop new ones (see chapter 7), they may use this as an excuse to withdraw from the NPT and pursue nuclear weapons themselves. Ultimately, of course, the continuing success of the NPT regime will largely depend on whether they think their national interests are better served without nuclear weapons or with them.

Yet the 2001 U.S. Nuclear Posture Review argues: "New [nuclear weapon] capabilities must be developed to defeat emerging threats such as hard and deeply buried targets, to find and attack mobile and relocatable targets, to defeat chemical and biological agents, and to improve accuracy and limit collateral damage. Developments of these capabilities, to include research and timely fielding of new systems to address these challenges, are imperative."[131]

Such statements might discourage nonaligned countries from remaining in the NPT and give them an incentive to begin uranium enrichment or to reprocess spent fuel to make plutonium—or even to sympathize with Iran rather than support the United States.

Regime Successes and Failures in Particular Countries

Future challenges for the regime may well depend on the present approach to proliferation in individual countries.

Successes

All significant countries but India, Israel, Pakistan, and probably North Korea are now members of the NPT.[132] Many countries have put aside nuclear weapon research programs because of the NPT. Even South Africa, which had actually built nuclear weapons, gave them up and joined the NPT as a non-nuclear weapon state. The NPT and efforts by the United States, among others, have persuaded perhaps twenty to thirty countries not to acquire nuclear weapons that otherwise would probably have done so.[133]

Three former Soviet republics—Belarus, Kazakhstan, and Ukraine—transferred the nuclear weapons on their territories to Russia, with the United States providing major funding to pay for the shipments. Like South Africa, all three countries agreed to become non-nuclear weapon parties to the NPT.[134]

Failures

Israel began a nuclear weapons program in the early 1960s. Despite secret negotiations with the United States during that decade, Israel refused to join the NPT and is today regarded as a nuclear weapon power though it has never officially admitted having nuclear weapons. During the 1960s and 1970s, the United States also tried hard to persuade India to join the NPT. India refused, even though it had participated actively in the negotiation of the NPT. India conducted its first nuclear explosion in 1974. When India refused to join the NPT, Pakistan followed suit, though it had entered Atoms for Peace cooperation agreements with both Canada and the United States. Pakistan had started its nuclear weapon program even before India's 1974 test but did not conduct its first test until 1998, following India's tests that year.

By 1985 the U.S. Congress suspected that Pakistan was on the road to acquiring nuclear weapons. As a condition of future U.S. foreign aid, it called on the president to certify that Pakistan did not "possess a nuclear explosive device." The president made such certifications in fiscal 1986 through 1990, during the war that followed the Soviet invasion of Afghanistan, at which time the United States turned to Pakistan for support in aiding those fighting against the Soviet Union. In November 1990, as the Soviet Union was collapsing, the first President Bush refused to renew the certification because U.S. intelligence suggested that Pakistan had been fabricating components for nuclear weapons and developing nuclear-capable missiles for several years. In 1998, when Pakistan tested a nuclear weapon after India did, the United States imposed sanctions on both countries—until it needed Pakistani and Indian support for the U.S.-led war of 2001–02 in Afghanistan against al Qaeda and the Taliban. The sanctions were then removed.[135]

Mixed Successes and Failures

The United States succeeded in keeping North Korea in the NPT during negotiations after North Korea's original notice of withdrawal from the treaty. Although North Korea then negotiated the Agreed Framework of 1994, which contained its promise not to acquire nuclear weapons, it hid from IAEA inspectors what the United States believed to be efforts to enrich uranium for weapons. Later, it issued a new notice of withdrawal from the NPT, after its secret uranium-enrichment efforts were announced by the United States. Because American officials concluded that these and other North Korean efforts to gain the ability to make nuclear weapons violated the Agreed Framework, the United States cut off North Korea's fuel oil supply promised by the Agreed Framework. Then the Six Parties (China, Japan, Russia, North Korea, South Korea, and the United States) held talks to bring North Korea back into the NPT and on September 19, 2005, arrived at an agreed goal for future talks: "the verifiable denuclearization of the Korean Peninsula in a peaceful manner." If past experience is any indication, it will take a long time to reach this goal.[136]

In 1974 Iraq acquired a large research reactor and a small plutonium-separation plant from France, reportedly for peaceful purposes and therefore not in violation of the NPT if put under IAEA safeguards—as they were. (At the time, Iraq was a party to the NPT, but France had not yet joined.) In 1981 the reactor was destroyed by an Israeli bombing attack, but by the time of the 1991 Gulf War, Iraqi scientists were pursuing a crash program to make a bomb from the highly enriched uranium (HEU) supplied mainly by France and the Soviet Union for use in research reactors. By combining HEU that had been irradiated (within a research reactor) with HEU that had not yet been so irradiated for a total of 35 kilograms of HEU, and then adding HEU from uranium-enrichment facilities that the Iraqis had built or were building, Iraqi scientists thought they would have enough for a bomb by the end of 1991.[137]

These and other Iraqi nuclear activities were disclosed in part by defectors from Iraq and in part by broader IAEA inspections authorized by the UN Security Council following the 1991 Gulf War. Except for the research reactors and their fuel, these Iraqi nuclear weapon efforts had not been declared by Iraq to IAEA inspectors before the Gulf War. Moreover, they had not been discovered during IAEA inspections before that war.[138]

Argentina and Brazil at first stayed out of the NPT and conducted research on how to make nuclear weapons. But they later damped down their nuclear rivalry and agreed to join the NPT as well as the Latin American Nuclear Weapon–Free Zone.[139] As noted earlier, Brazil is now building a new plant for enriching uranium that will be subject to periodic IAEA inspections and continuing Argentinean monitoring.[140]

Iran is a mixed success and failure. Unlike India, it joined the NPT long ago but for some years appears to have been seeking the capability to make nuclear weapons. President Bush's 2006 National Security Strategy gives Iran a higher nuclear-weapon threat rating: "We face no greater challenge from a single country than from Iran. . . . The Iranian regime's true intentions are clearly revealed by the regime's refusal to negotiate in good faith; its refusal to come into compliance with its international obligations by providing the IAEA access to nuclear sites and resolving troubling questions; and the aggressive statements of its president."[141]

Iran has negotiated with Britain, China, France, Germany, and Russia over several years because of its desire to enrich uranium and their fear that such enrichment capability will likely be used to produce highly enriched uranium for nuclear weapons. Its case has been before the IAEA repeatedly over more than three years. As of May 2006, Iran's case is before the UN Security Council, but negotiations among the interested parties, and Iranian efforts to enrich uranium, are likely to continue for some time.

Iran is much further away from nuclear weapons than is North Korea—which appears to be an even greater failure of the nonproliferation regime. Recall, too, that North Korea has withdrawn from the NPT to continue making nuclear weapons. While recognizing that North Korea "poses a serious nuclear proliferation challenge," President Bush's 2006 National Security Strategy says his administration has had more success with North Korea:

> This time the United States has successfully forged a consensus among
> key regional partners—China, Japan, Russia and the Republic of Korea

[South Korea] that the DPRK [North Korea] must give up all its existing nuclear programs. . . . In a joint statement on September 19, 2005,
in the Six Party Talks . . . the DPRK agreed to abandon its nuclear
weapons and all nuclear programs.[142]

The "joint statement" of the six parties to which President Bush referred
suggested an agreed goal for future negotiations: removing nuclear weapons
from the Korean Peninsula. Its issuance was followed by disputes between
North Korea and the United States over what the statement meant—North
Korea insisting that it meant that North Korea would be given modern
nuclear power reactors with which to generate electricity before it had to do
anything further, and the United States insisting that North Korea had first to
take major steps to eliminate its capacity for manufacturing nuclear weapons.
The joint statement's goal of removing nuclear weapons from North Korea
(there are none in South Korea so far as we know) is clearly worthy, but the
disagreement of how and when that will be done suggests that the statement
is only a first step.

Though a participant in the negotiation of the NPT during the 1960s,
India did not join it, apparently because it wanted to keep open its option to
acquire nuclear weapons. A test by India in 1974 led the United States to make
new efforts to restrain proliferation, including passage of the Nuclear Non-
Proliferation Act of 1978 limiting U.S. nuclear exports to countries such as
India that sought nuclear weapons. This was followed by agreement on NSG
supplier-country guidelines for control over the export of nuclear material,
equipment, and know-how.

The NSG guidelines list nuclear-related dual-use equipment, materials,
software, and technology that "could make a major contribution to 'nuclear
explosive activity' or an 'unsafeguarded nuclear fuel-cycle activity.'" Supplier
governments have agreed not to authorize transfers of such items "for use in
a non-nuclear-weapon state in a nuclear explosive activity or an unsafeguarded nuclear fuel cycle activity." In general, the guidelines say, there should
be no export of such items "when there is an unacceptable risk of diversion
to such an activity."[143] Because there are important "dual-use" items that can
be used both for making weapons and for operating reactors, these guidelines
cannot prohibit the export of these items altogether.

The United States and others persuaded the industrialized countries of
Western Europe as well as Argentina, Brazil, China, Czechoslovakia, Japan,
Romania, Russia, South Korea, and several other potential suppliers to accept
the NSG guidelines.[144] But nuclear suppliers such as Pakistan and North

Korea are not members of the NSG and have not observed the guidelines in dealing with the A. Q. Khan proliferation ring. The NSG cannot be as effective today as it once was because there are now several non-NSG suppliers of dual-use materials and technologies that can be used for making weapons. Some of these states, however, have declared their intention to follow the NSG guidelines (see chapter 4).

The U.S. Nunn-Lugar cooperative program to reduce the nuclear threat arose in the wake of U.S.-Russian agreements to remove nuclear weapons from Belarus, Kazakhstan, and Ukraine at the end of the cold war.[145] For a decade or more, it and a related nonproliferation assistance program have authorized funds for the U.S. Departments of Defense, Energy, and State to help Russia and other former Soviet republics protect nuclear weapons and weapon-usable nuclear material from acquisition by thieves, terrorists, or other countries. Significant achievements have been made through comprehensive security upgrades of weapon-usable material in the former Soviet Union. By October 2004, security upgrades (some rapid and some comprehensive) had been completed for about half of all this material.[146]

Begun a decade ago during the Clinton administration, these programs are receiving effective support from the Bush administration because they are devoted to keeping nuclear weapons and nuclear weapon–usable material in Russia and some other countries out of the hands of terrorists and thieves. The programs need more funds and have a long way to go to ensure that such material in the former Soviet republics (especially Russia) is secure.[147] In fact, the amount secured in the former Soviet republics in the two years following September 11, 2001, was no more than the amount secured in the two years preceding September 11, according to periodic reports by Harvard experts. Much work remains to be done in this regard, and the pace has been slow, for a variety of reasons.[148]

In February 2005, Presidents Bush and Putin agreed that their countries would continue to cooperate on nuclear security matters and would appoint senior officials from participating agencies from both countries "to oversee implementation efforts" for their cooperation.[149] This is a good idea, which the two countries should expand upon in providing effective security for their nuclear weapons and weapons-usable nuclear materials.

Conclusion

To date, the nonproliferation regime has had a mixed record. Certainly its greatest success is that only eight or nine countries appear to have nuclear weapons, not the two dozen or more that would probably have them by now if the regime did not exist. This is a major achievement due to the efforts of the United States and many other countries that have actively supported the regime over the years. At the same time, some notable failures have occurred over the past decade or so. For example, U.S.-initiated multilateral nuclear export controls have been unable to prevent Pakistan, North Korea, and Iran from acquiring technology for enriching uranium for bomb-making purposes. According to an analyst at the Institute for Science and International Security:

> The existing system [of export controls] is a patchwork of legal and political commitments with varying adherents and application. . . . The NSG . . . does not include many supplier states, and it lacks the legal and normative status of a treaty and the threat of enforcement. . . . None of the existing measures [including UN Security Council Resolution 1540 discussed in this chapter] sets a clear standard for what makes an adequate system of nuclear export controls.[150]

In addition, recent actions of the United States do not coincide with its NPT obligations (especially its commitment to limit and reduce its own nuclear weapons). They have generated strong criticism among nonaligned NPT members—who form the majority of the NPT's membership. A growing concern is that countries wanting to go nuclear might use such U.S. actions as an excuse for withdrawing from the NPT. The United States has also been widely criticized for its invasion of Iraq in 2003, which was initiated just as inspectors authorized by the Security Council were inspecting Iraq for nuclear, biological, and chemical weapons. The United States justified the invasion on the grounds that Iraq had these weapons and that U.S. efforts were needed to find them. It then substituted its inspectors for those authorized earlier by the Security Council (who had had to leave Iraq because of the U.S. invasion).

The Bush administration also claimed the invasion was necessary to deal with terrorists in Iraq. Since September 11, 2001, many in the United States have come to believe that the greatest threat to the nonproliferation regime is the possibility that nuclear weapons will fall into the hands of a terrorist group such as al Qaeda. If anything, the invasion seems to have attracted terrorists to Iraq, rather than preventing any there from acquiring nuclear weapons.

Other initiatives of the Bush administration appear more helpful in preventing terrorists from acquiring nuclear weapons. It led the way after September 11 in proposing two useful additions to the nonproliferation regime to address this issue. The first was UN Security Council Resolution

1540 of April 2004, which in effect altered two existing global nuclear non-proliferation treaties, the NPT and the Convention on Physical Protection of Nuclear Material, for the benefit of nonproliferation. For example, Resolution 1540 makes the NPT's nuclear nonproliferation objective applicable to terrorists and thieves, not just to nation-states, the NPT's primary focus. Moreover, it requires nation-states to adopt national laws and regulations prohibiting the sale or other transfer of nuclear materials to persons not authorized to receive them.

In addition, the administration's Proliferation Security Initiative has provided a basis for stopping ships at sea, or inspecting them in port, if they are suspected of carrying nuclear material or related technology and equipment to terrorists or nation-states desiring to acquire nuclear weapons. This has the potential to help limit the trade in weapon-usable nuclear material, equipment, and technology in the future. The PSI and UN Security Council Resolution 1540 are useful additions to the nuclear nonproliferation regime spearheaded by the United States and are supported by many other governments.

Notes

1. See, for example, Henry Sokolski, *Best of Intentions: America's Campaign against Nuclear Weapons* (New York: Praeger, 2001); Frank von Hippel, "A Comprehensive Approach to Elimination of Highly-Enriched-Uranium from All Nuclear-Reactor Fuel Cycles," *Science and Global Security* 12, no. 3 (2004): 137–39; George Bunn and Chaim Braun, "Terrorism Potential for Research Reactors Compared with Power Reactors," *American Behavioral Scientist* 46 (February 2003): 714–19.

2. For a history and description of IAEA efforts to verify the NPT and otherwise control nuclear weapons, see IAEA, "2005 NPT Review Conference: International Atomic Energy Agency," in *Review Conference of the Parties to the NPT* (New York: UN Secretariat, April 2005), chap. 2.

3. Joint Chiefs of Staff, *DOD Dictionary of Military and Associated Terms* (Government Printing Office, 2004).

4. "Treaty on the Non-Proliferation of Nuclear Weapons between the United States and Other Governments," signed at Washington, London, and Moscow, July 1, 1968. Consent to ratification advised by the U.S. Senate, March 13, 1969. Proclaimed (ratified) by the U.S. president, March 5, 1970, and entered into force March 5, 1970. See *Treaties and Other International Acts* Series 6839 (1970). For parties, text, and efforts to achieve full compliance, see "Treaty on the Nonproliferation of Nuclear Weapons (NPT)," *Inventory of International Organizations and Regimes* (Monterey, Calif.: Center for Nonproliferation Studies, 2004), p. NPT-1 (cns.miis.edu/pubs/inven/index).

5. See UN General Assembly Resolution 1665, Documents on Disarmament (GPO 1962), p. 694.

6. See George Bunn, *Arms Control by Committee: Managing Negotiations with the Russians* (Stanford University Press, 1992), pp. 64–65.

7. NPT membership includes even Switzerland, which is not a member of the United Nations. Though it signed the NPT, Taiwan is not considered a member by China and by some other members that have agreed not to recognize Taiwan as a separate state from China.

8. When North Korea withdrew again in 2003, it gave only one day's notice, having used up eighty-nine days of the required notice period in its prior withdrawal. Japan and some other countries questioned the withdrawal's validity, arguing that a new ninety-day notice and new statement of reasons were required and that North Korea could not rely upon a notice given ten years earlier stating reasons that were inadequate then and no longer applicable now. See George Bunn and Roland Timerbaev, "What Does the NPT Withdrawal Clause Mean?" *Yaderny Kontrol,* Moscow, September 2005. Some also argued that North Korea had to relinquish benefits acquired—a nuclear reactor, plutonium-separation technology, and a great deal of useful nuclear information—when it promised to join the NPT and finally did. See "Preventing Nuclear Proliferation and Nuclear Terrorism: Essential Steps to Reduce the Availability of Nuclear-Explosive Materials," Center for International Security and Cooperation Report (Stanford University, 2005).

9. Bunn, *Arms Control by Committee*, pp. 72–80.

10. David Fischer, *History of the IAEA: The First Forty Years* (Vienna: IAEA, 1997), pp. 29–31. This, the official IAEA account, begins with Eisenhower's "Atoms for Peace" speech to the UN General Assembly and continues: "Eisenhower's proposals led to the creation of the IAEA and helped to shape international co-operation in the civilian use of nuclear energy up to 1978, when a far reaching change in American nuclear law signaled the end of Eisenhower's programme of 'Atoms for Peace'" (p. 9). In 1978 Congress enacted a law based on President Jimmy Carter's proposals that attempted to "use the influence of the USA, as the world's major supplier of nuclear plants and enriched fuel, to limit and eventually put an end to the separation of plutonium and the production of high enriched uranium (HEU) for civilian purposes." The Carter administration tried to persuade other countries to agree to this plan, without much success, in part because its assumptions about a rapid expansion of nuclear power, a shortage of uranium and a rise in its price, and the likely use of breeder reactors all turned out to be incorrect. Although the reprocessing of spent fuel can lead directly to the acquisition of weapon-usable material while the "once-through" fuel cycle cannot, the international discussions failed to reach a consensus on whether the former was more "proliferation prone." Hence nonproliferation made almost no progress. A 1987 UN conference, the Promotion of International Cooperation in the Peaceful Uses of Nuclear Energy, produced similarly meager results. See ibid., pp. 100–01.

11. Bunn, *Arms Control by Committee*, chap. 5.

12. See NPT, art. II: "Each non-nuclear weapon State Party to the Treaty undertakes . . . not to manufacture or otherwise acquire nuclear weapons or other nuclear explosive devices."

13. See NPT, art. III ; also Bunn, *Arms Control by Committee*, chap. 5.

14. See NPT, arts. I, II, and IV.

15. See NPT, art. III.

16. See, for example, IAEA, "2005 NPT Review Conference," p. 3. Some forty countries that are non-nuclear weapon members of the NPT have not yet brought the 1970s version

of IAEA safeguards into effect. Saudi Arabia recently signed a safeguards agreement with the IAEA that is less than that required by IAEA INFIRC/153 of 1972, apparently because the country has no nuclear reactors.

17. IAEA, "The Structure and Content of Agreements between the Agency and States Required in Connection with the Treaty on the Non-Proliferation of Nuclear Weapons," Information Circular 153 (1971). For the history of the negotiations that produced these safeguards, see Fischer, *History of the IAEA,* chap. 8.

18. IAEA, "Model Additional Protocol to the Agreements between States and the International Atomic Energy Agency for the Application of Safeguards," Information Circular 540 (1998).

19. See www.iaea.org/ourwork/SV/safeguards/sg_protocol.html. By the end of November 2005, additional protocols had been signed by 106 NPT parties but had been put into legal effect (by being ratified, entered into statutory revisions, or given regulatory status) by only 69. The number 188 assumes that North Korea is no longer a party to the NPT, though some NPT members argue that its withdrawal was legally ineffective.

20. G-8 Gleneagles Statement on Non-Proliferation, July 2005.

21. See Larry A. Niksh, "UN Security Council Consideration of North Korea's Violations of Its Nuclear Treaty Obligations," Report 94–299 F (Congressional Research Service, April 6, 1994).

22. See Mohamed ElBaradei, "Implementation of the NPT Safeguards Agreement in the Islamic Republic of Iran," Report GOV/2004/34 (IAEA, June 1, 2004), pp. 5–6; Mohamed ElBaradei, "Implementation of the NPT Safeguards Agreement in the Islamic Republic of Iran," Report GOV/2003/xx (IAEA, November 2003), pp. 3–6; Elaine Sciolino, "UN Agency Says Iran Falls Short on Nuclear Data," *New York Times,* April 29, 2006.

23. See, for example, Mohamed ElBaradei, "IAEA Verification System at a Cross-Road," statement to Carnegie Endowment for International Peace Conference on Nuclear Non-Proliferation, Washington, January 30–31, 1995; George Bunn, "Inspection for Clandestine Nuclear Activities: Does the Nuclear Non-Proliferation Treaty Provide Legal Authority for the IAEA's Proposals for Reform?" *Nuclear Law Bulletin* 57 (June 1996): 9–12.

24. See Joseph Cirincione, with Jon Wolfstahl and Miriam Rajkumar, *Deadly Arsenals: Tracking Weapons of Mass Destruction* (Washington: Carnegie Endowment for International Peace, 2002), pp. 30, 381, 384.

25. Ibid., p. 228.

26. See IAEA, "Nuclear Security—Measures to Protect against Nuclear Terrorism, Progress Report and Nuclear Security Plan for 2006–2009," Report of the Director General GC(49)/17 (2005), p. 1, n. 2.

27. See UN General Assembly, "International Convention on the Suppression of Nuclear Terrorism," Ad Hoc Committee Report A/59/766 (April 4, 2005) (www.un.int/usa/a-59-766.pdf).

28. See Ibid., arts. 2, 5, and 6 of the International Convention.

29. Steven C. Welsch, "Nuclear Terrorism Convention: International Convention of the Suppression of Acts of Nuclear Terrorism" (Washington: National Science Foundation, Center for Defense Information, May 17, 2005) (www.nuclearpathways.org).

30. See IAEA, "Convention on Physical Protection of Nuclear Material," Information Circular 274 (February 28, 1997), rev. 1, add. 6.The convention went into effect in 1991 for many countries. It has over sixty parties, and a consensus was developed during the

period 1998–2003 for its amendment to apply within countries, not just in international transit (its present coverage). Such an amendment was agreed in 2005.

31. Proposals to amend the convention go back to at least 1997. See George Bunn, "How to Strengthen International Norms against Stealing or Smuggling Nuclear Material?" in *Proceedings of the Workshop at Stanford University, July 28–30, 1997, Comparative Analysis of Approaches to the Protection of Fissile Materials* (Lawrence Livermore National Laboratory, 1998), pp. 133, 135–36; Matthew Bunn, "Security for Weapons-Usable Nuclear Materials: Expanding International Cooperation, Strengthening International Safeguards," in *Proceedings of the Workshop at Stanford University, July 28–30, 1997*, pp. 13, 25.

32. See IAEA, "Nuclear Security," p. 1.

33. The 1974 and 1976 treaties were the Threshold Test Ban and the Peaceful Nuclear Explosions Treaty. See Bunn, *Arms Control by Committee*, pp. 49–50.

34. For a useful review of the current status of the CTBT, see Keith Hansen, "Implications of Alternative CTBT Futures for the Nuclear Nonproliferation Regime," *Bulletin of the Atomic Scientists* 61 (January/February 2005).

35. National Academy Committee, *Technical Issues Related to Ratification of the Comprehensive Test Ban Treaty* (Washington: National Academies Press, 2002), p. 1.

36. Ibid., pp. 7, 8, 9, 11.

37. See www.ctbto.org.

38. See Hansen, "Implications of Alternative CTBT Futures."

39. See "Vienna Convention on the Law of Treaties," *American Journal of International Law* 63 (October 1969): 875–903 ; American Law Institute, *Restatement of the Law of Treaties,* vol. 1 (Chicago, 1987), pt. 3, pp. 144–45.

40. Text of India-U.S. Joint Statement of July 19, 2005, Indo-Asian News Service, July 19, 2005.

41. United States, "Recommendations for achieving the objective of nuclear disarmament and non-proliferation of nuclear weapons," submitted to the UN Disarmament Commission, 2006 Substantive Session, A/CN.10/2006/WG.I/WP.1 (April 18, 2006).

42. NPT preamble, par. 11.

43. NPT, art. VI. See 1995 NPT Extension Conference Decision 2, par. 4 (a), in Rebecca Johnson, "Indefinite Extension of the Non-Proliferation Treaty: Risks and Reckonings," *Acronym* (September 1995): app. 1, p. 73.

44. See "Roundtable Discussion: The Comprehensive Test Ban Treaty: Next Steps," report of conference sponsored by Center of International Security and Cooperation, Stanford Institute of International Studies, and Lawyers Alliance for World Security (CISAC and LAWS, 2000), pp. 22–23.

45. See Douglas Roche, *Deadly Deadlock: A Political Analysis of the Seventh Review Conference of the Non-Proliferation Treaty* (San Francisco: Middle Powers Initiative, 2005), p. 37.

46. U.S. Department of Defense, *Nuclear Posture Review [Excerpts]* (GPO, 2002), p. 18 (www.globalsecuity.org/wmd/library/policy/dod/npr.htm [January 30, 2003]).

47. See Graham Allison, *Nuclear Terrorism: The Ultimate Preventable Catastrophe* (New York: Henry Holt, 2004), pp. 19–42; and Charles D. Ferguson and William C. Potter, with Amy Sands, Leonard Spector, and Fred Wehling, *The Four Faces of Nuclear Terrorism* (Monterey, Calif.: Monterey Institute, 2004), chap. 2.

48. See White House website, www/whitehous.gov/news/releases/20030904-11html (available as of May 20, 2004).

49. See John R. Bolton, "An All-Out War on Proliferation," *Financial Times*, September 6, 2004, op-ed page.

50. See President Bush, address to UN General Assembly, September 23, 2003 (www.whitehouse.gov/news/releases/2003/09/20030923-r.html).

51. Any amendment must be approved by a majority, including *all* of the P-5 plus *all* of the forty members of the Board of Governors of the IAEA. See NPT, art. VIII.

52. "UN Security Council Unanimously Passes Resolution Preventing Proliferation of WMD," April 28, 2004 (www/acronym/org.uk/docs/0404/doc16.html).

53. See George Bunn, "The Legal Status of U.S. Negative Security Assurances to Non-Nuclear Weapon States," *Nonproliferation Review* 4 (Spring/Summer 1997): 8.

54. For a history of these promises, see ibid. For a description of the George W. Bush administration's position on what should be required, see Harold A. Feiveson and Ernst J. Hogendoorn, "No First Use of Nuclear Weapons," *Nonproliferation Review* 10 (Summer 2003): 90.

55. See UN Security Council Resolution 984 (April 11, 1995).

56. See George Bunn, "Security Assurances for Non-Aligned NPT Parties against Nuclear Attack: The Legal Framework," unpublished manuscript for Carnegie Endowment meetings on the Role of Security Assurances in Nuclear Nonproliferation Policy (1995–96); Mohamed I. Shaker, "Security Guarantees and the Role of the Security Council," report for Clingendael Project on Nonproliferation (1994); George Bunn and Roland M. Timerbaev, "Security Assurances to Non-Nuclear-Weapon States," *Nonproliferation Review* 1 (Fall 1993): 11–13.

57. See Article XII of the treaty creating the IAEA, the Statute of the International Atomic Energy Agency of 1956, as amended. Article XII.B(c) requires the IAEA Board of Governors to report noncompliance with IAEA safeguards by any nation to the UN Security Council.

58. For the views of a reporter who covered the conference and is a nonproliferation expert, see Rebecca Johnson, "Politics and Protection: Why the 2005 NPT Review Conference Failed," *Disarmament Diplomacy* 80 (Autumn 2005): 3.

59. See NPT Review and Extension Conference, "Principles and Objectives for Nuclear Non-Proliferation and Disarmament," Decision 2 (1995), pars. 3–4; NPT Review Conference, "'Thirteen Steps' to Implement NPT Article VI (Control and Reduction of Nuclear Weapons)," Final Document (2000). The FMCT proposal is for a treaty that would prohibit its members from producing fissile material for nuclear weapons. This proposal has been advanced by the United States for decades, but agreement to put it on the agenda of the Geneva Conference on Disarmament was recently prevented by Bush administration opposition to describing the agenda item as an FMCT that could be verified. The administration said it supported an FMCT but that such a treaty could not be verified effectively without unduly intrusive inspections.

60. See, for example, Rebecca Johnson, "Spineless NPT Conference Papers Over Cracks and Ends with a Whimper," May 27, 2005 (www.acronym.org.uk).

61. U.S. Assistant Secretary of State Stephan Rademaker, statement to NPT Review Conference (2005); and Roche, *Deadly Deadlock*, pp. 2, 19–20.

62. See Nicolas Schmidt, statement for the European Union, NPT Review Conference

(May 4, 2005); U.S. Department of State, Bureau of Nonproliferation, "United States Initiatives to Prevent Proliferation," May 2, 2005 (www.state.gov/t/np/rls/other/45456.htm). For an interesting analysis of the Bush administration's preferences for unilateral and cooperative initiatives over multilateral treaty and related efforts, see Jofi Josef, "The Exercise of Sovereignty: The Bush Administration's Approach to Combating Weapons of Mass Destruction," *Nonproliferation Review* 12 (July 2005): 373.

63. For an excellent summary and analysis of the 2005 NPT Review Conference, see Johnson, "Politics and Protection."

64. See President George W. Bush and Prime Minister Manmohan Singh, Text of India-U.S. Joint Statement of July 19, 2005, Indo-Asian News Service, July 19, 2005.

65. Ibid.

66. See Sharon Squassoni, "U.S. Nuclear Cooperation with India: Issues for Congress," Report RL 33018 (Congressional Research Service, July 29, 2005).

67. See Nuclear Non-Proliferation Act of 1978, Title III, "Export Organization and Criteria," secs. 302–08. According to a congressional explanation of the act, one of its central purposes was "encouragement for universal ratification of the Non-Proliferation Treaty, and a comprehensive set of controls, procedures and incentives designed to provide a framework for predictable international nuclear cooperation and commerce, . . . and to limit the further diffusion of nuclear explosive capabilities." See *Brief Summary of the "Nuclear Nonproliferation Act of 1978"* (GPO, 1978).

68. Bush and Singh, Joint Statement of July 19, 2005; see also U.S. State Department, "Administration to Seek Congress' Support for Nuclear Pact with India: State Department's Burns Praises India's Record on Nonproliferation" (July 20 and 22, 2005) (www.usinfo.state.gov).

69. George Perkovich, "Faulty Promises: The U.S.-India Nuclear Deal," in *Policy Outlook* (Washington: Carnegie Endowment for International Peace, September 2005) (www.CarnegieEndowment.org).

70. See Fred McGoldrick, Harold Benglesdorf, and Lawrence Scheinman, "The U.S.-India Nuclear Deal: Taking Stock," *Arms Control Today* 35 (October 2005): 6.

71. See Rebecca Johnson, "United Nations First Committee: 2005 First Committee Resolutions," Acronym Institute for Disarmament Diplomacy (Winter 2005) (www.acronym.org.uk/un/2005unfc.htm).

72. See NPT, art. III.

73. The NSG now includes China and the Russian Federation, as well as the EU countries and the United States, which have long been NSG members. It also includes former Warsaw Pact allies of the Soviet Union such as Poland, and former Soviet republics such as Kazakhstan. Finally, it includes Argentina, Brazil, Australia, New Zealand, South Korea, and Japan. It numbers forty-four states in all.

74. See Jacob Blackford, "Multilateral Nuclear Export Control after the A. Q. Khan Network" (Washington: Institute for Science and International Security, August 2, 2005).

75. See Nuclear Suppliers Guidelines, pt. 1, par. 7: "[If] enrichment or reprocessing facilities, equipment or technology are to be transferred, suppliers should encourage recipients to accept, as an alternative to national plants, supplier involvement and/or other appropriate multinational participation in resulting facilities. Suppliers should also promote international (including IAEA) activities concerned with multinational

regional fuel cycle centres." See Carlton E. Thorne, *A Guide to Nuclear Export Controls* (Springfield, Va.: Proliferation Data Services, 2001), p. 101.

76. See IAEA, "Multilateral Approaches to the Nuclear Fuel Cycle," Expert Group Report to the Director General, Information Circular 640 (February 22, 2005), pp. 37, 38.

77. See, for example, Elaine Sciolino, "Iran, Defiant, Insists It Plans to Restart Nuclear Program," *New York Times*, January 10, 2006; Richard Bernstein and Steven R. Weisman, "Europe Joins with U.S. in Urging Action by U.N. on Iran," *New York Times*, January 13, 2006.

78. U.S. Department of State, "The Nuclear Suppliers Group," Bureau of Nonproliferation Fact Sheet, July 29, 2004, pp. 1–2 (www.state.gov/t/np/fw/34729.htm).

79. For the U.S. "weapons of mass destruction" claims to the UN Security Council just before the March 2003 U.S.-U.K. invasion of Iraq, see Secretary of State Colin Powell, speech to the Security Council, March 7, 2003. Also "In the Delegates' Words: Hawks and Doves Debate at the Security Council," *New York Times*, March 8, 2003.

80. See Bolton, "An All-Out War on Proliferation."

81. See Matthew Bunn and Anthony Wier, *Securing the Bomb 2005: The New Global Imperatives* (Washington: Project on Managing the Atom, May 2005), pp. v–vi, 19–24.

82. See Ariel E. Levite, "Never Say Never Again: Nuclear Reversal Revisited," *International Security* 27 (Winter 2002/3): 59, 62; George Perkovich and others, *Universal Compliance: A Strategy for Nuclear Security* (Washington: Carnegie Endowment for International Peace, 2004), table 2. For a history of efforts to secure nuclear weapons in many of these countries, see Mitchell Reiss, *Bridled Ambition: Why Countries Constrain Their Nuclear Capabilities* (Washington: Woodrow Wilson Center Press, 1995).

83. In response to a question at a March 21, 1963, press conference about possible hope for a test ban treaty, given all the years of failure in negotiations with the Soviet Union to end testing, President John F. Kennedy said he had not given up hope: "I am haunted by the feeling that by 1970, unless we are successful, there may be 10 nuclear powers instead of four, and by 1975, 15 or 20. . . . I see the possibility in the 1970s of the President of the United States having to face a world in which 15 or 20 or 25 nations may have these weapons. I regard that as the greatest possible danger and hazard." President John F. Kennedy, News Conference 52, March 21, 1963, John F. Kennedy Library and Museum, Washington. See also U.S. Arms Control and Disarmament Agency, *Documents on Disarmament, 1963* (1964), pp. 112–13.

84. See, for example, Garry Dillon, "The IAEA in Iraq: Past Activities and Findings," *IAEA Bulletin* 44, no. 2 (2002).

85. See "G-8 Action Plan on Nonproliferation," June 9, 2004 (www.reachingcriticalwill.org/action/listindex.html).

86. For the 1995 agreement, see "Principles and Objectives for Nuclear Non-Proliferation and Disarmament," in Johnson, "Indefinite Extension of the Non-Proliferation Treaty," p. 73.

87. United States, "Recommendations for Achieving the Objective of Nuclear Disarmament and Non-proliferation of Nuclear Weapons," Report A/CN.10/2006/WG.I/WP.1 (UN Disarmament Commission, April 2006).

88. See Allison, *Nuclear Terrorism*, pt. 1; Ferguson and others, *The Four Faces of Nuclear Terrorism*, chap. 1.

89. NPT, art. IV.

90. NPT, art. IV (1). See Mohamed I. Shaker, *The Nuclear Non-Proliferation Treaty: Origin and Implementation: 1959–1979* (New York: Oceana, 1980), chap. 6, particularly pp. 293–99.

91. See Lawrence Scheinman, "The Nuclear Fuel Cycle: A Challenge for Nonproliferation," *Disarmament Diplomacy* 76 (March/April 2004): 7.

92. See Nuclear Control Institute, "Iran's Claim of Absolute 'Inalienable Right' under the NPT to Pursue Production of Uranium and Plutonium Is Not Supported by Treaty's Terms or History, NCI Legal Analysis Shows," NCI Press Conference, May 3, 2005.

93. See Mohamed ElBaradei, "Saving Ourselves from Destruction," *New York Times*, February 12, 2004, op-ed page.

94. See White House, "President Bush Announces New Measures to Counter the Threat of WMD," remarks by the president on weapons of mass destruction proliferation, February 11, 2004 (www.whitehouse.gov/news/releases/2004/02/print/20040211-5.html).

95. See Joseph Cirincione, Jon B. Wolfstahl, and Miriam Rajkumar, *Deadly Arsenals*, 2nd ed. (Washington: Carnegie Endowment for International Peace, 2005), pp. 395–99.

96. See Matthew Bunn, Anthony Wier, and John P. Holdren, *Controlling Nuclear Warheads and Materials: A Report Card and Action Plan* (Harvard University, Project on Managing the Atom, 2003), pp. 11–13.

97. See "G-8 Action Plan on Nonproliferation."

98. United Nations, *A More Secure World: Our Shared Responsibility*, Report of the Secretary-General's High-Level Panel on Threats, Challenges and Change (New York, 2004), pars. 130–31.

99. See Perkovich and others, Universal Compliance, p. 9.

100. See White House, "President Bush Announces New Measures to Counter the Threat of WMD."

101. NPT, art. X.

102. See ElBaradei, "Saving Ourselves from Destruction"; and *A More Secure World*, pars. 129, 134.

103. In explaining the addition to the Limited Test Ban Treaty withdrawal clause for NPT purposes of the notice to the UN Security Council, the Soviet representative to the negotiating conference said that observance of the NPT and its effectiveness "are bound to be related to the powers of the Security Council." See Shaker, *The Nuclear Non-Proliferation Treaty*, pp. 894–99.

104. Ibid.

105. See UN Charter, chap. VII.

106. See *A More Secure World*, pars. 129, 134, 139–41.

107. See Ashton B. Carter and William J. Perry, *Preventive Defense: A New Strategy for America* (Brookings, 1999), pp. 130–33.

108. For a chronological account, see Nautilus Institute, "The DPRK Briefing Book," "Fact Sheet on DPRK Nuclear Safeguards: IAEA, January 8, 2003," available then at www.nautilus.org/DPRKBriefingBook/monitoringVerification/Factsheet.html.

109. See George Bunn and John B. Rhinelander, "NPT Withdrawal: Time for the Security Council to Step In," *Arms Control Today* 35 (May 2005): 17; George Bunn and John B. Rhinelander, "The Right to Withdraw from the NPT: Article X Is Not Unconditional," *Disarmament Diplomacy* 79 (April/May 2005): 39. In the view of the United States, the Security Council had already made clear that the proliferation of nuclear weapons

constituted a threat to international peace and security giving the council jurisdiction to consider a withdrawal and that, upon doing so, the council "should consider the full range of options provided by the Charter," obviously including authorizing the use of force to prevent withdrawal. See U.S. representative Sally Horn, statement to the 2005 NPT Review Conference, May 23, 2005. The EU position was that the Security Council was "the final arbiter in maintaining international peace and security" in the event of a withdrawal from the NPT and that the council should consider withdrawal with a sense of urgency to determine whether it would constitute a threat to international peace and security. See "Withdrawal from the Treaty on the Non-Proliferation of Nuclear Weapons," NPT/CONF.2005/WP.32 (www.un.org/events/npt2005/working%20papers.html). Earlier, the UN Secretary-General's High-level Panel on Threats, Challenges and Change had concluded: "A State's notice of withdrawal from the [NPT] should prompt immediate verification of its compliance with the Treaty, if necessary, mandated by the Security Council. . . . Those who withdraw should be held responsible for violations committed while still a party to the Treaty." *A More Secure World*, par. 134.

110. At the 2005 NPT Review Conference, the consensus among the twenty-five EU members was that "all" nuclear materials, equipment, and facilities developed for peaceful purposes should remain under IAEA safeguards in case a nation using them withdrew from the NPT and that those acquired from other countries "must be frozen with a view to having them dismantled and/or returned to the supplier state, under IAEA control." See "Withdrawal from the Treaty on the Non-Proliferation of Nuclear Weapons." See also Center for International Security and Cooperation, *Preventing Nuclear Proliferation and Nuclear Terrorism: Essential Steps to Reduce the Availability of Nuclear-Explosive Materials* (Stanford University, 2005), pt. 2.

111. NPT, art. III, par. 2; art. I; art II; and art. IV, par. 2.

112. NPT/CONF.2005/WP32.

113. See NPT Review Conference, "Review of the Operation of the Treaty, Taking into Account the Decisions and the Resolution by the 1995 NPT Review and Extension Conference," art. IV and preamble, pars. 6, 7, 2 (April 14–May 19, 2000).

114. For the Latin American treaty, which is less well known, see Interamerican Treaty of Reciprocal Defense ("Rio Treaty") of September 2, 1947.

115. UN Security Council Resolution 984 (April 11, 1995).

116. See Bunn, "The Legal Status of U.S. Negative Security Assurances," p. 1.

117. For an analysis of security assurances in today's world, including a call for their reassessment, see Joseph F. Pilat, "Reassessing Security Assurances in a Unipolar World," *Washington Quarterly* 28 (February 2005): 159.

118. See Bunn, "The Legal Status of U.S. Negative Security Assurances."

119. See UN Security Council Resolution 984 (April 11, 1995).

120. See Bunn, "The Legal Status of U.S. Negative Security Assurances," p. 10. The United States has not yet ratified some of the treaty agreements it has signed pertaining to nuclear weapon–free zones.

121. See Charles P. Blair and Jean P. du Preez, "Visions of Fission: The Demise of Nuclear Negative Security Assurances on the Bush administration's Pentomic Battlefield," *Nonproliferation Review* 12 (March 2005): 38, 52–56.

122. See George Bunn, "Expanding Nuclear Options: Is the U.S. Negating Its Non-Use Pledges?" *Arms Control Today* 26 (May/June 1996): 7.

123. Blair and du Preez, "Visions of Fission," pp. 52–56.

124. See Thomas C. Schelling, "The Nuclear Taboo," *Wall Street Journal,* October 24, 2005.

125. See Robert S. Norris and Hans M. Kristensen, "U.S. Nuclear Weapons in Europe, 1954–2004," *Bulletin of the Atomic Scientists* 60 (November/December 2004): 76.

126. For a description of reciprocal unilateral measures to withdraw U.S. and Soviet tactical nuclear weapons from deployment in other countries and at sea, see George Bunn and David Holloway, *Arms Control without Treaties? Rethinking U.S.-Russian Strategic Negotiations in Light of the Duma-Senate Slowdown in Treaty Approval* (Stanford University, Center for International Security and Arms Control, 1998), p. 16.

127. See Douglas Jehl, "Iraq Study Finds Desire for Arms, but Not Capacity," *New York Times,* September 17, 2004, national ed., p. A-1.

128. Ambassador Tim Caughley, statement to NPT 2003 Preparatory Committee for 2005 Review Conference, in Rebecca Johnson, "NPT PrepCom Second Interim Report May 4, 2003: Nuclear Disarmament" (www.acronym.org.uk/npt [May 10, 2003]).

129. See Rebecca Johnson, "The 2003 UN First Committee Considers Disarmament and Reform," *Disarmament Diplomacy* 74 (December 2003): 3, 4, 7.

130. See, for example, David S. Yost, "The U.S. Nuclear Posture Review and the NATO Allies," *International Affairs* 80, no. 4 (2004): 705, 724–25; Vladimir Orlov, "Arms Control and Security Letter No. 1" (Moscow: PIR Center, February 2003).

131. U.S. Department of Defense, *Nuclear Posture Review [Excerpts],* p. 15 (www.globalsecuity.org/wmd/library/policy/dod/npr.htm [January 30, 2003]).

132. There were disputes about the validity of North Korea's withdrawal—for example, whether the treaty-required waiting period of ninety days had expired, making the withdrawal effective at the time North Korea said it had. (North Korea insisted that this period was reduced to one day because, in its prior withdrawal in 1993, it did not set aside its withdrawal until eighty-nine of the ninety days had run. Therefore, according to North Korea, one day's notice was sufficient.) This argument now appears irrelevant because more than ninety days have expired. Japan, among others, insists that the withdrawal is still invalid. A good argument can be made that the weak reasons North Korea gave in its notice of withdrawal in 1993 were not even applicable a decade later when North Korea insisted again on withdrawing. Moreover, because North Korea was out of compliance with the NPT at the time it withdrew, its withdrawal could not be valid until it complied. According to the language of the withdrawal clause, the interpretation depends on the decisions of the withdrawing party rather than the views of others. The clause says that the withdrawing party may "in exercising its national sovereignty" have a "right" to withdraw "if it decides that extraordinary events, related to the subject matter of this Treaty, have jeopardized the supreme interests of its country." This language is drawn from the U.S.-U.K.-Soviet negotiation of the Limited Test Ban Treaty (LTBT) in 1963, when the U.S. delegates wanted to be sure they could tell the U.S. Senate, to gain a two-thirds majority for ratification of the Test Ban Treaty, that the United States could withdraw easily—for example, if China tested nuclear weapons. See Bunn, *Arms Control by Committee,* p. 38. On the other hand, the LTBT language was strengthened for the NPT. In any event, these arguments are likely to make little difference *unless* the UN Security Council takes jurisdiction over the issue and considers whether to direct North Korea to comply with the NPT.

133. See, for example, Levite, "Never Say Never Again," pp. 59, 62, table 1.

134. Reiss, *Bridled Ambition,* chap. 4; Rodney Jones and Mark G. McDonough, *Tracking Nuclear Proliferation* (Washington: Carnegie Endowment for International Peace, 1998), pp. 71–100.

135. Cirincione, with others, *Deadly Arsenals: Tracking Weapons,* pp. 208–13, 214–15.

136. See Joint Statement on the Fourth Round of the Six-Party Talks, Beijing, September 19, 2005 (usinfo.state.gov/eap/Archive/2005/Sep/19-210095.html).

137. See George Bunn, "The Nuclear Non-Proliferation Treaty: History and Current Problems," *Arms Control Today* 33 (December 2003): 4; David Albright and Robert Kessey, "Has Iraq Come Clean at Last?" *Bulletin of the Atomic Scientists* 52 (November/December 1995): 53–55; Greg Dillon, "The IAEA Iraq Action Team Record: Activities and Findings," in *Iraq: A New Approach* (Washington: Carnegie Endowment for International Peace, 2002), pp. 41–42. By the end of 1998, IAEA inspectors were satisfied that Iraq had produced no nuclear weapons and no longer retained the capability to produce amounts of weapon-usable nuclear material of practical significance for bomb-making purposes. Dillon, "The IAEA Iraq Action," p. 42.

138. Leonard Spector and Mark McDonough with Evan Madeiros, *Tracking Nuclear Proliferation* (Washington: Carnegie Endowment for International Peace, 1995), pp. 28, 33–34. Under the NPT, Iraq was required to accept IAEA safeguards on "all source and special fissionable material in all peaceful nuclear activities within its territory" and was prohibited from acquiring any such nuclear material for weapons purposes. See IAEA Information Circular 153 (1972) and NPT arts. II and III.

139. Reiss, *Bridled Ambition,* chap. 3.

140. See Wise Uranium Project, Uranium Enrichment and Fuel Fabrication, Uranium Enrichment Plant, Resende (Brazil) (www.antenna.nl/wise/uranium/eproj.html#SAM); Larry Rohter, "If Brazil Wants to Scare the World, It's Succeeding," *New York Times,* October 31, 2004, national ed., News of the Week, p. 3.

141. White House, National Security Strategy of the United States of America, March 2006 (www.whitehouse.gov/nsc/nss/2006/nss2006.pdf), p. 20.

142. Ibid., p. 21.

143. Nuclear Suppliers Guidelines, pt. 2 (2000), pp. 144–45.

144. Spector and others, *Tracking Nuclear Proliferation,* pp. 40–41, 307.

145. Ibid., pp. 59–60.

146. Matthew Bunn and Anthony Wier, *Securing the Bomb: An Agenda for Action* (Harvard University, Project on Managing the Atom, 2004), p. ix; Bunn and Wier, *Securing the Bomb 2005,* pp. vi, 30–32.

147. Bunn and Wier, *Securing the Bomb: An Agenda for Action,* p. ix; Bunn and Wier, *Securing the Bomb 2005,* pp. v–viii, 30–32.

148. See Bunn and Wier, *Securing the Bomb 2005,* pp. 31–32, 72–74. See also National Research Council, "Overcoming Impediments to U.S.-Russian Cooperation on Nuclear Nonproliferation," Report of a Joint Workshop (Washington: National Academies Press, 2004); Allison, *Nuclear Terrorism,* pp. 147–51.

149. See Joint Statement by President Bush and President Putin on Nuclear Security Cooperation, February 24, 2005 (www.whitehouse.gov/news/releases/2005/02/2005 0224-8.html).

150. Blackford, "Multilateral Nuclear Export Control," p. 19.

four

New Challenges to the Nonproliferation Regime

Christopher F. Chyba, Chaim Braun, and George Bunn

Since the end of the cold war, the nuclear nonproliferation regime has faced new challenges. These include the spread of nuclear weapon technology to more states as well as the danger that a terrorist group could acquire the material needed for a nuclear explosion. While these challenges have always been present, the increased vulnerability to theft of plutonium and highly enriched uranium (HEU) after the collapse of the Soviet Union, coupled with the rise of nuclear smuggling networks and the visibility of mass casualty terrorism, suggests that the nonproliferation regime faces a new world of risk.

State Proliferation

The Nuclear Non-Proliferation Treaty (NPT) counts all but four countries of the world as its members. Only five NPT members are allowed to possess nuclear weapons: the United States, Russia, the United Kingdom, France, and China. These are called the nuclear weapon states (NWS). All other members—known as the non-nuclear weapon states—are prohibited from acquiring nuclear weapons (see chapter 3). A latent proliferator is a non-nuclear weapon state that works within, or maintains the façade of working within, its formal obligations under the NPT but nevertheless develops the capabilities needed for a nuclear weapons program. A latent proliferator may either withdraw from the NPT and build actual weapons on short notice or simply remain within the NPT while maintaining the capability for the rapid realization of nuclear weapons as a hedge against future threats. At one time, Iraq, North Korea, and Libya all followed a strategy of latent proliferation in pursuing nuclear weapons, and Iran may be doing so today.

Another challenge for the regime in the past decade has been the elaboration, then partial dismantlement, of illicit "proliferation rings" consisting of substate organizations, individuals, and companies that trade in components, technology, and materials for making nuclear weapons. When there were only a few nuclear suppliers, such exports were easier to control. Most suppliers agreed to Nuclear Suppliers Group (NSG) criteria for nuclear exports, particularly exports useful for enriching uranium and separating plutonium. But countries that are not members of the NSG are now acquiring nuclear technology and components not fully controlled by NSG members. Nonmember governments such as those of Pakistan, North Korea, Iran, and Libya, as well as individuals and companies from these and other countries (including Malaysia, South Africa, and Turkey, but also many European nations that are in the NSG) have traded in technology, components, or nuclear materials useful for making weapons. For example, nuclear experts in Pakistan apparently traded uranium-enrichment technology for missile technology with North Korea. Iran and Libya acquired nuclear materials, components, and technologies in similar ways. A representative of Pakistan has said that entities in two dozen countries were involved in these proliferation networks.[1]

If such proliferation rings were to expand further, a group of countries or substate actors in the developing world might be able to cut loose from traditional nuclear suppliers and trade among themselves for the nuclear capabilities (and also missile technologies) that their individual programs lack. That would make it far harder to curtail the transfer of missile and uranium-enrichment technology.

With increasing transfers among proliferating states and companies, there could be less difficulty, cost, and time involved in acquiring nuclear weapons for countries with the capacity to take advantage of them.[2] Worse, terrorists might find it easier to steal nuclear weapons or weapons-usable nuclear materials or obtain them from nationals of states having such materials.

Terrorist Acquisition of Nuclear Weapons

In the 2004 presidential election campaign, President George W. Bush and his opponent, Senator John Kerry, both stated that nuclear proliferation, particularly the possibility that terrorists might obtain and use nuclear weapons, is the gravest threat the United States now faces.[3] Many nuclear weapons experts agree.[4] As they also point out, the threat of retaliation may be an unreliable deterrent against terrorist organizations.[5] At the same time, a non-state group would have difficulty acquiring nuclear weapons unless a government or rogue elements within it decided to intentionally transfer a weapon to such a group. In the absence of that kind of direct proliferation, a weapon would either have to be stolen or built.

Terrorist Theft of Nuclear Warheads

The prospect of a complete warhead being stolen from a national program seems unlikely but cannot be ruled out. Publicly available information suggests that as of late 2004 comprehensive upgrades to security at Russian sites containing nuclear warheads covered only about 10 percent of the warheads. At the same time, rapid, initial upgrades had been completed at 60 percent of such sites.[6] Few details about the actual locations of, and security provided for, nuclear weapons throughout the world are publicly available.[7] In particular, little is known about the reliability of personnel and the physical security in place for most programs, or the extent to which permissive action links (PALs) are used.[8] PALs are devices that are intended to prevent detonation of a nuclear warhead without an authorized code. All told, it would seem to be difficult to steal and smuggle a complete warhead from a state program, overcome whatever security measures might be installed on it, and then gain operational use of that warhead—but it cannot be ruled out, and the dangers of insider assistance must be addressed.[9]

Terrorist Theft of Nuclear Weapons Material

A more likely path a terrorist group might take would be to steal nuclear explosive material (NEM) in the form of plutonium or highly enriched uranium.[10] There are already anecdotal examples of thefts of kilogram quantities of HEU from Russian facilities.[11] To put these reports in context, published estimates of the amount of HEU needed to build nuclear weapons suggest that the first U.S. bomb exploded over Japan, the gun-type Hiroshima uranium weapon, contained about 60 kilograms of HEU, whereas more advanced uranium implosion designs require only 25 kilograms of HEU, or as little as 15 kilograms or less for increasingly sophisticated designs.[12]

Nor is Russia the only possible target for nuclear theft; HEU is present at some 350 sites in 58 countries around the world, of which two dozen sites are of greatest concern.[13] In 2003 the 350 sites included over 100 research reactors in some 40 countries.[14]

While in principle a nonstate group could produce a working fission nuclear warhead with either stolen plutonium or HEU, plutonium warheads would be difficult to make because they require spherical implosive compression with precision timing.[15] However, a gun-type HEU weapon would be less of a challenge, and, according to the former director of one of the U.S. nuclear weapons laboratories, some substate groups could likely assemble such a weapon if they had the HEU.[16] Documents captured by the United States in Afghanistan, in addition to statements by Pakistani officials, suggest that al Qaeda was interested in nuclear weapon construction. However, al Qaeda seems not to have physically begun such a program.[17]

In the 1990s, Soviet nuclear material security efforts began receiving more attention through financial assistance from the U.S. Nunn-Lugar program. As of October 2004, rapid or comprehensive security upgrades had been completed on less than 50 percent of potentially vulnerable former Soviet nuclear material outside of nuclear weapons, leaving about 300 tons of material for which security upgrades had not yet been completed.[18]

The first line of defense against terrorist acquisition of nuclear weapons is to improve nuclear materials protection, control, and accounting (MPC&A). This must be done globally, although understandably the security of material in the former Soviet Union has received the lion's share of attention and funds. A "global cleanout" campaign of the most vulnerable sites has now been begun by the United States and other Group of Eight (G-8) countries. This will include the expansion of the U.S. Reduced Enrichment for Research and Test Reactors (RERTR) program, which is gradually converting many U.S.-supplied HEU research reactors around the world to run on low-enriched-uranium fuel, which could not be used for weapons without further enrichment, a demanding industrial process.[19] It is not realistic to expect a nonstate group to develop its own uranium-enrichment or plutonium-reprocessing facilities.

If effective steps continue to be taken to prevent the theft and smuggling of weapons-usable nuclear materials, the only route for terrorists to obtain nuclear weapons would be to divert them from national programs—by persuading national operators to sell to the terrorists or their agents. Though unlikely, this cannot be ruled out altogether. Two nuclear scientists from the Pakistani program did, in fact, provide technical information to al Qaeda.[20] A terrorist group could already have access to plans for a spherical implosion nuclear warhead design. Apparently, the nuclear equipment smuggling network put in place by Abdul Qadeer (A. Q.) Khan—former director of the Khan Research Laboratory (KRL) in Pakistan and leader of the Pakistani uranium centrifuge enrichment program to produce HEU for Pakistani atomic bombs—sold the design of a workable uranium implosion warhead to Libya.[21] The design is thought to be one that China originally provided to Pakistan and that is suitable for a missile warhead.[22] The Khan network may also have offered to provide this design to Iraq in 1990 and possibly made similar offers to other nations.[23] The possibility that copies of this warhead design are now available elsewhere in the world, perhaps outside of state control, cannot be discounted.

A clearly important component of the prevention of nuclear terrorism is the prevention of the proliferation of nuclear weapons to more and more states, since the opportunities for illicit transfer to nonstate groups will only increase as the technology spreads. Preventing terrorists from acquiring nuclear weapons therefore depends upon preserving the nuclear nonproliferation regime. In sum, the first essential move against nuclear terrorism is to secure stocks of nuclear warheads and material worldwide, and the second is to take the steps on the supply and demand side needed to strengthen the nuclear nonproliferation regime.

Radiological Weapons

A radiological weapon, or radiological dispersal device (RDD), is designed to spread radioactive contamination over a large area. If the dispersal is done using high explosives, it is also called a dirty bomb.[24] But unlike a nuclear weapon, it does not produce a nuclear explosion; it just blows radioactive debris into the air. In the case of terrorist use, the radioactive materials might come from industry, hospitals, research reactors, nuclear power plants, or other enterprises. Millions of radioactive sources are used worldwide for medicine, industry, and scientific research; of these, tens of thousands are perhaps suitable for use in an RDD. According to a study by the International Atomic Energy Agency (IAEA), more than half the world's countries have inadequate regulatory controls on certain radioactive sources.[25]

A dirty bomb is unlikely to immediately kill those outside of the blast zone itself. But it could disperse radioactive materials over a much wider area. The size and shape of the dispersal area would depend upon the size of the explosive, the size of the radioactive particles produced, and in what direction and how hard the wind was blowing. The dispersal could cause some radiation sicknesses and terror in a populated area.[26] Cleanup of contaminated areas would present major problems. Even if this did greatly reduce the radioactivity, many might fear moving back in.[27]

This book focuses on nuclear, not radiological, weapons. A nuclear weapon, even a low-yield terrorist nuclear weapon, would cause far more casualties and have far greater political implications than a dirty bomb. Even so, many experts believe that radiological weapons are a more likely mode of terrorist attack than nuclear weapons. This is because ordinary high explosives can be used to disperse the material, and radioactive material is much easier to acquire than weapons-usable nuclear material.[28] Cobalt-60, for example, is used in tens of thousands of industrial and medical locations worldwide, and every year it is stolen, abandoned, or lost from many hundreds of such places (about 200 in the United States alone).[29] However, the very highly radioactive industrial material that would be most dangerous if used in a radiological dispersal device would also be very difficult to handle safely. This is why few radiation deaths are likely to result from a dirty bomb—it most likely would make use of less radioactive material. Nevertheless, such a weapon could disrupt society, with decontamination presenting an enormous challenge.[30] Therefore it is essential to ensure that first responders can work safely and that the public receives reliable and timely information about steps to take.[31]

Various measures have already been introduced at the international level to better protect nuclear reactor fuel and other significant radiation sources.[32] Similar attention should be given to deterring the smuggling of radioactive materials, but this will come at the cost of a global inspection and control system for trade. The challenge is admittedly daunting: U.S. seaports alone receive and offload about 9 million cargo containers every year. It is in each country's interest to scan containers upon embarkation; by the time they reach the possible target port, it is too late should there be a nuclear detonation. This problem could be addressed through a program of container "scans" at ports of embarkation, the cost of which would be partly offset by reduced loss and theft.[33] A program along these lines begun in January 2002, the U.S. Container Security Initiative (CSI), is now operating in over forty foreign ports. All twenty of the world's largest ports are committed to CSI but are at various stages of implementation. The CSI works with host governments to identify and prescreen containers judged to pose a risk for terrorism. The initiative is a start, but a great deal more remains to be done.[34]

Latent Proliferation

A foremost challenge in addressing latent proliferation is to determine a country's intentions in pursuing nuclear capabilities ostensibly permitted by the NPT. Over the years, a number of NPT nations that have agreed not to acquire nuclear weapons have built, or participated in the building of, uranium-enrichment facilities for peaceful purposes, notably Argentina, Brazil, Germany, Japan, and the Netherlands.[35] Some facilities in Germany and the Netherlands are operated by a multilateral company, Urenco, owned by the governments of Britain, Germany, and the Netherlands. These facilities are open to regular inspection by Euratom, a regional multilateral nuclear inspection organization composed of Western European members, and by Urenco's resident Euratom inspectors. Periodic checks are also made by IAEA inspectors. To ensure that their uranium enrichment is not for weapons, Argentina and Brazil have agreed to a mutual monitoring arrangement in addition to IAEA inspections.

A number of countries in good standing with the NPT appear to have followed "hedging" strategies over the past several decades. Japan may provide the most important example.[36] By contrast, North Korea chose a more clandestine course. It joined the NPT in 1985, but then resisted signing the NPT-required safeguards agreement with the IAEA until 1992 and hid some of its nuclear activities from agency inspectors. It built reactors said to be for peaceful purposes and burned uranium fuel rods in them to produce spent fuel containing plutonium mixed with other elements. Its nuclear scientists learned how to separate ("reprocess") the plutonium from these other elements. The plutonium could then be used either for nuclear reactors or in nuclear weapons. North Korea's mastery of reprocessing, while at first ostensibly for peaceful (nuclear power) purposes, gave it a latent ability to meet many of the requirements for building nuclear weapons. It chose nuclear weapons. When its intentions were discovered, it withdrew from the NPT and now claims to have nuclear weapons[37]

For a time, Libya also followed a clandestine nuclear weapons course. Eventually, it turned over its uranium-enrichment equipment and designs to the United Kingdom and the United States as part of a deal to escape sanctions imposed for earlier transgressions.[38]

Iraq also pursued a secret uranium-enrichment program for nuclear weapons prior to the 1991 Gulf War, although it had ratified the NPT in 1969. These efforts were discovered and dismantled after that war.[39]

Many countries also are worried that Iran is pursuing a latent proliferation strategy for nuclear weapons acquisition.[40] Using largely imported technology, Iranian scientists learned how to assemble a uranium-enrichment centrifuge at undeclared nuclear sites, contrary to NPT requirements, and therefore avoided IAEA inspections.[41] Thus Iran's uranium-enrichment efforts and other nuclear activities were for a time hidden from the IAEA.[42]

Ongoing negotiations with Iran over its uranium-enrichment program may help determine which way it will go: toward peaceful nuclear uses, nuclear weapons, or both. So far, it appears to want to keep all its options open, although Iran's desire to experiment with uranium enrichment seems paramount.[43]

Proliferation Rings

Early in the history of the nuclear nonproliferation regime, countries moved to curtail the spread of technology used in building nuclear weapons by forming two groups to oversee the export of such technology: the Nuclear Exporters Committee (or Zangger Committee) and subsequently the Nuclear Suppliers Group.[44] Nevertheless, nuclear-weapons-relevant technology has leaked through and around these regimes to additional countries. *First-tier* or primary proliferation may be defined as the spread of nuclear weapons technology or know-how from states that are members of the Zangger Committee or NSG, or from private entities or individuals within those states. *Second-tier* suppliers are other states, or private entities or individuals within those states, that may be supplying relevant material or know-how on the international market. The past decade has seen a surge in second-tier proliferation, often abetted by first-tier suppliers.

Recent revelations about activities in Iran, Libya, Malaysia, Pakistan, Turkey, and other nations have shed considerable light on the dynamics of second-tier proliferation of nuclear technologies, weapons designs, and delivery systems, as well as its connections with latent and first-tier proliferation. Second-tier proliferation is particularly challenging to the supply-side approaches that have been central to the existing nonproliferation regime. This is evident from the second-tier proliferation emanating from Pakistan (not a member of either suppliers group) and its effect on nuclear weapon proliferation in Iran, Libya, and North Korea (also not a member of either group). In the missile programs in Pakistan, Iran, and Libya, missile proliferation activities emanating from North Korea have intersected with nuclear proliferation networks. Nuclear and missile second-tier proliferation challenges are interrelated, and the clandestine supply rings for the two have often been intertwined.

Unless dismantled, these "second-tier" proliferation rings could render the current export control regimes much less effective. With nuclear weapons technologies and manufacturing bases of their own, a set of developing countries could eventually disconnect themselves from first-tier state or corporate suppliers and trade among themselves for the capabilities that their individual programs lack.

Second-tier proliferation is hardly a new phenomenon.[45] What is new is that the proliferation routes established by the Pakistani and North Korean networks are larger, more widespread, and more varied than first recognized. The resulting proliferation has had a significant impact on the nuclear weapons and missile programs of several developing countries. Until 1990, second-tier suppliers' capabilities were at the lower end of the nuclear export spectrum, and their exports were for the most part cautious and of limited consequence.[46] This is obviously no longer the case. Proliferation-ring members support one another either directly, at the state-to-state level, or indirectly, through once-removed private-sector supplier networks.

An effective response must address both the supply and demand sides of the problem. On the supply side, it is essential to continue limiting the transfer of weapons-grade material and nuclear weapons technology from first-tier suppliers to potential proliferators. Second-tier networks must continue to be shut down. On the demand side, the nonproliferation regime needs to address the balance of factors that states consider in determining whether to acquire nuclear weapons and missile delivery systems.[47]

More specifically, supply-side solutions need to focus on increasing the security of nuclear weapons–grade material in the former Soviet Union (FSU) and elsewhere. If the Nunn-Lugar Cooperative Threat Reduction (CTR) program is successful in the FSU and expands to include poorly protected fissile material in other countries, nuclear theft and smuggling should decline over time, given an ongoing commitment and effort by the G-8 and other states.[48] Thus, in addition to maintaining a robust and successful CTR program, the various export controls must also be broadened and strengthened.[49]

The supply-side "push" to proliferation is complemented by the demand-side proliferation "pull" arising from national prestige, regional security, and internal political considerations, all requiring responses that go well beyond the NPT itself. Nevertheless, the nonproliferation regime plays an important role in framing the balance of factors that states consider when determining their nuclear weapons choices. As currently structured, however, the regime presents potential proliferators with a mixed set of positive and negative inducements for compliance versus noncompliance. If the nuclear nonproliferation regime is to be preserved, a better balance must be struck, one that increases the benefits of adhering to the regime, decreases the drawbacks, makes clear the negative impact of abandoning the regime, and reassures adherents that the regime protects them from the nuclear ambitions of their adversaries. Any discussion of how the nonproliferation regime might better respond to second-tier proliferation in the future must begin with an understanding, albeit imperfect, of the actions taken by, and motivations of, the proliferating nations that have brought the regime to the crisis it faces today, particularly those of North Korea, Libya, Iran, and Pakistan.

North Korea's Plutonium Program

North Korea began reprocessing plutonium in 1989 using its 5 MW(e) graphite-moderated reactor and its "radiochemical laboratory," a medium-sized reprocessing plant located at the Yongbyon nuclear center about 100 kilometers north of Pyongyang.[50] North Korea's reactors are thought to be based on the British Calder Hall–type reactors of the 1950s, described in detail in the open technical literature. IAEA inspections of the Yongbyon site in 1992 uncovered North Korea's diversion of several kilograms of plutonium following its reprocessing.[51]

The Agreed Framework between the United States and North Korea signed in October 1994 froze North Korea's ability to reprocess the remaining unreprocessed spent fuel from its 5 MW(e) reactor at Yongbyon, but not before it had extracted enough plutonium for about two nuclear weapons, according to published CIA estimates.[52] It is not clear whether North Korea successfully manufactured nuclear warheads from this extracted plutonium, although this is commonly thought to be the case.[53]

In December 2002, North Korea gave notice of withdrawal from the NPT and removed the monitoring devices installed by the IAEA on the Yongbyon facilities. It also expelled the IAEA's safeguards inspectors.[54] In addition, it restarted the 5 MW(e) Yongbyon reactor in March 2003 and then prepared to reopen the radiochemical laboratory at that site for separating plutonium from spent fuel, with the aid of 20 tons of tributyl phosphate (TBP) organic solvent reportedly obtained from a Chinese company.[55]

After the signing of the Agreed Framework, North Korea had a stock of 8,000 spent fuel rods discharged from the 5 MW(e) nuclear reactor. IAEA inspectors monitored these rods. Reprocessing of this accumulated stockpile could have provided adequate plutonium for perhaps six additional nuclear warheads, depending on the reactor's capacity factor and the efficiency of North Korea's reprocessing facilities.[56] When an unofficial U.S. delegation visited North Korea in 2004, it found that the 8,000 rods had been removed from their storage ponds; North Korean scientists claimed that these had all been reprocessed to separate out the plutonium during a six-month work campaign.[57]

Operation of the 5 MW(e) reactor will probably produce enough plutonium for one additional weapon a year. If North Korea was able to complete construction of two other partly built reactors (a 50 MW(e) reactor at Yongbyon and a 200 MW(e) reactor at Taechon), it could produce adequate plutonium for thirty to fifty nuclear weapons a year, depending on reprocessing capacity.[58] In January 2004 a group of U.S. experts found the larger Yongbyon reactor in an apparent state of bad disrepair, but in June 2005 North Korea had reportedly informed a U.S. visting scholar and the U.S. government that it had resumed work on the two reactors.[59] It seems likely that North Korea's plutonium-based stockpile could increase (using just the 5 MW(e) reactor's plutonium) at about one warhead a year over the next several years, unless and until the 50 MW(e) or 200 MW(e) reactors are brought into production. While a stockpile of just one or two nuclear warheads would likely be jealously guarded by the North Korean regime, North Korea's leaders might think a larger number of warheads would permit them to conduct nuclear testing—or even, in a worst case, to sell plutonium (or warheads) on the black market.[60]

North Korea's Uranium-Enrichment Program

The status of North Korea's clandestine uranium-enrichment program remains unclear. At one point, North Korea reportedly acknowledged having a uranium-enrichment program, a statement that North Korea at first denied and later admitted.[61] If North Korea does have an enrichment program, it would appear that after signing the Agreed Framework in 1994 the government decided to pursue an alternative route to acquiring nuclear weapons material. It apparently turned to Pakistan, which had a fully developed uranium-enrichment program.[62] This seems to have led to a barter of missiles for enrichment technology, a benchmark event in global proliferation. According to unnamed Pakistani, South Korean, and U.S. officials, this relationship began as early as 1993 with plans for North Korea to provide the Nodong missile to Pakistan.[63] In 1998 Pakistan successfully tested the Ghauri-1 missile, its version of the Nodong. Pakistan's lack of hard currency putatively coincided with North Korea's desire for a uranium route to nuclear weapons, and in that same year the Khan Research Lab reportedly began to provide Pyongyang with blueprints and components for gas centrifuges for uranium enrichment. Pakistani officials denied this deal until April 2004, when the

Pakistani government made public portions of the confession of A. Q. Khan, attesting to the transfer of Pakistani enrichment technology to North Korea.[64] In August 2005 President Pervez Musharraf of Pakistan confirmed that A. Q. Khan had provided North Korea with uranium centrifuges.[65]

According to Khan's reported testimony, his network provided North Korea with centrifuge designs based on Pakistani versions of both early and second-generation centrifuges developed at the Urenco enrichment plants in Almelo, in the Netherlands, and Gronau, Germany. Famously, Khan had been employed in the Almelo plant and took design information and listings of component suppliers with him to Pakistan in 1975 when he left Urenco.[66] Using that information, the KRL developed and built two centrifuge models, the P-1 and the more sophisticated and capable P-2.[67]

By 2001 North Korea had apparently developed centrifuge enrichment technology to the point where it could start shopping for the large-scale supply of machine components required to construct about 4,000 centrifuges. North Korea's procurement agents appear to have bought British-manufactured high-tensile-strength aluminum tubes from a German company and shipped a consignment of them with freight papers indicating their destination to be the Shenyang Aircraft Corporation in China. However, the shipment was halted in Egypt while en route.[68] Had 4,000 rotor tubings and other centrifuge components ultimately been obtained by North Korea and the enrichment plant completed, the plant could have produced enough highly enriched uranium for one or two weapons a year, depending on weapon design.[69]

In this pursuit, as in 1992, North Korea appears to have underestimated the technical capabilities of IAEA inspectors. In 1992 the North Koreans seemingly failed to foresee that IAEA swipes of surfaces in buildings within the Yongbyon nuclear complex would provide data on their recent pluto-nium-reprocessing activities.[70] In 2001 they apparently hoped to procure large quantities of dual-use items related to centrifuge manufacturing in the global markets without alerting the export control regimes. They were wrong both times, and in that sense the inspection and export control regimes performed as designed. The problem is that in each case North Korea advanced the technical scope of its proliferation efforts before being discovered.

Pakistan, Europe, Libya, and the Private Sector Network

In late 2003, Libya's president Muammar al-Qadhafi decided to break with his past proliferation activities, renounce Libya's nuclear and chemical weapons programs, disclose and dismantle them, and forswear missiles that do not conform to 1987 Missile Technology Control Regime (MTCR) guidelines.[71] This decision followed years of negotiations with the United Kingdom and United States to relieve U.S. sanctions imposed on Libya after attacks by Libyan agents on civilians and U.S. soldiers in Berlin. President Ronald Reagan responded to these attacks in 1986 by bombing a number of Libyan targets. This was followed by the 1988 destruction of an American airliner flying over Lockerbie, Scotland, by a bomb on board the airliner. In 2003 Libya accepted civil liability for the Lockerbie bombing.[72] President Qadhafi's decision to break with past proliferation activities came after Libya approached Britain in March 2003 at the outset of the second war against Iraq, and after a German-owned ship, the BBC *China,* proved to be carrying the components for several thousand P-2 centrifuges for Libya's uranium-enrichment program.[73]

The revelations flowing from President Qadhafi's decision were remarkable. Evidently Pakistan's A. Q. Khan and a few of his senior associates at KRL were at the center of a private sector proliferation network for the clandestine export of centrifuge uranium-enrichment technology; the network reportedly included German, South African, Swiss, Turkish, and U.K. nationals.[74] Besides North Korea and Libya, it appears that Iran, Iraq, possibly Syria, and perhaps other countries were approached with offers of nuclear weapons–related deals.[75] The network obtained centrifuge components from Scomi Precision Engineering, a firm in a third-party country, Malaysia. The factory staff may not have known the purpose of the products they manufactured. The ultimate destination to Libya was hidden by transshipment through Dubai. The network reportedly purchased motors and frequency converters for the centrifuges from the Turkish electrical components firm Elektronik Kontrol Aletleri (EKA). These components were discovered on the ship when it docked in Tripoli in March 2004.[76] The transshipments were facilitated by a Dubai-based Sri Lankan businessman, Buhary Syed Abu Tahir, the controlling shareholder of Gulf Technical Industries and the "chief financial officer and money launderer" of the Khan network, according to President Bush.[77] The network also relied on a group of former European colleagues of Khan who worked as engineers in technology and components supply companies serving Urenco. They later branched out to form their own consulting companies specializing in centrifuge technologies.[78] Even more disturbing, Khan's network evidently sold the Chinese-origin nuclear warhead design to Libya and made overtures to other nations.[79]

The support provided for the Libyan nuclear program was likely the most ambitious and elaborate activity undertaken by Khan's network. The Libyan purchases alone netted an estimated $100 million for the network, while providing Libya with a workable centrifuge enrichment plant and a centrifuge components manufacturing facility—though it appears that Libya had insufficient capacity to make good use of this equipment.[80] Further help with plant design and piping arrangements for the enrichment facility evidently came from South African engineers.[81] An intriguing question is how private consultants and equipment suppliers from many countries, and especially Europe, evidently continued operating in support of Khan's network over many years without action being taken by law enforcement agencies.

Iran and Pakistan

Iran has been a party to the NPT since 1970. In 1996 Director of Central Intelligence John Deutch testified that Iran was "actively pursuing an indigenous nuclear weapons capability" by "attempting to develop the capability to produce both plutonium and highly enriched uranium."[82] A pilot uranium-enrichment centrifuge plant in Natanz was reported in the media in August 2002. In February 2003 Iran informed the IAEA director general of two enrichment facilities at Natanz: a pilot plant nearing completion and a large commercial-scale fuel-enrichment plant under construction.[83] Iran stated that more than 100 of the 1,000 planned centrifuge rotor casings had been installed at the pilot plant and that those remaining would be installed before the end of 2003. The commercial enrichment facility was intended ultimately to contain 50,000 centrifuges.[84] In June 2003 Iran introduced gaseous uranium hexafluoride into the first centrifuge for testing purposes, and in August 2003 a small, ten-machine cascade for the centrifuge started test operations.[85] A French government document provided to the Nuclear Suppliers Group in May 2003 concluded that Iran was concealing a military program within its civilian nuclear program and appeared "ready to develop nuclear weapons within a few years."[86] The Iranian foreign ministry denied the existence of a nuclear weapons program.[87]

According to unnamed Western intelligence sources, Iran obtained design information and component parts for the pilot facility from Pakistan, starting in 1987.[88] Some support from other nations was also suspected.[89] A. Q. Khan's private sector associate B. S. A. Tahir has admitted that he sold Iran two containers of surplus Pakistani centrifuge equipment in 1994 and 1995 for a payment of $3 million.[90] These shipments and other components purchased abroad or manufactured in Iran reportedly allowed Iran to assemble 500 P-1 centrifuges by 1995.[91]

In February 2003 Iran informed the IAEA that there was an enrichment test-bed facility in the Kalaye Electric Company's workshop but refused to permit IAEA environmental sampling at the site until August 2003, when significant recent modifications to the site facilities were noted.[92] IAEA inspectors found traces of highly enriched uranium at the Natanz plant in June 2003 and in the Kalaye workshop in September 2003. Iran has stated that these traces were on the equipment when it was purchased from another country, thus denying the production of HEU at its own plants but acknowledging outside help in their construction.[93] After conducting tests, IAEA inspectors did not dispute this claim. Evidence collected in Iran by the IAEA reportedly implicates Pakistan as a supplier of critical technology and parts.[94] The IAEA is also said to suspect that Pakistan may be the source of the 90 percent HEU found on some samples.[95] Iran has allegedly obtained assistance from other nations as well, perhaps including China, North Korea, and Russia.[96] The IAEA has identified two other Iranian facilities related to the centrifuge program engaged in development work on the more advanced P-2 centrifuges; in March 2004 the Iranian military acknowledged having produced P-1 centrifuges in a facility located at the Doshen-Tappen air base near Tehran.[97]

The scope of the P-2 centrifuge program may be larger than originally reported by Iran. Iranian representatives have apparently inquired through European middlemen about purchasing "tens of thousands" of magnets for P-2 centrifuges. A centrifuge cascade at the scale this implies would be enough, were it to be completed, to produce several warheads' worth of HEU a year.[98]

Iran's nuclear program also includes a planned heavy-water reactor and its ancillary facilities at Arak, close to Isfahan. In May 2003 Iran declared to the IAEA that it intended to build a 40 MW(th) heavy-water-moderated, natural-uranium-fueled nuclear research reactor (designated IR-40). The stated purpose of that reactor is radioisotope production and reactor research development and training.[99] A radioisotope production plant referred to as the Molybdenum, Iodine, and Xenon (MIX) facility is now under construction at the Tehran nuclear research center.[100] There is a heavy-water production plant in Khondab, near the Arak site. A related facility is the Fuel Manufacturing Plant. It will fabricate the fuel elements for the IR-40 research reactor and perhaps ultimately for the Bushehr Nuclear Power Plant, which began construction in 2003.[101]

The Iranian nuclear program has a broad technological base, includes redundant facilities, and is well dispersed at many different sites. Dispersal is a particular advantage for a centrifuge enrichment-based program for any country pursuing a covert program. In contrast to plutonium-production reactors, centrifuge operations can be carried out in small-scale, distributed facilities that can be difficult to detect. However, it is harder to conceal the associated conversion facilities at the front and back end of the enrichment process—those required to produce gaseous uranium hexafluoride at the front end and metallic uranium at the back end.

The IAEA Board of Governors set a deadline of October 31, 2003, for Iran to provide extensive additional information on its nuclear activities, and to suspend all further uranium-enrichment-related activities.[102] In October 2003 Iran promised to freeze all uranium-enrichment and reprocessing activities, provide full information to the IAEA, and open all requested facilities to IAEA inspectors. In December 2003 it signed the Additional Protocol.[103] But Iran's compliance was grudging and characterized by attempts to limit the agreement's scope, and by threats to cancel it. Indeed, in June 2004 Iran announced that it would resume centrifuge production in response to an IAEA resolution critical of its poor cooperation with the agency.[104] Later, it pulled back from this position. But after a further IAEA report resolving some questions but raising others, and after negotiations with representatives from Britain, France, and Germany (called the EU-3), Iran agreed in November of 2004 to suspend its uranium-enrichment program pending further negotiations.[105]

In 2005, however, after the election of a new, more conservative president (Mahmoud Ahmadinejad), Iran rejected a detailed offer from the EU-3, removed the IAEA seals from its stores of nuclear materials at a uranium conversion plant, and resumed operations.[106] In a speech to the UN General Assembly, President Ahmadinejad suggested that Iran would enrich uranium in concert with other countries to ensure that the uranium was not diverted to nuclear weapons.[107] This idea apparently drew upon an IAEA suggestion for multilateral enrichment facilities in which personnel from several countries would cooperate to operate a common enrichment facility, allowing mutual inspections intended to ensure that the plant's enriched uranium was not diverted to nuclear weapons.[108] At the end of 2005, Iran appeared to open the door to negotiations with Russia for an enrichment plant in Russia for Iran's use in which both countries would participate.[109] But as of January 2006, Iran had broken IAEA seals at its uranium-enrichment facility in Natanz.[110] In February 2006 Iran was referred to the UN Security Council by a vote of the IAEA board.[111]

Linked Missile and Uranium Proliferation Rings

China, North Korea, and Russia are also suspected of supporting Iran's missile program.[112] Companies in Taiwan, Macedonia, and Belarus have allegedly helped as well.[113] According to Israeli sources, a follow-on missiles-for-centrifuges barter deal was struck between North Korea and Iran.[114] Under this putative arrangement for Iranian help with uranium enrichment, North Korea provided Iran with engines for Nodong missiles (the precursors for the development of the Iranian Shahab-3 missile) and helped work out Shahab-3 manufacturing problems in Iran. The Shahab-3 successfully completed its test program in July 2003 and is thought to be able to carry a 1,000-kilogram payload 1,500 kilometers.[115] Such a payload could be large enough to include a nuclear weapon, especially if range were traded for payload mass.

North Korea has proved willing to sell its missile technologies worldwide. Since that country and its customers are not members of the MTCR, these sales violate no agreements. The North Korean network of missile sales resembles the hub and spokes of a wheel, with North Korea the hub and Pakistan and Iran at the end of two spokes. North Korea has also sold missiles to Egypt, Iraq, Libya, Syria, and Yemen and approached other nations.[116] The importance of export controls is illustrated by the fact that North Korea started its entire missile development and export program in the late 1970s with the purchase, from Egypt, of several Soviet-supplied Scud-B missiles, which it then proceeded to reverse-engineer and further develop.[117]

An analogous group of countries that trade among themselves in uranium-centrifuge-enrichment technologies appears to have evolved during the 1990s, centered in Pakistan. China was the major historical supporter of the Pakistani nuclear program, putatively providing Pakistan with a complete design of one of its early uranium nuclear warheads, sufficient quantities of HEU for two such weapons, short-range ballistic missiles and construction blueprints, assistance in developing a medium-range missile and second-generation uranium-enrichment centrifuges (including providing 5,000 ring magnets in 1994–95), and a 40 MW(th) heavy-water plutonium and tritium production reactor located at Khushab.[118] Smuggling from a number of Western nations, particularly the acquisition of an entire plant for converting uranium powder to uranium hexafluoride from West Germany between 1977 and 1980, also played an important role.[119]

Links among these missile and uranium-enrichment technology rings may accelerate technology transfer within each ring, reduce the total development cost, and, if not disrupted, potentially shorten the time period needed for the successful development of the technology. Without details on the origin and success of the North Korean, Pakistani-derived gas centrifuge program, however, it is difficult to evaluate this claim quantitatively.[120] Foreign assistance appears to have telescoped the timescale for ballistic missile development and production.[121] Obviously, purchasing or trading the blueprints for a working HEU warhead could also greatly shorten the time required to complete a nuclear weapons program.

Motives for Proliferation

The motives that drive nuclear proliferation are complex, with reasons of national security, prestige, organizational politics, international pressure, and others all playing a role.[122] Even in the case of South Africa, where the trajectory of the construction and destruction of its six-warhead nuclear stockpile is known and dozens of interviews with nuclear policymakers have taken place, it is difficult to determine the relative importance of various motivating factors.[123] Case studies for a number of countries suggest that security concerns, the prestige of being a nuclear power, and domestic politics are especially important factors.[124] Regime type—whether or not a country is a democracy—seems not to be especially significant.[125]

What motives have been driving second-tier proliferation? Why did the Pakistani Khan network assist North Korea, and evidently Iran, Libya, and other countries, with their nuclear programs? What kind of calculations (political or otherwise) went into these decisions? These questions are hard to answer. It is difficult enough on the basis of open sources, relying largely on unnamed officials who may be pursuing their own agendas, to sketch what actually occurred in these exchanges. Going from these results to conclusions about motivations is even more challenging. Moreover, the nations involved in the exchanges may well not be unitary actors in their proliferation actions. Successive heads of Pakistan's government, for example, have held varying authority over the country's military, intelligence, and nuclear bureaucracies.[126] Yet cooperation with other nations in uranium centrifuge enrichment was evidently continued under three of its governments.[127]

The rivalry between the KRL and the Pakistani Atomic Energy Commission (PAEC) may also have played a significant role in the development of the Khan network.[128] Given the gravity of the Pakistani–North Korean deal, however, including decisions regarding the possible acquisition of nuclear-strike systems, it would seem surprising if Khan and the KRL were acting independently of higher authorities. However, at least for those outside the Pakistani government, the relative roles of the covert nature of the Pakistani nuclear program, the authority of successive civilian governments, and Khan's motives, including simple greed, remain difficult to specify.[129] Information as to how Khan obtained the warhead design he evidently shared with Libya and possibly others might shed light on these issues. The extent to which Khan was an independent "rogue actor" or, at the other extreme, that there was deep and ongoing government involvement remains incompletely answered.[130]

Prime Minister Zulfikar Ali Bhutto apparently decided to put Pakistan on a nuclear weapons course after its devastating loss in the 1971 war with India.[131] The relationship with North Korea may have been driven by a desire to secure appropriate nuclear weapons delivery systems.[132] In the mid-1980s, the United States provided forty F-16 aircraft to Pakistan. With appropriate modifications, these aircraft could serve as nuclear delivery vehicles, though unlike ballistic missiles, they are vulnerable to air defenses. In 1985, however, the U.S. Congress passed the Pressler amendment to the Foreign Assistance Act, requiring the president to certify annually "that Pakistan does not possess a nuclear explosive device."[133] Ronald Reagan and George H. W. Bush made these annual certifications to Congress, but with increasing discomfort and caveats in successive years. In 1989 the Soviet army completed its withdrawal from Afghanistan, and in October 1990 the Pressler amendment was finally invoked, terminating most military aid to Islamabad, including the transfer of additional F-16s that were on order. Not until after September 11, 2001, did U.S. military aid to Islamabad once again increase significantly.

In 1989, through PAEC connections, Pakistan agreed with China to buy thirty-four solid-fueled M-11 ballistic missiles having a 300-kilometer range if carrying a 500-kilogram payload. By the early 1990s, however, Beijing was under increasing U.S. pressure to comply with MTCR restrictions on missile transfers, and Pakistan evidently sought missiles from other suppliers.[134] It apparently negotiated with North Korea for liquid-fueled Nodong missiles with a range of 1,000–1,300 kilometers and a payload of 700–1,000 kilograms. This permitted Pakistan to threaten a much larger set of targets deeper in India than was possible with the M-11 missiles. In addition, some speculate that North Korea supplied the plutonium for the fifth Pakistani nuclear test in May 1998.[135]

At whatever level it was made, Pakistan's decision to share centrifuge uranium-enrichment technology with North Korea may have been driven by a perceived strategic need to acquire a less vulnerable, longer-range nuclear warhead delivery system with which to hold Indian targets at risk. Pakistan's motives in assisting the Iranian nuclear program seem harder to understand.[136]

North Korea's motives are generally difficult to assess, but in the case of the centrifuge-missile deal they seem easier to discern. The acquisition of uranium centrifuge technology provided North Korea with an alternative pathway to nuclear weapons after its plutonium program attracted international attention. The deal seems to have been reached sometime between 1993 and 1997.[137] North Korea stated in 2002 that it would seek a negotiated settlement over its nuclear programs on three conditions: "Firstly, if the U.S. recognizes the DPRK's [North Korea's] sovereignty, secondly, if it assures the DPRK of non-aggression and thirdly, if the U.S. does not hinder the economic development of the DPRK."[138] These conditions have remained prominent through North Korean Ambassador Li Gun's detailed remarks in 2003, and in the Joint Statement of the Fourth Round of the Six-Party Talks held in Beijing in September 2005.[139] (Attempts to negotiate an end to North Korea's nuclear weapons program are described in chapter 5.) North Korea's nuclear program may serve either as an ultimate guarantor of the regime or as a bargaining chip, but even in the latter role it serves at least in part as a security guarantee, and this aspect of their approach has been constant.

As for Iran, at least two motives seem to lie behind its apparent pursuit of nuclear weapons: security concerns in relation to the United States, Israel, and possibly Pakistan (and in the past, Iraq and the Pakistani-supported Taliban); and nationalism and nationalist-fueled resentment of other nations' perceived hypocrisies.[140] On October 26, 2005, President Ahmadinejad announced: "As the Imam said, Israel must be wiped off the map."[141] The UN Security Council denounced the statement as being contrary to the commitments made by all members of the United Nations.[142]

Conclusion

Latent proliferation and proliferation rings represent two major and broad challenges to the survival of the nonproliferation regime. Proliferation rings compound the latent proliferation problem and make it clear that current export controls are inadequate. First-tier proliferation, from the countries of the Nuclear Suppliers Group, has played an important role in helping potential proliferators in developing countries acquire the ability to make both nuclear weapons and the missiles with which to deliver them. The world may be entering a period in which those countries will acquire sufficient knowledge, technology, and manufacturing capabilities to allow them to disconnect from first-tier suppliers and fill technological gaps in their nuclear and missile programs by trading with other developing countries. A critical question is whether the discovery of second-tier proliferation networks represents the unraveling of a uniquely ambitious set of proliferation relationships, or whether these networks are harbingers of the proliferation landscape to come, driven by continuing regional instabilities and abetted by the spread of technological know-how throughout the world.

Whatever the answer may be, the required response is clear. It would be foolish to think that rolling up the programs of all the countries known to have been involved in the Khan network would guarantee that additional copies of the warhead design that the network provided Libya were not available elsewhere.[143] The international community must act as if the proliferation rings described here are the shape of the future, while taking steps to ensure that history will view them as a fiscal challenge to the nonproliferation regime from a few last proliferators. Both state-sponsored and privately sponsored nuclear proliferation must be checked. The current proliferation networks must be shut down and measures put in place to prevent or detect their rise elsewhere.

Centrifuge enrichment technology, while now the most economically appealing uranium-enrichment technology, remains demanding, expensive, and beyond the capacity of today's terrorist groups. Producing the HEU for making nuclear weapons may require "roughly $1 billion and a decade of intensive effort."[144] Producing HEU for nuclear weapons is the most difficult step in making a uranium nuclear weapon. Rather than trying to enrich uranium, terrorists may seek the nuclear weapons themselves, or the HEU with which to make them.[145] Therefore, better security from thieves and terrorists for weapons-usable nuclear materials and for the weapons themselves is essential.[146]

The possibility that nuclear weapons or weapons-usable nuclear materials might be stolen, or even intentionally transferred to terrorists by a government or substate group, cannot be discounted—though intentional transfer would be an extraordinarily dangerous decision for any country to make. But these possibilities emphasize the importance of curtailing further proliferation to additional countries. Chapter 5 turns to what may be done to preserve and strengthen the nonproliferation regime in light of these challenges.

Notes

1. The discussion in this section is drawn from Chaim Braun and Christopher F. Chyba, "Proliferation Rings: New Challenges to the Nuclear Nonproliferation Regime," *International Security* 29 (Fall 2004): 5–49. For a skeptical view, see Alexander H. Montgomery, "Ringing in Proliferation: How to Dismantle an Atomic Bomb Network,"

International Security 30 (Fall 2005): 153–87. For the Pakistani claim, see UN General Assembly First Committee debates during the week of October 11, 2004 (www.reaching criticalwill.org/political/1com/FCM/2004wk2.html#prolif).

2. This does not mean that these networks would make it easy to develop nuclear weapons, only easier. Montgomery, "Ringing in Proliferation," emphasizes the many barriers facing any such program, including tacit knowledge, knowledge that must be learned through trial and error, possibly under the instruction of an individual already possessing it. See also Donald MacKenzie and Graham Spinardi, "Tacit Knowledge, Weapons Design, and the Uninvention of Nuclear Weapons," *American Journal of Sociology* 101 (July 1995): 44–99.

3. Senator John Kerry and President George W. Bush, remarks at their first presidential debate on September 30, 2004 (www.debates.org/pages/trans2004a.html). In response to a question asking him to identify "the single most serious threat to the national security of the United States," Senator Kerry said: "Nuclear proliferation. Nuclear proliferation. There's some 600-plus tons of unsecured material still in the former Soviet Union and Russia. At the rate that the president is currently securing it, it'll take 13 years to get it.... Now, there are terrorists trying to get their hands on that stuff today." In his reply, President Bush agreed with his opponent "that the biggest threat facing this country is weapons of mass destruction in the hands of a terrorist network."

4. Senator Richard Lugar, member or chairman of the Senate Foreign Relations Committee for many years, took this position long before President Bush and Senator Kerry did in the 2004 campaign. See Lugar, "Redefining NATO's Mission: WMD Terrorism," *Washington Quarterly* 25 (Summer 2002): 7. See also Matthew Bunn and Anthony Wier, *Securing the Bomb: The New Global Imperatives* (Harvard University, Project on Managing the Atom, May 2005), pp. 2–4; and Graham Allison, *Nuclear Terrorism: The Ultimate Preventable Catastrophe* (New York: Henry Holt, 2004), pp. 17–120. Compare the somewhat more cautious assessment by Sidney D. Drell and James E. Goodby, *The Gravest Danger: Nuclear Weapons* (Stanford, Calif.: Hoover Institution Press, 2003), pp. 44–49.

5. See, for example, Charles D. Ferguson and William C. Potter, *The Four Faces of Nuclear Terrorism* (Monterey, Calif.: Monterey Institute, Center for Nonproliferation Studies, 2004), pp. 1–2. They argue that "this reality requires a profound change in the way the United States thinks about nuclear policy.... Terrorist organizations are the only entities that are seeking to rain nuclear destruction on the United States without regard to the potential consequences to themselves or to the innumerable innocent victims of such action." For a somewhat contrary view, see Robert Trager and Dessislava Zagorcheva, "Deterring Terrorism: It Can Be Done," *International Security* 30 (Winter 2005/06): 87–123.

6. Bunn and Wier, *Securing the Bomb: The New Global Imperatives*, fig. ES-2, p. vii. Compare Allison, *Nuclear Terrorism*, pp. 43–46, 68–74.

7. Ferguson and Potter, *The Four Faces of Nuclear Terrorism*, pp. 65–80.

8. For a discussion of the security of Russian nuclear warheads, see Matthew Bunn and Anthony Wier, *Securing the Bomb: An Agenda for Action* (Harvard University, Project on Managing the Atom, May 2004), pp. 51–56. Evaluating the security of nuclear weapons in a number of other programs, especially in the Pakistani program, is more difficult. In January 2002, Pakistani general Khalid Kidwai reportedly stated that Pakistani warheads do not have PALs, although the bombs are normally kept in a disassembled state. See Paolo Cotta-Ramusino and Maurizio Martellini, *Nuclear Safety, Nuclear*

Stability, and Nuclear Strategy in Pakistan (Como, Italy: Landau Network, Centro Volta, February 11, 2002) (lxmi.mi.infn.it/~landnet/Doc/pakistan.pdf).

9. Some assert that PALs on a stolen warhead could eventually be overcome, but that this would be challenging for a nonstate or unsophisticated state program. See Richard L. Garwin and Georges Charpak, *Megawatts and Megatons: A Turning Point in the Nuclear Age?* (New York: Alfred A. Knopf, 2001), p. 342.

10. NEM refers to any mixture of materials that can be made to support an exponentially growing chain reaction triggered by "fast" neutrons. For a list of the most important such materials, see "Physics and Technology of Nuclear Explosive Materials," in Committee on International Security and Arms Control, *Monitoring Nuclear Weapons and Nuclear-Explosive Materials* (Washington: National Academies Press, 2005), app. A, pp. 221–44.

11. For an account of recent attempts of the theft of NEM, see "Anecdotes of Nuclear Insecurity," in Matthew Bunn, Anthony Wier, and John Holdren, *Controlling Nuclear Warheads and Materials: A Report Card and Action Plan* (Harvard University, Project on Managing the Atom, March 2003), app. A, pp. 166–78. See also U.S. National Intelligence Council, "Annual Report to Congress on the Safety and Security of Russian Nuclear Facilities and Military Forces" (December 2004) (www.cia.gov/nic/special_russiannuke04. html); and Lyudmila Zaitseva and Kevin Hand, "Nuclear Smuggling Chains: Suppliers, Intermediaries, and End-Users," *American Behavioral Scientist* 46 (February 2003): 282.

12. See Garwin and Charpak, *Megawatts and Megatons*, p. 59; and Leonard Spector with Jacqueline Smith, *Nuclear Ambitions: The Spread of Nuclear Weapons 1989–1990* (Boulder, Colo.: Westview Press, 1990), app. A.

13. Robert Schlesinger, "24 Sites Eyed for Uranium Seizure," *Boston Globe*, August 24, 2002. See also Bunn and others, *Controlling Nuclear Warheads and Materials*, pp. 71–72.

14. George Bunn and Chaim Braun, "Terrorism Potential for Research Reactors Compared with Power Reactors," *American Behavioral Scientist* 46 (February 2003): 714–19. For more recent estimates, see Bunn and Wier, *Securing the Bomb: The New Global Imperatives*, p. 15; Ferguson and Potter, *The Four Faces of Nuclear Terrorism*, p. 110.

15. See Garwin and Charpak, *Megawatts and Megatons*, pp. 347–50.

16. Albert Narath, "The Technical Opportunities for a Sub-National Group to Acquire Nuclear Weapons," *XIV International Amaldi Conference on Problems of Global Security* (Rome: Accademia Nazionale Dei Lincei, 2003), pp. 19–32. See also Francesco Calogero, "The Risk of Nuclear Terrorism," Second Pugwash Workshop on Terrorism: Consequences of the War on Terrorism, Como, Italy, October 9–12, 2003.

17. David Albright, "Al Qaeda's Nuclear Program: Through the Window of Seized Documents" (Nautilus Institute, November 2002) (www.nautilus.org/archives/fora/Special-Policy-Forum/47_Albright.html). Albright states that "al Qaeda's determination to get nuclear weapons along with its increased ability to obtain outside technical assistance, lead to the conclusion that if al Qaeda had remained in Afghanistan, it would have likely acquired nuclear weapons eventually."

18. Bunn and Wier, *Securing the Bomb: An Agenda for Action*, pp. 27–32.

19. For a discussion of the "cleanout" campaign, see Kevin N. Luongo and W. E. Hoehn, "Reform and the Expansion of Cooperative Threat Reduction," *Arms Control Today* 33 (June 2003): 11–15. The Reduced Enrichment for Research and Test Reactors program, now part of the "global cleanout" plan initiated by the U.S. Department of Energy (DOE), is described at the DOE NNSA website (www.nnsa.doe.gov/na-20/rertr.shtml).

20. Pakistani nuclear scientists Sultan Bashiruddin Mahmood and Chaudiri Abdul Majeed have admitted that they had long discussions with al Qaeda officials in August 2001 about nuclear, chemical, and biological weapons, according to Pakistani intelligence officials. See Kamran Khan and Molly Moore, "2 Nuclear Experts Briefed Bin Laden, Pakistanis Say," *Washington Post*, December 12, 2001.

21. See, for example, Robin Wright and Glenn Kessler, "Iran, Libya, and Pakistan's Nuclear Supermarket," *Disarmament Diplomacy* 75 (January/February 2004): 39–42.

22. See references in Joseph Cirincione, with Jon B. Wolfsthal and Miriam Rajkumar, *Deadly Arsenals: Tracking Weapons of Mass Destruction* (Washington: Carnegie Endowment for International Peace, 2002), p. 172; and John Pike, "Pakistan Nuclear Weapons," *GlobalSecurity.org* (www.globalsecurity.org/wmd/world/pakistan/nuke.htm).

23. See discussion and citations in Braun and Chyba, "Proliferation Rings," p. 16.

24. For a more technical discussion, see Peter D. Zimmerman with Cheryl Loeb, "Dirty Bombs: The Threat Revisited," *Defense Horizons* 38 (January 2004): 1–11. See also Stanford University Center for International Security and Cooperation "'Dirty Bomb' Fact Sheet" (iis-db.stanford.edu/pubs/20769/dirty_bomb_facts.pdf).

25. Cited in Charles D. Ferguson and Joel O. Lubenau, "Securing U.S. Radioactive Sources," *Issues in Science and Technology Online* (Fall 2003) (www.issues.org/issues/20.1/ferguson.html). See also International Atomic Energy Agency (IAEA), *Categorization of Radioactive Sources*, IAEA-TECDOC-1344 (Vienna, June 2003) (hps.org/documents/IAEATecDoc1344.pdf); and Stanford University Center for International Security and Cooperation, "Understanding the Risks and Realities of Nuclear Terrorism" (cisac.stanford.edu/publications/understanding_the_risks_and_realities_of_nuclear_terrorism/).

26. Analysts sometimes comment that dirty bombs or other terrorist attacks will cause "panic"; in fact, studies of disasters show that people usually do not panic. See the discussions in Lee Clarke, *Mission Improbable: Using Fantasy Documents to Tame Disaster* (University of Chicago Press, 1999).

27. For an illustration of the likely dispersal pattern from a dirty bomb and a discussion of its consequences, including health risks, see Tonya L. Putnam, *Communicating Nuclear Risk: Informing the Public about the Risks and Realities of Nuclear Terrorism*, Workshop Report (Stanford University Center for International Security and Cooperation, October 2002) (cisac.stanford.edu/publications/communicating_nuclear_risk_informing_the_public_about_the_risks_and_realities_of_nuclear_terrorism). See also Bunn and Braun, "Terrorism Potential for Research Reactors Compared with Power Reactors," pp. 714, 719; and Lynne L. Snowden, "How Likely Are Terrorists to Use a Nuclear Strategy?" *American Behavioral Scientist* 46 (February 2003): 699–702

28. See Zaitseva and Hand, "Nuclear Smuggling Chains"; Snowden, "How Likely Are Terrorists to Use a Nuclear Strategy?" p. 699.

29. George Bunn and Lyudmila Zaitseva, "Efforts to Improve Nuclear Material and Facility Security," *SIPRI Yearbook 2002* (Oxford University Press, 2003), app. 10D, pp. 598, 605.

30. See Morton B. Maerli, Annette Schaper, and Frank Barnaby, "The Characteristics of Nuclear Terrorist Weapons," *American Behavioral Scientist* 46 (February 2003): 727, 729.

31. See Putnam, *Communicating Nuclear Risk*.

32. For summaries of the existing treaties and other international arrangements intended to help raise existing standards (and provide standards where none existed) for the protection of nuclear and other radioactive materials from terrorists and thieves, see Bunn and Braun, "Terrorism Potential for Research Reactors Compared with Power

Reactors," pp. 722–25; Maerli and others, "The Characteristics of Nuclear Terrorist Weapons," p. 739. In addition, UN Security Council Resolution 1540, requiring states to report the regulatory steps they have taken to protect nuclear and other radioactive materials from terrorists, was adopted in April 2004. See chapter 3 of this volume. Amending the Convention on Physical Protection of Nuclear Material so that it will apply to domestic storage and use of civilian nuclear material (rather than just international transport) has been the subject of international negotiations for many years. Finally, on January 19, 2005, a majority of the parties reached a sufficient consensus on what the amendment should say. A conference in July 2005 adopted an amendment, but it will take some time before enough countries sign and ratify it to put it into force. At their summit conference on February 24, 2005, Presidents Bush and Putin issued a joint statement calling for enhancement of security at nuclear facilities. They promised that their two governments would "continue our cooperation on security upgrades of nuclear facilities and develop a plan of work through and beyond 2008 on joint projects." Joint Statement on Nuclear Security Cooperation, White House, February 24, 2005 (www.whitehouse.gov/news/releases/2005/02/20050224-8.html).

33. See Michael May, Tonya Putnam, and Dean Wilkening, *Detecting Nuclear Material in International Container Shipping: Criteria for Secure Systems* (Stanford University Center for International Security and Cooperation, 2003) (iis-db.stanford.edu/pubs/20127/1-Container_Security.pdf).

34. See U.S. Customs and Border Protection, "Keeping Cargo Safe: Container Security Initiative" (www.cbp.gov/xp/cgov/border_security/international_activities/csi); but see also Stephen E. Flynn, "The Continued Vulnerability of the Global Maritime Transportation System," written testimony before the House Committee on Transportation and Infrastructure, Subcommittee on Coast Guard and Maritime Transportation, 109th Cong., 2nd sess., March 9, 2006 (www.house.gov/transportation/cgmt/03-09-06/flynn.pdf).

35. See Cirincione, with others, *Deadly Arsenals*, pp. 258–59, 344, 346, 349, 351; and Leonard S. Spector, *The Undeclared Bomb* (Washington: Carnegie Endowment for International Peace, 1988), p. 72.

36. Ariel Levite argues, for example, that "Japan provides the most salient example of nuclear hedging to date." See Ariel Levite, "Never Say Never Again: Nuclear Reversal Revisited," *International Security* 27 (Winter 2002/3): 71. See also Kurt Campbell and Tsuyoshi Sunohara, "Japan: Thinking the Unthinkable," in *The Nuclear Tipping Point: Why States Reconsider Their Nuclear Choices*, edited by Kurt Campbell, Robert Einhorn, and Mitchell Reiss (Brookings, 2004), pp. 218–53.

37. For a discussion of the North Korean claim, see Paul Kerr, "Examining North Korea's Nuclear Claims," *Arms Control Today* 35 (March 2005).

38. See Bruce Jentleson and Christopher Whytock, "Who 'Won' Libya: The Force-Diplomacy Debate and Its Implications for Theory and Policy," *International Security* 30 (Winter 2005/06): 47–86.

39. See, for example, International Institute for Strategic Studies, "Iraq's Weapons of Mass Destruction: A Net Assessment" (2002).

40. For one discussion of latent proliferation in the context of Iran, see George Perkovich, "Dealing with Iran's Nuclear Challenge" (Washington: Carnegie Endowment for International Peace, April 28, 2003) (www.ceip.org/files/projects/npp/pdf/Iran/

iraniannuclearchallenge.pdf). In January 2004 Iran's president Mohammad Khatami stated publicly that Iran's nuclear program was peaceful and that Iran was "vehemently" opposed to the production of nuclear arms. See "Iran Denies Receiving Nuclear Material from North Korea," Agence France-Presse, Davos, Switzerland, January 21, 2004 (www.spacewar.com/2004/040121200135.i5cph0v8.html).

41. The role of the IAEA, the requirements of its inspections, and efforts to make these inspections harder to circumvent are described in chapters 3 and 5.

42. IAEA, Director General's report to the IAEA Board of Governors, November 2004.

43. See, for example, Steven R. Weisman, "A Test of Wills between Iran and the West," *New York Times*, January 12, 2006.

44. The discussion in this and the remaining sections draws substantially from Braun and Chyba, "Proliferation Rings." The Zangger Committee and the NSG are described in chapter 3.

45. Analyses of second-tier proliferation prior to the 1990s include those in Joseph Pilat and William Potter, eds., *The Nuclear Suppliers and Nonproliferation* (Lexington, Mass.: Lexington Books, 1985); Spector with Smith, *Nuclear Ambitions*, pp. 29–48; and William Potter, ed., *International Nuclear Trade and Nonproliferation* (Lexington, Mass.: Lexington Books, 1990).

46. See Lewis Dunn, "The Emerging Nuclear Suppliers: Some Guidelines for Policy," in *International Nuclear Trade and Nonproliferation*, edited by Potter, p. 398. Dunn notes the exception of China to his statement that "the emerging suppliers have so far acted relatively cautiously as nuclear exporters."

47. There is an extensive literature on the reasons that countries choose to develop nuclear weapons, including Etel Solingen, "The Political Economy of Nuclear Restraint," *International Security* 19 (Fall 1994): 126–69; Mitchell Reiss, *Bridled Ambition: Why Countries Constrain Their Nuclear Capabilities* (Johns Hopkins University Press, 1995); Scott D. Sagan, "Why Do States Build Nuclear Weapons? Three Models in Search of a Bomb," *International Security* 21 (Winter 1996/97): 54–86; George Perkovich, *India's Nuclear Bomb: The Impact on Global Proliferation* (University of California Press, 1999), pp. 444–68; Peter Liberman, "The Rise and Fall of the South African Bomb," *International Security* 26 (Fall 2001): 45–86; Levite, "Never Say Never Again"; Sonali Singh and Christopher R. Way, "The Correlates of Nuclear Proliferation: A Quantitative Test," *Journal of Conflict Resolution* 48 (December 2004): 859–85; and Dong-Joon Jo and Erik Gartzke, "Determinants of Nuclear Weapons Proliferation," November 2005 (www.columbia.edu/~eg589/pdf/jo_gartzke_nuke_11222005.pdf).

48. For a review of CTR programs, see Matthew Bunn, Anthony Wier, and John P. Holdren, *Controlling Nuclear Warheads and Materials: A Report Card and Action Plan* (Harvard University, Project on Managing the Atom, March 2003); for an update see Bunn and Wier, *Securing the Bomb: An Agenda for Action*.

49. For a summary and evaluation of export control regimes, see U.S. General Accounting Office, *Nonproliferation Strategy Needed to Strengthen Multilateral Export Control Regimes* (October 2002) (www.state.gov/documents/organization/14867.pdf).

50. The abbreviation MW(e) stands for "megawatt electric." A megawatt, or million watts, is a unit of power; 1,000 MW(e) is a typical electrical power output for a large commercial power reactor. MW(e) measures the electrical power output of the plant, as opposed to MW(th), or "megawatt thermal," which measures the plant's thermal power.

The plant's thermal output is converted, at an efficiency cost (about a factor of 1/3 for a commercial reactor), into electrical power. For terminology and basic reactor physics, see Garwin and Charpak, *Megawatts and Megatons*.

51. For descriptions of the North Korean plutonium program, see David Albright and Kevin O'Neill, eds., *Solving the North Korean Nuclear Puzzle* (Washington: Institute for Science and International Security Press, 2000); Michael M. May and others, "Verifying the Agreed Framework," CGSR-CISAC report, April 2001 (cisac.stanford.edu/publications/12020); and Jonathan Pollack, "The United States, North Korea, and the End of the Agreed Framework," *Naval War College Review* 56 (Summer 2003): 11–49.

52. Central Intelligence Agency, *Unclassified Report to Congress on the Acquisition of Technology Related to Weapons of Mass Destruction and Advanced Conventional Munitions, 1 July to 31 December 2001*, released in January 2003 (www.nti.org/e_research/official_docs/cia/cia_cong_wmd.pdf). See also David Albright, "North Korea's Current and Future Plutonium and Nuclear Weapons Stocks," *ISIS Issue Brief* (Institute for Science and International Security, January 15, 2003).

53. See Siegfried S. Hecker, "Visit to the Yongbyon Nuclear Scientific Research Center in North Korea," statement before the Senate Committee on Foreign Relations, 108th Cong., 2nd sess., January 21, 2004 (www.foreign.senate.gov/testimony/2004/HeckerTestimony 040121.pdf). For a discussion of inconsistencies in unclassified intelligence assessments of whether North Korea has produced nuclear warheads from its extracted plutonium, see Pollack, "The United States, North Korea, and the End of the Agreed Framework." A. Q. Khan, a key figure in the Pakistani nuclear program, reportedly told Pakistani authorities that during a visit to North Korea in 1999 he was shown what he believed to be three nuclear warheads. See David E. Sanger, "Pakistani Tells of North Korean Nuclear Devices," *New York Times*, April 13, 2004.

54. IAEA, "Fact Sheet on DPRK Nuclear Safeguards" (May 2003).

55. See www.cnn.com/2002/WORLD/asiapcf/east/12/22/n.korea.nukes; and John Pike, "Yongbyon" (www.globalsecurity.org/wmd/world/dprk/yongbyon.htm).

56. The capacity factor of a reactor over a given period of time is the energy actually produced by the reactor divided by the energy that would have been produced had the reactor run nonstop at 100 percent power for that time. For an analysis suggesting that both the capacity factor and reprocessing efficiencies of North Korea's weapons program are lower than many Western estimates have assumed, see Montgomery, "Ringing In Proliferation," pp. 158–60. For periodically updated reviews of the North Korean nuclear program, see Larry A. Niksch, "North Korea Nuclear Weapons Program," Issue Brief IB 91141 (Congressional Research Service, October 6, 2005); and Sharon A. Squassoni "North Korea's Nuclear Weapons: How Soon an Arsenal?" Report RS21391 (Congressional Research Service, August 1, 2005).

57. See Hecker, "Visit to the Yongbyon Nuclear Scientific Research Center."

58. For the potential rate of accumulation of fissile materials within North Korea's nuclear program, see Henry Sokolski, "Beyond the Agreed Framework: The DPRK's Projected Atomic Bomb Making Capabilities, 2002–2009," an analysis of the Nonproliferation Education Center, December 3, 2002 (www.npec-web.org/pages/fissile.htm); and Jon B. Wolfsthal "Estimates of North Korea's Unchecked Nuclear Weapons Production Potential" (Washington: Carnegie Endowment for International Peace, August 2003).

59. For a summary of these reports, see "Yongbyon 50-MW(e) Reactor," *GlobalSecurity.org* (www.globalsecurity.org/wmd/world/dprk/yongbyon-50.htm).

60. Unnamed U.S. officials claimed that at an April 2003 meeting in Beijing, North Korea threatened to export or test a nuclear weapon. See Glenn Kessler, "N. Korea Says It Has Nuclear Arms: At Talks with U.S. Pyongyang Threatens 'Demonstration' or Export of Weapon," *Washington Post*, April 25, 2003. Two different unnamed officials, however, warned that the North Koreans' words were vague. "No one talked about testing directly, or selling," one official stated. Rather, "there was language about 'taking physical actions.'" See David E. Sanger, "North Korea Says It Now Possesses Nuclear Arsenal," *New York Times*, April 23, 2003. For an analysis of mistranslation and misunderstanding of North Korean assertions, see Daniel Pinkston and Phillip Saunders, "Seeing North Korea Clearly," *Survival* 45 (Autumn 2003): 79–102. See also Marina Malenic, "North Korea Could Give Nuclear Weapons to Terrorist Groups U.S. Military Officials Warn," NTI *Global Security Newswire*, April 1, 2004.

61. A senior Chinese official said in June 2004 that "the U.S. has not presented convincing evidence" that a North Korean uranium program exists. See Joseph Kahn and Susan Chira, "Chinese Official Challenges U.S. Stance on North Korea," *New York Times*, June 9, 2004. See also Paul Kerr, "N. Korea Uranium Enrichment Efforts Shrouded in Mystery," *Arms Control Today* 33 (May 2003).

62. Central Intelligence Agency, *Report to Congress on North Korea's Nuclear Weapons Potential* (November 19, 2002) (www.fas.org/nuke/guide/dprk/nuke/cia111902.html). See also David E. Sanger and James Dao, "U.S. Says Pakistan Gave Technology to North Korea," *New York Times*, October 17, 2002; and Carla Anne Robbins and Zahid Hussain, "North Korea Had Russian Parts Suppliers," *Wall Street Journal*, October 21, 2002.

63. For accounts of the missiles for centrifuges deal, see Gaurav Kampani, "Second-Tier Proliferation: The Case of Pakistan and North Korea," *Nonproliferation Review* 9 (Fall/Winter 2002): 107–16; Mark Hibbs, "CIA Assessment on DPRK Presumes Massive Outside Help on Centrifuges," *Platts Nuclear Fuel*, November 25, 2002, pp. 1, 12–13; International Institute for Strategic Studies (IISS), "Pakistan and North Korea: Dangerous Counter-Trades," *IISS Strategic Comments* 8 (November 2002): 1–2; Daniel A. Pinkston, "When Did WMD Deals between Pyongyang and Islamabad Begin?" (Center for Nonproliferation Studies, December 2002); David E. Sanger, "In North Korea and Pakistan, Deep Roots of Nuclear Barter," *New York Times*, November 24, 2003; David E. Sanger "U.S. Widens View of Pakistan Link to Korean Arms," *New York Times*, March 14, 2004; and Christopher Clary, "Dr. Khan's Nuclear WalMart," *Disarmament Diplomacy* 76 (March/April 2004): 31–36. North Korean assistance to the Ghauri program was affirmed by the U.S. National Intelligence Council in December 2001, in *Foreign Missile Developments and the Ballistic Missile Threat through 2015* (www.cia.gov/nic/PDF_GIF_otherprod/missilethreat2001.pdf).

64. See David E. Sanger and William J. Broad, "From Rogue Nuclear Programs, Web of Trails Leads to Pakistan," *New York Times*, January 4, 2004; and George Jahn, "AP: Pakistan Knew of Nuclear Black Market," *Washington Times*, March 7, 2004. For reports on Khan's admissions, see David Rhode and David E. Sanger, "Key Pakistani Is Said to Admit Atom Transfers," *New York Times*, February 2, 2004; John Lancaster and Kamran Khan, "Pakistani Scientist Apologizes," *Washington Post*, February 5, 2004; and Peter

Edidin, "Dr. Khan Got What He Wanted, and He Explains How," *New York Times*, February 15, 2004.

65. See Salman Masood and David Rohde, "Pakistan Now Says Scientist Did Sell Koreans Nuclear Gear," *New York Times*, August 25, 2005.

66. For reviews of Khan's activities, see Douglas Frantz, "Iran Closes In on Ability to Build a Nuclear Bomb," *Los Angeles Times*, August 4, 2003; and Maggie Farley and Bob Drogin, "1 Man, 3 Nations, a World of Peril," *Los Angeles Times*, January 6, 2003.

67. Using URENCO data, the KRL built the P-1 centrifuge, which uses aluminum tubes and has a capacity of 2–3 separative work units (SWU) per year. (A SWU is a measurement of the effort needed to enrich uranium; about 200 SWUs are required to make 1 kilogram of HEU from natural uranium.) By 1995 the KRL switched to the P-2 centrifuge, based on a maraging steel rotor and rated at twice the SWU capacity of the P-1. See David Albright and Corey Hinderstein, "The Centrifuge Connection," *Bulletin of the Atomic Scientists* 60 (March/April 2004): 61–66.

68. The halted consignment reportedly contained only 214 tubes. For accounts of this incident, see Mark Hibbs, "DPRK Sought Enough Aluminum Tubing in Germany for 4,000 Centrifuges," *Platts Nuclear Fuel*, May 12, 2003, pp. 1, 16–17; Joby Warrick, "N. Korea Shops Stealthily for Nuclear Arms Gear; Front Companies Step Up Efforts in European Market," *Washington Post*, August 15, 2003; Joby Warrick, "U.S. Followed the Aluminum," *Washington Post*, October 18, 2003; and Mark Hibbs, "DPRK Enrichment Not Far Along, Some Intelligence Data Suggest," *Nucleonics Week*, October 24, 2003, pp. 1, 12–14; Central Intelligence Agency Nonproliferation Center, *Unclassified Report to Congress on the Acquisition of Technology Relating to Weapons of Mass Destruction and Advanced Conventional Munitions, 1 July through 31 December 2003* (www.cia.gov/cia/reports/721_reports/july_dec2003.htm).

69. According to Garwin and Charpak, *Megawatts and Megatons*, p. 59, the gun-type Hiroshima weapon contained about 60 kilograms of HEU. According to Spector and Smith, *Nuclear Ambitions*, app. A, more difficult implosion designs require 25 kilograms of HEU, or as little as 15 kilograms or less for increasingly sophisticated designs. According to Albright and Hibbs, citing an unnamed U.S. official interviewed in 1991, the nuclear warhead design China provided to Pakistan used about 15 kilograms of HEU. See David Albright and Mark Hibbs, "Pakistan's Bomb: Out of the Closet," *Bulletin of the Atomic Scientists* 48 (July/August 1992): 38–43. Since it requires about 200 SWUs to make 1 kilogram of HEU, about 3,000 SWUs are needed to produce one weapon's worth of HEU, or 1,000 to 1,500 P-1 centrifuges operating for one year. For the production capacity goal of the North Korean enrichment plant, see Central Intelligence Agency, *Unclassified Report to Congress on the Acquisition of Technology Related to Weapons of Mass Destruction and Advanced Conventional Munitions, 1 January through 30 June 2002* (www.fas.org/irp/threat/bian_apr_2003.htm#5).

70. See May and others, "Verifying the Agreed Framework"; and Albright and O'Neill, *Solving the North Korean Nuclear Puzzle*.

71. Robin Wright and Glenn Kessler, "Analysis: Two Decades of Sanctions, Isolation Wore Down Gaddafi," *Washington Post*, December 20, 2003; and Wright and Kessler, "Iran, Libya, and Pakistan's Nuclear Supermarket." Libya's efforts to meet its obligations to the IAEA are given in IAEA Board of Governors, "Implementation of the NPT Safeguards Agreement of the Socialist People's Libyan Arab Jamahiriya," Report

GOV/2004/12 (February 20, 2004); see also Paul Kerr, "U.S. Says Libya Implementing WMD Pledge," *Arms Control Today* 34 (March 2004): 28–29.

72. See Jentleson and Whytock, "Who 'Won' Libya."

73. Stephen Fidler, Mark Huband, and Roula Khalaf, "Comment: Return to the Fold: How Gaddafi Was Persuaded to Give Up His Nuclear Goals," *Financial Times*, January 27, 2004; Ray Takeyeh, Statement before the Committee on International Relations, U.S. House of Representatives, March 10, 2004; and "Qaddafi's Son Says Libya Was Promised Economic, Military Gains for WMD Disarmament," NTI *Global Security Newswire*, March 10, 2004.

74. See Peter Slevin, John Lancaster, and Kamran Khan, "At Least 7 Nations Tied to Pakistani Nuclear Ring," *Washington Post*, February 8, 2004; William J. Broad, David E. Sanger, and Raymond Bonner, "A Tale of Nuclear Proliferation: How Pakistani Built His Network," *New York Times*, February 12, 2004; and Christopher Clary, "Dr. Khan's Nuclear WalMart." For official Malaysian investigation results, see Polis Diraja Malaysia, "Press Release by Inspector General of Police in Relation to Investigation on the Alleged Production of Components for Libya's Uranium Enrichment Programme," February 20, 2004 (www.rmp.gov.my/rmp03/040220scomi_eng.htm). According to this document, European participants allegedly involved in the Malaysian/Libyan centrifuge efforts included Heinz Mebus and Gotthard Lerch from Germany; Friedrich Tinner and his son, Urs Friedrich Tinner, from Switzerland; Gunas Jireh and Selim Alguadis from Turkey, and Peter Griffen from the United Kingdom.

75. See David Albright and Corey Hinderstein, "Documents Indicate A. Q. Khan Offered Nuclear Weapons Designs to Iraq in 1990. Did He Approach Other Countries?" *ISIS Issue Brief* (Institute for Science and International Security, February 4, 2004) (www.isis-online.org); Douglas Frantz, "Nuclear Ring May Have Aided Syria," *Los Angeles Times*, June 25, 2004. Possible nuclear links between Pakistan and Saudi Arabia are discussed in Simon Henderson, *Towards a Saudi Nuclear Option: The Saudi-Pakistani Summit*, Policy Watch 750 (Washington Institute for Near East Policy, April 22, 2003); and "Pakistan, Saudi Arabia Reach Secret Nuclear Weapons Deal, Pakistani Source Says," NTI *Global Security Newswire*, October 21, 2003. An offer of "nuclear power" to Nigeria by a visiting senior Pakistani military officer was asserted, then rescinded; see "Nigerian Military Asserts, Then Denies, Interest in Acquiring Pakistani Nuclear Technology," NTI *Global Security Newswire*, March 4, 2004.

76. Stephen Fidler and Mark Husband, "Turks and South Africans Helped Libya's Secret Nuclear Arms Project," *Financial Times*, June 10, 2004; Stephen Fidler, "Turkish Businessman Denies Nuclear Goods Claim," *Financial Times*, June 11, 2004.

77. Rohan Sullivan and Patrick McDowell, "'Chief Financier' in Nuclear Network Had Ties with Malaysian Leader's Son," *AP Online*, February 18, 2004 (24hour.startribune.com/24hour/world/story/1151188p-8021305c.html); and Raymond Bonner, "Salesman on Nuclear Circuit Casts Blurry Corporate Shadow," *New York Times*, February 18, 2004.

78. See Slevin and others, "At Least 7 Nations Tied to Pakistani Nuclear Ring"; and Broad and others, "A Tale of Nuclear Proliferation." For estimates of the network's earnings, see David E. Sanger and William J. Broad, "Pakistan's Nuclear Earnings: $100 Million," *New York Times*, March 16, 2004; and Clary, "Dr. Khan's Nuclear WalMart."

79. The warhead is thought to be based on a design tested by the Chinese and later provided to Pakistan in the 1980s. See Pike, "Pakistan Nuclear Weapons." See also

William J. Broad, "Libya's A-Bomb Blueprints Reveal New Tie to Pakistani," *New York Times,* February 9, 2004; "Libyan Inspections Find Evidence of Collaboration with Egypt," *World Tribune.com,* March 29, 2004 (216.26.163.62/2004/me_egypt_03_29.html). The possibility that a package of centrifuge technology, uranium hexafluoride, and nuclear warhead designs was provided by the Pakistani network to North Korea, citing a CIA assessment, is reported in Sanger, "U.S. Widens View of Pakistan Link to Korean Arms." Reportedly according to that assessment, Dr. Khan's network sold a similar package to Libya for $60 million.

80. The scope of the Libyan nuclear and chemical programs is discussed in Mark Huband, Roula Khalaf, and Stephen Fidler, "Libya Nuclear Deal Exposes Black Market," *Financial Times,* January 21, 2004; Raymond Bonner and Craig Smith, "Pakistani Said to Have Given Libya Uranium," *New York Times,* February 21, 2004; Judith Miller, "Libya Discloses Production of 23 Tons of Mustard Gas," *New York Times,* March 6, 2004; and George Jahn "Japan Company Sold Atomic Plant to Libya," *Manchester Guardian,* March 12, 2004. Reportedly, in February 2001 North Korea transferred 1.7 tons of uranium hexafluoride to Libya in support of the uranium centrifuges provided by the Khan network. See David E. Sanger and William J. Broad, "Evidence Is Cited Linking Koreans to Libya Uranium," *New York Times,* May 23, 2004. For a discussion of the ability to use the imported equipment, see Montgomery, "Ringing in Proliferation."

81. South African Council for the Non-Proliferation of Weapons of Mass Destruction, Press Release, Department of Foreign Affairs, Republic of South Africa, September 7, 2004, (www.dfa.gov.za/docs/2004/weap0906.htm); "South Africa Makes Nuclear Arrest in Libyan Proliferation," *Financial Times,* September 4, 2004.

82. CIA director John Deutch's 1996 congressional testimony quoted by the Carnegie Endowment for International Peace, "Iran" (www.ceip.org/programs/npp/iran.htm).

83. Mohamed ElBaradei, "Implementation of the NPT Safeguards Agreement in the Islamic Republic of Iran," Report GOV/2003/40 (IAEA, June 6, 2003), p. 2.

84. Ibid., p. 6.

85. Mohamed ElBaradei, "Implementation of the NPT Safeguards Agreement in the Islamic Republic of Iran," Report GOV/2003/63 (IAEA, August 26, 2003), p. 7.

86. Reported by Frantz, "Iran Closes In on Ability to Build a Nuclear Bomb."

87. Iranian Foreign Ministry spokesman Hamid Reza Asefi has called these allegations "poisonous and disdainful rumors" that were spread by the United States. Quoted in ibid.

88. Mark Hibbs, "Pakistan Believed Design Data Source for Centrifuges to Be Built by Iran," *Platts Nuclear Fuel,* January 20, 2003, pp. 1, 14–16.

89. See Joby Warrick and Glenn Kessler, "Iran's Nuclear Program Speeds Ahead," *Washington Post,* March 10, 2003; and David Albright and Corey Hinderstein, "Furor over Fuel," *Bulletin of the Atomic Scientists,* vol. 60 (May/June 2003), pp. 12–15.

90. Polis Diraja Malaysia, "Press Release by Inspector General," February 20, 2004; and Bonner, "Salesman on Nuclear Circuit Casts Blurry Corporate Shadow."

91. Albright and Hinderstein, "The Centrifuge Connection."

92. ElBaradei, "Implementation of the NPT Safeguards," GOV/2003/63, pp. 6–8.

93. Felicity Barringer, "Traces of Enriched Uranium Are Reportedly Found in Iran," *New York Times,* August 27, 2003; and Joby Warrick, "Iran Admits Foreign Help on Nuclear Facility; UN Agency's Data Point to Pakistan as the Source," *Washington Post,* August 27, 2003.

94. Warrick, "Iran Admits Foreign Help on Nuclear Facility."

95. Joby Warrick, "Nuclear Program in Iran Tied to Pakistan," *Washington Post*, December 21, 2003; and Craig S. Smith, "Alarm Raised over Quality of Uranium Found in Iran," *New York Times*, March 11, 2004.

96. According to an unnamed non-U.S. intelligence officer and an unnamed former Iranian intelligence officer, North Korea is providing Iran with help on nuclear warhead design. See Frantz, "Iran Closes In on Ability to Build a Nuclear Bomb." For claims of other nations' participation in the Iranian program, see Glen Kessler, "Group Alleges New Nuclear Site in Iran," *Washington Post*, February 20, 2003; and Leonard S. Spector, "Iran's Secret Quest for the Bomb," *YaleGlobal Online*, May 16, 2003 (yaleglobal.yale.edu/article.print?id=1624).

97. "IAEA Inspectors Find Centrifuge Equipment at Iranian Air Base," NTI *Global Security Newswire*, February 19, 2004; "Iran Talks Quiet in Vienna, but High-Grade Uranium Reportedly Found," NTI *Global Security Newswire*, March 11, 2004.

98. Louis Charbonneau, "UN Sees Signs of Massive Iran Nuke Plans—Diplomats," Reuters, June 10, 2004; Mohamed ElBaradei, "Implementation of the NPT Safeguards Agreement in the Islamic Republic of Iran," Report GOV/2004/34 (IAEA, June 1, 2004). Two other enrichment facilities allegedly began operating in 2000 near the villages of Lashkar-Abd and Ramandeh, about 40 kilometers west of Tehran. See Sheryl Gay Stolberg, "Group Says Iran Has 2 Undisclosed Nuclear Laboratories," *New York Times*, May 27, 2003. At the Lashkar-Abd site the IAEA found an active laser program that could be used for uranium enrichment. See ElBaradei, "Implementation of the NPT Safeguards," GOV/2003/63, p. 8.

99. "Iran Set to Announce Work on Heavy Water Reactor; Nuclear Inspections Timetable Set," NTI *Global Security Newswire*, April 9, 2004.

100. ElBaradei, "Implementation of the NPT Safeguards," GOV/2003/40, pp. 5–7.

101. Since a heavy-water reactor operates with natural uranium fuel, plutonium can be produced without a uranium-enrichment facility. India and Israel based their nuclear weapons programs on such reactors. A description of the Iranian facilities may be found in ElBaradei, "Implementation of the NPT Safeguards," GOV/2003/40, pp. 5–8, and GOV/2003/71, November 10, 2003, "Heavy Water Reactor Programme" section.

102. Joby Warrick, "Iran Given Deadline to Lay Bare Nuclear Program," *Washington Post*, September 13, 2003.

103. Christine Hauser and Nazila Fathi, "Iran Signs Pact Allowing Inspections of Its Nuclear Sites," *New York Times*, December 18, 2003; Mohamed ElBaradei "Implementation of the NPT Safeguards Agreement in the Islamic Republic of Iran," Report GOV/2004/11 (IAEA, February 24, 2004), sec. B.5, p. 10.

104. Dafna Linzer, "Iran Says It Will Renew Nuclear Efforts," *Washington Post*, June 25, 2004.

105. Mohamed ElBaradei, "Report by the Director General, Implementation of the NPT Safeguards Agreement in the Islamic Republic of Iran," IAEA report GOV/2004/83 (IAEA, November 15, 2004); Peter Ford, "Europe Persuades Iran to Cool Nuclear Program, For Now," *Christian Science Monitor*, November 15, 2004; EU-Iran Nuclear Agreement of November 15, 2004 (www.albwaba.com/news/index.php3?sid=288927&lang=e&dir=news); Elaine Sciolino, "Europeans Say Iran Agrees to Freeze Uranium Enrichment," *New York Times*, November 16, 2004, p. A-3; Steven Weisman, "Bush Confronts New Challenge on Issue of Iran," *New York Times*, November 19, 2004.

106. Nazila Fathi, "Iran Rejects European Offer to End Its Nuclear Impasse," *New York Times,* August 7, 2005; Joel Brinkley and Steven R. Weisman, "Rice Urges Israel and Pakistan to Sustain Momentum," *New York Times*, August 18, 2005.

107. See Joel Brinkley, "Iranian Leader Refuses to End Nuclear Effort," *New York Times*, August 18, 2005.

108. Expert Report to IAEA Director General, "Multilateral Approaches to the Nuclear Fuel Cycle," INCIRC/640 (IAEA, February 2005), pp. 13–14.

109. Richard Bernstein and David E. Sanger, "New Twist in Iran Plan for Nuclear Fuel: Aide Seems Ready to Have Enrichment Done Outside Country," *New York Times*, December 29, 2005.

110. Richard Bernstein and Steven R. Weisman, "Europe Joins U.S. in Urging Action by UN on Iran," *New York Times*, January 13, 2006.

111. CBS News, "Iran Referred to Security Council," February 4, 2006 (www.cbsnews.com/stories/2006/02/04/politics/main1281378.shtml).

112. Cirincione, with others, *Deadly Arsenals*, pp. 262–64; Donald H. Rumsfeld and others, "Executive Summary of the Report of the Commission to Assess the Ballistic Missile Threat to the United States," July 15, 1998 (www.fas.org/irp/threat/bm-threat.htm).

113. John R. Bolton, "Iran's Continuing Pursuit of Weapons of Mass Destruction," testimony before the House International Relations Committee, Subcommittee on the Middle East and Central Asia, 108th Cong., 2nd sess., June 24, 2004.

114. See Ze'ev Schiff, "North Korea Got Nuclear Know-How from Iran," *Ha'aretz* English ed., November 21, 2002; and Schiff, "Weapons of Mass Destruction and the Middle East: The View from Israel," James A. Baker III Institute for Public Policy paper (March 2003).

115. Barringer, "Traces of Enriched Uranium Are Reportedly Found in Iran."

116. Cirincione, with others, *Deadly Arsenals*, pp. 250–51. North Korean offers of missile sales to Myanmar and Nigeria are reported in "Intelligence Officials Suspect North Korean WMD Exports to Myanmar," NTI *Global Security Newswire,* November 18, 2003; and Nicholas Kralev, "North Korea Offers Nigeria Missile Deal," *Washington Times*, January 29, 2004. For a more detailed analysis of the topology of these uranium and missile networks, see Montgomery, "Ringing in Proliferation."

117. Cirincione, with others, *Deadly Arsenals*, pp. 250–51; see also Federation of American Scientists, "Weapons of Mass Destruction—WMD around the World—North Korea Missiles—Hwasong 5/SCUD B" (www.fas.org/nuke/guide/dprk/missile/hwasong-5.htm).

118. Cirincione, with others, *Deadly Arsenals*, pp. 148–50, 152, 212–15. China's supply of HEU to Pakistan has been called unconfirmed by an unnamed U.S. official; see Albright and Hibbs, "Pakistan's Bomb."

119. Spector with Smith, *Nuclear Ambitions*, p. 91. Uranium hexafluoride is the gaseous form of uranium needed for uranium centrifuge enrichment.

120. A relevant comparison timescale would include the time needed for HEU production in Pakistan's program. This program was launched in 1972 and was expedited by Khan's return to Pakistan in 1975 from the URENCO plant in the Netherlands. Apparently Pakistan began producing HEU in 1985–86. See Cirincione, with others, *Deadly Arsenals*,

pp. 210–11. For discussions of the timescales for North Korea's enrichment program, see Braun and Chyba, "Proliferation Rings"; and Montgomery, "Ringing in Proliferation."

121. Duncan Lennox, "Co-operation Boosts Missile Proliferation," *Jane's Intelligence Review,* January 2002, pp. 39–41; and Rumsfeld and others, "Executive Summary of the Report of the Commission to Assess the Ballistic Missile Threat to the United States."

122. Sagan, "Why Do States Build Nuclear Weapons?" p. 54.

123. Liberman, "The Rise and Fall of the South African Bomb"; and Helen E. Purkitt and Stephen F. Burgess, with reply by Peter Liberman, "South Africa's Nuclear Decisions," *International Security* 27 (Winter 2002/3): 59–88.

124. See, for example, Liberman, "The Rise and Fall of the South African Bomb"; Perkovich, *India's Nuclear Bomb*, pp. 446–55; and Perkovich, "Dealing with Iran's Nuclear Challenge."

125. See Sonali Singh and Christopher R. Way, "The Correlates of Nuclear Proliferation: A Quantitative Test," *Journal of Conflict Resolution* 48 (December 2004): 859–85; and Dong-Joon Jo and Erik Gartzke, "Determinants of Nuclear Weapons Proliferation," November 2005 (www.columbia.edu/~eg589/pdf/jo_gartzke_nuke_11222005.pdf).

126. See Sagan, "Why Do States Build Nuclear Weapons?" For a discussion of this issue during the 1970s and 1980s, see Spector with Smith, *Nuclear Ambitions*, pp. 89–112.

127. A concern of the Clinton administration was "whether the Pakistani government was sufficiently in control of its nuclear labs and certain nuclear scientists." Unnamed Clinton administration official quoted in Dan Stober and Daniel Sneider, "Bush Knew about North Korea's Nuclear Program for More than a Year," *San Jose Mercury News*, October 25, 2002.

128. Relations between Khan's KRL and the PAEC in the context of the Pakistani weapons program are discussed in Simon Henderson, *Pakistan's Nuclear Proliferation and U.S. Policy*, Policy Watch 826 (Washington Institute of Near East Policy, January 12, 2004); and Pervez Hoodbhoy, "Pakistan: Inside the Nuclear Closet," *Open Democracy*, March 3, 2004 (www.opendemocracy.net/debates/article-2-95-1767.jsp).

129. The hypothesis that Khan was acting on his own is criticized by Kampani, "Second-Tier Proliferation," and in IISS, "Pakistan and North Korea: Dangerous Counter-Trades." Kampani also discusses the bureaucratic rivalry between the KRL and PAEC, and its possible effects. The U.S. State Department determined that North Korean–Pakistani cooperation in missile technology violated the MTCR and imposed sanctions on the KRL and North Korea's Ch'anggwang Trading Company. For a journalist's discussion of the Khan-government link, see William Langewiesche, "The Point of No Return," *Atlantic* 297 (January/February 2006): 96–118.

130. Clary, "Dr. Khan's Nuclear WalMart"; and Sharon Squassoni, "Closing Pandora's Box: Pakistan's Role in Nuclear Proliferation," *Arms Control Today* 34 (April 2004): 8–13.

131. Spector with Smith, *Nuclear Ambitions*, p. 90; see also Stephen Philip Cohen, *The Idea of Pakistan* (Brookings, 2004).

132. For details, see ibid., pp. 107–12; Cirincione, with others, *Deadly Arsenals*, pp. 207–16; Kampani, "Second-Tier Proliferation"; and IISS, "Pakistan and North Korea: Dangerous Counter-Trades."

133. The texts of the 1985 Pressler amendment, as well as the 1976 Symington and Glenn amendments, are given in the appendixes to Richard N. Haass and Morton H.

Halperin, *After the Tests: U.S. Policy toward India and Pakistan* (New York: Council on Foreign Relations, 1998).

134. Cirincione, with others, *Deadly Arsenals*, p. 152; and Dinshaw Mistry, "Beyond the MTCR: Building a Comprehensive Regime to Contain Ballistic Missile Proliferation," *International Security* 27 (Spring 2003): 119–49.

135. See David E. Sanger and William J. Broad, "Pakistan May Have Aided North Korea A-Test," *New York Times*, February 27, 2004; and Paul Watson and Mubashir Zaidi, "Death of N. Korean Woman Offers Clues to Pakistani Nuclear Deals," *Los Angeles Times*, March 1, 2004.

136. For speculations about possible motives, see Perkovich, "Dealing with Iran's Nuclear Challenge"; and Sultan Shahin, "Iran, Nukes, and the South Asian Puzzle," *Asia Times*, September 8, 2003.

137. Pinkston, "When Did WMD Deals between Pyongyang and Islamabad Begin?"

138. North Korea, Foreign Ministry Statement, October 25, 2002 (www.kcna.co.jp/index-e.htm).

139. Li Gun, "Requisites for Resolving the Nuclear Issue," Center for National Policy, December 16, 2003 (www.cnponline.org/Issue%20Briefs/North%20Korea/Li%20Gun%20Paper.pdf); and "Joint Statement of the Fourth Round of the Six-Party Talks," Beijing, September 19, 2005 (www.state.gov/r/pa/prs/ps/2005/53490.htm).

140. Ibid. Perkovich, "Dealing with Iran's Nuclear Challenge," assesses the evidence available for the different motives fueling Iranian nuclear demand. For a discussion of the utility of Iranian nuclear weapons in meeting Iran's national security needs, see Sharam Chubin, "Iran's Strategic Environment and Nuclear Weapons," in *Iran's Nuclear Weapons Options: Issues and Analysis*, edited by Geoffrey Kemp (Washington: Nixon Center, 2001), pp. 17–34; and for a discussion of the public debate over nuclear weapons within Iran, see Farideh Farhi, "To Have or Not to Have: Iran's Domestic Debate on Nuclear Options," in *Iran's Nuclear Options,* edited by Kemp. See also "Iran's Nuclear Ambitions: Full Steam Ahead?" *IISS Strategic Comments* 9 (March 2003).

141. See, for example, "Ahmadenijad: Wipe Israel Off Map," Aljazeera.net, October 26 2005 (english.aljazeera.net/NR/exeres/15E6BF77-6F91-46EE-A4B5-A3CE0E9957EA.htm); see also "Iranian Leader: Wipe Out Israel" (edition.cnn.com/2005/WORLD/meast/10/26/ahmadinejad/index.html).

142. See "Security Council Condemns Anti-Israel Words" (edition.cnn.com/2005/WORLD/meast/10/28/iran.un.reaction).

143. For example, the IAEA is trying to determine whether Egypt may have received the Pakistani nuclear warhead designs from Libya. See "Libyan Inspectors Find Evidence of Collaboration with Egypt," *World Tribune.com*, March 29, 2004.

144. Allison, *Nuclear Terrorism*, p. 212,

145. Ibid., pp. 20–41, 74–86.

146. See Bunn and Zaitseva, "Efforts to Improve Nuclear Material and Facility Security," app. 10D; Bunn and Wier, *Securing the Bomb: An Agenda for Action*, pp. 9–16.

five

Strategies for Tackling Proliferation Challenges

Christopher F. Chyba, Chaim Braun, and George Bunn

The nuclear nonproliferation regime faces grave challenges.[1] The most serious of these (see chapters 3 and 4) include illicit nuclear smuggling networks, latent proliferation under the guise of the Nuclear Non-Proliferation Treaty (NPT), three or four states with nuclear weapons outside the NPT, the extent to which the nuclear weapon states are living up to their NPT obligations, and the ongoing diffusion of technology relevant to nuclear weapons.[2] The regime is particularly threatened if NPT signatories such as North Korea or Iran successfully pursue nuclear weapons. It has been argued that failure to stop North Korea and Iran from acquiring nuclear weapons "could trigger an avalanche of decisions to acquire nuclear weapons in Asia, the Middle East and elsewhere," and that, as a result, the NPT "could become a dead letter."[3]

A world without a reasonably effective nuclear nonproliferation regime would be a far more dangerous world. The greatest nuclear threat to the United States may be the acquisition of nuclear weapons by terrorists, and that threat is increased as nuclear weapons spread to more states.[4] According to the UN Secretary General's High-Level Panel on Threats, Challenges and Change, terrorist groups might already be able to obtain the necessary weapons-usable nuclear material, "and, with purchases on the open market, assemble a simple 'gun-type' nuclear device."[5] This chapter explores effective responses to these dangers via national and international policies to prevent or curtail the spread of nuclear weapons, technology, and materials.

Nuclear Weapons and Materials: Supply and Demand

As described in chapter 4, nuclear proliferation has both a supply and demand side. Addressing the *supply* side means controlling the export and other transfer of weapons-grade material or nuclear-weapons-relevant technology from both developed and developing countries. Addressing the *demand* side means confronting the factors that states are likely to take into consideration when deciding whether to acquire nuclear weapons, including those factors specific to individual countries.[6]

Supply-side action first requires increasing the physical security of nuclear weapons-usable material in developed and developing countries alike, especially in Russia and the former Soviet republics. This material is the focus of the Nunn-Lugar Cooperative Threat Reduction program and related programs, referred to collectively here as CTR.[7] But even with these programs, the threat of theft and smuggling of weapon-usable nuclear material cannot be reduced overnight. It will take years and will require continuing attention, commitment, and funding from many countries.[8]

In addition, it is essential to strengthen export control regimes such as the Zangger Committee of Nuclear Exporters and the Nuclear Suppliers Group (NSG).[9] NSG members have traditionally been technologically developed nuclear supplier states, rather than countries in the developing world.[10] But as the history of the A. Q. Khan proliferation network (detailed in chapter 4) shows, the developing world is where the NSG has been least effective in curtailing nuclear weapons–related transfers among traders and manufacturers—although the Khan network also benefited directly from individuals in NSG member states.

Nonproliferation policies must roll up the Khan network and other networks involved in smuggling nuclear or missile components. But they must also be attentive to the possibility that these networks are harbingers of future challenges that it would be wise to take steps to counter now.[11]

The nonproliferation regime plays an important role in establishing the balance of factors that states consider when determining their nuclear weapon policies. If the regime is to remain effective, it must increase the benefits to states of adhering to it, decrease the negative consequences of adherence, make clear the dangers of abandoning the regime, and reassure adherents that the regime protects them from their adversaries' nuclear ambitions.

Buttressing Existing Supply-Side Approaches

Policy options for strengthening the nonproliferation regime begin with incremental measures for buttressing the existing regime. These are important but will not be enough; new approaches are also needed. We consider these in turn.[12]

Cooperative Threat Reduction Programs

The theft and smuggling of weapons-usable material are serious concerns. Although stealing a complete warhead from a state program is probably more difficult to do, it cannot be ruled out.[13] There are already anecdotal examples of the theft of nuclear explosive material in the form of plutonium or highly enriched uranium (HEU). At least kilogram quantities of HEU (including 90 percent HEU, which is ideal for making the lowest-mass uranium warheads) have been stolen from Russian facilities.[14] With CTR support, by October 2004 Russia had completed rapid or comprehensive security upgrades of 46 percent of the 600 metric tons of its vulnerable weapons-usable nuclear material.[15]

The first line of defense against bomb building from stolen HEU or plutonium is to deter and erect barriers against theft, and to detect it if it should occur. This must be done worldwide, in a "global cleanout" campaign, given that there are substantial quantities of poorly safeguarded HEU outside Russia and the other former Soviet republics.[16] The CTR programs are central to this effort.[17] In June 2002 the Group of Eight industrialized nations (G-8) meeting at the Kananaskis summit in Canada reached a "10 plus 10 over 10" agreement to increase funding for cleanout, to distribute the total funding more equitably while committing the United States to do more, and to ensure that the G-8 would continue to address this problem throughout the coming decade. For its part of the agreement, the United States has promised $10 billion in assistance over ten years to be matched by $10 billion over the same period from the other G-8 members.[18] At the 2003, 2004, and 2005 G-8 summits, these plans and the efforts to implement them continued to be on the agenda. Some progress has been made, but much more needs to be done. If CTR efforts are successful, the danger posed by poorly secured fissile material stocks should decline over the next several years. Other measures will still be necessary, including IAEA assistance to improve the security of nuclear research reactors in many countries.

Strengthening the IAEA

Under Article III of the NPT, the IAEA implements a safeguards and inspections regime intended to ensure that non-nuclear weapon NPT parties meet their treaty obligations not to use their existing nuclear programs to develop nuclear weapons. A measure already taken to strengthen the safeguards regime, the so-called Additional Protocol, should make latent proliferation by this route more difficult, and should also constrain the building of illegal programs through second-tier proliferation.[19]

Starting in 1970, the IAEA safeguards requirements for non-nuclear weapon states were negotiated by safeguards experts from interested NPT members. These were codified in 1972 as IAEA Information Circular 153. The stated goal of these regulations was the timely detection of the diversion of significant quantities of nuclear material from permitted peaceful nuclear activities to nuclear weapons programs.[20] But monitoring and inspections under Information Circular153 were typically carried out only at facilities declared by the nation being inspected. By the early 1990s, it had become clear that these safeguards could be sidestepped, as in Iraq and North Korea, by using covert nuclear facilities not revealed to the IAEA in safeguards agreements, and not otherwise reported to the IAEA.[21] Although the IAEA had requested a special inspection under Information Circular153 for access to undeclared facilities in North Korea, that country refused to give the IAEA inspectors access, and the UN Security Council did not enforce the IAEA request for inspection.[22] Also under the Information Circular153 regime, Iranian authorities refused to allow the IAEA to sample nuclear materials at two uranium-enrichment-related sites that it had not reported to the IAEA.[23]

In 1993 the IAEA embarked on a project to strengthen the existing safeguards system. The measures considered were divided according to whether they could be implemented under existing IAEA authority (so-called part 1 measures) or would require additional provisions in a new safeguards agreement (part 2 measures). The additional provisions for part 2 were proposed by the IAEA Board of Governors in 1997. These were the Additional Protocol, a new agreement that goes beyond the IAEA Information Circular 153 safeguards. The new IAEA standards for the Additional Protocol appear in a document called IAEA Information Circular 540.[24]

As the IAEA explains: "While the chief object of safeguards under INFCIRC/153 is to verify that declared nuclear material was not diverted, the chief object of the new measures under INFCIRC/540 is to obtain assurance that the State has no undeclared activities."[25] Under Information Circular 540, states are required to make expanded, comprehensive declarations of all nuclear material and activities related to the nuclear fuel cycle, and the IAEA may conduct both location-specific and wide-area environmental sampling at locations specified by the Agency.[26] As interpreted by most NPT members, the treaty's safeguards provision does not require acceptance of the Additional Protocol, but states have been strongly encouraged to comply with it.[27]

As of 2005, only a little more than a third of the NPT's 188 parties had ratified the Additional Protocol, and another third had signed but not yet ratified it.[28] Iran had signed but refused to ratify.[29] The slow acceptance of the Additional Protocol goes to the heart of the bargain of the NPT. The Additional Protocol represents a significantly greater intrusion into a country's sovereignty than does IAEA Information Circular153. Adherents to the Additional Protocol must divulge ten-year fuel-cycle research and development plans to the IAEA, the activities and identities of persons or entities carrying out these plans, export/import information, and descriptions of many facilities. Adherents may be subject to far more intrusive inspections. A country joining the protocol is likely to see these as negative factors. What does it gain in return?

It is important to answer that question to persuade states that their adherence to the protocol, and to the NPT itself, is worth the price they pay. Increasingly onerous reporting and inspection requirements of the Additional Protocol, as well as perceived inequalities in its requirements for nonnuclear weapon states in comparison with those for nuclear weapon states (including those outside of the NPT), may be mitigated with appropriate inducements from the United States and other developed countries that have supported the new protocol. Such inducements are not necessarily inconsistent with the influence that the United States or others may unilaterally bring to bear to delay, stop, or roll back a particular state's nuclear program if it appears to be headed toward weaponization.[30] After all, one important inducement is simply that the broad adoption and implementation of the protocol should give countries greater assurance that their neighbors and rivals do not have nuclear weapon ambitions. This is the primary argument for the Additional Protocol given by representatives of the United States at NPT conferences.[31]

Effective implementation of the Additional Protocol has faced budgetary obstacles. From 1985 until recently, member states (which provide the money to run the IAEA) applied a policy of zero growth to the agency, despite its increasing responsibilities.[32] Its regular budget for 2004 was less than $269 million, of which nuclear verification received about $102 million, the largest single budget category. With U.S. support, the IAEA Board of Governors accepted a budget increase of $25 million to be phased in over 2004–07.[33] Given the centrality of IAEA inspections to the nonproliferation regime, and given the IAEA's expanding responsibilities related to the protocol's new requirements for routine inspections and for special investigations in places such as Iran and Libya, the no-growth policy in place for so long was self-defeating. An underfunded IAEA, with limited means to verify safeguards compliance, is then open to blame for being insufficiently capable of verification. A robust IAEA should be a high priority of U.S. foreign policy. To be robust, the agency must both be well funded and widely viewed as credible, independent, and fair.

Strengthening Export Control Regimes

The activities of proliferation rings have been abetted by suppliers in developed and developing countries alike. More robust inspections following a broad adoption of the Additional Protocol should help to interrupt these networks by deterring or revealing illicit transfers of equipment. Export control regimes are supply-side measures that have been adopted mostly by the world's nuclear supplier states. These regimes must be extended to capture developing-country exporters as well. At the same time, it is essential to strengthen existing controls on developed-country suppliers. Progress in both respects may appear to conflict with Article IV of the NPT, which declares the "inalienable right of all the Parties to the Treaty to develop research, production and use of nuclear energy for peaceful purposes without discrimination" and "in conformity with Articles I and II of this Treaty." Under Article I, nuclear weapon states agree not to assist those that do not have nuclear weapons to acquire them; under Article II, non-nuclear weapon states agree not to receive any assistance in the manufacture of nuclear weapons or to seek to build them on their own. Given these obligations, export controls designed to ensure that nuclear weapons technology does not spread are consistent with the NPT.

However, the Nuclear Suppliers Group has not banned the export of uranium-enrichment or plutonium-reprocessing technology. In the case of enrichment, its earlier recommendation was that "suppliers should encourage recipients to accept, as an alternative to national plants, supplier involvement and/or other appropriate multinational participation in resulting facilities." In 2004 the NSG recommendation was strengthened to state: "For a transfer of an enrichment facility or technology . . . the recipient nation should agree that neither the transferred facility, nor any facility based on such technology, will be designed or operated for the production of greater than 20% enriched uranium without the consent of the supplier nation, of which the IAEA should be advised."[34]

An IAEA-appointed panel of nuclear experts from twenty-six IAEA members (including all of the P-5) later examined multilateral nuclear approaches

(MNAs) to address both the "front end" and "back end" of the nuclear fuel cycle: the production of enriched uranium and the reprocessing and disposition of plutonium, respectively. Multilateral approaches, they said, could help meet "prevailing concerns about assurances of supply and non-proliferation." The panel suggested several ways of doing this: by developing and implementing international supply guarantees, to give reactor operators that do not yet have major uranium-enrichment or plutonium-separation facilities (such as Iran) an assurance of supply from others, guaranteed by the IAEA; by promoting the voluntary conversion of existing facilities to MNAs, so that MNA members could check on each other to prevent the enrichment of uranium or separation of plutonium at the facility for nuclear weapons purposes; and by creating multinational and regional MNAs for new facilities based on joint ownership, drawing rights, or co-management for front-end and back-end nuclear facilities.[35]

These recommendations would be implemented on a voluntary basis— not required by any treaty—as is also the case with both NSG standards and the export control regime for missiles and missile technology called the Missile Technology Control Regime (MTCR).[36] There is no specified sanction for any "violations" of these recommendations, even if a nuclear supplier violated them. If some of the recommendations of the IAEA Expert Group were adopted by the IAEA Board of Governors as requirements for the future, cases of violation might at least come before that board, and, if significant, might be reported to the UN Security Council as the ultimate official enforcer of the NPT.

The MTCR should be considered an integral part of the nuclear nonproliferation regime. The MTCR text states that the reason for restrictions on exports of missile technology "is to limit the risks of proliferation of weapons of mass destruction (i.e. nuclear, chemical and biological weapons), by controlling transfers that could make a contribution to delivery systems (other than manned aircraft) for such weapons."[37] Ballistic missiles are such delivery systems. A missile with a range of 1,500 kilometers has little utility as a conventional weapon without "smart" (very accurate) targeting ability. Unless it has a nuclear warhead, its chances of damaging the target at which it is aimed may be slight. As a result, damage effectiveness calculations will favor the quest for nuclear warheads for such missiles. As noted in chapter 4, missile technology has apparently been a key element in some of the swaps involved in the proliferation of nuclear weapons technology. If better controlled, missile technology would be less of a threat to nuclear proliferation.

In an assessment of the NSG and MTCR, the U.S. Government Account-ability Office (GAO) has recommended a number of commonsense improve-ments that we endorse.[38] These would require regime members to share information on their export licensing decisions, including denials and approvals of exports, and to do so in a timely manner; reduce the length of time members can take to adopt agreed-upon changes to control lists;[39] rec-oncile differences in how members implement agreed-upon controls; and ensure that new members have effective export control systems in place at the time they join the regime.[40]

The first measure would improve intelligence concerning the question-able actions of some countries simply by capturing and sharing existing information among export control regime members. Some NSG and MTCR members have never reported any denials of export licenses. The reasons for this have not been evaluated systematically; perhaps some countries provide informal denials to would-be exporters even before any formal applications for export licenses are made. If these are not reported, other regime members will not necessarily be alerted that potential proliferators may be seeking par-ticular items, and a chance to develop a more complete picture of those coun-tries' actions or intentions may be lost.[41]

While the steps described so far are important, they represent incremen-tal improvements in the current regime. More ambitious measures are also needed, particularly to control exports relevant to nuclear weapons. For example, at least two suppliers in countries not members of the NSG (or the Zangger Committee) contributed to Libya's efforts to make nuclear weapons. The Malaysian firm Scomi Precision Engineering and the Turkish EKA elec-trical equipment company produced centrifuge technology for shipment to Libya (see chapter 4). Export controls (including controls for dual-use equip-ment) clearly need to be adopted in countries beyond the suppliers that make up the NSG, though the immediate benefits of such controls may be less clear to developing countries.

In some cases, the appropriate measure will be to bring additional mem-bers into the NSG, as in the case of China, Estonia, Lithuania, and Malta, which joined in May 2004.[42] Some authors have suggested that the NSG should in fact be globalized, and that it should adopt majority rule in place of consensus decisionmaking.[43] However, such a move risks pushing its deci-sions toward a lowest common denominator. Yet as the Scomi Precision Engineering and EKA examples demonstrate, not all exporters of relevant dual-use nuclear equipment are within countries that are members of the Zangger Committee or the NSG. Moreover, effective export controls must be maintained by all three of the nuclear weapon non-NPT states—India, Israel, and Pakistan—as well.[44]

New Supply-Side Approaches to Nonproliferation

More ambitious than the incremental approaches just described are proposals made in 2003–05 by the Bush administration and the director general of the IAEA.[45] The heart of the Bush administration's approach to the nonproliferation threat has been to improve *enforcement* of the supply-side strictures and, without formally amending the NPT (which is nigh impossible), to close what it sees as NPT loopholes that allow proliferation under the guise of good standing within the treaty. The Iran and Brazil cases are examples. In contrast to U.S. criticism of Iran's pursuit of uranium enrichment capability, the United States has not criticized Brazil's pursuit of that technology.[46] Both countries maintain that their enrichment technology is to be used for peaceful purposes rather than for making nuclear weapons. But a major difference is that Brazil has an agreement with Argentina for mutual monitoring (in addition to IAEA inspection) of the nuclear facilities that the two neighbors (and sometime rivals) operate. Assuming that Argentina will have resident inspectors at the Brazilian enrichment facility, the arrangement could satisfy IAEA director general Mohamed ElBaradei's proposals for bilateral or multilateral monitoring of enrichment plants in addition to periodic IAEA inspection.

The Bush administration has not often pursued multilateral treaty-based approaches to close what it perceives as NPT loopholes. Its reports and statements to the 2005 NPT Review Conference emphasized its own nontreaty efforts. In a remarkable move, it and the United Kingdom succeeded in gaining unanimous UN Security Council approval of global nonproliferation standards for national action in UN Security Council Resolution 1540 (see chapter 3). These included a requirement that nations adopt national export controls to prevent terrorists from gaining access to nuclear, chemical, or biological weapons or the missiles that might carry them. Security Council Resolution 1540 also added global requirements for the protection of nuclear material against theft by terrorists or thieves, complementing the NPT's provisions for detecting the diversion of nuclear material to nonpeaceful purposes.[47]

Some of the Bush administration's proposals have the same goals as those of Director General ElBaradei but are not as closely related to the NPT or to any other multilateral, treaty-based approach. They were achieved in much less time than it would take to reach a broad, international consensus on a new treaty or to amend the NPT, if that were even possible.[48]

The possibilities for rapid adoption of new measures in the Bush administration's approach are a clear advantage. The question remains whether these less-than-global supply-side approaches will achieve their objectives in the long term, or if other approaches produce stronger, longer-lasting results.

The Proliferation Security Initiative

President Bush's Proliferation Security Initiative (PSI) announced in Krakow, Poland, on May 31, 2003, provides a way to inspect ships, aircraft, and land vehicles for "contraband" related to nuclear, chemical, or biological weapons.[49] To implement this initiative, the United States and ten allies agreed on some practical steps to interdict shipments of missiles, chemical and biological agents, and nuclear components traveling through their national territories, or on the high seas in their flag vessels.[50] In a formal Statement of Interdiction Principles issued in September 2003, these countries called on all states to undertake such interdiction measures, streamline procedures for the rapid exchange of relevant information, strengthen their national legal authority to accomplish these objectives, and take a series of specific actions in support of interdiction efforts. These included measures not only to interdict land vehicles or aircraft in their own territories or on their own flag vessels at sea, but also to "seriously consider" consenting to letting other states board their flag vessels if their cargo needed to be inspected.[51]

Since then, the PSI has expanded to fifteen or more core members, including Russia. The United States claims that more than sixty states support the initiative.[52] It has also signed boarding-permission agreements with Liberia and Panama, whose flags fly from more ships than those of any other nations in the world. These agreements allow vessels carrying Liberian and Panamanian flags to be stopped and searched by the United States (or other states that are core PSI members), unless Liberia or Panama object, within two hours of being notified of the intention to board the ships given by the United States (or another core member).[53] The United States has pursued similar boarding-permission agreements with other nations.

Unlike traditional export controls, the PSI is a supply-side measure that directly addresses both second-tier and first-tier proliferation as well as proliferation to terrorists. A ship carrying nuclear technology from a developing country would be subject to search just as much as if it carried goods from a developed country. The success of the PSI will depend strongly on intelligence. Its best-known claimed success is the discovery by German and Italian authorities of nuclear-enrichment centrifuge parts aboard the BBC *China,* a German-owned ship bound for Libya carrying cargo from Malaysia, among other states.[54]

One of PSI's limitations is that some nuclear material of consequence could still be transported by means that are not inspected by PSI members or that are hard to detect and track even with inspections. Moreover, nuclear materials or technology could travel by small air- or seacraft not routinely checked at airports and seaports. Despite U.S. efforts to enlist more countries into the PSI regime, important ones along the transfer routes may choose not to participate, intelligence is still imperfect, and timely "actionable" intelligence may be scarce. Although the PSI is but one supply-side component in what must be a web of measures to counter proliferation, it does represent an important new step in that it directly addresses both second-tier and first-tier proliferation.

The IAEA Director General's Proposals

In October 2003 IAEA director general Mohamed ElBaradei called for a new nonproliferation framework "more suited to the threats and realities of the 21st century."[55] Criticizing the behavior of both the nuclear weapon states and the non-nuclear weapon parties to the NPT, he proposed three measures focused mainly on the dangers of latent proliferation: limit the production of separated plutonium or highly enriched uranium to facilities under multinational control or, at least, under continuous inspection by representatives of a country other than the controlling/operating country; convert existing uranium-enrichment facilities to low-enriched uranium; only deploy new systems that are proliferation resistant; and consider multinational approaches to the disposal of spent fuel and radioactive waste. He also called for renewed attention to the Fissile Material Cut-Off Treaty (FMCT).[56] And in an editorial of February 12, 2004, responding to President Bush's speech on related topics a few days earlier, ElBaradei urged greater adherence to the NPT's Additional Protocol and argued that "no country should be allowed to withdraw" from the NPT and that the export control system must be universalized with the enactment of "binding, treaty-based controls."[57] The combination of these measures, if realized, would make it much more difficult for countries to use civilian nuclear capacity acquired pursuant to Article IV of the NPT to create a de facto nuclear weapons capability and then withdraw from the NPT to produce nuclear weapons—as North Korea has done.

After analyzing existing and proposed multilateral approaches to the nuclear fuel cycle, the IAEA-appointed Expert Group on Multilateral

Approaches concluded that the "objective of increasing non-proliferation assurances concerning the civilian nuclear fuel cycles, while preserving assurances of supply . . . could be achieved through a set of gradually introduced multilateral nuclear approaches (MNA)."[58] Their recommendations are being considered by governments and by the IAEA. Such approaches have, in part, long been employed in specific cases in which countries retain their rights under the NPT but choose for particular reasons not to exercise particular options. For instance, South Korea decided, under U.S. pressure, not to develop a plutonium-reprocessing capacity.[59] But what can be achieved multilaterally remains to be seen.

How could these multilateral approaches be enforced? Suppliers could deny new applicants the technology for uranium enrichment or plutonium separation unless the applicants agreed to multilateral ownership, or reciprocal inspections in addition to IAEA inspection, so that participants could check on one another. Such multinational approaches would reinforce IAEA inspections. Multinational inspection arrangements would also be more trustworthy than bilateral ones. If implemented, ElBaradei's recommendations and those of the IAEA Expert Group would also make it more difficult to construct an illicit program, whether supplied by smuggling or otherwise.

At the same time, these recommendations would place further restrictions on non-nuclear weapons states and even limit their sovereignty. If the recommendations required a global treaty-based approach, they would likely be very difficult to negotiate. However, the IAEA Expert Group discussed other options for multilateral approaches that would not require a global treaty, or that could be achieved by negotiating treaties among a small group of states, such as the treaties that produced the Urenco and EURODIF multilateral enrichment facilities in Western Europe.[60]

Multinationalizing uranium enrichment for non-nuclear weapon states has a legal basis in NPT Articles I, II, and IV, although this interpretation is not without controversy. NPT Article I promises that nuclear weapon parties to the treaty will "not in any way . . . assist . . . any non-nuclear-weapon State to manufacture or otherwise acquire nuclear weapons." In Article II, the non-nuclear weapon parties themselves agree "not to seek or receive any assistance in the manufacture of nuclear weapons." But because of Article IV, not all NPT parties have interpreted the treaty this way. Article IV says: "Nothing in this Treaty shall be interpreted as affecting the inalienable right of all Parties to the Treaty to develop research, production and use of nuclear energy for peaceful purposes without discrimination in conformity with Articles I and II." It also says that all NPT parties have a "right" to "participate in the fullest possible exchange of information for . . . the further development of the applications of nuclear energy for peaceful purposes." But Article IV also requires "conformity with Articles I and II." If a non-nuclear weapon party acquires technology for an enrichment plant for the purpose of making nuclear weapons, for example, it has violated the NPT. To make this rule effective requires more than periodic IAEA inspection because some enrichment plants can be quickly shifted from a low enrichment of uranium for supplying nuclear power reactors to a high enrichment for making bomb material. This is the type of problem that multinational enrichment plant owners and operators could solve by having employees from more than one participating country trained and on duty all the time. Even without multilateral agreement on this interpretation of Article IV, it could still be adopted in a regional context on the basis of being in the nuclear transparency interest of the parties involved.

President Bush's Seven 2004 Proposals

In a speech at the National Defense University on February 11, 2004, President Bush announced seven proposals "to strengthen the world's efforts to stop the spread of deadly weapons":[61] (1) expand the PSI; (2) gain UN Security Council approval for a proposal (which became UN Security Council Resolution 1540) that "all states criminalize proliferation, enact strict export controls, and secure all sensitive materials within their borders"; (3) broaden the Nunn-Lugar Cooperative Threat Reduction (CTR) program beyond Russia and other former Soviet republics; (4) ask the Nuclear Suppliers Group to deny enrichment and reprocessing equipment and technologies "to any state that does not already possess full-scale, functioning enrichment and reprocessing plants," while ensuring that states renouncing enrichment and reprocessing have reliable access at reasonable cost to civilian reactor fuel; (5) deny civilian nuclear reactor program equipment to states that have not joined the Additional Protocol; (6) create a safeguards and verification committee of the IAEA Board of Governors; and (7) deny membership on this committee or the IAEA board to any state (such as Iran) "under investigation for proliferation violations."

These proposals address several issues. Proposals (1) and (2) endeavor to prevent or interdict nuclear weapons–related shipments and therefore are directly concerned with proliferation rings. Proposal (3) speaks to the basic need to prevent nuclear theft. Proposals (4) and (5) build on but go beyond Director General ElBaradei's suggestions without calling for new treaties. Proposal (6) has been implemented by the creation of an IAEA committee of state representatives called the Committee on Safeguards and Verification. It will "review the IAEA's ability to ensure compliance with NPT obligations and safeguards agreements in light of recent non-proliferation challenges."[62]

Some of the Bush proposals lack universal appeal and would have difficulty gaining acceptance in multilateral negotiations requiring a consensus or near consensus for adoption. The PSI is a coalition that has been well received by many friends and allies of the United States, but not by all countries. UN Security Council Resolution 1540 is an important addition to the nonproliferation regime because it *requires* countries around the world to criminalize proliferation, to regulate their suppliers, and to adopt security protections for their nuclear facilities and materials, but whether the Security Council will take action against reluctant countries to force adoption of effective measures remains to be seen. How President Bush's proposal that only members of the Additional Protocol be allowed to import civilian reactor equipment would be enforced is not specified, but Bush's speech implies that this would be attempted through NSG decisions. Most global reactor equipment vendors are in countries that are members of the NSG. But, as the A. Q. Khan proliferation ring revealed, not all potential suppliers are NSG members.

UN Security Council Resolution 1540

The proposal for widespread export controls, criminal statutes against proliferation, and efforts to secure sensitive materials from thieves and terrorists was put forth in a Security Council resolution rather than a new negotiated treaty or a broadly agreed reinterpretation of the NPT. President Bush first mentioned such a resolution in his address to the UN General Assembly on September 23, 2003.[63] In December 2003 a draft resolution that had British support began circulating to some other governments, including China, France, and Russia; subsequent negotiations among the P-5 produced a draft resolution in March 2004, which the United States and United Kingdom then presented to the ten elected, nonpermanent Security Council members. After further negotiations, the Security Council adopted a modified version that became Resolution 1540 of April 2004.[64]

The resolution lists twelve numbered points, many of which "call upon" states to take certain voluntary steps. However, the first three points represent Security Council lawmaking in a new approach to global enforcement of nonproliferation requirements. In effect, this approach adds to the NPT's provisions without amending the treaty, which, as already mentioned, is an almost impossible task.[65]

Point (2) of Resolution 1540 requires states to adopt internal legislation to prevent "nonstate actors" from acquiring nuclear (or chemical or biological) weapons or their means of delivery: "All States . . . shall adopt and enforce appropriate effective laws which prohibit any non-State actor to manufacture, acquire, possess, develop, transport, transfer or use nuclear, chemical or biological weapons and their means of delivery." Point (3) requires that states "(a) develop and maintain appropriate effective measures to account for and secure" nuclear, chemical, or biological weapons and materials; "(b) develop and maintain appropriate effective physical protection measures; (c) develop and maintain appropriate effective border controls and law enforcement efforts" to prevent illicit trafficking in these materials; and "(d) establish, develop, review and maintain appropriate effective national export and trans-shipment controls over such items, including appropriate laws and regulations to control export, transit, trans-shipment and re-export" of such items along with appropriate penalties for violations. Members of the P-5 have thus mandated the adoption of a requirement for supply-side measures to be taken by every nation in the world.[66]

Compliance with New Supply-Side Approaches

The Bush and ElBaradei proposals recognize the importance of reducing latent proliferation—incrementally through the universal adoption of the Additional Protocol and more radically through limits on HEU production and plutonium reprocessing.[67] These are supply-side measures to address first- and second-tier proliferation as well as that related to terrorists. ElBaradei called for "treaty-based" universalization of export controls. But universalizing the NSG risks reducing its effectiveness, even as it expands. Negotiating a universal regime at periodic NPT conferences would not directly include India, Israel, and Pakistan; and negotiating a new universal regime for all members of the United Nations would be a labor of many years—yet the problem requires immediate attention. Not surprisingly, the Bush administration has favored working through either a Security Council resolution (UN Security Council Resolution 1540) or a coalition of willing states (the PSI), but neither of these arrangements would lead to a new global treaty-based regime.

Of course, a precedent for this approach is the NSG, created as a voluntary group of major suppliers at the initiative of the United States in 1974. But unlike the NSG, which *recommends* provisions for export controls by participating states, Resolution 1540 *requires all* nations to adopt and implement export controls without first reaching global consensus. It requires that states develop and maintain "appropriate" export controls "to prevent the proliferation of nuclear, chemical, or biological weapons and their means of delivery." It recognizes the need for "effective national export and trans-shipment controls." But the resolution is silent on what "appropriate" and "effective" controls are and by what standards they will be measured. More than a year later, 1540 compliance was still a problem, which the G-8 attempted to deal with at their 2005 Gleneagles Summit:

> The majority of UN members have responded to UNSCR 1540 by submitting reports on their domestic provisions including export controls, and their contribution to international cooperation. We urge those who have not yet done so to submit reports without delay. It is essential that all states meet their obligations in full, by enacting and enforcing national legal and regulatory measures including appropriate criminal and civil penalties for violations, and by committing to international cooperation on non-proliferation.[68]

To consider responses to Resolution 1540 and to achieve better compliance, the Security Council created a 1540 Committee after the resolution was adopted in 2004. At the Gleneagles Summit of 2005, the G-8 asked this committee to "work quickly and effectively" and urged the Security Council "to consider how best to ensure the work of the committee makes an enduring contribution to non-proliferation."[69] Although Resolution 1540 is being implemented slowly, progress is being made. It is important that implementation of 1540 be effective, lasting, and as broad as possible.

Resolution 1540 was silent on whether some countries are to be prohibited from *receiving* certain items, and by what criteria. That is left to treaties such as the NPT and the Chemical and Biological Weapons Conventions, as well as to less formal arrangements.

The PSI bears greater resemblance to the NSG, and the two have many members in common. The PSI Statement of Interdiction Principles of September 2003 calls on members of the PSI to interdict the transfer of nuclear, chemical, and biological weapons (and of missiles to carry them) "to and from states and non-state actors of proliferation concern," meaning in general "those countries or entities that . . . should be subject to interdiction activities because they are engaged in proliferation," as established by PSI participants.[70] Similarly, the NSG agreed in 1994 that a nuclear supplier should authorize a transfer of NSG "trigger list" items only when satisfied that the transfer would not contribute to nuclear weapons proliferation, recognizing that formal adherence to the NPT may not in itself guarantee that a recipient state shares a commitment to nonproliferation.[71] The PSI is more aggressive than the NSG, in that PSI countries have successfully pressured flag-carrier states to agree to the boarding of their flag ships on the high seas by navies of PSI member states. Under the agreements reached with Liberia and Panama, permission to stop a ship will be granted on a case-by-case basis. Failure to respond to a specific request within a two-hour period will be treated as consent to act.[72] The PSI's actual impact is hard to judge because the activities are generally kept secret.

The Bush proposals face at least two challenges. The first relates to universalizing the initiatives. The second concerns the incompleteness of a supply-side response.

Universalizing New Supply-Side Approaches

Security Council Resolution 1540 may preempt Director General ElBaradei's proposal to universalize export controls. Perhaps the Security Council will ultimately promulgate and update a trigger list of items to be under every nation's export controls. Such decisions might fall within the purview of the Security Council 1540 Committee created to report on the resolution's implementation. Every country will have a stake in seeing that export controls are effectively implemented by every other country. If violations are permitted, the system may not last long, except, perhaps, as a hollow shell of aspirations.

One step that might gain acceptance would be a global requirement that exports be made only to states that have signed Additional Protocol agreements with the IAEA, ratified these agreements, entered them into force, and complied with them. Could the Security Council create such an export regime? The NSG could continue to exist alongside it as a body that could agree on export standards (such as the Additional Protocol requirement) and implement them without the need for Security Council approval.

Attempts to universalize the PSI could also rely on good standing with the Additional Protocol to separate those countries that are "of proliferation concern" from those that are not. The strictest export controls would be applied universally to countries of concern under this definition. The countries of the PSI, like those of the NSG, could continue to apply their own criteria as well.

Addressing the Demand for Nuclear Weapons

Resolution 1540 suggests that the United States and the P-5 do not expect the proliferation problem to be resolved by tackling a few "hard cases." Rather,

Resolution 1540 and the PSI see the need for measures with a global reach that will continue indefinitely. This long-term perspective is wise, but it must also be recognized that nuclear weapons–relevant technology will undoubtedly become increasingly available in countries that are not traditionally nuclear suppliers, either through illicit trade within proliferation rings (if that trade is not interdicted) or through the creation of indigenous capability. The shipments of centrifuge technology to Libya and the manufacture of centrifuge-relevant components by Scomi Precision Engineering in Malaysia and EKA in Turkey show that while the PSI may successfully interdict shipments of equipment, it will not prevent the globalization of technology and know-how. More and more countries will learn to manufacture such equipment for themselves, especially since many of the required items represent dual-use technologies with other legitimate civilian applications. Therefore supply-side steps will likely not be enough to halt proliferation, and demand-side measures must be given greater attention.

The Need for Further Demand-Side Steps

Addressing the demand for nuclear weapons must confront the motives for acquiring them. As discussed in chapter 4, state motives for nuclear weapons are diverse and sometimes difficult to discern, but desires for national security or national prestige often play key roles; other important factors may include organizational politics and international reassurances or pressure.[73] (It remains the case that terrorist groups will acquire nuclear weapons only by obtaining warheads or nuclear explosive material from state programs, so even in the case of terrorism, addressing state demand is an important element in our response.) Security and prestige are complicated objectives that can be threatened, or buttressed, in a wide variety of ways.

Supply-side proposals such as UN Resolution 1540 tighten NPT Article II and III requirements for NPT members that do not have nuclear weapons. (They also restrict business opportunities for the nuclear weapon states.) For the long-term viability of the NPT, these new burdens should be balanced by demand-side incentives for adherence to the NPT regime. For many states, this will include the advantage, under NPT Article II, of being assured that similar proliferation restraints are imposed on neighbors or rivals, at times reinforced by positive security assurances from the United States or other countries. But for states that suspect their neighbors or rivals of having engaged in long-term clandestine or semi-overt nuclear weapons programs, the basic elements of the NPT agreement may not seem to provide adequate long-term security.

More states are likely to defect from the regime if this uncertainty cannot be adequately compensated by the mix of economic benefits expected from peaceful nuclear uses under Article IV of the NPT, the security benefits both from alliances and security assurances given by the P-5, and NPT Article II promises of neighbors and rivals that they will not acquire nuclear weapons. Defection may even seem tempting for the security and prestige it can bring, if nations such as North Korea are held up as an example of a state that has acquired nuclear weapons despite the NPT. In this light, defection is not an irrational decision by a rogue nation, but rather a rational response to an unfavorable balance of incentives and disincentives.

As a result, supply-side measures are not a sufficient response to nonproliferation, though a crucial part. Furthermore, they will become more difficult to monitor and enforce as the capability to manufacture uranium centrifuge components, for example, becomes increasingly widespread. Nor will it be easy for supply-side measures to address what occurs on the territory of especially weak governments. Even if a government adopts the national regulatory requirements called for by UN Security Council Resolution 1540, this will not extend its authority into a range of activities it does not in fact control.

Demand-side measures are also needed to blend with, and in some cases strengthen and extend, traditional approaches. Security guarantees (such as treaty alliances based on protection or nontreaty assurances that states will refrain from nuclear attack) and the imposition or lifting of economic sanctions have and will continue to play important roles. These methods have been applied in varying ways and with varying success in the case of most countries that have been part of the proliferation rings described here. The easing of regional security concerns will also be a crucial objective even as supply-side steps are being taken to slow down a state's ability to develop a nuclear arsenal. Of course, all these issues must be addressed on a case-by-case basis, although a sweetener for many countries could be a program providing energy support in return for restraint in weapons development. This would be consistent with, but would expand, the implicit bargain in Article IV of the NPT, namely, that the benefits of nuclear technology will be available, under controls, to NPT members without nuclear weapons.

An ESI to Complement the PSI

A major benefit of the NPT, made explicit in Article IV, is preferred access to presumed abundant and low-cost nuclear electricity supplies, as envisioned in President Eisenhower's Atoms for Peace program of 1953.[74] It is now clear that nuclear power is not a low-cost energy option, but rather an expensive and demanding technology to construct and operate. Early hopes for using nuclear energy to "bootstrap" economies to a higher level of technical development level and raise standards of living through the supply of low-cost power have at best been only partly met. And now states are being asked to accept even more intrusive and costly safeguards on their nuclear activities, if not a ban on the development of indigenous nuclear fuel-cycle facilities, while in some cases having neighbors who pursue, openly or clandestinely, nuclear weapons programs.

The NSG guidelines for nuclear transfers call on suppliers to "encourage" recipients to accept, "as an alternative to national plants," supplier involvement or multinational participation in enrichment or reprocessing facilities.[75] The nonproliferation benefits of the resulting transparency are clear; such an approach, however, should be coupled with incentives to make the bargain more appealing to recipient countries. A menu of possible energy-related benefits could be clustered under a new Energy Security Initiative that would take into account the burdens imposed on non-nuclear weapons states by the PSI, the Additional Protocol, and Resolution 1540.

In particular, this nuclear assistance approach could be tied to fuel-leasing arrangements, in which countries in good NPT standing (and having an IAEA Additional Protocol) could receive (by lease, not ownership) subsidized, lower-cost fuel for their nuclear plants, with the subsidy costs borne by the nuclear weapon or NSG states. Subsidized fuel leasing should be coupled with programs for taking back spent fuel and, at a later stage, could be tied in with the storage of that fuel at regional facilities to be run by regional organizations and monitored by their own participating members as well as by the IAEA. Such suggestions have been made for North Korea and Iran.[76] Although Article IV of the NPT speaks exclusively of cooperation in the provision of nuclear energy, consideration should be given to expanding the scope of assistance to other energy alternatives under appropriate commercial terms, as well as to electric transmission grid enhancements, in return for demonstrable adherence to NPT obligations.

Some aspects of this approach can be detected in proposals for improving Iran's oil and gas industries as a means of meeting the country's energy needs and dealing with its nuclear program.[77] A similar approach was proposed to help resolve the North Korean nuclear standoff during six-party talks held in Beijing in June 2004. This approach seems to parallel that reportedly pursued by the United States and United Kingdom with Libya.[78] The Energy Security Initiative would present an international policy declaration up front, providing a menu of potential incentives to be tailored as appropriate to the specific needs of particular countries. In this way the two sides of the NPT bargain would be visibly brought into closer balance. The intent of NPT Article IV on peaceful uses of nuclear energy was to support the provision of energy services to NPT members in good standing. However, nuclear power is not the only available source; many countries now have other means of providing relatively low-cost energy.

Cooperation under NPT Article IV need not be limited to the area of electric power. Indeed, the IAEA's technical cooperation program funds public health and environmental assistance as well as programs with a nuclear component.[79] The total 2004 budget for the IAEA technical cooperation program was about $75 million.[80] Further incentives along these lines could be explored as well.

A Fissile Material Cut-Off Treaty

A Fissile Material Cut-Off Treaty (FMCT) is a long-standing proposal for an international agreement to prohibit all signatories from producing enriched uranium or separated plutonium for use in nuclear weapons.[81] An FMCT could strengthen the nonproliferation regime in several ways: it would prohibit the P-5 from increasing their stocks of weapons material (in fact, the P-5 have already all reportedly suspended their production of fissile material for nuclear weapons); it would demonstrate further movement by the United States and the other P-5 members toward meeting their arms limitation and reduction requirements under Article VI of the NPT and the agreed goals of both the 1995 NPT Extension Conference and the 2000 NPT Review Conference; and it would end nuclear weapons material production in India, Israel, and Pakistan and thus place a cap on their stockpiles, were they to join the treaty.[82] The nuclear Expert Group appointed by IAEA director general ElBaradei endorsed an FMCT as a way of imposing multilateral restrictions on the nuclear fuel cycle.[83] From the U.S. point of view, there is a strategic advantage to freezing the size of other countries' nuclear weapons materials at current levels.

Under most versions of the proposal, parties to the FMCT would be permitted to enrich uranium and separate plutonium for peaceful purposes, under effective international inspection. Therefore international inspectors would still have to deal with the old problem of distinguishing between uranium enrichment for peaceful purposes and its enrichment for weapons. Strict inspection, including in the national territories of the P-5, should therefore be an important component of such a treaty.

The FMCT would make the nuclear nonproliferation regime more equitable by putting restraints on countries with nuclear weapons as well as on those without. This idea was supported in a 1993 consensus resolution of the UN General Assembly calling for the negotiation of a "non-discriminatory multilateral and internationally and effectively verifiable treaty banning the production of fissile material for nuclear weapons or other nuclear explosive devices."[84] For NPT members without nuclear weapons, the FMCT would be a step toward reducing the NPT's discrimination between the P-5 and all the other NPT parties that are prohibited from having nuclear weapons. It would restrict the P-5's use of nuclear energy in the same way as it would restrict the use by NPT parties without nuclear weapons. The P-5 promised an FMCT in 1995 if the parties not having nuclear weapons would agree to the indefinite extension of the NPT that year.[85] At the 2000 NPT Review Conference, one of the thirteen steps listed as agreed requirements for compliance with NPT Article VI's disarmament negotiating requirements was the achievement of an FMCT with effective verification within five years.[86]

The FMCT has been under negotiation for such a long period in part because China and the United States have, at different times, prevented a consensus of the potential negotiators. The treaty was first proposed for discussion at the Geneva Conference on Disarmament, at the urging of the United States. If participants were to engage in such negotiations, China countered, they should also consider limiting the military uses of outer space (limitations that China favored but the United States opposed). This disagreement prevented negotiations on either measure for several years.[87] Finally, in 2003, China agreed to negotiate toward an FMCT—while the United States continued to refuse to negotiate on outer space.[88]

The change in China's position apparently was a surprise to the United States. The U.S. delegation asked for a delay to determine what its position should be. After more than a year of study, the United States announced, at the end of the Conference on Disarmament in 2004, that it would agree to an FMCT negotiation provided that the treaty would contain no significant inspection requirements, on the grounds that realistic, effective verification of the FMCT was not achievable.[89] This position contradicted long-standing U.S. insistence on the need for an "effectively verifiable" FMCT.[90]

The United States should return to supporting appropriate verification measures for the FMCT and vigorously pursue the treaty. Even if the prospects look poor for gaining the agreement of nuclear weapon states outside the NPT (India, Israel, Pakistan), the United States should pursue the FMCT rather than provide a shield on this issue for countries that may wish to continue producing fissile material for weapons.[91] The pressure to cap the production of material for nuclear weapons should be on those countries, not on the United States.

The Role of U.S. Nuclear Weapons Policy in Constraining (or Increasing) Demand

U.S. nuclear weapons policy has historically played an important role on the demand side of controlling proliferation.[92] In treaties with allies that have no nuclear weapons, for example, the United States has issued positive assurances that the protection of the U.S. defense umbrella spares allies of the need for their own nuclear weapons program. The United States has also applied pressure on allies and their nuclear suppliers in certain cases where positive assurances were not sufficient.[93] The P-5 as well have given positive nontreaty assurances to nonaligned, non-nuclear weapon NPT members. Although these efforts may not appear to carry as much weight, they may nevertheless have some utility (see chapter 3).

Nontreaty declarations also include negative security assurances—reassurances against a nuclear first strike. In its Nuclear Posture Review of 2001, the Bush administration states that "in setting requirements for nuclear strike capabilities," the United States must be prepared for certain contingencies, which "can be categorized as immediate, potential or unexpected." It identifies North Korea, Iraq, Iran, Syria, and Libya as "among the countries that could be involved in immediate, potential, or unexpected contingencies."[94] Policy documents such as these, along with "axis-of-evil" rhetoric, may be taken by other countries to mean that they risk future nuclear attack by the United States and therefore need to pursue nuclear weapons of their own, or at least maintain a nuclear weapons option as a hedge. Further nuclear policy statements by the Bush administration, such as its December 2002 National Strategy to Combat Weapons of Mass Destruction, its opposition to U.S. ratification of the Comprehensive Test Ban Treaty (CTBT), and its previous proposals to fund research on a new generation of nuclear weapons may signal to other nations that nuclear weapons play a growing, not diminishing, role in U.S. security decisions—despite substantial overall reductions in the U.S. operational nuclear weapons stockpile.[95]

In its September 2002 National Security Strategy, the Bush administration indicated that the United States would engage in preventive (which it called "preemptive") war to counter emerging threats.[96] But as the case of North Korea suggests, it may be possible for even small developing nations to deter the United States from military actions by conventional threats (such as artillery and missile concentrations aimed at South Korea, particularly at the capital city Seoul). Overall, preventive wars to enforce nonproliferation obligations are likely to carry significant costs and unforeseen consequences for the United States, as has been the case with the 2003 invasion of Iraq. Indeed, given the ongoing costs and demands of the Iraq war, future options for preventive war to counter proliferation are likely to remain limited. It is to reduce the need or perceived need for such wars that new means of strengthening the nonproliferation regime must be found, latent proliferation curtailed, and the emergence and expansion of the proliferation rings prevented or disrupted.

Nonproliferation Policies of the European Union

The European Union—which is composed of most NATO allies of the United States as well as non-NATO friends such as Ireland and Sweden—was deeply split on whether to support the U.S.-led 2003 invasion of Iraq. The United States justified the invasion on counterproliferation grounds, stating it was necessary to prevent Iraq's development or use of "WMD." Britain was an early supporter; France and Germany were vigorous opponents. The remaining twenty-five EU members were divided. In June 2003, in substantial part as a result of this disagreement on what was regarded as an important nonproliferation matter, the European Union began a major effort to draft a common EU Strategy against the Proliferation of Weapons of Mass Destruction.[97] In contrast to the U.S. approach, which many EU members viewed as a unilateral strategy, the Europeans called for "effective multilateralism" to implement nonproliferation goals. This included promoting the universalization of multilateral treaties; providing financial and technical support for multilateral efforts to implement nonproliferation verification regimes; encouraging the Nuclear Suppliers Group to deal more effectively with illicit trafficking of materials for making nuclear, biological, and chemical weapons and the missiles for their delivery; and improving the physical security of proliferation-sensitive material within the European Union.[98]

Continuing rifts were evident at the NATO Summit in June 2004, following the adoption of the EU strategy earlier that year. U.S. officials had hoped that after the UN Security Council agreed unanimously in 2003 to the transfer of sovereignty to a new interim Iraqi government, NATO members would provide more troops for Iraq. But President Jacques Chirac of France ruled out any French troop support and opposed any significant NATO-led operation in Iraq. Only a group of 300 NATO trainers for Iraqi military, police, and related forces was agreed upon. NATO members such as the United Kingdom and Poland that provided troops for the Iraq war did so in their national capacities, not as EU or NATO members. The debate between some major EU members and the United States over the implementation of nonproliferation strategies and policies continues.[99]

As the EU strategy makes clear, the European Union ranks nonproliferation much higher in its priorities than in the past. It mentions new coercive measures, for example, including the use of trade sanctions against NPT violators and the possible use of force after all other possible means of persuasion have been exhausted. The strategy supports the Proliferation Security Initiative and UN Security Council Resolution 1540, produced as the result of U.S. initiatives. But the core argument of the strategy is that multilateral nonproliferation regimes based on the norms of the NPT and the Chemical and Biological Weapon Conventions can be effective if properly implemented. EU members focus primarily on multilateral treaty efforts to prevent additional countries from acquiring nuclear weapons. By contrast, the United States has been primarily engaged in nontreaty efforts (ranging from the invasion of Iraq to UN Security Council Resolution 1540) to prevent dangerous states or terrorists from acquiring these weapons. Though the EU strategy reflects concerns about terrorists, it does not concentrate on them to the same extent that U.S. nonproliferation strategy does.[100] The difference between European and U.S. attitudes was particularly evident at the NPT Review Conference in 2005.[101] The EU spokesperson presented a statement about the community's common strategy, and several working papers reflected a common theme. But the United States did not support the EU approach or some of the measures proposed in the EU's common strategy. The conference failed to reach a consensus on any substantive recommendations.[102]

EU members have joined together to ratify the IAEA Additional Protocol. They have also adopted common positions urging implementation of the Comprehensive Test Ban Treaty. Unlike the United States, they have supported negotiation of a Fissile Material Cut-off Treaty with verification measures.[103] Among the most important nonproliferation policies adopted by the Europeans are those relating to controls on the export of nuclear equipment and technology. These are especially welcome in light of the long-running support the A.Q. Khan network received from certain European centrifuge experts. Since adoption of the EU strategy, the EU Council secretariat has criticized the slow implementation of stronger export controls within the community itself.[104] The union wants not only other countries but also its own members to make an all-out multilateral effort to prevent the spread of nuclear weapons to additional countries as well as to terrorists.[105]

Two Difficult Cases: North Korea and Iran

Many of the foregoing recommendations for strengthening the nonproliferation regime were intended to lessen the likelihood that states would pursue a nuclear weapons option in violation of their NPT obligations. They did not directly address the acute problems raised by states already in violation of these obligations and in crisis with the nonproliferation regime, most notably North Korea and Iran. Although the measures discussed so far can help meet the challenges posed by these countries (for example, the Additional Protocol and the Proliferation Security Initiative may both play important roles in the two cases, and elements of our proposed ESI have been pursued with each), they do not in themselves provide a solution. What, then, can the United States do about North Korea and Iran?

North Korea

The Soviet Union began training North Koreans in nuclear matters in the early 1950s, and in 1965 provided them with a research reactor fueled with HEU. But until 1985 North Korea resisted Soviet requests for it to join the NPT, and until 1992 it resisted IAEA requests for inspections. It then resisted IAEA requests for a special examination of questionable activities beyond the areas that North Korea had declared open for regular, periodic IAEA inspections. In 1993, when the IAEA Board of Governors insisted on these special inspections, North Korea gave its first notice of withdrawal from the NPT.[106]

In 1992 North Korea had entered into an agreement with South Korea for a Korean Peninsula free of nuclear weapons.[107] However, the two countries could not agree on the areas where reciprocal inspections would be permitted. In 1993, after it had begun its withdrawal from the NPT, North Korea began direct negotiations concerning its nuclear weapon efforts with the United States. As an early result of the negotiations, it stopped its withdrawal from the NPT on the last day of the ninety-day withdrawal period required by the treaty. Negotiations with the United States (which was cooperating closely with South Korea and Japan) produced the Agreed Framework of 1994 between North Korea and the United States, under which North Korea agreed to permit IAEA inspections, which would be limited for the time being to areas previously inspected by the IAEA. These areas would be expanded later, after a "significant portion" of the work promised by the Agreed Framework had been completed. That "work" consisted of new nuclear reactors for generating electric power. In the meantime, the United

States would supply oil to keep North Korea's steam-driven electric generators in operation.[108] Over the next eight years, the work moved forward slowly, with the building of reactor components in South Korea, preparation of the site in North Korea, and supply of fuel oil to North Korea by the United States.

In 2002 the United States began six-party talks with North Korea and its neighbors (China, Japan, Russia, and South Korea) with the aim of preventing North Korea from making nuclear weapons. But after learning of North Korean uranium-enrichment activities (which North Korea had not declared to the IAEA inspectors), the United States halted the supply of fuel oil. In response, North Korea announced a new withdrawal from the NPT, this time giving only one day's notice on the grounds that only one day remained on its three-month NPT withdrawal notice given at the beginning of its first withdrawal. Its withdrawal was not opposed by the UN Security Council on either occasion, probably because China could not be persuaded not to veto such an order.[109]

In 2003, according to the U.S. representative to the six-party talks, a North Korean representative admitted that the IAEA had not been told about his country's efforts to enrich uranium for nuclear weapons.[110] The uranium centrifuge equipment that North Korea seems to have obtained from the A. Q. Khan network sometime between 1993 and 1997 provided North Korea with an HEU pathway to nuclear weapons while its plutonium pathway was being inspected by the IAEA following the Agreed Framework.[111] The situation in North Korea, IAEA director general ElBaradei told the Board of Governors in 2004, "is currently the most immediate and most serious threat to the nonproliferation regime."[112]

North Korea had stated in 2002 that it would seek a negotiated settlement with the United States regarding its nuclear programs on three conditions: that the United States recognize North Korea's sovereignty, that there be no U.S. aggression, and that the United States not hinder North Korea's economic development.[113] In 2005 the six-party talks resumed with more bilateral discussions between the United States and North Korea, but greater demands from North Korea.[114] In September 2005 the talks produced a statement of common goals for a future agreement including that:

—The Korean Peninsula would be verifiably denuclearized "in a peaceful manner."

—North Korea would abandon "all nuclear weapons."

—North Korea would rejoin the NPT and accept IAEA safeguards.

—The parties would discuss, "at an appropriate time," the provision of a light-water reactor to North Korea, and would provide "energy assistance" to the North.

—North Korea and the United States would "respect each other's sovereignty" and "take steps to normalize their relations subject to their respective bilateral policies." The United States affirmed that it "has no intention to attack or invade [North Korea] with nuclear or conventional weapons."[115]

The United States said later that no light-water reactor was promised to North Korea until after all its existing nuclear weapons and facilities were dismantled and its territory had been thoroughly inspected by the IAEA. In response, one North Korean representative said that North Korea would not dismantle its nuclear weapons until it received the new light-water reactor.[116] Another representative said North Korea understood that the reactor would come later. Further negotiations to achieve specific agreements on these issues are likely to take a long time. In the meantime, North Korea, freed from the constraints on its plutonium program that had been set by the Agreed Framework, continues to produce about one plutonium bomb's worth of nuclear explosive material a year.[117] It is likely, though not certain, that North Korea is able to build nuclear weapons with this material.[118]

We recommend continued determined negotiations with North Korea to test whether its desire for security guarantees, economic assistance, and other incentives is sufficient for it to relinquish its nuclear weapons activities. However, it is unclear how much progress will be made in the remaining years of the Bush administration. South Korea and China do not feel the same urgency as the United States with respect to the North's nuclear weapons program; these countries seem to put greater priority on avoiding the dangers of sudden regime change in the North, and look toward a slow peaceful transition.[119]

A number of U.S. officials, including Vice President Dick Cheney, have in the past warned that "time is not on our side" with respect to resolving the North Korean dilemma.[120] It is useful to ask in what sense this might be the case. Currently, North Korea can produce about one warhead's worth of plutonium a year in its 5 MW(e) Yongbyon reactor. Assuming that it is able to produce warheads, the slow accumulation of warheads that the 5 MW(e) Yongbyon reactor allows does not radically change the situation in the short term; the difference between eight warheads, or nine, or ten, does not seem likely to be significant in itself. (The line between one or two and, say, eight is significant because the regime would seem less likely to test or sell its only warhead, or one of its two only warheads. But that line has probably already been crossed.)

However, there are several actions that North Korea could take that would make the situation dramatically worse:

—Most dangerous would be if North Korea made an effort to provide one of its warheads to any other party. But reliable evidence of this would be so likely to lead to the end of the Pyongyang regime upon discovery that we must hope that it is very unlikely.

—Next would be a decision by North Korea to test a weapon. The immediate security implications of such an action would likely be worse for China than for the United States, because of the effect that a test might have on the nuclear calculations of non-nuclear states in the region, especially those of Japan. However, a collapse of the nonproliferation regime in northeast Asia would not serve any country's long-term interests.

—A third dangerous escalation would be for North Korea to complete and resume operations at either the 50 MW(e) reactor at Yongbyon or the 200 MW(e) reactor at Taechon. Nongovernment experts in the United States have estimated that North Korea's reprocessing facility could extract up to 60–70 kilograms of plutonium a year from spent gas-graphite fuel; reactor completion and operation could therefore put North Korea in a position to produce not one but perhaps around ten warheads a year (or more if further reprocessing capacity were added).[121] This would be a qualitatively worse situation.

—The situation on the Korean peninsula represents an ongoing corrosion of the nuclear nonproliferation regime. Continued ballistic missile development by North Korea will only add to the military pressure felt by its neighbors, pressure that is not in the long-term interest of stability in northeast Asia.

It seems likely, though hardly certain, that in the next two years North Korea will neither sell a nuclear warhead to a terrorist group, test a nuclear warhead, nor finish rebuilding its 50 MW(e) or 200 MW(e) reactors. In this case, there is a kind of slowly evolving status quo on the Korean peninsula, and the price paid for continuing lack of progress in the six-party talks may not be too high. The coming years should be spent in continued negotiations with North Korea in pursuit of real progress, but they should also be used in preparation for what might come next, and especially in dialogue with China, Japan, and South Korea. Such preparations should include efforts to elucidate the verification measures required to fulfill the 2005 Six-Party Agreement, and to reach a common understanding as to what these would entail.[122]

Iran

Iran's interest in a nuclear weapons capability may have several sources. Iran may be motivated in part by security concerns regarding the United States, Israel, and its Arab and Pakistani neighbors. It may see a nuclear weapons capability as giving it a freer hand in the region. It may also be motivated by nationalism and nationalist-fueled resentment of other nations' perceived hypocrisies, including those in the nuclear realm.[123] To the extent its weapons program is a hedge built on top of a nuclear power program, the Iranian government itself may not have had to reach unified decisions about either motives or endpoints for its program.

Over the years, Iran's nuclear activities had been inspected by the IAEA without major controversy at first. But questions arose when it was discovered that Iran had been experimenting with steps toward uranium enrichment and separation of spent reactor fuel. These experiments took place away from IAEA-inspected sites and had not been reported to the IAEA, as Iran was required to do. Low-level uranium enrichment is, of course, useful for making fuel for nuclear reactors, but high-level enrichment is useful for making nuclear weapons. Plutonium separated from spent reactor fuel is also useful for making weapons. Iran's violations of its IAEA reporting requirements have been questioned by the United States and others, as well as by the IAEA, for several years. The IAEA Secretariat has agreed with many, though not all, U.S. concerns. Perhaps the most important issue has been Iran's efforts to build uranium-enrichment facilities, evidently using technology acquired from the A. Q. Khan network. In September 2003 the IAEA Board of Governors called on Iran to cooperate by providing full transparency for its nuclear activities, by suspending further uranium-enrichment and spent-fuel reprocessing efforts, and by accepting IAEA inspections.[124]

In contrast to, but in cooperation with, the U.S. approach of making charges against Iran to the IAEA, the foreign ministers of France, Germany, and the United Kingdom (the EU-3) went to Iran to negotiate in October 2003. According to the EU-3, Iran agreed to resolve all outstanding issues with the IAEA, sign and ratify the Additional Protocol, and suspend uranium-enrichment and spent-fuel reprocessing activities. The three foreign ministers promised that "once international concerns, including those of the three Governments, are fully resolved, Iran could expect easier access to modern technology and supplies in a range of areas."[125] The agreement was "reluctantly accepted" by then U.S. secretary of state Colin Powell.[126]

Iran, however, continued to have major differences with the IAEA, to be criticized by the United States, and to produce new concerns in Britain, France, and Germany. The EU-3 questioned whether Iran had in fact complied with the first agreement they thought they had negotiated. Before the 2003 agreement, the IAEA had reported that Iran had not been forthcoming about its activities and thus had "failed to meet its obligations." Starting in 1991, Iran had withheld information about its nuclear activities and hindered the IAEA inspectors' efforts to find out the extent of its nuclear program, including its uranium-enrichment efforts.[127]

After the 2003 agreement, Iran signed the IAEA Additional Protocol (but did not ratify it) and gave IAEA inspectors much greater access to its nuclear facilities (but did not show them everything they wanted to see). In June 2004 the IAEA Board of Governors criticized Iran for obstructing the inspectors' efforts to inspect uranium centrifuge facilities and asked why environmental sampling by the inspectors showed contamination of Iranian facilities with HEU as well as low-enriched uranium. The board adopted a resolution criticizing Iran's inspection-delaying tactics and its refusal to answer all the inspectors' questions about its enrichment program and where the equipment and designs for enriching uranium had come from.[128] This resolution was supported by China, France, Germany, Russia, the United Kingdom, and the United States—among many other countries.[129]

After further negotiations with Britain, France, and Germany, Iran offered to suspend its uranium enrichment in return for normal relations with them and an end to threats of sanctions. IAEA inspectors reported that as early as 1995 the Khan network had begun providing Iran with designs for uranium-enrichment centrifuges.[130] The United States urged the IAEA Board of Governors to refer Iran's case to the UN Security Council, presumably for issuance of an order commanding Iran to comply with the IAEA's demands, on the peril of sanctions if Iran refused.[131] The board decided instead to try again to continue inspections if Iran could be persuaded to comply.[132] Iran continued negotiations with the EU-3 but took steps to gasify some of its uranium so that it could later be enriched. The IAEA board then called on Iran to refrain from uranium enrichment and asked the IAEA inspectors to continue their work in Iran. Again, the board did not refer the Iran case to the UN Security Council. The EU-3 presented a new proposal to Iran that it promptly rejected. The IAEA board then called upon Iran to permit further inspections.

An election in Iran produced a new, more conservative president, Mahmoud Ahmadinejad. His government rejected a new EU-3 proposal. Leading developing countries in the Non-Aligned Movement (NAM) sympathized with Iran's desire to enrich uranium—so long as it was not doing so to make weapons. They argued that permitting Japan and Germany to enrich uranium but denying that right to developing countries was discriminatory.[133] President Ahmadinejad then said that he wanted to continue negotiations with the EU-3, a statement that President Bush greeted as a "positive sign."[134] This was a more conciliatory gesture toward Iran than past U.S. demands that Iran's case be referred to the UN Security Council for enforcement.[135]

In September 2005 Director General ElBaradei reported to the IAEA Board of Governors that Iran had not provided all the necessary information, emphasizing that its "full transparency is indispensable and long overdue." Iran's "past concealment efforts over many years" indicated that the IAEA staff was "still not in a position to conclude that there are no undeclared nuclear materials or activities in Iran."[136] As a result, the board decided that Iran's noncompliance with its IAEA safeguards agreement were of Security Council concern, but put off any referral of Iran's case to the council pending further inspections of Iran's activities. China, Russia, and a number of non-aligned countries that opposed referral to the council chose to abstain rather than dissent; only Venezuela dissented.[137] In early 2006, Iran took steps to restart uranium-enrichment research and development at its Natanz nuclear complex. This program had been suspended during the long negotiations with the EU-3; preventing uranium enrichment in Iran had been the EU-3's long-term goal. Various countries represented on the IAEA board continued negotiations on what the NPT permitted Iran to do and what actions the IAEA board and the UN Security Council should take.[138] In February 2006, the IAEA director general issued a report describing the IAEA's concern that "uncertainties related to the scope and nature of Iran's nuclear programme have not been clarified after three years of intensive Agency verification." Iran's failure to disclose some of its uranium-enrichment efforts were a particular problem.[139] In March, the IAEA Board of Governors referred this report to the UN Security Council. On April 27, Director General ElBaradei reported to the council that Iran had promised to resolve the outstanding issues in the February report. But, he added, the agency had repeatedly requested that Iran "provide additional information on certain issues related to its enrichment programme." He listed many issues but focused on the "gaps [that] remain in the Agency's knowledge with respect to the scope and content of Iran's centrifuge program."[140] Debate continued, particularly among the P-5, as to what action the council should take. Iran's president Ahmadinejad has threatened to withdraw from the NPT, but that would not affect the power of the UN Security Council to require Iraq to permit inspectors access, or to take other action.

Why would not a guarantee of enriched uranium from Russia, or for that matter even from the multinational EURODIF or Urenco, be sufficient to meet Iran's needs if it seeks enriched uranium only for peaceful purposes?[141] Iran's claim is that it is a matter of international equity, as well as national sovereignty and pride. Iran's nuclear negotiator Hassan Rohani has said:

> Termination of fuel cycle activities as demanded of Iran means that you have killed the NPT. If you take out Article IV, all developing countries will step out of the treaty. . . . Termination is war between the North and the South. The Americans say forget about Article IV, forget about the disarmament promised in Article VI. . . . The U.S. today is trying to create a second discrimination, one between those that have peaceful nuclear technology and those not allowed to have peaceful technology.[142]

Similarly, in a speech to the UN General Assembly in September 2005, President Ahmadinejad decried a "nuclear apartheid" that would allow some nations to manufacture nuclear fuel while condemning others for doing so.[143] A Tehran professor has been quoted as saying: "We want what Japan has. If Japan can have the fuel cycle and stay happily within the NPT, why can't we?"[144]

In fact, it is inaccurate to say that the United States "today is trying to create a second discrimination" by working to limit the number of countries that have the full nuclear fuel cycle, if the implication is that U.S. or European behavior is new or unique. The United States and other countries have not been consistent in their efforts to enforce such limits, but they have done so in certain cases for decades. That work has often served the cause of peace and international security well. For example, the United States brought pressure to bear on South Korea at least twice in the 1970s to force it to abandon its efforts to purchase or develop reprocessing technology and a heavy-water reactor, out of concern that these were really steps in a covert nuclear weapons program.[145] U.S. tactics reportedly included communicating to the South Korean government the risk of the loss of U.S. security commitments; intervention with France, Belgium, and Canada to block sales; the receipt of information from South Korean sources, and, according to a South Korean official, a threat to cancel a $300 million loan for Korea's civilian nuclear reactor program—thereby holding civilian nuclear power hostage to Korean assurances that fuel-cycle activities were abandoned and would not be resumed.[146]

A similar dynamic has played out in the relationship of the United States and Taiwan. The United States successfully put pressure on Taiwan in the 1970s and again in the 1980s to abandon its pursuit of nuclear reprocessing, in the context of discoveries about initially undeclared facilities and inspection discrepancies and concern that Taiwan might in fact be pursuing nuclear weapons.[147] And because of political sensitivities over the construction of a uranium-enrichment plant in Germany, a decision was made to build the first German-owned enrichment capacity in the Netherlands, as a joint Dutch/German-owned facility, operated by an international team.[148]

Northeast Asia is more secure, not less, because the United States intervened to impede the development of the nuclear fuel cycle in South Korea and Taiwan. Even if one regards the Taiwan political situation as sui generis, South Korea had joined the NPT in 1975, so the pressure brought to bear on it not to pursue reprocessing during President Jimmy Carter's administration took place in the context of the republic's enjoyment of whatever "rights" Article IV of the NPT confers. The negotiations between the EU-3 and Iran over its efforts to develop the nuclear fuel cycle were not unprecedented within the NPT. The issue should not be framed as a matter of giving up rights inherent in the NPT, but rather as making wise decisions not to exercise certain capabilities, or to exercise them only with particular multilateral monitoring arrangements in place—as a number of countries in particularly sensitive political situations (such as Brazil, Germany, and the Republic of Korea, each in different ways) have done in the past.

It remains to be determined whether a grand bargain involving nuclear technology, terrorism, security guarantees, relaxation of sanctions (especially in the energy sector), and normalization of relations could be struck with Tehran. If Iran insists on having its own enrichment facility, however limited, then a final option short of further sanctions or military action would be for Iranian enrichment facilities to be examined periodically by IAEA inspectors but also constantly by resident monitors from other countries, perhaps from Britain, France, and Germany—an arrangement for which there is a great deal of precedent in the nonproliferation regime.[149]

The U.S.-India Nuclear Deal

In their 2005 and 2006 summit meetings, President Bush and Prime Minister Manmohan Singh of India agreed to a new Indian-U.S. "broad partnership," including close cooperation in peaceful nuclear affairs. Cooperation on nuclear matters between these two countries began during President Eisenhower's

Atoms for Peace program, before the NPT was negotiated. But resisting U.S. pleas, India refused to join the NPT when the treaty was opened for signature in 1968, and in 1974 it conducted a nuclear test explosion. India said the test was for peaceful purposes.[150]

Many then in the U.S. Congress were angry that India had used not only a Canadian reactor, but also U.S. nuclear assistance (which Congress intended for peaceful purposes) to produce its 1974 nuclear explosion.[151] As a result, in 1976 Congress passed legislation denying U.S. economic or military assistance to any country (such as India) that had not joined the NPT.[152] Later Congress amended the U.S. Atomic Energy Act to prevent future U.S. nuclear assistance provided "for peaceful purposes" from being used to make weapons. The amended statute required countries without nuclear weapons to guarantee that no U.S. nuclear assistance provided to them would be used to make nuclear explosive devices, and that no reprocessing of nuclear fuel from their U.S-supplied reactors to produce plutonium could take place without U.S. consent.[153]

In 1998 India conducted its first nuclear explosions since the one in 1974. It did not claim that these tests were for peaceful purposes. In 2005 President Bush agreed to provide nuclear assistance for peaceful purposes to India, assuming that Congress would amend or waive the statutory prohibitions adopted in the 1970s. In a meeting with Prime Minister Singh, President Bush said that he would seek "agreement from Congress to adjust U.S. laws and policies" to permit U.S. nuclear exports to India. To this end, the State Department submitted draft legislative amendments to Congress. These would authorize civilian nuclear agreements between the United States and India, including formal agreements based on the Bush-Singh joint statement. The goal of the Bush plan, the president said, was to "achieve full civil nuclear energy cooperation with India."[154] It was reported that an additional goal was to counter the rise of China by accelerating India's ascent to global power.[155]

President Bush promised that the United States would "work with friends and allies to adjust international regimes" to permit nuclear energy cooperation with India.[156] The most important of these regimes is the NSG, an enforcing agent for the NPT bargain that countries without nuclear weapons agree to give up the right to acquire them in exchange for the promise of cooperation on nuclear technology and materials. The Bush-Singh joint statement constitutes a major departure from this bargain. In initial U.S. contacts with many members of the NSG, France, Russia, and the United Kingdom expressed support for accepting India into the NSG as a nuclear-weapon state. Many other NSG members expressed reservations—Sweden and

Switzerland, for example. Before the NPT was signed, these two countries, like India, conducted exploratory research to learn about nuclear technology, including how to make nuclear weapons.[157] But unlike India, these two ended their nuclear-weapon efforts and joined the NPT. At an informal March 2006 meeting of NSG members, Sweden and Switzerland joined several other countries in questioning whether India should be given the benefits promised to non-nuclear weapon NPT members and admitted into the NSG. Indeed, at this meeting, only France, Russia, and the United Kingdom supported the U.S. proposal to accept India into the NSG. Twenty-seven other delegations asked questions or remained silent. Since unanimity is required for NSG approval of the U.S.-India agreement, achieving that approval may be difficult.[158]

Before this NSG meeting, the United States had drafted a proposed new NSG rule, which would permit nuclear suppliers to transfer NSG export-banned nuclear technology items to civilian nuclear facilities in India that are under IAEA safeguards. Without an amendment such as this, many would see transfers to India as a violation of the NSG principle against nuclear transfers when "there is an unacceptable risk of diversion" of the transferred material to a "nuclear explosive activity."[159] At the March 2006 NSG meeting, however, no action was taken on the U.S. proposal.

Given the failure of these initial U.S. efforts, it may be hard to achieve the NSG consensus needed for approval of the Bush-Singh proposed nuclear shipments to India. Unless NSG approval is achieved, or some other way is found to provide an exception to the NSG guidelines, this part of the Bush-Singh agreement will be hard to implement. If President Bush goes ahead with the agreement despite the lack of approval, the U.S. action would directly undermine the NSG. A unilateral exception by the United States for India's sake would call into question the utility of having a suppliers group to reach consensus on export restrictions—although there have been inconsistencies on the part of other states in the past. Nevertheless, the consensus rule has been key to the prevention of nuclear weapons–related exports by NSG members.[160]

Gaining majority votes in the U.S. House and Senate for the Bush-Singh agreement may be less difficult, but is not guaranteed. In his meetings with Prime Minister Singh, President Bush promised to ask Congress to amend the U.S. Atomic Energy Act, and Singh promised to separate Indian nuclear facilities into civilian and military categories, and to place those designated as civilian under IAEA safeguards.[161] This would give India a relationship to the IAEA much like that now enjoyed by NPT members with nuclear weapons.

Draft legislation proposed to Congress by the Bush administration assumed that Congress would provide legal authority for the proposed cooperative nuclear arrangement before a detailed agreement between India and the United States was actually negotiated. Secretary of State Condoleezza Rice strongly supported the Bush-Singh joint statement in her testimony to the Senate Foreign Relations and the House International Affairs committees. She argued that the initiative "will deepen the strategic partnership" between the two countries, would benefit the natural environment because India would burn much less coal if it generated electricity with nuclear reactors, and would "strengthen the international nuclear nonproliferation regime."[162]

If a detailed agreement based on the Bush-Singh joint statement were negotiated and implemented, one likely result would be that India would be able to use its stock of uranium and plutonium from its existing sources for making nuclear weapons. This would be possible because India could use American-supplied uranium for its electricity-generating reactors under IAEA safeguards. The various Indian nuclear materials and facilities not under IAEA safeguards would then be available to make nuclear weapons. By one estimate, India would then have the capacity to produce several dozen nuclear weapons a year rather than six to ten, its present estimated capacity.[163] Some argue that the United States would thereby "assist" India in the "manufacture" of nuclear weapons, in violation of the NPT.[164] However, the American supply of fissionable material to India would itself be used for peaceful, not weapons, purposes, so this argument may be debated. The Bush-Singh agreement would certainly serve India's goal of gaining a twentyfold increase in nuclear-generated electricity by 2020.[165]

The Bush-Singh deal is difficult because it requires disparate factors to be weighed. It would bring some elements of India's nuclear program under international inspection for the first time but would then allow India to exclude its self-designated "military" facilities. The Bush administration has put greatest weight on factors that stand apart from nonproliferation issues:

—*The need to improve U.S. relations with India.* Secretary of State Rice said that India, like the United States, is "a multi-ethnic and multi-religious democracy . . . characterized by individual freedom and the rule of law . . . [and is] a natural partner for the United States."[166] India could cooperate with the United States in many endeavors.

—*Assisting India's economic growth.* The Bush administration considers India's economic growth to be in U.S. interests, accepts India's need for a major increase in electric power generation to support that growth, and accepts the advantages of nuclear-powered electricity over that provided by burning oil or coal. Implementation of the Bush-Singh joint statement would permit U.S. assistance for India's pursuit of nuclear reactors to generate electricity. It would help India shift from a largely coal-based electricity system to a nuclear-based electricity system, and would open a market for U.S. nuclear energy exports.[167]

—*Helping India "become a major power in the 21st century."* This would help offset the "growing and utterly more capable nuclear forces Beijing is likely to possess by 2025."[168]

India's gains from the deal are concrete, whereas U.S. gains are comparatively long-term and, in many cases, more abstract (although some unofficial diplomatic benefits, such as India's support with respect to Iran, may already have been realized). How to weigh these many factors is a dynamic issue, the more so since middle-ground positions may be staked out. One such position would be to weigh the progress India makes in reducing its production of nuclear explosive material. The United States could supply nuclear fuel for India's peaceful power plants but refuse its request for new reactors until India is willing to halt the production of fissile material for nuclear weapons—as the United States, Britain, China, France, and Russia have done.[169] This could be tied to the eventual achievement of international agreement on a multilateral Fissile Material Cut-off Treaty. However, the United States would need consensus with its NSG partners for such criteria, or else risk having its restrictions undercut. However the U.S.-India deal proceeds, it should be a priority that the deal not do serious, lasting damage to that important suppliers group restraint on illicit nuclear activity.

Multilateral Enforcement of the Nuclear Non-Proliferation Treaty

The IAEA has no enforcement power of its own, except to deny violators any assistance it is authorized to give. It must rely on the UN Security Council for enforcement.[170] But fear of adverse decisions by the IAEA Board of Governors motivates states to comply if they want to stay in good standing with the regime and avoid the risk of having their cases referred to the Security Council. This may well remain true as long as the nonproliferation regime is perceived as reasonably effective and continues to be supported by the overwhelming majority of countries.

In the Iranian case, EU-3 promises to Iran of "easier access to modern technology and supplies in a range of areas" if it cooperated may have further motivated Iran to negotiate with them.[171] In contrast, the United States imposed sanctions on thirteen traders with Iran from seven countries, traders who had allegedly sold equipment and expertise to Iran that it could use in nuclear, chemical, or biological weapons programs.[172] IAEA board decisions of NPT noncompliance may thus sometimes be "enforced" without the Security Council because an IAEA noncompliance conclusion could damage the violator's trade and other relations with important countries.

Enforcement Mechanisms: Role of the UN Security Council

According to the IAEA's governing treaty and the UN Charter, the ultimate organ for sanctions is the UN Security Council. Absent a veto by one of the P-5, the Security Council may authorize sanctions or the use of force to achieve compliance with the nonproliferation regime. Referral of a noncompliance case by the IAEA Board of Governors to the Security Council happens infrequently. And when it does, the council may not act. When North Korea gave its first NPT withdrawal notice in 1993, the board reported the withdrawal to the council. Efforts among the P-5 to agree on a UN Security Council sanctions resolution against North Korea failed to gain China's assent. As a result, the council took no enforcement action. It simply called on North Korea to comply, a request that North Korea ignored.[173]

In September 2004 France suggested that it would likely support an IAEA board decision to refer Iran's case to the Security Council if Iran were not more cooperative.[174] The IAEA Board of Governors then adopted a resolution calling on Iran to suspend all of its uranium-enrichment activities and meet related demands by November 2004, the time of the board's next meeting. This was based upon a British-French-German draft of the proposed IAEA board resolution modified to coincide with, on the one hand, the U.S. effort to make it stronger and, on the other hand, the effort of Brazil and South Africa to make it weaker. During the negotiations, Iran agreed to permit IAEA inspection of a site that the United States wanted examined but that the IAEA had not been permitted to inspect. In the end, the resolution did not ask that the case be referred to the UN Security Council.[175] After further similar negotiations, the IAEA board reached much the same result in November 2004 and in several decisions in 2005.[176] The decision of September 2005 concluded that Iran's breaches of its safeguards obligations and its "history of concealment" of those breaches were of a kind requiring an IAEA report to the UN Security Council, but it postponed such a report until a later meeting. In March 2006 the IAEA board referred the director general's February 2006 report to the Security Council.

After the Gulf War of 1991, Security Council resolutions authorized the IAEA to conduct much stronger, more penetrating inspections in Iraq than had been conducted pursuant to Iraq's safeguards agreement with the IAEA based on the safeguards standards of 1971. The stronger inspections uncovered major efforts by Iraq to make nuclear weapons, efforts that Iraq had successfully hidden from previous IAEA inspectors operating under the 1971 safeguards agreement. Indeed, it was the evidence of Iraq's nuclear weapons efforts that IAEA inspectors found, after they were given the much broader inspection authority by the Security Council, that convinced many countries that stronger IAEA safeguards inspections were necessary in other countries as well.[177] The resulting negotiations among members of the IAEA Board of Governors eventually produced the Additional Protocol for strengthened NPT inspections.[178]

Apart from UN Security Council orders requiring Iraq to submit to IAEA inspections just after the 1991 Gulf War and again in 2002, none of the past cases alleging NPT violation included Security Council action to require compliance. This was true even after the IAEA board had referred North Korea's NPT noncompliance to the Security Council and North Korea had given notice of its withdrawal from the NPT in 1993. What is the power of the Security Council in such a case?

The NPT permits a party to withdraw if it "decides that extraordinary events, related to the subject matter of this Treaty, have jeopardized the supreme interests of its country." The withdrawing party must give three months' notice of its intention to withdraw to all the other NPT parties and to the UN Security Council. Its notice must state the "extraordinary events it regards as having jeopardized its supreme interests."[179] North Korea's statement made at the time of its withdrawals seemed inadequate to many members of the Security Council. However, China refused to agree with the United States not to veto a Security Council command that North Korea accept IAEA inspections.

The NPT withdrawal clause was modeled, with important changes, on a similar clause in the Limited Test Ban Treaty of 1963, which stated that a party had a "right to withdraw from the Treaty if it decided that extraordinary events related to the subject matter of this Treaty have jeopardized the supreme interests of its country." The Limited Test Ban Treaty clause required that a notice of withdrawal be sent to all other parties "three months in advance" but did not require that the notice include a statement of reasons for withdrawal and be submitted to the Security Council, two additions to the NPT withdrawal clause at the suggestion of the United States and Soviet

Union.[180] The new language was clearly intended to authorize the council to consider whether a party's withdrawal threatened the maintenance of international peace and security, within the meaning of the UN Charter, and if so, to take action to restrain withdrawal or require other action.[181]

How might this be applied in light of North Korea's withdrawal from the NPT? North Korea's obvious reason for withdrawal was to pursue nuclear weapon development without IAEA inspections, using materials, technology, and equipment at least some of which was acquired while it was an NPT member.[182] The Security Council should adopt a resolution to warn those considering withdrawal that they would face continuing NPT obligations with respect to the nuclear materials, technology, and equipment acquired earlier because of their membership in the NPT.[183]

Challenges to Multilateral Enforcement of the NPT

In 2002 the UN Security Council authorized renewed inspections in Iraq when the United States and the United Kingdom alleged that Iraq was violating the post–Gulf War UN Security Council resolutions requiring it to give up nuclear, chemical, and biological weapons and missiles that could carry them. Buildup of military force by the United States likely played a crucial role in Iraq's decision to accept these renewed inspections.[184] The inspections found little to suggest significant violations of these requirements in the first months of their inspections.[185] When France, Germany, and others prevented the Security Council from adopting a resolution explicitly authorizing the invasion of Iraq to conduct the searches sought by the United States, the United States and the United Kingdom invaded, arguing that Iraq was in fact deceiving the UN inspectors regarding its "weapons of mass destruction," and that a Security Council resolution from the preceding year authorized their military action.[186]

The Iraq crisis, leading up to and including the U.S.-led invasion in 2003, was a challenge to multilateral action through the United Nations. This challenge was an important motive behind UN Secretary-General Kofi Annan's appointment of his High-Level Panel on Threats, Challenges and Change. In its 2004 report, this panel made recommendations on multilateral enforcement of the nonprolifesration regime, urging "global instruments that reduce the demand" for nuclear weapons as well as "global instruments that operate on the supply side." An additional effort, the panel concluded, had to be "Security Council enforcement activity underpinned by credible, shared information and analysis."[187] In the past, the United States had hoped to see the NPT's nonproliferation requirements enforced by the council—in Iraq

(2003), Iran (2004), and North Korea (1994 and 2003). In all of these cases, other countries threatened to veto or otherwise disagreed, and no council enforcement action was taken.

In the view of the nuclear Expert Group appointed by IAEA director general ElBaradei, strengthened safeguards resulting from widespread adoption of the Additional Protocol or other multilateral approaches "will not serve their full purpose if the international community does not respond with determination to serious cases of non-compliance. Responses are needed at four levels, depending on the specific case: the partners of the non-compliant state, the IAEA, the States Parties to the NPT, and the UN Security Council."[188] But the parties to the NPT, if their conduct at the NPT Review Conference of May 2005 is any measure, may not be able to reach a consensus on enforcement actions of significance. After many proposals and four weeks of meetings and debate, they were unable to agree on a final report providing much more than procedural information.[189]

Lessons Learned from War with Iraq

The 2003 invasion of Iraq for nonproliferation reasons appears to have been a mistake. In late 2002 the UN Security Council had authorized experienced inspectors to conduct inspections in Iraq. More than two months of these inspections revealed no biological, chemical, or nuclear weapons in Iraq. Nevertheless, in March 2003 the United States invaded Iraq. After the invasion, further inspections by U.S. investigators failed to find any such weapons.[190]

The failure to find "weapons of mass destruction" in Iraq and the subsequent difficulties facing the United States in securing the country are reminders of the intelligence demands, high costs, and unintended consequences of preventive war as a nonproliferation tool.[191] This does not mean that coercive diplomacy, backed by the threat of military force, should never be employed; and it certainly does not alleviate concern over the difficulty of achieving UN Security Council action for the enforcement of the nonproliferation regime. But it does emphasize the need to employ all other tools first, including bilateral and multilateral negotiation, before choosing military action.

Recent U.S. efforts to restrain the North Korean and Iranian nuclear programs have by and large been unsuccessful. (The Agreed Framework had shut down North Korea's plutonium program for nearly a decade, but that agreement no longer applies.) Preventive war against Iran or North Korea seems impractical even if it could be justified by those accepting President Bush's "preemptive" war strategy for invading Iraq (see chapter 2). War with North Korea or Iran could greatly stress the military resources of the United States. War with North Korea would probably require large numbers of U.S. troops.[192] War with Iran might at first be limited to air strikes by the United States or Israel.[193] Iran's responses to such strikes are, however, of concern to U.S. policymakers, as should be the longer-term consequences of any such attacks.[194] The United States would not, under current circumstances, have the support of many allies for attacking Iran or North Korea. The European Union continues to emphasize multilateral efforts. Nor do the other participants in the six-party talks with North Korea—and especially South Korea—favor the use of force against the North Korean nuclear program.

A vital challenge for the United States is to find the combination of approaches to avoid again having to face threatening nuclear programs comparable in development to those of North Korea or Iran. The circumvention of nuclear weapons programs before they reach an advanced stage must be a central foreign policy objective. Moreover, to the extent that proliferation to additional countries heightens the risk that nuclear weapons or materials might become available to terrorists, a strong nonproliferation regime is a backbone of protection against the worst terrorist threats. The United States will be able to fight only so many wars of counterproliferation, and in the face of high costs. It should therefore place a high priority on maintaining the strongest reasonable nonproliferation regime. No single proposal for improvement can be a solution, for the regime has many weaknesses, and careful and strategic trade-offs will need to be made. But the "silver bullet fallacy," which disdains useful measures that are less than complete solutions, must be resisted. Rather, each step must be recognized as but one strand in the web of a determined and multifaceted nonproliferation strategy that must be maintained for decades to come.

Notes

1. In chapter 3, the nuclear nonproliferation regime is defined as "international agreements and cooperative national actions to prevent the spread of nuclear weapons to additional countries or to terrorists."

2. For a different accounting of the challenges the nonproliferation regime faces, see IAEA Expert Group, "Multilateral Approaches to the Nuclear Fuel Cycle," Report to the Director General, Information Circular 640 (February 22, 2005), chap. 2, par. 18.

3. Of course, North Korea may already have had nuclear weapons for more than the past decade. The quotation is from James E. Goodby and others, *Cooperative Threat*

Reduction for a New Era (National Defense University, Center for Technology and National Security Policy, 2004), Executive Summary. Similar concerns were expressed by Henry Kissinger, "A Nuclear Test for Diplomacy," *Washington Post*, May 16, 2006.

4. See remarks by Senator John Kerry and President George W. Bush at their first presidential debate on September 30, 2004 (www.debates.org/pages/trans2004a.html).

5. Secretary-General's High-level Panel on Threats, Challenges and Change, *A More Secure World: Our Shared Responsibility* (New York: United Nations, 2004), pp. 40, 45.

6. There is an extensive literature on the reasons countries choose to develop nuclear weapons, including Mitchell Reiss, *Bridled Ambition: Why Countries Constrain Their Nuclear Capabilities* (Johns Hopkins University Press, 1995); Scott Sagan, "Why Do States Build Nuclear Weapons? Three Models in Search of a Bomb," *International Security* 21 (Winter 1996/97): 54–86; George Perkovich, *India's Nuclear Bomb: The Impact on Global Proliferation* (University of California Press, 1999), pp. 444–68; Peter Liberman, "The Rise and Fall of the South African Bomb," *International Security* 26 (Fall 2001): 45–86; Ariel Levite, "Never Say Never Again: Nuclear Reversal Revisited," *International Security* 27 (Winter 2002/3): 59–88; Sonali Singh and Christopher R. Way, "The Correlates of Nuclear Proliferation: A Quantitative Test," *Journal of Conflict Resolution* 48 (December 2004): 859–85; and Dong-Joon Jo and Erik Gartzke, "Determinants of Nuclear Weapons Proliferation," November 2005 (www.columbia.edu/~eg589/pdf/jo_gartzke_nuke_11222005.pdf).

7. The "Nunn-Lugar" program was begun at the end of the cold war to increase the security of nuclear weapons material in the former Soviet Union; the program takes its name from its bipartisan sponsors, Senators Sam Nunn and Richard Lugar. In this book, Nunn-Lugar Cooperative Threat Reduction (CTR) refers not only to the programs of the Department of Defense, the initial Nunn-Lugar effort, but also to the related programs of the Departments of Energy, State, and Commerce, all of which came after, but are related to, the purpose of the original 1991 Nunn-Lugar program. Officially, CTR refers only to the Defense Department program. But there is no other common name for all these programs and they are all often referred to together as CTR.

8. See Matthew Bunn and Anthony Wier, *Securing the Bomb 2005: The New Global Imperatives* (Harvard University, Project on Managing the Atom, May 2005), pp. 1–3.

9. The Zangger Committee was organized in the early 1970s to achieve agreement among NPT-member suppliers on the meaning of NPT language dealing with exports to non-nuclear weapon countries. At that time, agents and exporters in nations such as China, France, and Germany (that had not yet joined the NPT or the Zangger Committee) were sometimes exporting uranium-enrichment and plutonium-separation technology to developing countries. The NSG was formed in 1974 following India's first nuclear test, which demonstrated to the world that developing countries could make nuclear weapons. (India had earlier received exports such as a research reactor intended for peaceful purposes from Canada with participation by the United States.) At the time, countries from many parts of the world were pursuing nuclear power in part because of the higher prices for oil brought about by the pricing agreements of the Organization of Petroleum Exporting Countries. Given all these concerns, the United States initiated formation of the NSG to go beyond Zangger Committee measures. After it was formed, France and Germany joined, and China joined recently. See Leonard S. Spector, *The Undeclared Bomb* (Cambridge, Mass.: Ballinger, 1988), app. F; and the

discussion in chapters 3 and 4 of this book. For a summary and evaluation of export control regimes, see U.S. General Accounting Office (GAO), *Nonproliferation Strategy Needed to Strengthen Multilateral Export Control Regimes,* GAO-03-43 (Government Printing Office, October 2002) (www.state.gov/documents/organization/14867.pdf).

10. This has begun to change. As of April 2006, the forty-five members of the NSG are Argentina, Australia, Austria, Belarus, Belgium, Brazil, Bulgaria, Canada, China, Croatia, Cyprus, Czech Republic, Denmark, Estonia, Finland, France, Germany, Greece, Hungary, Ireland, Italy, Japan, Kazakhstan, Republic of Korea, Latvia, Lithuania, Luxembourg, Malta, Netherlands, New Zealand, Norway, Poland, Portugal, Romania, Russian Federation, Slovakia, Slovenia, South Africa, Spain, Sweden, Switzerland, Turkey, Ukraine, United Kingdon, and United States (http://www.nuclearsuppliersgroup.org/).

11. For specific recommendations aimed at further dismantling existing proliferation networks, see Alexander H. Montgomery, "Ringing in Proliferation: How to Dismantle an Atomic Bomb Network," *International Security* 30 (Fall 2005): 153–87. Montgomery analyzes the structure of the proliferation networks described here and argues that because these networks have structures closer to a star (with Pakistan at the center in the case of uranium enrichment) rather than rings or "cliques," "proliferation can be halted or slowed through proper application of country-specific incentives selected from a broad range of options" (p. 156). We agree that country-specific approaches are needed and have said so explicitly. See Chaim Braun and Christopher F. Chyba, "Proliferation Rings: New Challenges to the Nuclear Nonproliferation Regime," *International Security* 29 (Fall 2004): 5–49. However, we also note that many of the "global measures," as Montgomery calls them, that we proposed for strengthening or broadening (see Braun and Chyba, "Proliferation Rings") and reiterate here are urged by him as well (though details may differ) in the context of their application to specific countries or problems. So, for example, Montgomery argues (p. 185) that Pakistan should be urged to join the MTCR and the NSG, and that a Fissile Material Cut-off Treaty would undercut suppliers to proliferation networks generally. But the global measures need to be in place or at least pursued for them to be available to apply to specific cases. Except in detail, we see little disagreement between our prescriptions and Montgomery's, although our emphasis is less on specific immediate challenges and more on the possibility that today's problems may be harbingers of future challenges that it would be wise to take steps to counter now. See also Geoffrey Forden, "Avoiding Enrichment: Using Financial Tools to Prevent Another Khan Network," *Arms Control Today* 35 (June 2005) (www.armscontrol.org/act/2005_06/Forden.asp).

12. This section draws heavily from Braun and Chyba, "Proliferation Rings."

13. See Bunn and Wier, *Securing the Bomb 2005*, pp. 28–30, 34–37. It is difficult to evaluate, for example, the security of warheads against insider and outsider threats in the Pakistani or Indian programs. General Khalid Kidwai of Pakistan stated in January 2002 that Pakistani warheads do not have permissive action links (PALs, devices designed to prevent the explosion of the warhead by an unauthorized user), although the bombs are kept in a disassembled state. See Paolo Cotta-Ramusino and Maurizio Martellini, *Nuclear Safety, Nuclear Stability, and Nuclear Strategy in Pakistan* (Como, Italy: Landau Network, Centro Volta, February 11, 2002) (lxmi.mi.infn.it/~landnet/Doc/pakistan.pdf). Garwin and Charpak state that PALs on a stolen weapon could eventually be overcome, but this would be challenging for a terrorist group or unsophisticated state

program to do. See Richard L. Garwin and Georges Charpak, *Megawatts and Megatons: A Turning Point in the Nuclear Age?* (New York: Alfred A. Knopf, 2001), p. 342.

14. See Lyudmila Zaitseva and Kevin Hand, "Nuclear Smuggling Chains: Suppliers, Intermediaries, and End-Users," *American Behavioral Scientist* 46 (February 2003): 822.

15. Bunn and Wier, *Securing the Bomb 2005*, pp. 29–32.

16. But the conversion of HEU research reactors worldwide to run on low-enriched uranium (LEU) fuel proceeds slowly. There are 128 nuclear research reactors or associated facilities around the world with 20 kilograms of HEU or more. See Bunn and Wier, *Securing the Bomb 2005*, p. 15. The reactor conversion program is discussed in "Reduced Enrichment for Research and Test Reactors" (www.nnsa.doe.gov/na-20/rertr.shtml). On May 26, 2004, Department of Energy secretary Spencer Abraham during a visit to the IAEA announced the launch of a Global Threat Reduction Initiative to expedite the conversion of research reactors to LEU and other related goals (www.energy.gov/engine/content.do?BT_CODE=PR_SPEECHES).

17. See Goodby and others, *Cooperative Threat Reduction for a New Era.*

18. The agreement is formally called the Global Partnership against the Spread of Weapons and Materials of Mass Destruction. See "The G8 Global Partnership against the Spread of Weapons and Materials of Mass Destruction," Statement by the Group of Eight Leaders, Kananaskis, Canada, June 27, 2002 (www.state.gov/e/eb/rls/othr/11514.htm). For analyses of subsequent progress, see Matthew Bunn, Anthony Wier, and John Holdren, *Controlling Nuclear Warheads and Materials: A Report Card and Action Plan* (Harvard University, Project on Managing the Atom, March 2003), pp. 54–55.

19. As discussed in chapter 4, "latent proliferation" refers to a country's development of nuclear technology that is ostensibly for peaceful (nuclear power) purposes that gives it a latent ability to meet many of the requirements for building nuclear weapons.

20. IAEA, "The Structure and Content of Agreements between the Agency and States Required in Connection with the Treaty on the Non-Proliferation of Nuclear Weapons," Information Circular 153 (Corrected) (June 1972). A "significant quantity" is the approximate amount of material from which a nuclear explosive device could be manufactured. The IAEA defines a significant quantity as 8 kilograms of plutonium or Uranium-233, or 25 kilograms of U-235 in HEU. See IAEA, *IAEA Safeguards Glossary,* 2001 Edition (Vienna, International Atomic Energy Agency, 2002) (www-pub.iaea.org/MTCD/publications/PDF/nvs-3-cd/Start.pdf).

21. Under Information Circular 153, the IAEA did request a "special inspection" of North Korea after its inspectors found reason to believe that a violation may have occurred. North Korea declined the request. The IAEA reported this to the UN Security Council, precipitating North Korea's threat to withdraw from the NPT. See IAEA, "The Evolution of IAEA Safeguards," International Verification Series 2 (1998), pp. 21–22.

22. See Ephraim Asculai, *Verification Revisited: The Nuclear Case* (Washington: Institute for Science and International Security, 2002), pp. 13–18.

23. "Iran: IAEA Inspectors Turned Away from Nuclear Site, Leave Iran," NTI *Global Security Newswire,* June 12, 2003; and Craig S. Smith "Iran Postpones a Visit by U.N. Inspectors until April," *New York Times,* March 13, 2004.

24. IAEA, "Model Protocol Additional to the Agreement(s) between State(s) and the International Atomic Energy Agency for the Application of Safeguards," Information Circular 540 (Corrected) (September 1997).

25. IAEA, "The Evolution of IAEA Safeguards."

26. IAEA, "The Evolution of IAEA Safeguards." For a summary of both Part 1 and Part 2 provisions, see Ming Shih Lu, "The IAEA Strengthened International Safeguards Systems," Sixth ISODARCO Seminar on Arms Control, Beijing, October–November 1998.

27. George Bunn argued that the NPT could have been interpreted to make the Agreed Framework compulsory for all non-nuclear weapon NPT members; this argument did not prevail. See Bunn, "Inspection for Clandestine Nuclear Activities: Does the Nuclear Non-Proliferation Treaty Provide Legal Authority for the International Atomic Energy Agency's Proposals for Reform?" *Nuclear Law Bulletin* 57 (June 1996): 9–22. In 2005 the G-8 urged that the Additional Protocol become the "universally accepted norm for verifying compliance with NPT safeguards obligations" in the field of nuclear supply arrangements and vowed to "work together to strengthen NSG guidelines accordingly." G-8 Gleneagles Statement on Non-Proliferation, July 2005, par. 12.

28. For a list of signatories with dates of signature and entry into force, see www.iaea. org/worldatom/Programmes/Safeguards/sg_protocol.shtml.

29. The U.S. Senate had given its consent to ratification by the United States, but additional changes in U.S. legislation, administrative practices, and regulations were necessary before the president could send a ratification notice to the IAEA. For the text of the U.S. protocol, see "Additional Protocol to the U.S.-IAEA Safeguards Agreement," 67 Fed. Reg. 70049, December 20, 2002.

30. A taxonomy of these approaches with historical examples has been presented by Levite, "Never Say Never Again," pp. 76–85.

31. Deputy Assistant Secretary of State Andrew K. Semmel, statement to the Second Session of the Preparatory Committee for the 2005 NPT Review Conference, May 5, 2003 (www.us-mission.ch/press2003/0505IAEASafe.htm).

32. IAEA, "How Much Do Safeguards Cost?" (www.iaea.org/Publications/Booklets/Safeguards2/contents.html).

33. *IAEA Programme and Budget for 2004–2005* (www.iaea.org/About/budget.html). For U.S. support, see Semmel, statement to the Second Session of the Preparatory Committee for the 2005 NPT Review Conference.

34. Uranium enriched to only 20 percent U-235 or less ("low-enriched uranium") is not regarded as weapon usable. See IAEA, "Nuclear Suppliers Group Guidelines," Information Circular 254/Rev.4/Part 1 (May 2003), par. 7.

35. IAEA Expert Group, "Multilateral Approaches," pp. 13–15.

36. The current memberships and guidelines of the NSG and MTCR may be found at www.nuclearsuppliersgroup.org and www.mtcr.info/english, respectively.

37. Missile Technology Control Regime, par. 1 (projects.sipri.se/expcon/mtcrguidelines.htm).

38. GAO, *Nonproliferation Strategy.* (After this report was issued, the GAO's name was changed to Government Accountability Office.) See also www.australiagroup.net and www.wassenaar.org.

39. GAO, *Nonproliferation Strategy.* This process can take as long as a year for some members.

40. In 2001 George Tenet, then director of Central Intelligence, reported that Russia did not have an effective export control system owing to weak enforcement and insufficient penalties for violations. See Central Intelligence Agency, *Unclassified Report to*

Congress on the Acquisition of Technology Relating to Weapons of Mass Destruction and Advanced Conventional Munitions, 1 January through 30 June 2001, released in January 2003 (www.fas.org/irp/threat/bian_apr_2003.html).

41. GAO, *Nonproliferation Strategy*.

42. "The NSG—Strengthening the Nuclear Non-proliferation Regime," NSG Plenary Meeting, Göteborg, Sweden, May 27–28, 2004 (www.nuclearsuppliersgroup.org/PRESS/2004-05-goteborg.pdf).

43. See, for example, Michael Beck and Seema Gahlaut, "Creating a New Multilateral Export Control Regime," *Arms Control Today* 33 (April 2003): 12–18.

44. See Anupam Srivastava and Seema Gahlaut, "Curbing Proliferation from Emerging Suppliers: Export Controls in India and Pakistan," *Arms Control Today* 33 (September 2003): 12–16.

45. Much of the discussion in the first subsections of this section derives from Braun and Chyba, "Proliferation Rings."

46. Steven R. Weisman, "Warming to Brazil, Powell Says Its Nuclear Program Isn't a Concern," *New York Times*, October 6, 2004.

47. See UN Security Council Resolution 1540 of April 28, 2004, www.un.org/Docs/sc/unsc_resolutions04.html.

48. John R. Bolton, "An All-out War on Proliferation," *Financial Times*, September 7, 2004, op. ed. page (www.state.gov/t/us/rm/36035.htm).

49. White House, "Remarks by the President to the People of Poland," Krakow, Poland, May 31, 2003 (www.whitehouse.gov/news/releases/2003/05/20030531-3.html).

50. The eleven original PSI countries were Australia, France, Germany, Italy, Japan, the Netherlands, Poland, Portugal, Spain, the United Kingdom, and the United States.

51. Proliferation Security Initiative, "Statement of Interdiction Principles," Paris, September 4, 2003.

52. The additional adherents are Canada, Norway, Singapore, and Russia. See Jofi Joseph, "The Proliferation Security Initiative: Can Interdiction Stop Proliferation?" *Arms Control Today* 34 (June 2004): 6–13. Russia joined the PSI in May 2004; see George Jahn, "U.S. Welcomes Russia Arms Security Effort," Associated Press, June 1, 2004 (www.ransac.org/Projects%20and%20Publications/News/Nuclear%20News/2004/612004123906PM.html#1C).

53. Flag states permit foreign-owned ships to operate under their national flag, often for reasons of lower costs or more lenient operating rules. See Wade Boese, "U.S., Panama Agree on Boarding Rules for Ships Suspected of Carrying WMD," *Arms Control Today* 34 (June 2004): 38–39.

54. See White House, "President Announces New Measures to Counter the Threat of WMD" (www.whitehouse.gov/news/releases/2004/02/20040211-4.html). Whether the interdiction of the shipment aboard the BBC *China* is accurately described as being due to the PSI is controversial; for an account of the controversy see Wade Boese, "Key U.S. Interdiction Initiative Claim Misrepresented," *Arms Control Today* 35 (July/August 2005) (www.armscontrol.org/act/2005_07-08/Interdiction_Misrepresented.asp).

55. Mohamed ElBaradei, "Towards a Safer World," *Economist*, October 16, 2003, pp. 48–50.

56. The FMCT is a proposed treaty long discussed at the Conference on Disarmament that would ban the production of fissile material for nuclear weapons. See Jean du

Preez, "The Fissban: Time for Renewed Commitment or a New Approach," *Disarmament Diplomacy* 79 (April/May 2005) (www.acronym.org.uk/dd/dd79/index.htm).

57. Mohamed ElBaradei, "Saving Ourselves from Self-Destruction," *New York Times*, February 12, 2004.

58. IAEA Expert Group, "Multilateral Approaches," p. 102.

59. Technical details of South Korea's attempts to pursue the fuel cycle, and the U.S. response, may be found in Jungmin Kang and H. A. Feiveson, "South Korea's Shifting and Controversial Interest in Spent Fuel Reprocessing," *Nonproliferation Review* 8 (Spring 2001): 71–78. Political accounts, including quotations from U.S. and Korean diplomats, may be found in Jonathan D. Pollack and Mitchell B. Reiss, "South Korea: The Tyranny of Geography and the Vexations of History," in *The Nuclear Turning Point: Why States Reconsider Their Nuclear Choices,* edited by Kurt M. Campbell, Robert J. Einhorn, and Mitchell B. Reiss (Brookings, 2004), pp. 254–92; and in Don Oberdorfer, *The Two Koreas: A Contemporary History* (New York: Basic Books, 2001), pp. 68–74.

60. IAEA Expert Group, "Multilateral Approaches," pp. 54–57.

61. White House, "President Announces New Measures to Counter the Threat of WMD.

62. G-8 Gleneagles Statement on Non-Proliferation, July 2005, par. 12.

63. White House, "President Bush Addresses United Nations General Assembly," United Nations, New York, September 23, 2003 (www.whitehouse.gov/news/releases/2003/09/20030923-4.html).

64. UN Security Council Resolution 1540 (2004) (www.un.org/Docs/sc/unsc_resolutions04.html).

65. Amending the NPT requires a majority of the votes of all the parties of the treaty, including unanimous agreement of the P-5 and all the other members of the IAEA's thirty-five-member Board of Governors. See NPT, art. VIII (2).

66. The UN Security Council declared in UNSCR 1540 that it was acting under the authority of Chapter VII of the Charter of the United Nations, which permits (Article 39) the Security Council to "determine the existence of any threat to the peace . . . and . . . decide what measures shall be taken in accordance with Articles 41 and 42, to maintain or restore international peace and security." Article 41 states that "The Security Council may decide what measures not involving the use of armed force are to be employed to give effect to its decisions." Article 42 permits the Security Council to take armed action. A precedent for UNSCR 1540 was UNSCR 1373 (September 28, 2001), in which the Security Council required all states to deny safe haven to terrorists.

67. The conceptual analysis in much of this discussion derives from Braun and Chyba, "Proliferation Rings."

68. G-8 Gleneagles Statement on Non-Proliferation, July 2005, par. 6.

69. Ibid.

70. Proliferation Security Initiative, "Statement of Interdiction Principles."

71. IAEA, "The Nuclear Suppliers Group: Its Origins, Role and Activities," Information Circular 539 (Attachment) (projects.sipri.se/expcon/infcirc_539_1.htm).

72. Boese, "U.S., Panama Agree on Boarding Rules."

73. Understanding motives for the South African bomb project has been especially difficult; see Liberman, "The Rise and Fall of the South African Bomb"; and Helen E. Purkitt and Stephen F. Burgess with reply by Peter Liberman, "Correspondence: South

Africa's Nuclear Decisions," *International Security* 27 (Winter 2002/3): 59–88. Former South African president F. W. de Klerk stated in May 2006 that although he had not been part of the inner circle that had developed the South African bomb, "as it was explained [to me] then, it was built never to be used, but to have it as a deterrent—to almost be used as a shield. It was built in the face of a definite threat, a definite strategy by the U.S.S.R., to directly or indirectly gain control of the whole of southern Africa." See Arlene Getz, "Lessons of History," *Newsweek*, May 13, 2006 (www.msnbc.msn.com/id/12758097/site/newsweek/).

74. For a description and critique of this program, see Henry Sokolski, *Best of Intentions: America's Campaign against Strategic Weapons Proliferation* (Westport, Conn.: Praeger, 2001), pp. 25–37.

75. Section 6 of the NSG part 1 guidelines reads in part: "If enrichment or reprocessing facilities, equipment or technology are to be transferred, suppliers should encourage recipients to accept, as an alternative to national plants, supplier involvement and/or other appropriate multinational participation in resulting facilities. Suppliers should also promote international (including IAEA) activities concerned with multinational regional fuel cycle centers." See IAEA, "Communications Received from Certain Member States Regarding Guidelines for the Export of Nuclear Material, Equipment and Technology," Information Circular 254/Rev.5/Part 1 (Corrected) (www.nsg-online.org/guide.htm).

76. William J. Perry and Ashton B. Carter "The Crisis Last Time," *New York Times*, January 19, 2003; Daniel Poneman and Robert Gallucci, "U.S. Should Offer a Better Deal to N. Korea," *Los Angeles Times*, May 24, 2004; Brent Scowcroft, "A Critical Nuclear Moment," *Washington Post*, June 24, 2004.

77. For a U.S. government view of Iran's oil and gas reserves and their role in a proposed nuclear power program, see John R. Bolton, "U.S. Efforts to Stop the Spread of Weapons of Mass Destruction," testimony before the House International Relations Committee, 108th Cong., 1st sess., June 4, 2003.

78. See, for example, "Qaddafi's Son Says Libya Was Promised Economic, Military Gains for WMD Disarmament," NTI *Global Security Newswire*, March 10, 2004.

79. For example, the sleeping sickness–carrying tsetse fly was eliminated from Zanzibar through the release of radiation-sterilized male flies. See IAEA, "Campaign Launched to Eliminate Tsetse Fly," WorldAtom Press Release, PR2002/0219 (February 2002).

80. *IAEA Programme and Budget for 2004–2005.*

81. Much of the analysis in this section is drawn from Braun and Chyba, "Proliferation Rings."

82. For the status of fissile material production in the P-5 and other countries, see Christopher F. Chyba, Harold Feiveson, and Frank von Hippel, "Preventing Nuclear Proliferation and Nuclear Terrorism: Essential Steps to Reduce the Availability of Nuclear-Explosive Materials," CISAC/PS&GS (March 2005) (cisac.stanford.edu/publications/reports/); and Nuclear Threat Initiative, "Fissile Material Cut-Off Treaty (FMCT)" (www.nti.org/db/china/fmctorg.htm).

83. IAEA Expert Group, "Multilateral Approaches," par. 325.

84. United Nations General Assembly, "Prohibition of the Production of Fissile Materials for Weapons or Other Nuclear Explosive Devices," UNGA 48/75L (December 16, 1993).

85. Paragraph 4(b) of "Principles and Objectives for Nuclear Non-Proliferation and Disarmament," adopted by consensus by the parties to the NPT at the May 1995 extension conference, called for "the immediate commencement and early conclusion of negotiations on a non-discriminatory and universally acceptable convention banning the production of fissile material for nuclear weapons or for other nuclear explosion devices."

86. Final Document, 2000 NPT Review Conference, May 2000, par. 15.3. The United States has stated that it "no longer supports all 13 steps." See, for example, U.S. Department of State Fact Sheet Provided to the Second Session of the Preparatory Committee for the 2005 NPT Review Conference, "Article VI of the Non-Proliferation Treaty," May 1, 2003 (www.state.gov/t/np/rls/fs/20288pf.htm).

87. See, for example, the statement by Hu Xiaodi, ambassador for disarmament affairs of China, at the Plenary of the 2003 Session of the Conference on Disarmament, August 7, 2003 (www.china-un.ch/eng/53991.html).

88. For example, in 2002 U.S. under secretary of state for arms control and nonproliferation John Bolton told the Conference on Disarmament that "the current international regime regulating the use of space meets all our purposes. We see no need for new agreements." Quoted in Hui Zhang, "Action/Reaction: U.S. Space Weaponization and China," *Arms Control Today* 35 (December 2005): 6–11.

89. Jackie W. Sanders, permanent representative to the Conference on Disarmament and special representative of the president for the nonproliferation of nuclear weapons, "U.S. Proposals to the Conference on Disarmament," July 29, 2004 (www.state.gov/t/ac/rls/rm/2004/34929.htm).

90. See, for example, Wade Boese, "Bush Shifts Fissile Material Ban Policy," *Arms Control Today* 34 (September 2004) (www.armscontrol.org/act/2004_09/FMCT.asp).

91. For example, Israel has reportedly at various times privately told the United States that it "will never sign the treaty." See Joseph Cirincione, Jon B. Wolfsthal, and Miriam Rajkumar, *Deadly Arsenals: Nuclear, Biological, and Chemical Threats,* 2nd ed. (Washington: Carnegie Endowment for International Peace, 2005), pp. 268–69.

92. For a review, see Levite, "Never Say Never Again."

93. See discussions of the cases of the Republic of Korea and Taiwan, in Kurt M. Campbell, Robert J. Einhorn, and Mitchell B. Reiss, *The Nuclear Tipping Point* (Brookings, 2004).

94. Excerpts from the leaked Nuclear Posture Review are posted at www.globalsecurity.org/wmd/library/policy/dod/npr.htm.

95. National Strategy to Combat Weapons of Mass Destruction (www.whitehouse.gov/news/releases/2002/12/WMDStrategy.pdf). See also Carl Hulse and James Dao, "Cold War Long Over, Bush Administration Examines Steps to a Revamped Arsenal," *New York Times,* May 29, 2003.The Bush administration regards the reductions agreed under the Moscow Treaty as strong evidence of its fulfillment of its Article VI obligations; see Assistant Secretary of State John S. Wolf, "Remarks to the Second Meeting of the Preparatory Committee," April 28, 2003 (www.state.gov/t/np/rls/rm/20034.htm).

96. White House, National Security Strategy of the United States of America, September 17, 2002 (www.whitehouse.gov/nsc/nss.html), p. 15.

97. Council of the European Union, EU Strategy against the Proliferation of Weapons of Mass Destruction, adopted in final form on December 12, 2003. See also Clara Portela,

"The EU and the NPT: Testing the New European Nonproliferation Strategy," *Disarmament Diplomacy* 78 (July/August 2004): 38, 39; Clara Portela, *The Role of the EU in the Non-Proliferation of Nuclear Weapons* (Frankfurt: Peace Research Institute, 2003); and Ulla Jasper, "The Challenge of Biological Weapons: Proposals for Greater EU Effectiveness," *Disarmament Diplomacy*, 78 (July/August 2004): 31, 35.

98. Council of the European Union, EU Strategy against the Proliferation of Weapons of Mass Destruction.

99. See Nicola Butler, "Deep Divisions over Iraq at NATO's Istanbul Summit," *Disarmament Diplomacy* 78 (July/August 2004): 47–48; and Roger Cohen, David E. Sanger, and Steven Weisman, "Challenging the Rest of the World with a New Order," *New York Times*, October 12, 2004.

100. See, for example, Portela, "The EU and the NPT," pp. 40–43 ; and Jasper, "The Challenge of Biological Weapons," p. 35.

101. Portela, "The EU and the NPT," pp. 41–43.

102. See statement of Luxembourg's representative for the European Union to NPT Review Conference, May 3, 2005.

103. Portela, "The EU and the NPT," p. 42.

104. See Council of European Union, "EU Strategy against Proliferation of Weapons of Mass Destruction—Draft Progress Report on the Implementation of Chapter II Strategy," EU Doc. 10448/04 (Brussels, June 10, 2004).

105. See Cohen and others, "Challenging the Rest of the World." This report quotes Javier Solana, the European Union's chief representative for foreign policy, as expressing concern that U.S. policies are presented to the union as a fait accompli, without opportunity for debate before they are implemented.

106. See Michael May and others, *Verifying the Agreed Framework* (Lawrence Livermore National Laboratory, Center for Global Security Research, 2001), pp. 15–18.

107. Joint Declaration on the Denuclearization of the Korean Peninsula, entered into force February 19, 1992.

108. May and others, *Verifying the Agreed Framework*, pp.17–20.

109. David E. Sanger, "U.S. to Withdraw from Arms Accord with North Korea," *New York Times*, October 20, 2002.

110. Ibid. A senior Chinese official said in June 2004 that "the U.S. has not presented convincing evidence" that a North Korean uranium program exists. See Joseph Kahn and Susan Chira, "Chinese Official Challenges U.S. Stance on North Korea," *New York Times*, June 9, 2004. In August 2005 President Pervez Musharraf of Pakistan confirmed that A. Q. Khan had provided North Korea with uranium centrifuges. See Salman Masood and David Rohde, "Pakistan Now Says Scientist Did Sell Koreans Nuclear Gear," *New York Times*, August 25, 2005.

111. Daniel A. Pinkston, "When Did WMD Deals between Pyongyang and Islamabad Begin?" (Monterey, Calif.: Center for Nonproliferation Studies, December 2002).

112. See IAEA, "Implementation of the Safeguards Agreement between the Agency and the DPRK Pursuant to the Treaty on the Nonproliferation of Nuclear Weapons," Director General's Report, GC(48)/17 (August 16, 2004), p. 2.

113. North Korean Foreign Ministry Statement, October 25, 2002 (www.kcna.co.jp/index-e.htm).

114. Joseph Kahn, "North Korea Sets New Demand for Ending Arms Program: Money to Buy a Civilian Reactor," *New York Times*, September 15, 2005.

115. See Joint Statement of the Fourth Round of the Six-Party Talks, Beijing, September 19, 2005 (usinfo.state.gov/eap/Archive/2005/Sep/19-210095.html).

116. See Joseph Kahn and David E. Sanger, "U.S.-Korean Deal on Arms Leaves Key Points Open," *New York Times*, September 20, 2005.

117. This assumes that North Korea continues to operate only its 5 MW(e) plutonium production facility.

118. See Siegfried S. Hecker, "Visit to the Yongbyon Nuclear Scientific Research Center in North Korea," statement before the Senate Committee on Foreign Relations, 108th Cong., 2nd sess., January 21, 2004. For periodically updated reviews of North Korea's nuclear program, see Larry A. Niksch, "North Korea Nuclear Weapons Program," Issue Brief IB 91141 (Congressional Research Service, October 6, 2005); and Sharon A. Squassoni, "North Korea's Nuclear Weapons: How Soon an Arsenal?" Report RS21391 (Congressional Research Service, August 1, 2005).

119. See, for example, David Shambaugh, "China and the Korean Peninsula: Playing for the Long Term," *Washington Quarterly* 26, no. 2 (2003): 43–56; David C. Kang, "Rising Powers, Offshore Balancers, and Why the U.S.-Korea Alliance is Undergoing Strain," *International Journal of Korean Unification Studies* 14, no. 2 (2005): 115–40; Scott Snyder, "A Comparison of U.S. and South Korean National Security Strategies: Implications for Alliance Coordination toward North Korea," in *North Korea: 2005 and Beyond*, edited by Philip Yun and Gi-Wook Shin (Stanford, Calif.: Shorenstein APARC, 2006), pp. 149–66; and Bong-Geun Jun, "North Korean Nuclear Crises: An End in Sight?" *Arms Control Today* 36 (January/February 2006): 6–10.

120. See, for example, Vice President Cheney quoted in David Sanger and William Broad, "Atomic Activity in North Korea Raises Concerns," *New York Times*, September 12, 2004.

121. See David Albright and Holly Higgins, "Setting the Record Straight about Plutonium Production in North Korea," in *Solving the North Korean Nuclear Puzzle* (Institute for Science and International Security, 2000).

122. Verifying the dismantlement of North Korea's uranium-enrichment program will likely prove especially challenging and require greater access to records and personnel than verification of North Korea's plutonium inventory, for example, would entail.

123. In a speech to the UN General Assembly in September 2005, for example, Iranian president Mahmoud Ahmadinejad decried a "nuclear apartheid" that would allow some nations to manufacture nuclear fuel while others are condemned for doing so. See remarks by President Mahmoud Ahmadinejad, quoted in "Iran Is Resolved to Pursue Nuclear Program," *CNN International*, September 18, 2005 (edition.cnn.com/2005/WORLD/meast/09/17/iran.president). George Perkovich assesses the scant evidence available for the different motives fueling Iranian nuclear demand in "Dealing with Iran's Nuclear Challenge" (Washington: Carnegie Endowment for International Peace, April 28, 2003) (www.ceip.org/files/projects/npp/pdf/Iran/iraniannuclearchallenge.pdf). In January 2004, Mohammad Khatami, then president of Iran, gave public assurances that Iran's nuclear program is peaceful, stated that Iran "vehemently" opposed production of nuclear arms, and denied that Iran had received nuclear material from North Korea. See "Iran Denies Receiving Nuclear Material from North Korea," Agence France-Presse, Davos, Switzerland, January 21, 2004 (/www.spacewar.com/2004/040121200135.i5cph0v8.html). For a discussion of the utility of Iranian nuclear weapons in meeting its national security needs, see Sharam Chubin, "Iran's Strategic Environment and Nuclear

Weapons," in *Iran's Nuclear Weapons Options: Issues and Analysis,* edited by Geoffrey Kemp (Washington: Nixon Center, 2001), pp. 17–34; and for a discussion of the public debate over nuclear weapons within Iran, see Farideh Farhi, "To Have or Not to Have: Iran's Domestic Debate on Nuclear Options," in *Iran's Nuclear Weapons Options,* edited by Kemp, pp. 35–53.

124. For a description of the many IAEA questions about Iran's nuclear activities as of September 2003, see Mohamed ElBaradei, "Implementation of the NPT Safeguards Agreement in the Islamic Republic of Iran," Report GOV/2003/75 (IAEA, November 10, 2003).

125. U.K. Foreign and Commonwealth Office, Agreed Statement by the Foreign Ministers of Britain, France and Germany, October 21, 2003. See "Iran's Pact: Full Cooperation," *New York Times,* October 22, 2003. The many IAEA issues that needed resolution are described in ElBaradei, "Implementation of the NPT Safeguards Agreement," GOV/2003/75.

126. Elaine Sciolino, "Iran Will Allow U.N. Inspections of Nuclear Sites," *New York Times,* October 22, 2003.

127. See Mohamed ElBaradei, "Implementation of the NPT Safeguards Agreement by the Republic of Iran," Report GOV/2003/40 (IAEA, June 6, 2003), released to the press June 19, 2003; see also Mark Landler, "U.S. and U.N. Agency Press Iran on its Nuclear Program," *New York Times,* June 18, 2003.

128. IAEA, "Implementation of the NPT Safeguards: Agreement with the Islamic Republic of Iran," Resolution adopted by the Board of Governors, Report GOV/2004/49 (June 18, 2004).

129. Mark Landler, "U.N. Agency to Rebuke Iran for Obstructing Inspections," *New York Times,* June 18, 2004. IAEA-Iran negotiations and the inspections that were carried out from March through May 2004 are described in Mohamed ElBaradei, "Implementation of the NPT Safeguards Agreement in the Islamic Republic of Iran," Report GOV/2004/34 (IAEA, June 1, 2004).

130. David Sanger, "Pakistan Found to Aid Iran Nuclear Efforts," *New York Times,* September 2, 2004.

131. Steven R. Weisman, "Allies Resist U.S. Efforts to Pressure Iran on Arms," *New York Times,* September 9, 2004.

132. Landler, "U.N. Agency to Rebuke Iran."

133. Craig S. Smith, "Iran's Plans of Nuclear Fuel Widen Global Rift over Technology," *New York Times,* September 23, 2004.

134. Thomas Graham, "Iran: A Crisis of Choice," 2005 (www.TomPaine.commonsense.com).

135. See Steven R. Weisman and Douglas Jehl, "Estimate Revised on When Iran Could Make Nuclear Bomb," *New York Times,* August 3, 2005; IAEA Board of Governors, "Implementation of the NPT Safeguards Agreement in the Islamic Republic of Iran and Related Board Resolutions," Report GOV/2005/64 (August 11, 2005). This IAEA board resolution says various "outstanding issues relating to Iran's nuclear programme have yet to be resolved, and . . . the Agency is not yet in a position to conclude that there are no undeclared nuclear materials" (p. 1). It also expresses serious concern that Iran had resumed uranium conversion activities (p. 2).

136. Mohamed ElBaradei, "Implementation of the NPT Safeguards Agreement in the Islamic Republic of Iran," Report GOV/2005/67 (IAEA, September 2, 2005), pars. 50, 51.

137. IAEA Board of Governors, "Implementation of the NPT Safeguards Agreement in the Islamic Republic of Iran," resolution adopted September 24, 2005.

138. See, for example, Elaine Sciolino, "Iran Proposes New Talks with Europeans, Who Are Mostly Dismissive," *New York Times*, January 18, 2006.

139. IAEA Director General, "Implementation of the NPT Safeguards Agreement in the Islamic Republic of Iran," Report to the Board of Governors, GOV/2006/15.

140. BBC News, Nuclear Report on Iran: Excerpts, April 29, 2006 (http://news.bbc.co.uk/go/pr/fr/-//2/hi/middle_east/4956882.stm).

141. EURODIF (Usine EUROpéenne d'enrichissement par DIFfusion gazeuse [European Gaseous Diffusion Uranium Enrichment Consortium]) is a multilateral enrichment organization with a plant in France. Urenco (Uranium Enrichment Company) is another enriched uranium supplier owned by West European states. Iran originally had a significant share in EURODIF. The other partners were Belgium, Italy, and Spain. The technological enrichment secrets were held by France, but Belgium, Iran, Italy, and Spain were assured a supply of enriched uranium for peaceful purposes. Iran does not now receive enriched uranium from EURODIF. See IAEA Expert Group, "Multilateral Approaches," pars. 124, 126.

142. Hassan Rohani, quoted in George Perkovich, "For Tehran, Nuclear Program Is a Matter of National Pride," *YaleGlobal*, March 21, 2005 (www.carnegieendowment.org/publications/index.cfm?fa=print&id=16694).

143. President Mahmoud Ahmadinejad, quoted in "Iran Is Resolved to Pursue Nuclear Program."

144. Perkovich, "For Tehran, Nuclear Program Is a Matter of National Pride."

145. Technical details of South Korea's attempts to pursue the fuel cycle, and the U.S. response, may be found in Kang and Feiveson, "South Korea's Shifting and Controversial Interest in Spent Fuel Reprocessing." Political accounts, including quotations from U.S. and Korean diplomats, may be found in Pollack and Reiss, "South Korea: The Tyranny of Geography and the Vexations of History," pp. 254–92; and in Oberdorfer, *The Two Koreas*, pp. 68–74.

146. See the discussion in Pollack and Reiss, "South Korea," pp. 261–65.

147. See Derek J. Mitchell, "Taiwan's Hsin Chu Program: Deterrence, Abandonment, and Honor," in *The Nuclear Turning Point*, edited by Campbell and others, pp. 293–313.

148. See IAEA Expert Group, "Multilateral Approaches," par. 123.

149. For a discussion by the IAEA Expert Group of the advantages and disadvantages of several multilateral or bilateral enrichment approaches that could include both IAEA safeguards and resident inspectors from another country at a national enrichment plant, see ibid., pars. 144–53.

150. See Perkovich, *India's Nuclear Bomb*, pp. 49–52, 104, 115, 118–19, 124, 127, 137–39, 170–83.

151. Ibid., pp. 197–98.

152. Ibid., p. 198.

153. Atomic Energy Act, as amended in 1978, Section 123.

154. Ileana Ros-Lehtinen and Gary Ackerman, cochairs of the Congressional Caucus on India and Indian Affairs, Nuclear Cooperation with India (Library of Congress, Feb. 14, 2006), p. 2.

155. Glenn Kessler, "India Deal May Face Hard Sell," *Washington Post*, April 3, 2006.

156. Kessler, "India Deal May Face Hard Sell."

157. State Department Undersecretaries Nicholas Burns and Robert Joseph, Answers to "Questions for the Record" from Senate Foreign Relations Committee Chairman Richard G. Lugar, Noveember 2, 2005.

158. See Arms Control Association, "U.S. Proposal for Changes to Nuclear Suppliers' Group (NSG) Guidelines Ciculated March 2006" (http://www.armscontrol.org/projects/India/).

159. See Nuclear Suppliers' Group Guidelines (Part 2), Basic Principle 2.

160. See Michael Krepon, "The U.S.-India Deal; Another Wrong Turn in the War on Terror" (March 29, 2006) (http://www.stimson.org/pub.cfm?id=283).

161. "Implementation of the India-United States Joint Statement of July 18, 2005: India's Separation Plan," tabled in the Indian Parliament on March 7, 2006.

162. Condoleezza Rice, "India Is a Natural Partner for the United States," Opening Statement to the Senate Foreign Relations Committee, April 5, 2006 (http://www.rediff.com//news/2006/apr/05ndeal7.htm); Rice, "U.S.-India Civil Nuclear Cooperation Agreement," Opening Statement to the House International Relations Committee, April 5, 2006, Department of State, Bureau of Public Affairs, Office of Electronic Information.

163. See Daryl Kimball, "Arms Control Association Media Advisory," March 2, 2006; and Zia Mian and M. B. Ramana, "Wrong Ends, Means and Needs: Behind the U.S. Nuclear Deal with India," *Arms Control Today* 36 (January–February 2006): p. 11.

164. In Article I of the NPT, the United States promised not "in any way to assist" a "non-nuclear-weapon state" to "manufacture" nuclear weapons. For the purposes of the NPT, India is a non-nuclear weapon state because it did not have nuclear weapons "prior to January 1, 1967," the cut-off date established by the NPT to include as nuclear weapon states only those that had nuclear weapons before that date. India did not. See NPT Art. IX (3). Thus, if implementation of the Bush-Singh agreement would help India make more nuclear weapons, it would constitute assistance to India to "manufacture" nuclear weapons and would arguably violate the NPT.

165. See Under Secretary of State Burns's answer to "Questions for the Record #4" submitted by the State Department to the Senate Foreign Relations Committee, November 2, 2005.

166. Rice, Opening Statement to the House International Relations Committee.

167. See Rice, Opening Statement to Senate Foreign Relations Committee; Ashley Tellis, Council on Foreign Relations meeting, New York City, March 13, 2006, Federal News Transcript. (Tellis was one of the Bush administration's advisers during the negotiations of the Bush-Singh joint statement and a former aide to the U.S. ambassador to India.)

168. See Kessler, "India Deal May Face Hard Sell," quoting Ashley Tellis.

169. This argument is due to George Perkovich. See Perkovich, "Faulty Promises: The U.S.-India Nuclear Deal," in *Policy Outlook* (Washington: Carnegie Endownment for International Peace, September 2005) (www.CarnegieEndowment.org), p. 12.

170. See, for example, Statute of the IAEA (treaty providing its basic authority), as amended on December 28, 1989 (the most recent amendment), arts. XII C and III B.4.

171. See Portela, *The Role of the EU in the Non-Proliferation of Nuclear Weapons*, pp. 17–19.

172. Judith Miller, "Bush Puts Penalties on Nuclear Suppliers," *New York Times*, April 3, 2004.

173. See May and others, *Verifying the Agreed Framework*, pp. 16–17.

174. "North Korea Is Told to End A-Bomb Work," *New York Times*, September 25, 2004.

175. Craig S. Smith, "Atomic Agency Votes to Censure Iran over Its Nuclear Program," *New York Times*, September 19, 2004.

176. See, for example, Weisman and Jehl, "Estimate Revised on When Iran Could Make Nuclear Bomb"; and Elaine Sciolino, "Europe Threatens to Punish Iran if Nuclear Work Restarts," *New York Times*, August 3, 2005.

177. For this history, see David Sloss, "It's Not Broken, So Don't Fix It: The IAEA Safeguards System and the Nuclear Nonproliferation Treaty," *Virginia Journal of International Law* 35 (Summer 1995): 841–45.

178. IAEA, "Model Protocol Additional to the Agreements between States and the IAEA for the Application of Safeguards," Information Circular 440 (1997).

179. NPT, art. X.1.

180. Limited Test Ban Treaty, art. IV. The second requirement in the NPT withdrawal clause was challenged at the negotiating conference by Brazil on the grounds that it would add a new limitation on withdrawal. In response, the Soviet representative explained that "observance of the non-proliferation treaty and its effectiveness are bound to be related to the powers of the Security Council, which according to the United Nations Charter, Article 24, has the primary responsibility for the maintenance of international peace and security." Eighteen-Nation Disarmament Conference, Provisional Verbatim 377, March 12, 1968, pars. 24–31; Mohamed Shaker, *The Nuclear Nonproliferation Treaty: Origin and Implementation: 1959–1979* (New York: Oceana, 1980), p. 895.

181. Ambassador Mohamed Shaker, a member of Egypt's delegation to the Geneva Disarmament Conference during most of the NPT negotiations, authored a major history of those negotiations. Considering what must have been intended by adding the Security Council to the parties as an entity entitled to notice of withdrawal and by requiring a statement of reasons for withdrawal, he concluded: "There is no doubt that withdrawal from a treaty such as the NPT would be of direct concern to the Security Council, which should be given the opportunity to examine the grounds for withdrawal and its possible impact on the viability of the NPT. Since the decision to withdraw might most probably be based on security considerations, as can be implied from the text of [the NPT withdrawal clause] and its negotiating history, the Security Council would be a suitable forum for meeting security preoccupations of the withdrawing Party. Moreover, [there is] the possibility that withdrawal might imply or indicate an imminent acquisition of nuclear weapons [or, quoting the Charter] . . . 'a situation which might lead to international friction' justifying an investigation by the Security Council. . . . The entire situation might thereafter be characterized as a 'threat to the peace' [quoting the charter again] justifying the application of appropriate sanctions" by the Security Council. See Shaker, *The Nuclear Nonproliferation Treaty*, p. 896.

182. A report in April 2005 by a group of nonproliferation experts organized by Princeton and Stanford Universities concluded that the NPT should not be interpreted to "allow a party to withdraw from the treaty and then use fissile materials or production facilities acquired while they were parties to the treaty to make nuclear weapons." The Princeton-Stanford report recommended that the Security Council declare that it would authorize "an escalating series of measures" against a country proposing to do what North Korea did. See Stanford University Center for International Security and

Cooperation, *Preventing Nuclear Proliferation and Nuclear Terrorism* (April 2005), p. 4. At the May 2005 NPT Review Conference, European Union members proposed an agreed interpretation of the withdrawal clause that would countervail North Korea's approach, were the Security Council to adopt it. The twenty-five-member EU "common approach" to interpreting the NPT withdrawal clause was that the Security Council was "the final arbiter on maintaining international peace and security"; that the Security Council should give "urgency" to withdrawal cases; that the withdrawing party "will remain internationally liable for violations of the Treaty committed prior to withdrawal"; that withdrawing "with a view of conducting a military nuclear program constitutes a violation of the objectives of the Treaty"; that "withdrawal from the Treaty could in a given case constitute a threat to international peace and security," giving the council authority to take action against it; and "that all nuclear materials, equipment, technologies and facilities, developed for peaceful purposes . . . remain, in case of withdrawal from the Treaty, restricted to peaceful purposes only." See "Withdrawal from the Treaty on Non-Proliferation of Nuclear Weapons: European Union Common Approach," NPT/CONF.2005/WP.32.

183. See George Bunn and John B. Rhinelander, "NPT Withdrawal: Time for the Security Council to Step In," *Arms Control Today* 35 (May 2005): 17.

184. For instance, Hans Blix writes: "The military force, whose buildup had begun in the summer of 2002, . . . had been an essential reason why Iraq had accepted the inspectors back." Hans Blix, *Disarming Iraq* (New York: Pantheon, 2004), p. 4.

185. See, for example, the discussion in ibid.; Mohamed ElBaradei, "The Status of Nuclear Inspections in Iraq," statement to the UN Security Council, February 14, 2003; ibid., March 7, 2003.

186. The official U.S. legal justification relies on a 2002 UN Security Council Resolution to justify the U.S. invasion in 2003. The 2002 resolution was not understood as giving this authority by most of the countries that voted for it, but it contained language that the State Department's legal adviser relied on to conclude that the resolution justified invasion of Iraq if the Iraqi government made false statements to, or failed to cooperate fully with, the inspectors authorized by the resolution to look for nuclear, biological, and chemical weapons and missiles for their delivery. See William H. Taft IV and Todd F. Buchwald, "Preemption, Iraq and International Law," *American Journal of International Law* 97 (July 2003): 557, 562–63. (Taft was then legal adviser to the State Department and Buchwald was a senior member of the legal adviser's office.)

187. See Secretary-General's High-Level Panel on Threats, Challenges and Change, *A More Secure World: Our Shared Responsibility* (New York: United Nations, 2004), p. 40.

188. IAEA Expert Group, "Multilateral Approaches," Executive Summary, par. 43.

189. A frustrated, long-time reporter on NPT conferences wrote: "The failure of the conference to adopt consensus agreements was due to politics, especially the entrenched positions and proliferation-promoting policies of a tiny number of influential states, including the United States and Iran. . . . The so-called 'final document' the conference delegates managed to adopt did little more than list the participants and officials of the conference and how many meetings they held. As for the important issues they had all identified before and during the conference—such as entry into force of the CTBT, nuclear disarmament, the nuclear fuel cycle and strengthening safeguards and the institutional powers of states parties—the governments lacked the political will and backbone . . . to adopt measures that would strengthen the world's capacity to deal with [these

issues]." See Rebecca Johnson, "Spineless NPT Conference Papers Over Cracks and Ends with a Whimper," May 27, 2005 (www.acronym.org.uk).

190. See Charles Duelfer, Iraq Survey Group Report (September 2004), "Nuclear" chapter, p. 1; and Commission on the Intelligence Capabilities of the United States Regarding Weapons of Mass Destruction, *Report to the President of the United States* (GPO, March 31, 2005), pp. 43–249.

191. "Weapons of mass destruction" was a term frequently used by the Bush administration, the press, and many scholars during the lead-up to the war in Iraq. We prefer not to use this term, first, because radiological and chemical weapons are poorly described as "weapons of mass destruction" since they are unlikely to achieve casualties greater than those achieved by conventional explosives, and second, the term "WMD" lends itself to intellectual confusion as it tends to blur the important differences among nuclear, biological, and other weapons. For a discussion of these points, see Christopher F. Chyba, "Toward Biological Security," *Foreign Affairs* 81 (May/June 2002): 122–36.

192. See, for example, Scott Stossel, "North Korea: The War Game," *Atlantic* 296 (July/August 2005), pp. 97–108.

193. Anthony H. Cordesman and Khalid R. Al-Rodhan, "Iranian Nuclear Weapons? The Options if Diplomacy Fails," Center for Strategic and International Studies Working Draft, April 7, 2006 (www.csis.org/media/csis/pubs/060407_irannucoptions.pdf); and Whitney Raas and Austin Long, "Osirak Redux? Assessing Israeli Capacities to Destroy Iranian Nuclear Facilities," Security Studies Program Working Paper (MIT, April 2006) (web.mit.edu/ssp/Publications/working_papers/wp_06-1.pdf).

194. See, for example, Dana Priest, "Attacking Iran May Trigger Terrorism," *Washington Post*, April 2, 2006; and Cordesman and Al-Rodhan, "Iranian Nuclear Weapons?" pp. 36–39.

six

Defenses against Nuclear Attack on the United States

W. K. H. Panofsky and Dean A. Wilkening

During the cold war, U.S. defenses against nuclear attack focused primarily on interdicting ballistic missile and air delivery by the former Soviet Union. Since then the emphasis has shifted to defending against such attack by hostile regional powers and, more important, the interdiction of clandestine delivery by nonstate actors. Although ballistic missile defense occupies a prominent place in the American defense debate and therefore merits some attention here, the emphasis is on interdicting air and covert delivery, specifically, controlling U.S. borders and interdicting air attacks that employ commercial aircraft or cruise missiles launched from nearby territories or seas, with only a brief comment on civil defense.

As a general proposition, the nuclear age is an era of "offense dominance." That is, nuclear offense has an advantage over the defense. This results from several fundamental attributes of nuclear weapons. First, nuclear weapons have increased by a factor of about 1 million the destructive energy that can be delivered by an object of given size and weight. Because of their enormous destructive power, even a few nuclear weapons leaking through a defense would cause tremendous damage. Therefore the probability with which the defense must intercept an incoming warhead must be very high to provide meaningful protection. Second, nuclear weapons are relatively small and light (100–1,000 kilograms) and thus suited to a myriad of delivery means (such as ballistic missiles, aircraft, or covert delivery). This complicates attempts at defense. Furthermore, once their means of production is established, nuclear weapons are relatively inexpensive to make. This low incremental cost permits nuclear arsenals to be large, as they were during the cold war, thus allowing the offense to saturate the defense. Together, these attributes suggest that a true defense against nuclear attack will be very difficult to achieve.

These arguments do not prove that defensive intercepts are technically impossible, or that the defenses might not have some effect under some conditions, at least against small attacks. However, they do suggest that a comprehensive defensive strategy against a large nuclear arsenal will have little, if any, success. It is even debatable whether defenses can ever be effective enough against any size of attack to convince a U.S. president to take some course of action that he or she otherwise would not consider without the defense when just one nuclear warhead leaking through the defense could kill upward of 100,000 people in a U.S. city.

History is equivocal on this point. During the Cuban Missile Crisis, President John F. Kennedy decided against a conventional air strike to destroy, preemptively, Soviet ballistic missiles in Cuba that could have had nuclear warheads. He did so out of fear that one Soviet missile might survive and be launched against the United States. This suggests that defenses that are less than perfect will not allow leaders to escape the dilemma created by an opponent that can arguably deliver a single nuclear warhead on U.S. territory. On the other hand, President Kennedy did alert U.S. air defenses in the southeastern United States, giving him some confidence that the country was not totally vulnerable to a nuclear air strike, since some of the Soviet IL28 bombers deployed to Cuba were allegedly nuclear capable. Thus the presence of some defenses may have emboldened President Kennedy to take a more aggressive stance—namely, to blockade the island—than might otherwise have been the case. A blockade, after all, is an act of war.[1]

The Character of the Defense

Defenses prevent an attacker from achieving his objectives by preventing weapons from arriving on target (through so-called active defenses against air or ballistic missiles, for example), or by mitigating the damage after the weapons detonate (through so-called passive defenses such as civil defense). Passive defenses to mitigate the deadly consequences of a nuclear explosion—the blast, heat, and prompt and delayed radiation—are highly limited, in contrast to those available for chemical and biological weapons. Therefore this discussion focuses on active defenses and interdiction of clandestine delivery.

However, one should keep in mind that during the cold war the United States rejected civil defenses against nuclear attack because most of the scenarios involved hundreds, if not thousands, of megaton-class thermonuclear weapons. In an era where nonstate delivery of a single, relatively small, fission bomb constitutes a primary threat, passive defenses would have more value. Thus bomb shelters, efforts to preserve the continuity of local governments, evacuation strategies, communication efforts aimed at mitigating public panic, rapid medical intervention, decontamination of radioactive areas, and reconstitution of essential services may all be quite important, if not effective, in reducing casualties from such an event. The question is whether they can reduce the casualties enough to be worth their cost. Clearly, the physical destruction of infrastructure will be difficult to prevent owing to the tremendous blast and heat effects of any nuclear explosion. However, it is conceivable that civil defense preparations, some of which are occurring to protect against covert biological, chemical, or radiological attacks, may reduce the casualties from a nuclear attack by a factor of 2 to 10, depending on the scenario.

It is often said that defenses "deter" an opponent from attacking because he has less confidence that his attack will succeed. Defenses may dissuade an opponent because the prospects for success are diminished or because defenses complicate his attack plans. But this is a very different calculus from one based on a fear of the consequences. Hence it is useful to avoid confusing defense (sometimes called "deterrence by denial") with deterrence, as is quite common in the literature. Deterrence, in this discussion, is reserved for situations in which opponents are dissuaded from attacking because they fear the consequences of reprisal.

Defense against nuclear attack has been an important policy issue since the dawn of the nuclear age. An examination of the merit of such defenses should consider all means of delivering nuclear weapons, including ballistic missiles, aircraft of all kinds, cruise missiles and attacks launched from nearby ships, and covert delivery by ship, rail, truck or assembly in situ by specially trained teams. Even an "insider threat" of nuclear weapons delivery by a dissident U.S. group is conceivable.

Unfortunately, the discourse about defenses has been highly politicized. Many people equate "defense" with ballistic missile defense (BMD), as though other delivery modes do not exist. Given the variety of available modes of delivery, this approach has made it difficult for U.S. political leaders to formulate a comprehensive policy for the defense of the United States and its allies, along with a rational allocation of resources.

In assessing the role of defense against nuclear weapon delivery, one must recognize that the perpetrator of a nuclear attack is likely to be acquainted with the nature of the available defensive measures. He can therefore adopt countermeasures, evasive tactics, or choose an alternate means of delivery. The relative economic burden of this offense-defense competition can be measured by the cost "at the margin" of efforts to improve the offense and efforts by the defense to counter these improvements to restore defense effectiveness. Because of the extreme damage, both in human and material terms, wrought by the detonation of even a single nuclear weapon, this "exchange ratio," however measured, will generally lead to a result favorable to the offense.

The cost-exchange ratio is, of course, not in itself conclusive if the country supporting the defense commands much larger resources than the country with the offense, but it must not be ignored. For example, the United States has vastly greater resources for ballistic missile defense than, for example, North Korea has for its offensive missile program. Hence the United States might pursue ballistic missile defenses despite the poor cost-exchange ratio because it can afford the disproportionate cost. Less rational strategic preferences may also influence the decision to pursue defenses. During the cold war, for example, the Soviet Union spent vast sums on civil defense, air defense, and, to a lesser extent, ballistic missile defense, despite the poor cost-exchange ratio of all of these defensive measures and despite the fact that it had fewer resources than the United States. The reason may have been a deep-seated preference for measures that protect the Russian homeland whether by defenses or preemptive attack—a preference that is understandable in light of Russia's history of repeated invasions—although most Russian leaders acknowledged that mutual assured destruction between the United States and the former Soviet Union was a fact of life.

For the reasons already described, there should be no expectation that defenses against nuclear weapons could relieve the condition of "offense dominance," at least for large attacks. In other words, defenses should raise no hope that conflicts in which substantial arsenals of nuclear weapons are used can prevent unacceptable damage. But defenses may have some limited utility. They can complicate attack planning and they can undermine a potential attacker's confidence in success. Defenses may even provide some protection against very limited attacks—for example, those with less than a few tens of weapons. Defenses can also raise the costs of delivery and consequently may persuade an attacker to pursue alternate delivery means, or perhaps to abandon the idea of nuclear attack altogether.

Defenses, in principle, are more effective against technically unsophisticated attacks with a small number of targets because the defense can concentrate its assets, provided the nature and location of the attack is known. U.S. theater air defenses demonstrated this during the 1991 Gulf War when they shot down, or turned back, all Iraqi aircraft that were able to take off from airfields surviving allied attacks. Within one week, the Iraqi Air Force rarely took to the air except to escape to Iran.[2] If the defense is unaware that a surprise attack might occur, however, then the defense has less opportunity to concentrate its assets.

In a war between nations, defenses are much more effective against non-nuclear attacks than nuclear attacks because the former require repeated sorties for high effectiveness; therefore the defense has multiple opportunities to intercept the delivery vehicles. This was clearly demonstrated by the German air defense during World War II where attrition rates approaching 10 percent per sortie, and sometimes higher, forced U.S. and British bomber forces to alter their tactics to remain viable.[3] Similarly, despite the repeated air attacks by the German air force against London and other British cities, enough attrition was wrought on German pilots and aircraft that on balance the attacks were ineffective in defeating Great Britain. Conversely, had the German air force carried nuclear weapons, Great Britain would have been defeated. Defenses against conventional weapons are effective even in an era of precision-guided munitions because, even though each sortie is much more effective, multiple sorties still are required to inflict operationally meaningful damage against a wide range of military targets.

A simple numerical example illustrates the potential value of defenses against small nuclear attacks; this value disappears rapidly as the attack size increases. Suppose that a single defensive missile has a 70 percent chance of intercepting a nuclear delivery vehicle or warhead. Then the chance that a single vehicle or warhead will penetrate the defense would be approximately 1 percent if four attempts were made to intercept it—assuming each intercept attempt is statistically independent, a questionable assumption under realistic battlefield conditions for single defensive systems, although "layered" defenses, to some extent, approximate statistically independent intercept attempts. In a hypothetical attack by 10 vehicles or warheads against a defense with the above characteristics, the probability that all 10 vehicles or warheads would be intercepted is 0.92, the probability that one vehicle or warhead would leak through the defense is approximately 0.08, and there is a negligible chance that more than one warhead would penetrate the defense. For an attack by 100 warheads, however, there is a better than 50-50 chance that one or more warheads will leak through such a defense. Therefore, in principle, defenses with performance characteristics as good as those just described can be effective against small nuclear attacks even if they cannot be effective against large attacks.

Again, statistical independence may not be a good assumption for real defense systems because common failure modes can occur, and when they do, they make this simple arithmetic inappropriate. Taking common mode failures into account, the likelihood that a single nuclear weapon will leak through a defense increases. Thus one returns to the fundamental political question: can defenses ever provide sufficient protection, even against small nuclear attacks, so that U.S. leaders can act confidently in the face of a presumed small, but fundamentally unknowable, likelihood that one nuclear weapon will leak through the defense, killing perhaps 100,000 people? In most scenarios, the answer is likely to be "no." However, one should not dismiss the possibility that defense might have some impact on U.S. decisions in the midst of a crisis. The question, as always, is whether the benefit of defenses is worth their cost in the light of other options available to the United States, as discussed in the preceding chapters, such as deterring nuclear attacks with the threat of overwhelming reprisal or concerted diplomatic efforts to forestall a potential crisis, or launching a preemptive strike if attack is clearly imminent.

Against major nuclear powers like Russia and China, defenses would only induce these countries to augment their offensive forces at a cost lower than the cost to the United States of augmenting its defenses. For example, after deciding to deploy a national missile defense system, the Bush administration found it necessary to reassure both Russia and China that the proposed defense was not intended to reduce the effectiveness of their deterrent, although China remains skeptical about its purpose. At the time of this writing, there is no persuasive evidence that the U.S. decision to deploy a national missile defense has accelerated the already existing Chinese and Russian programs to modernize their offensive missile forces, although both countries objected to the U.S. decision.

In the nuclear age, the role of defenses must be evaluated not only in terms of their "first-order" effectiveness in a potential conflict but also in terms of their impact on the long-term strategic relationship among nations. Indeed, during the Cold War, both the United States and the former Soviet Union were persuaded that nuclear defenses would be escalatory.

Summary of Past Defense Efforts against Nuclear Weapons

After World War II, the United States implemented an extensive air defense system against nuclear-armed long-range aircraft. However, this system was allowed to deteriorate, recognizing the large growth in the Soviet ballistic missile arsenal in the late 1960s and 1970s, against which there was no effective defense.[4] The Soviet Union, on the other hand, maintained a large strategic air defense throughout the cold war despite its limited effectiveness.[5]

In the 1950s, the United States also developed plans, with limited implementation, for civil defenses, although these too were abandoned after considerable public debate in the early 1960s because they provided little protection to centers of population from the large nuclear arsenal the Soviet Union was amassing. Again, the Soviet Union invested substantial resources in civil defenses during the cold war, especially for its top leadership and key industries, long after the United States had abandoned such efforts.[6]

The United States designed and deployed the Nike Zeus ballistic missile defense system with nuclear-tipped interceptors in the early 1960s and designed the Sentinel system with nuclear-tipped exo-atmospheric and endo-atmospheric interceptors in the late 1960s to provide limited defense against small attacks by the leading "state of concern" at the time, namely, China. In the early 1970s the Sentinel system was converted into the Safeguard system dedicated to point defense of American intercontinental ballistic missile (ICBM) silos. This system was canceled in 1974 after being operational for only several months. The Soviet Union deployed a similar system of nuclear-tipped interceptors around Moscow, which went through successive upgrades and is still in existence although in some state of disrepair.

President Ronald Reagan's proposal to erect a "penetration-proof" BMD shield based on space-based weapons for ballistic missile defense ("Star Wars") is well known but was clearly technically infeasible. The George H. W. Bush administration scaled back these ambitious plans but remained interested in a limited space-based BMD system to protect against accidental ballistic missile launches while it explored land-based systems for so-called theater ballistic missile defense. With the Clinton administration, U.S. ballistic missile defense efforts came back to earth, with efforts to develop and deploy theater missile defenses and to conduct research on land-based interceptors for national missile defense using kinetic-kill vehicles for midcourse intercept. The George W. Bush administration continued the work on midcourse intercept systems and, since the U.S. withdrawal from the ABM Treaty, has expanded the architecture to include multiple interceptor launch sites, naval interceptors, multiple BMD radars (some of which are located outside U.S. territory), and possibly interceptor sites deployed outside U.S. territory as well. A rudimentary version of this system was prematurely deployed in 2004 in Alaska and California, and on board Aegis cruisers, even though the system has not completed its developmental test and evaluation program and its naval component has no significant capability against ICBMs threatening the continental United States as that component is now configured. Currently, the Bush administration is spending approximately $10 billion to $11 billion a year on ballistic missile defense.[7] Since 1962 the United States has spent approximately $150 billion in today's dollars on ballistic missile defense.[8]

The next section presents a summary of the status of defenses against various potential means of delivering nuclear weapons. It does not include all possible defenses that the U.S. government has considered over the years but does cover the most important ones, given the current security environment.

Control of Land Borders

The United States has a 7,500-mile land border with Canada and Mexico that is crossed by approximately 500 million people, 130 million motor vehicles, and 2.5 million rail cars each year. About 200 million cruise and ferry passengers travel its 95,000 miles of shoreline and navigable waters each year, and approximately 10 million cargo containers arrive on 8,000 foreign-flag vessels at 361 U.S. ports. In addition, approximately 30,000 flights carrying 1.8 million passengers arrive every day at 422 primary airports and 124 commercial service airports.[9] These numbers reflect global business ties and open borders. At the same time, a country open to this extent is potentially vulnerable to terrorist attack. There are many ways a nuclear weapon or materials needed to construct a nuclear weapon could be smuggled into U.S. territory—via truck across the U.S.-Canadian or U.S.-Mexican border; via containers aboard commercial shipping traffic; via private boat, yacht, or minisubmarine; via airliners; or some other means. Individuals might also be able to smuggle small amounts of fissionable material across the border for later assembly within the United States, although smuggling an entire nuclear (or radiological) device would require a large vehicle.

The Homeland Security Act of 2002 consolidated several federal agencies that safeguard the U.S. homeland from illegal or terrorist activities into the Department of Homeland Security. Within this department, the Directorate for Border and Transportation Security (BTS) has responsibility for securing the land, air, and water borders of the United States and their associated ports of entry from illegal goods and people. As such, the BTS houses the U.S. Coast Guard, the Bureau of Customs and Border Protection, the Transportation Security Agency, and Immigration and Customs Enforcement. Its basic objectives are to interdict unwanted people and goods before they enter the United States, to employ technology to increase the chance of detecting illegal individuals and cargo attempting to enter the United States, to ease restrictions on the flow of legitimate travel and trade, to improve border control through more effective use of intelligence, and to improve interdiction through cooperation with other enforcement entities, both foreign and domestic.[10]

For example, the Department of Homeland Security created the U.S.-Visit program to track the arrival and departure of every foreign visitor to the United States. Its NEXUS and SENTRI programs speed entry into the United States from Canada and Mexico, respectively, for low-risk travelers. Air travel is also monitored, through BTS's improved Advanced Passenger Manifest program, Computer Aided Passenger Pre-Screening System, "no-fly" lists, and strengthened Federal Air Marshall program.

To monitor goods, BTS has initiated an Advance Electronic Cargo Manifest, which requires shippers to provide electronic manifests at least twenty-four hours before goods arrive at U.S. ports as maritime cargo, four hours before departure for air cargo, two hours before arrival by rail, and one hour before arrival by truck. The Free and Secure Trade program is designed to expedite commerce across the Canadian and Mexican borders. In addition, the Customs-Trade Partnership against Terrorism (C–TPAT) program offers expedited cargo processing for companies that secure their entire supply chain. The Container Security Initiative (CSI), launched in 2002, aims at improving the security of maritime shipping containers by developing criteria for identifying high-risk containers, screening containers with various sensor technologies at foreign ports prior to departure for the United States, and developing "smart containers" that are more intrusion-resistant. To date, forty foreign ports have signed on to the CSI. They account for approximately two-thirds of all container traffic to the United States. This program enables U.S. BTS personnel to work in conjunction with host nation customs officers to prescreen high-risk containers bound for the United States.

Taken together, current Homeland Security programs for monitoring the entry of foreigners into the United States and for monitoring and securing various trade routes represent substantial progress over the programs in place before September 11, 2001. However, implementation of these programs varies from planning only and sample pilot installations to various degrees of actual coverage. For all their efforts, these programs are still inadequate to the task of securing U.S. borders from the covert delivery of a single nuclear weapon or enough fissile material to assemble a crude nuclear device.[11] Note, however, that all of these measures focus on points of entry into the United States and have no effect on entry over the vast open borders. They may have some deterrent effect in raising a would-be terrorist's level of concern about being caught, but they still fail to provide confident security for the United States against covert nuclear delivery.

The obvious approach to interdicting this type of nuclear delivery is to identify suspected perpetrators as far from U.S. borders as possible and to apprehend them before they carry out their mission. This task poses a serious challenge for government agents, who must interrogate suspicious trucks, ships, airplanes, railroad cars, and containers far from U.S. borders, especially when the United States may not have the access, or authority, to carry out such interrogations. Even if it did, there would be the problem of searching for a single nuclear weapon or corresponding shipment of nuclear weapons–usable material in a large commercial or private shipment of goods via plane, ship, rail, and truck.[12] How does one detect such shipments against this background? How much screening in foreign countries is politically acceptable even if permission can be secured? And if such inspections are allowed, how easy will it be for terrorists or others to circumvent the system?

Nuclear weapons generate a radiation signature that could be exploited to detect them from a distance of tens of meters. However, heavy radiation shielding can reduce such signatures, and weapons based on uranium-235 rather than plutonium would be very difficult to detect because they emit much less radiation. All detection systems require that suspicious cargo pass through narrow portals equipped with radiation detectors; and even then, detection efficiency is moderate. No area surveillance is feasible. Clearly, intelligence is key to this form of defense. The more focused one's search becomes in terms of attack timing, likely perpetrators, countries of origin, modes of operation (means of transport, communication channels, command hierarchy in the group, and so on), delivery route, and likely targets, the better the chances of successful interdiction. It is beyond the scope of this chapter to suggest any concrete means by which intelligence can be improved for effective border control.

However, before one concludes that covert delivery is an easy way to introduce nuclear weapons into the United States, one should realize that covert delivery carries risks for the attacker as well. An emerging nuclear state or a terrorist organization is likely to have only a few nuclear weapons, at least initially. Covert delivery requires the leadership to part with what is arguably one of its most precious assets and hand it over to a special team for delivery. Fear that team members will defect or that the plot will be uncovered prematurely, thereby implicating the perpetrator, would weigh on the leadership's mind, especially in light of the severe retribution the group would face. From the time the weapon departs, delivery to U.S. territory may take several days to a week or more. Several more days may elapse before the weapon is ready for detonation at its intended site. During this time the leader sending the weapon may have little communication with the covert team, for fear of interception. Yet the leader would presumably need to make brief contact to tell the team when to detonate the device or to abort the mission if the attack is called off. This communication activity may provide opportunities for U.S. intelligence to intercept information related to the plan. And if the plan were called off, the leadership presumably would want to retrieve the weapon. On the other hand, a leader who merely wishes to "kill as many Americans as possible" may not feel constrained by the timing or target of the attack and may care less about weapon retrieval since the mission is a one-way operation by definition. Only the fear of interdiction and possible retaliation by the United States would weigh on such a leader's mind.

Shipping Containers

The border and transportation security problem regarding nuclear weapons and nuclear material can be illustrated with the example of shipping containers. The system of international maritime shipping handles over 100 million containers each year. A fraction of this, 9.6 million containers in 2004, come through U.S. ports. Shipping containers account for 95 percent of U.S. import-export cargo tonnage. Shipping containers are a particularly attractive means of clandestine delivery because they can handle heavy loads, which provide ample space for radiation shielding to impede the detection of nuclear weapons. Under normal conditions, the system of international maritime transport depends on the ability to maintain a steady flow of container traffic through the world's major ports. Efforts to achieve a secure system must not threaten the economic viability of the network and, by extension, the system of global trade.

Since criminal activities are not uncommon in the realm of international container shipping, increased security measures designed to counter nuclear weapons smuggling could also provide benefits by reducing other illegal activities, thus offsetting part of the cost for such measures by benefits associated with reduced contraband. Measures needed to counter the smuggling of nuclear weapons would have to be designed specifically to detect such weapons, and different sensors would be required to detect nuclear weapons as opposed to nuclear weapons–usable materials. Any serious attempt to reduce the risks associated with container shipments of nuclear materials would have to increase the probability of detection via this channel to such a degree that terrorists would opt for other delivery means. Again, the problem is how to detect nuclear shipments in the presence of a very large background of commercial traffic, and how to do so at a cost in time and money that does not disrupt the economic efficiency of the maritime shipping industry.

Securing shipping containers against nuclear delivery requires a layered approach, with containers screened at various stages. A first step would be to designate certified shippers whose containers would be allowed to bypass some of the inspection levels, thereby reducing the number to be scrutinized. Various levels of monitoring would then take place at the port of embarkation to ensure that no nuclear weapon or special nuclear material is loaded onto a ship. Monitoring could continue after the containers have been loaded onto a ship to determine the location of each container during transit and whether the container has been entered; this could include radiation monitoring to take advantage of the long integration time associated with container transit. A similar layered monitoring system would be in place at the port of debarkation in the United States. Finally, a data collection and fusion center would compile all the information obtained from sensors and intelligence on every container in the system. Such a system would make it much more difficult, but not impossible, to ship nuclear weapons via this route.[13]

This staged approach requires a number of technical tools, such as improved seals and tags for each container to discourage unauthorized intrusion and detect it if it occurs; special imaging and nonimaging radiation sensors to detect special nuclear materials and heavy shielding at ports of embarkation and debarkation; and appropriate "black boxes" placed inside the container for geolocating containers, detecting intrusions, integrating radiation signals during long transit times, and broadcasting this information to a data fusion center. As mentioned earlier, the Department of Homeland Security is already implementing elements of such a system as part of the Container Security Initiative. However, a great deal more effort is required, especially in the way of field-testing candidate systems to determine the rate at which false positives occur. Clearly, to be acceptable, the system must have a very low false alarm rate.

The consensus, at the time of this writing, is that it should be technically feasible to develop a monitoring system that does not significantly increase the cost of maritime shipping while substantially increasing the chances of intercepting a nuclear weapon transported via shipping containers. Of course, any such system will still be vulnerable to insider threats. Also, if terrorists are dissuaded from using shipping containers, they will likely channel their shipments into another delivery means. If interdiction programs similar to this included additional delivery modes, it would be more difficult for a terrorist to penetrate U.S. borders with a nuclear weapon or fissile material. Although invulnerability is an impossible goal, the hope should be that terrorists will recognize the large risks in trying to bring a nuclear weapon into the United States covertly.

Air Defense

In the 1950s and 1960s the United States had a substantial continental air defense system, consisting of Nike surface-to-air missiles, fighter interceptor aircraft, and land-based surveillance radar. With the deployment of a large Soviet ICBM force in the late 1960s, however, the decision was made to reduce the priority associated with modernizing its homeland air defense, since the United States could not interdict the much larger ballistic missile threat.

The post–cold war air threat facing the United States is much different. Potential enemy arsenals are smaller. In addition to bombers and fighters, U.S. planners must worry about civil aviation, private aircraft, and cruise missiles launched from ships off shore. In fact, the coastal threat may be one of the most serious air threats facing the United States and other countries in the decades to come.

The United States still retains assets that can be used for continental air defense. The First Air Force at Langley Air Force Base is responsible for U.S. continental air defense. Warning of air attack is centralized at the North American Aerospace Defense Command (NORAD) in Cheyenne Mountain, Colorado. The warning sensors consist of the North Warning System (formerly known as the Distant Early Warning or DEW line), a string of fifty-five radars stretching from Alaska across the northern border of Canada and into Greenland, and radars of the Joint Surveillance System, a network of approximately eighty radars around the periphery of the United States jointly operated by the Air Force and the Federal Aviation Administration. The Joint Surveillance System was to be replaced by Over-the-Horizon-Backscatter (OTH-B) radar, which operates by reflecting radar energy off the ionosphere and hence can detect aircraft at very long ranges over the horizon (up to 3,500 kilometers). At night, however, when electron densities in the ionosphere are lower, OTH-B radar has diminished, perhaps even marginal, capability against cruise missiles and small aircraft. Two of the four planned OTH-B sites have been built but are not operational. In addition, AWACS aircraft, which perform a central role in U.S. theater air defense, can be used to patrol the skies around the United States. The 552nd Air Control Wing based at Tinker Air Force Base, Oklahoma, maintains thirty-two operational AWACS aircraft.[14]

AWACS radar can provide continuous coverage for aircraft flying into U.S. airspace at high altitudes, as well as low-altitude coverage out to a distance of approximately 400 kilometers from the AWACS aircraft. Note that about four AWACS are required in the inventory to support one AWACS plane on station continuously. Therefore, if the entire U.S. AWACS fleet were to be designated for continental air defense, the United States could maintain adequate warning against high-altitude threats from any coastal approach to the United States, excluding the borders with Mexico and Canada. The actual number of aircraft available for continental air defense varies, depending on demands for AWACS abroad and the state of alert regarding air attack against the U.S. homeland.[15]

Low-altitude coverage would be spottier. The North Warning System provides low-altitude coverage of northern approaches. However, the Joint Surveillance System has many low-altitude gaps that the OTH-B radar was designed to fill. These gaps remain today. During heightened states of alert, AWACS, with a nominal detection range of at least 400 kilometers against fighter-sized targets, can fill these gaps sporadically, and then only in a small number of places, unless the entire AWACS fleet is deployed for continental air defense.

Despite the gaps in radar coverage around the periphery of the United States, especially for low-flying aircraft, it is not trivial to employ civilian airliners or small private airplanes for nuclear attack against the United States. During heightened states of alert, all civilian air traffic from hostile countries could be halted. Since private civilian aircraft that could fly through the many gaps in the Joint Surveillance System would have to depart from nearby territory, a nuclear weapon could only be boarded at such sites, and the operation would be open to detection if the relevant sites are kept under surveillance.

Perhaps the greatest airborne threats are cruise missiles launched from commercial ships located several hundred kilometers off the U.S. coast. Cruise missiles could penetrate gaps in the low-altitude radar coverage around the U.S. periphery, unless the ship was sufficiently suspicious that U.S. authorities decided to maintain continuous radar coverage with AWACS or to shadow the ship with an Aegis air defense cruiser.

In the 1950s and 1960s the United States deployed a large number of Nike surface-to-air missiles throughout the country. In addition, it had fighter interceptors with air-to-air missiles, sometimes carrying nuclear-tipped Genie missiles, on alert. Today U.S. air defenses consist almost entirely of F-15 and F-16 fighter interceptors armed with conventional air-to-air missiles (such as the AIM-7, AIM-9, and AIM-120 AMRAAM). Gone are the nuclear-tipped air-to-air missiles and surface-to-air missiles. The U.S. Army's Patriot PAC-2 and PAC-3 air defense missiles could be deployed around the United States in an emergency but otherwise are in storage awaiting deployment overseas.

How effective continental air defense might be against a few aircraft or cruise missiles carrying nuclear weapons is difficult to gauge. Air defense performance during the 9/11 attacks was highly deficient. Communication with command authorities was erratic, and some of the interceptors were unarmed—problems that have largely been addressed since then. But holes still exist in the defense that a clever opponent would not have too much difficulty penetrating. Yet any opponent's mishap that alerts the United States to a possible air attack from a neighboring country or a suspicious ship in advance could make it much more difficult to penetrate the defense, especially if a sufficient number of AWACS and fighter aircraft have been placed on airborne alert. The AWACS/F-15 combination using AIM-9 and AMRAAM missiles is difficult to penetrate, as has been demonstrated in several regional conflicts over the past few decades, most notably in the 1991 Gulf War. Even stealthy cruise missiles are potentially vulnerable to the AWACS/F-15 combination, although there is less chance of successful interception.[16] Thus the single most important determinant of U.S. air defense effectiveness is the presence or absence of warning regarding the time and place of attack. With warning, U.S. air defenses can be quite effective against small attacks. Without warning, the defense will likely be ineffective, as the events of September 11, 2001, demonstrate.

Smuggling by air poses some of the same defense challenges as those arising from other shipping routes. In general, however, security for air shipments is better today than for shipping on land or sea. Furthermore, since aircraft are less able to accommodate heavy shielding than trucks and ships, radiation detection is possible from nearby interrogating aircraft.

Ballistic Missile Defense

During the cold war, land-based ICBMs were the most menacing means of delivering nuclear weapons against the United States. At its peak, during the

1980s and early 1990s, the Soviet Union deployed approximately 6,400 ICBM warheads. The Russian Federation presides over a shrinking strategic arsenal that may fall to around 600 ICBM warheads in the next decade or so. The number of Russian intercontinental bombers and submarine-launched ballistic missiles (SLBMs) will also shrink. However, current total Russian strategic forces still contain approximately 3,500 nuclear warheads, and nonstrategic nuclear forces remain much larger.[17] Moreover, Russian strategic nuclear forces are being modernized with the introduction of land- and sea-based missiles with maneuvering warheads.

Because of its size and character, the Russian Federation's strategic nuclear force precludes effective or even significant defenses against that force. That was also the case in Soviet times. During the cold war, U.S. security relied on deterrence as opposed to defense to protect the homeland. Although planners could construct conceptual models of U.S. and Soviet first strikes—including attacks against the opponent's ICBM silos, long-range bomber bases, missile submarine bases, and nuclear command and control facilities—such attacks were never credible with or without added defenses. Such attacks could not conceivably have destroyed enough of the U.S. or Soviet nuclear arsenal to limit damage to the homeland from a retaliatory strike. Still, the existence of defenses on either side made each opponent nervous about the long-term viability of its retaliatory force, thus spurring modernization plans to overcome such defenses. This dynamic clearly was present in the competition between long-range bomber forces and strategic air defenses during the cold war. Recognizing this dynamic, the United States and the former Soviet Union eventually concluded that substantial deployment of BMD would be escalatory for the U.S.-Soviet arms competition. The Anti-Ballistic Missile (ABM) Treaty of 1972, amended in 1974, converted that conclusion into a severe limitation on nationwide BMD.

China currently has about twenty ICBMs capable of reaching the continental United States but is modernizing this force by adding an unspecified number of DF-31 solid-propellant mobile ICBMs over the next decade. These clearly are incapable of anything but a deterrent role but can be interpreted to limit U.S "freedom of action" in a conflict in Asia.

In the next decades, smaller actors capable of ICBM delivery may emerge, notably North Korea and possibly Iran. With the end of the cold war, defense against such "states of concern" has become the dominant justification for national missile defense. The feasibility of threats from such states is outlined in the Rumsfeld Commission report of 1998, although it did not go into their likelihood or make any recommendation on defenses. In 2002 the Bush administration withdrew from the ABM Treaty, notwithstanding the objections raised by Russia and China, to provide greater latitude to U.S. BMD deployments.

Note that our remarks about the cost-effectiveness of BMD are restricted to defenses against nuclear, and possibly biological, ballistic missile attacks. Defenses may indeed be cost-effective against conventionally armed ballistic missiles, even if the probability of successful intercept is low. Examples include defenses against intermediate and short-range conventionally armed ballistic missiles that China has aimed at Taiwan. Nuclear use by China against territory that China considers a "dissident province" is very unlikely. Similarly, defense against non-nuclear ballistic missile threats on the battlefield may generate attrition unacceptable to the offense, as German air defenses in World War II did against conventional bombing raids. Although ballistic missiles are a much more remote threat than other means of nuclear delivery, their status and technology merit attention because of their political prominence.

Ballistic Missile Defense Technologies

In principle, ICBMs or SLBMs can be intercepted during their boost phase, their midcourse phase (as the warhead traverses the near vacuum of outer space), or their terminal phase (after the warhead reenters the atmosphere). Each of these phases offers different technical options for detecting, tracking, and destroying the opponent's warheads. In addition, there are alternative basing modes for such defenses. ICBMs can also be attacked in the "preboost" phase, that is, before launch. This option is covered in the discussions on preemption in chapter 2 so is bypassed here, along with the technology or status of early warning systems designed to alert, or even to launch preemptively, the available offensive forces.

The proclaimed missions of the defense can be to erode a first strike against U.S. retaliatory (deterrent) forces or to prevent (or mitigate) attacks against population and industry. Defending U.S. cities is the most important current mission, given the small and inaccurate ICBM forces likely to be on hand in emerging ballistic missile states.

Despite the large literature on the technical feasibility of different BMD architectures, it is difficult to evaluate in detail the Bush administration's proposals in this regard because it has yet to specify the system architecture for its BMD developments.[18] Rather, the administration has promoted a "capabilities-based" approach—a term that lends itself to a variety of interpretations. The actual approach seems to be one that stresses fielding systems in their infancy, then improving or replacing them later as weaknesses are uncovered. This approach seems to sidestep cost-effectiveness analysis of possible responses to a projected threat. Moreover, it omits preparatory steps usually required by good industrial practice. The administration even appears to waive the legal requirement that major defense acquisition programs demonstrate performance in field tests before the government proceeds to acquisition and deployment.

Although the systems architecture remains undefined, the proposed concept centers on "layered defense," based on a combination of intercept modes: boost phase, midcourse, and terminal. However, the largest fraction of the total budget for fiscal 2005 was dedicated to developing midcourse intercept, following the pattern set by the Clinton administration.[19]

Boost-Phase Intercept

The boost phase of an ICBM lasts for a very short time (three to five minutes, depending on the booster type). The principal technical challenges associated with boost-phase intercept are the short booster burn times and the accelerating nature of the target. The short burn time imposes severe limits on the decision to launch an intercept and the implied short flight time, and hence range for boost-phase interceptors imposes geographic constraints on the location of the BMD platform. The acceleration of the target places greater demands on the kinetic-kill vehicle's homing guidance system compared with that for midcourse intercept. On the other hand, the target's exhaust plume radiates tens of megawatts of thermal energy, which makes target detection and tracking relatively easy and effective decoying of the thermal signal difficult, although not impossible.

The short decision time generally implies that the decision to fire an interceptor must be predelegated to local commanders. This puts a heavy burden on rapid launch detection and tracking and incurs the risk of destroying nonhostile rocket boosters. Since very few civilian activities look like a ballistic missile launch, this may not be a serious problem in a crisis or war.

After the initial booster's detection and tracking by radar, infrared sensors, or both, the defense will launch a high-acceleration interceptor with a kinetic-kill vehicle payload designed to home on the missile booster, causing the kill vehicle to collide with it at speeds in excess of 5–10 kilometers per second, depending on the target missile speed and the intercept geometry. At these speeds, the missile booster is destroyed by the kinetic energy of the impact. As a result, warhead delivery will fall short of its intended target or fail entirely.

The geographic constraint implies that not all potentially hostile launch sites are accessible from land, sea, or air. For example, North Korean sites could be covered from a ground-based interceptor location in Russia, or from interceptors based at sea or in the air, owing to the small size of the country and the presence of nearby international waters and friendly territory. However, Chinese and Russian ICBM launch sites cannot be covered by land-based or sea-based interceptors because they are too far from possible BMD interceptor launch sites. Air-based boost-phase interceptors could technically cover Russian or Chinese ICBM launch sites, but this would require a very large number of airborne launch platforms and aerial refueling aircraft to maintain continuous coverage, not to mention that these aircraft would be vulnerable to Russian or Chinese air defenses. Thus land, sea, or airborne interceptors pose little threat to geographically large states such as Russia or China, or for that matter to any state that can deploy strategic missiles (that is, SLBMs) into the vast regions of the world's oceans (such as Russia, France, Great Britain, or the United States). This is less true for naval boost-phase interceptors, which could conceivably be deployed on oceans around the world. Thus airborne, land, and, to a lesser extent, sea-based boost-phase BMD interceptors pose little or no threat to the strategic nuclear forces of the world's five major nuclear powers, thereby reducing political opposition to their deployment. They could, however, be effective in destroying ICBMs from small emerging missile states.

Space-basing, in principle, can provide global coverage including the ability to intercept accidental or unauthorized Russian or Chinese missile launches. However, this requires a large number of satellites and would thus be very expensive. Moreover, any deployment that can reasonably be presumed to threaten Russia's or China's deterrent capability is likely to provoke a response from those and possibly other countries, although proposals have been made to deploy such defenses multilaterally in the form of a defensive alliance. The United States currently is pursuing research on boost-phase intercept concepts, especially space-based interceptors, although recent budget cuts have by and large eliminated the "kinetic intercept program" that supported land-, sea- and air-based boost-phase interceptor concepts, and the testing of space-based components will not begin in earnest until 2012 with the planned space-based test bed.

Powerful lasers, another technology suggested for boost-phase missile defense, were proposed during the Strategic Defense Initiative as a possible space-based BMD system. In view of the technical challenges associated with lightweight megawatt-class lasers and very accurate optical pointing and tracking systems, however, this idea was shelved. Even today, these same challenges have caused the Bush administration to downgrade the space-based laser program from a development program to a research program. Research into space-based lasers is still too limited to predict when, if ever, such a system might become feasible.

The most advanced laser program for ballistic missile defense is the Airborne Laser Program, which is attempting to integrate a high-power (megawatt-class) chemical oxygen-iodine laser operating at an infrared wavelength of 1.3 microns with 1.5-meter adaptive optics aboard a 747-400 aircraft. The lethal range of such a laser has been estimated to be between 200 and 400 kilometers against theater ballistic missiles, depending on the exact missile characteristics and damage criteria.[20] The Airborne Laser Program is currently limited by the considerable weight of lasers of adequate power and again by the challenge of accurate pointing and tracking for the laser beam as it propagates through the thin upper reaches of the atmosphere. System integration on an airborne platform is challenging because of aircraft vibration and the need to reduce overall system weight because this affects the aircraft operating altitude (approximately 40,000 feet). The latter determines the amount of atmosphere through which the laser beam must propagate and, hence, the degree to which the laser beam must compensate for atmospheric distortion. Initial plans called for the first airborne laser flight test against a ballistic missile target by 2003, with a fleet of seven aircraft to become operational by 2008. However, these dates have slipped because of technical challenges regarding laser weight and system integration. At the time of this writing, it is not clear if or when the airborne laser will be tested against a ballistic missile target or when the first aircraft could become operational, though the latter is unlikely before 2010.

In summary, boost-phase intercept options appear to be technically feasible against North Korean long-range missiles, and possibly against those from some other emerging missile states. Operationally, such systems present some challenges. Their cost-effectiveness is unknown, and no candidate systems have as yet been built, let alone tested. Of the various basing options, space basing is the least technically viable, probably the most expensive, and certainly the most provocative politically. Naval and airborne systems have the advantage of being mobile, and airborne interceptors also may be effective against theater-range ballistic missiles. Naval and airborne boost-phase intercept systems, which offer the most realistic near-term prospect for boost-phase BMD, are no longer funded.[21]

Midcourse Intercept

Most U.S. resources for ballistic missile defense, including those supporting the current U.S. National Missile Defense program, focus on midcourse intercept systems. These systems use radars and space-based infrared (IR) optical sensors for early detection and tracking, followed by the launch of an interceptor equipped with a kinetic-kill vehicle using optical sensors to home on its target as it flies through the near-vacuum of outer space. Short-range systems of this type have been designed and deployed for midcourse intercept against theater-range missiles (for example, Theater High-Altitude Area Defense, or THAAD, and the Navy Theater Wide defense).

The National Missile Defense tests have been subject to much public scrutiny but to date have proved little about the fundamental merits of the system. The record up to 2005 is five successful intercepts out of ten attempts. The failures—malfunction of interstage separation of the interceptor, lack of adequate cooling of the IR sensor, a software glitch, and the failure of a support arm to retract inside the interceptor silo—resulted from defective quality control and hence do not shed much light on the fundamental technical feasibility of the system. Other components of the system were tested in these experiments and, according to Department of Defense reports, functioned reasonably well. Still, these have only been research and development, not operational, tests. That is to say, the test managers knew the target timing and trajectory in advance, the interceptors were prototypes whose design had not yet been finalized, and the closing velocity between interceptors and target reentry vehicle (RV) was below realistic values.

Moreover, the system has yet to go through a rigorous set of tests to examine its performance against a range of possible countermeasures designed to undermine the effectiveness of the defense, tests that one would not expect early in the R&D phase but that clearly ought to be conducted before a deployment decision is made. In this regard, it is troubling that the sophistication and the number of decoys to be used in later flight tests have been cut back, a move inconsistent with rigorous countermeasure testing. In addition, the space-based IR sensor systems—that is, the Space-Based Infrared System–low earth orbit (SBIRS-Low) and the Space-Based Infrared System–high earth orbit (SBIRS-High)—have been plagued by serious cost and schedule problems, raising doubts about whether the former will ever be deployed and when the latter might be deployed. Thus although there is little question about the basic soundness of the physical principles underlying midcourse intercept of simple (that is, not decoyed) targets quality control and cost continue to be major obstacles and are expected to be serious factors affecting future deployment decisions.

The principal technical challenge associated with midcourse ballistic missile defense is how to cope with a range of possible well-known countermeasures such as decoy balloons, antisimulation techniques where the warhead is made to look like a decoy (for example, by placing it inside a balloon), radar jammers or transponders, chaff, and other booster fragments that may complicate the radar and infrared image of the target. The midcourse countermeasure problem arises because reentry vehicles follow the same trajectories as those of lightweight decoys or other objects released by the missile while in space. Discrimination thus depends on a detailed comparison of the observed or expected signatures of the reentry vehicle compared with those of other objects such as decoys and booster fragments. If the opponent does not flight-test its reentry vehicles, or if the flight test cannot be monitored in sufficient detail, it remains doubtful that the signatures expected by the defense will match those under actual conditions the first time an attack is observed.

Discrimination also depends on the algorithms used to analyze optical and radar signals. For example, subtle motional differences, sunlight reflections, and temperature differences between reentry vehicles and decoys over time can be incorporated as discriminants. Advances in precision X-band radar and multispectral optical sensors, especially long-wave infrared sensors aboard the kinetic-kill vehicle and, in principle, on SBIRS-low, give the defense considerable data on which to base discrimination algorithms. Even so, antisimulation remains a challenging problem for midcourse defense. Whether antisimulation techniques can be successfully mastered by emerging ballistic missile states and whether U.S. midcourse defenses and sensor architectures can devise effective measures to defeat them remain open questions at the current time.

If the missile payload is fractionated early in flight, it presents a midcourse defense with a large number of objects to shoot at, thus potentially saturating the defense. This is the idea behind the deployment of multiple independently targeted reentry vehicles (MIRVs). Chemical and biological submunitions delivered by ballistic missile payloads would also present the defense with a large number of targets.

The expected performance of a midcourse system against countermeasures is a critical and contentious issue, and one that is difficult to analyze in the abstract. Elementary physics alone cannot determine the outcome of the measure-countermeasure competition, because this competition is affected by the actual deployment and realistic performance of measures and countermeasures by the two sides, by the relative technical sophistication of the offense and the defense, by the relative intelligence about each side's capabilities, and by the relative resources each side has to devote to the problem.[22] Thus the outcome of the measure-countermeasure competition depends on the capability of opponents and on the exact BMD architecture deployed. As a result, the question "Will the defense work?" has no meaning without specifying the detailed nature of the offense-defense engagement.

In the public debate, proponents of BMD often assume that the offense is simple and the defense is sophisticated, while opponents allow for sophisticated offensive countermeasures and limit the measures the defense can take in response. Since the defense must be tested and deployed years before it is used, the opponent has time to study the vulnerabilities of the defense. Conversely, if the offense tests its countermeasures, the United States may be able to monitor such tests and adapt its defense to handle such countermeasures in ways that are difficult for the offense to know since they may only involve software changes in the discrimination algorithms. In any case, the design of sophisticated decoys relies on an understanding of sensor performance and the signatures of objects in outer space, whereas ICBM design and construction are based on mechanical and chemical engineering. Thus the rhetorical argument that any country that can build an ICBM can also build effective BMD countermeasures is not prima facie obvious. Finally, high-quality decoys tend to be relatively heavy and hence add a substantial payload penalty.

On the other hand, one should not assume that "simple" offensive threats would be easy for the defense to handle. Tumbling warheads, for example, are more difficult to discriminate from simple decoys than spin-stabilized warheads, yet an emerging ballistic missile state may deploy tumbling warheads, either intentionally or unintentionally, in much the same way as Iraqi Scud missiles maneuvered in flight during the 1991 Gulf War because they broke apart upon reentry owing to poor design. This made them very difficult for the PAC-2 ballistic missile defenses to intercept, inasmuch as these defenses had not been tested against maneuvering warheads. At the time, maneuvering warheads were thought to be too sophisticated for emerging ballistic missile states to deploy.[23] In any case, since the algorithms designed to discriminate decoys from real warheads generally are statistical in nature, it seems difficult to achieve high intercept efficiency against a decoyed attack accompanying a modest number of real warheads. Defense performance will degrade rapidly as the number of decoys, even those barely similar to the real target, is increased.

Suffice it to say that countermeasures in a variety of categories present the biggest technical challenge to midcourse missile defenses. Hence midcourse defenses should be subject to extensive flight tests against the widest range of potential countermeasures before any significant deployment decision is made.

Indeed, the Bush administration's decision to begin deployment of a prototype operational midcourse intercept system in 2004, with bases in Alaska and California, has been quite premature for this very reason: developmental tests against countermeasures have been meager and operational testing nonexistent. Furthermore, the final interceptor design was not yet available, and the sensor architecture (notably one including an advanced X-band tracking radar) was inadequate. Nevertheless, as of June 2006, the administration had deployed a total of eleven interceptors in silos, nine at Fort Greely, Alaska, and two at Vandenberg Air Force Base in California, despite the very limited capability this system would likely have against a real attack. The sea-borne deployments on Aegis-class ships are also of limited capability against ICBM targets owing to the weak performance of the existing Aegis radar and interceptors, although the radar could provide early track data on a threatening missile if the ship were stationed near the missile launch location. This system likely will have greater capability against theater-range ballistic missiles.

Terminal Defenses

In the defense of a high-value "point" target, the intercept can take place close to that target after the reentry vehicle has entered the atmosphere. Then atmospheric drag slows light decoys in relation to the heavy warhead and thus "filters" out most decoys. This was the basis of the Safeguard System deployed during the Nixon administration. At that time, the high-value point targets were U.S. ICBM silos conceivably subject to a Soviet preemptive attack. Such a scenario is now highly implausible, and terminal defenses would probably be of value only if they could defend U.S. cities or possibly U.S. military bases overseas.

The ICBMs that emerging missile states might be able to deploy in the next decade and beyond are likely to be inaccurate and few in number, with U.S. cities as their likely targets. If point defense is to be an option for cities, then nearly all U.S. cities must be protected because the attacker can choose to threaten the next largest undefended city. Such a deployment would therefore require a large and probably impractical number of terminal defense sites. However, point defense of important military targets in a theater does make sense and is the rationale for such systems as the Patriot Advanced Capability-3 (PAC-3) system.

Nuclear Warheads on Interceptors

There has been some public discussion of the merits of reintroducing nuclear explosions to enhance the effectiveness of intercepts in space. The radiation from nuclear explosions can damage incoming warheads over distances of perhaps hundreds of meters by a number of mechanisms. For example, the absorption of thermal X-rays from a nuclear explosion will cause some of the outer layers of the reentry vehicle to boil off rapidly and thus cause damaging recoil to the reentry vehicle or failure upon reentry into the atmosphere. Also, the more penetrating radiations may destroy electronic components of the reentry vehicle. This could reduce the burdens of precision intercept and at the same time disable nearby decoys.

Despite these advantages, nuclear-tipped interceptors are strongly counterindicated. As has been experienced in earlier exo-atmospheric tests (named Starfish and Argus), nuclear explosions in space can disable space communications and even terrestrial systems at long distances and interfere with radar tracking, thus disrupting an essential component of the missile defense architecture. These disruptive effects can be long lasting. Furthermore, the increased payload weight, larger than that for "hit-to-kill" intercepts, would require larger interceptor missiles. If the yield of a nuclear-tipped interceptor is small, the disadvantages of using such an interceptor may be diminished, but the benefits will be fewer as well because its lethal range will be reduced. Testing nuclear explosions in space would, of course, violate the Limited Test Ban Treaty and the Outer Space Treaty and hence would draw widespread international criticism.

Summary

In view of the many means available to deliver nuclear explosives onto U.S. soil, the overriding budgetary priority given to ballistic missile defense in current U.S. policy appears unjustified. Today, deliberate nuclear attack against the United States by any of the other four NPT nuclear weapon states or by India or Pakistan is extremely unlikely. Small "states of concern," should they acquire nuclear weapons, may not choose an ICBM as the preferred means of delivery even if they could build one (as may be the case for North Korea in the not too distant future), because the launch of an ICBM identifies the attacking nation and retaliation would likely be fatal to its state and leadership. Deterrence, as practiced during the cold war, or other forms of dissuasion remain by far the most effective remedy.

Covert delivery by states with small arsenals is a risky operation. Should subnational groups acquire a nuclear weapon, their most likely mode of attack will be one of the various methods of clandestine delivery. They simply will not have any other means at their disposal. Terrorists armed with an ICBM are not a realistic threat.

Therefore the "capabilities-based" approach of the Bush administration is counterproductive. It fails to assess system effectiveness against concrete hypothetical threats or to compare the likely effectiveness of alternative means of delivery. Without such comparisons, one cannot judge the relative effectiveness of different forms of defense against nuclear attack or judge the absolute merit of defenses versus the available means of dissuasion. A broad assessment of defense against nuclear attack would likely conclude that improved security for weapons-usable fissionable materials (particularly in Russia) and improved screening for nuclear weapons and weapons-usable materials hidden in commercial shipping containers or other covert delivery modes coming into the United States should receive higher priority and greater resources than ballistic missile defense. However, research and development on the latter could still be pursued at a reduced level of effort.

It is difficult to make quantitative recommendations on the level of effort the United States should devote to defense aimed at interdicting nuclear weapons or fissile material. According to a recent JASON group report that draws estimates from the 9/11 experience, a small nuclear explosion would cause damage of the order of $1 trillion.[24] Thus assuming that a successful terrorist delivery might occur once in twenty years, an annual preventive effort of $50 billion might be justified according to this crude calculus.

U.S. nuclear weapons policy will have to accept the reality that offense dominates any defense in the delivery of large nuclear arsenals. Technical developments or preemptive military moves are not likely to change this situation. Therefore policymakers should focus on defending against realistic delivery means for small nuclear attacks, in particular covert nuclear terrorist attacks. But even here, defenses can never confidently be expected to prevent the detonation of a nuclear weapon on U.S. soil.

Notes

1. Graham T. Allison, *Essence of Decision: Explaining the Cuban Missile Crisis* (Boston: Little, Brown, 1971), pp. 123–26.

2. Thomas Keaney and Eliot Cohen, *Gulf War Air Power Survey, Summary Report* (Government Printing Office, 1993), p. 59.

3. Christopher J. Bowie, "Untying the Bloody Scarf: Casualties, Revolutions, and Aerial Combat," Northrop Grumman Corporation, unpublished manuscript.

4. Arthur Charo, *Continental Air Defense: A Neglected Dimension of Strategic Defense*, Harvard University Center for Science and International Affairs Occasional Paper 7 (Lanham, Md.: University Press of America, 1990).

5. For example, at no time during the cold war did the United States estimate that the Soviet strategic air defense could intercept more than about half of the air-delivered weapons in the U.S. strategic nuclear arsenal. Frequently, the estimate of the effectiveness of Soviet air defenses was much lower than this, particularly if defense suppression by the United States was taken into account.

6. Dietrich Schroeer, *Science, Technology, and the Nuclear Arms Race* (New York: John Wiley & Sons, 1984), pp. 219–35; and John Dowling and Evans M. Harrell, eds., *Civil Defense: A Choice Of Disasters* (New York: American Institute of Physics, 1987).

7. See Missile Defense Agency, Fiscal 2005 Budget Estimates (www.acq.osd.mil/bmdo/bmdolink/pdf/budget05.pdf [March 11, 2004]).

8. Stephen I. Schwartz, ed., *Atomic Audit: The Costs and Consequences of U.S. Nuclear Weapons since 1940* (Brookings, 1998), pp. 294–96.

9. Jennifer E. Lake, William H. Robinson, and Lisa M. Seghetti, *Border and Transportation Security: The Complexity of the Challenge*, Report RL32839 (Congressional Research Service, March 29, 2005).

10. Lisa M. Seghetti, Jennifer E. Lake, and William H. Robinson, *Border and Transportation Security: Selected Programs and Policies*, Report RL32840 (Congressional Research Service, March 29, 2005); and William H. Robinson, Jennifer E. Lake, and Lisa M. Seghetti, *Border and Transportation Security: Possible New Directions and Policy Options*, Report RL32841 (Congressional Research Service, March 29, 2005).

11. For a discussion of some current shortcomings in the C-TPAT and CSI programs, see Richard M. Stana, "Key Cargo Security Programs Can Be Improved," testimony before the Senate Committee on Homeland Security and Government Affairs, 109th Cong., 1st sess., Report GAO-05-466T (Government Accountability Office, May 26, 2005).

12. At present, less than one-third of the illegal drug shipments into the United States are intercepted. However, the analogy between the drug trade and clandestine delivery of nuclear weapons can be misleading because the former employs many shipments and hence can saturate border controls, while the latter would utilize very few deliveries.

13. Stanford Study Group, *Container Security Report* (Stanford, Calif.: Center for International Security and Cooperation, 2003); and *Concealed Nuclear Weapons*, Jason Report JSR-03-130 (Boston: MITRE Corporation, 2003), restricted circulation.

14. See www.fas.org/man/dod-101/sys/ac/e-3.htm (September 2, 2004).

15. The current AWACS fleet consists of thirty-three aircraft, the majority of which could be available for continental air defense if so ordered. See www.globalsecurity.org/military/systems/aircraft/e-3.htm (June 2004).

16. David A. Fulghum, "Secret Upgrades Target Stealthy Cruise Missiles," *Aviation Week & Space Technology*, August 24, 1998, p. 22.

17. See www.russianforces.org/eng (October 26, 2005).

18. See, for example, Office of Technology Assessment, *Ballistic Missile Defense Technologies*, OTA-ISC-254 (GPO, 1985); Ashton Carter and David Schwartz, eds., *Ballistic Missile Defense* (Brookings, 1984).

19. Missile Defense Agency, Fiscal 2005 Budget Estimates.

20. Geoffrey E. Forden, *The Airborne Laser: Shooting Down What's Going Up* (Stanford University, Center for International Security and Cooperation, September 1997).

21. Dean A. Wilkening, *Ballistic-Missile Defense and Strategic Stability*, Adelphi Paper 334 (London: International Institute for Strategic Studies, May 2000), pp. 59–70; American Physical Society Study Group, *Boost-Phase Intercept Systems for National Missile Defense* (July 2003) (www.aps.org/public_affairs/popa/reports/nmd03.cfm); and Dean A. Wilkening, "Airborne Boost-Phase Ballistic Missile Defense," *Science and Global Security* 12, nos. 1–2 (2004): 1–67.

22. For a perspective suggesting that the countermeasure problem will be too difficult for the defense to handle, see Andrew Sessler and others, *Countermeasures: A Technical Evaluation of the Operational Effectiveness of the Planned U.S. National Missile Defense System* (Cambridge, Mass.: Union of Concerned Scientists, 2000).

23. Ted Postol, "Lessons of the Gulf War Experience with Patriot," *International Security* 16 (Winter 1991/92): 119–71; and Robert Stein, *Patriot ATBM Experience in the Gulf War* (Raytheon Corporation, 1991).

24. JASON, *Concealed Nuclear Weapons*, Report JSR-03-130, 2003.

seven

Assessing the United States' Nuclear Posture

Roger Speed and Michael May

George W. Bush's National Security Strategy is a bold departure from previous U.S. policy. First announced in September 2002 and reiterated in March 2006, it declares that the United States now finds itself in a unique position of military and political dominance and that it has a moral duty to use this strength to establish a new liberal democratic world order, "with the ultimate goal of ending tyranny in our world."[1] To achieve this envisioned democratic, peaceful world, it argues, the United States must in effect establish and maintain a global military hegemony.[2]

According to the strategy, carrying out this mission requires that any challenge to U.S. military dominance must be blocked, by force if necessary. A significant challenge to world stability comes from terrorists and certain states that are seeking weapons of mass destruction (WMD).[3] Concerned that the cold war doctrines of deterrence and containment may no longer work, and that "if we wait for threats to fully materialize, we will have waited too long," President Bush proclaimed a new "preemption doctrine" against such threats.[4]

To implement this new strategy would, it was believed, require the transformation of the Defense Establishment. Thus the Bush administration had earlier (in 2001) undertaken a Nuclear Posture Review (NPR).[5] The NPR

An earlier, shorter version of this chapter appeared as Roger Speed and Michael May, "Dangerous Doctrine," *Bulletin of the Atomic Scientists* 61, no. 2 (March/April 2005), pp. 38–49.

report argued that the U.S. military should move beyond the old strategic Triad (intercontinental ballistic missiles [ICBMs], strategic submarines, and strategic bombers) to the creation of a New Triad consisting of offensive strike systems (both nuclear and non-nuclear), defenses (both active and passive), and a revitalized defense infrastructure that will provide new capabilities in a timely fashion to meet emerging threats.[6] A number of strategic missions (some old, some new) for the New Triad were also developed by the NPR and then presented in various presidential policy statements.

These strategic missions and the resulting call for new nuclear weapons to meet the requirements of these missions are the subject of this chapter. Specifically, it examines possible new weapons concepts, whether these weapons will meet the military/technical requirements dictated by the new strategy, how the new weapons might (or might not) fulfill their mission objectives, and what might be the strategic and political consequences of the new doctrine (hereafter called the Bush doctrine).

A New U.S. Strategic Doctrine

According to the NPR, the New Triad will have four primary missions: to assure, dissuade, deter, and defeat. The president, as noted, later added a fifth mission, preemption, which he characterized as "proactive counterproliferation"—meaning the use of military force to prevent or reverse proliferation.[7] Most of these missions do not originate entirely with the current Bush administration. Strategic deterrence was the cornerstone of U.S. nuclear policy throughout the cold war. America's policy of extending its nuclear umbrella over its allies was meant to assure them that they could rely on U.S. nuclear weapons rather than acquire their own. Warfighting has also been a component of nuclear policy, although a much debated and controversial element. On the other hand, the idea that states could be dissuaded from procuring weapons through the demonstration of U.S. superiority was never part of practical policy when dealing with major states such as the Soviet Union or China, both of which found it unacceptable to have the United States in a position to completely dominate them. To the extent that dissuasion was able to limit or prevent the development of nuclear, chemical, and biological weapons around the world, it was done in large part through negotiations and agreements, approaches now downplayed by the Bush administration.

It is the fifth mission of the Bush doctrine that represents the most radical departure from past U.S. strategic policy. This mission emphasizes the possibility of preemptive military action to disarm those regional powers (stigmatized as "rogue" states) that possess or are trying to obtain WMD. In the view of the administration, this will require a more dynamic and "flexible" nuclear policy than existed during the cold war: "Nuclear attack options that vary in scale, scope, and purpose will complement other military capabilities. The combination can provide the range of options needed to pose a credible deterrent to adversaries whose values and calculations of risk and of gain and loss may be very different from and more difficult to discern than those of past adversaries" (NPR, p. 7).

Weapons and Military Targets

Currently, the United States has more than 5,000 deployed strategic nuclear weapons, consisting of RVs (reentry vehicles) delivered by long-range ballistic missiles (ICBMs and submarine-launched ballistic missiles [SLBMs]), bombs carried by the B-2 bomber, and cruise missiles carried by the B-52 bomber.[8] About 3,000 additional intact warheads are retained in reserve or inactive stockpiles.[9] According to the Treaty on Strategic Offensive Reductions (SORT) signed with the Russians in May 2002 in Moscow, the number of operationally deployed strategic warheads will be reduced to 1,700–2,200 by 2012.[10]

In addition to the strategic weapons, a few hundred "tactical" (nonstrategic) nuclear bombs (variations of the B61) carried by relatively short-range dual-capable (conventional and nuclear) aircraft are stationed in Europe and a few hundred nuclear-armed submarine-launched cruise missiles (SLCMs) are kept in storage in the United States. The tactical bombs and SLCMs are not covered by the SORT agreement, and apparently no change to their current status was suggested in the NPR.

U.S. weapons reportedly have a wide range of yields.[11] U.S. ballistic missiles carry only high-yield (over 100 kilotons) warheads. On the other hand, nuclear bombs and cruise missiles reportedly have low-yield options. For example, according to Senator Dianne Feinstein, the B61 bomb "has a 'dial-a-yield' feature, allowing its yield to range from less than a kiloton to several hundred kilotons."[12] The B83 bomb and the W80 cruise missile warhead reportedly have a similar dial-a-yield capability. The accuracies of U.S. strategic delivery systems are reportedly around 100 meters.[13]

Perceived Shortcomings of U.S. Nuclear Weapons

The NPR argues that the several thousand nuclear weapons in the U.S. nuclear arsenal will not be adequate to meet the challenges faced by the United States in implementing its new doctrine:

Today's nuclear arsenal continues to reflect its Cold War origin, characterized by moderate delivery accuracy, limited earth penetrator capability, high-yield warheads, silo and sea-based ballistic missiles with multiple independent reentry vehicles, and limited retargeting capability. . . . New capabilities must be developed to defeat emerging threats such as hard and deeply buried targets (HDBT), to find and attack mobile and relocatable targets, to defeat chemical or biological agents, and to improve accuracy and limit collateral damage. Development of these capabilities, to include extensive research and timely fielding of new systems to address these challenges, are imperative to make the New Triad a reality.

The need to reduce "collateral damage" (unintended death and injury to civilians and unintended property damage) may be the key rationale for the development of new weapon concepts. Since future wars are most likely to be regional conflicts and not central to the survival of the United States, the use of nuclear weapons, or even the threat of their use, is fraught with potentially serious political consequences. The administration apparently believes that if the collateral damage can be limited, nuclear use would be more politically acceptable, and hence the credibility of U.S. use of nuclear weapons would be enhanced. Since most current weapons would produce unacceptably large collateral damage, the administration argues that new concepts must be sought—weapons generally with low yield and high accuracy.

New Weapon Concepts

To meet perceived future weapons needs, the Bush administration initially undertook two programs: the development of a Robust Nuclear Earth Penetrator (RNEP), designed to attack hard and deeply buried targets, and a more general "Advanced Concepts Initiative" that authorized the weapons laboratories to renew previous programs to examine a broad range of new nuclear weapons concepts. However, in November 2004 congressional opponents of these initiatives managed to delete their funding before research was completed. But the Bush administration was not ready to give up on these programs.

In the budget for fiscal 2006, the administration requested $8.5 million to complete the RNEP feasibility study. In addition, money was requested for planning a Modern Pit Facility, and for searching for a specific site on which to construct the facility (which was forbidden by Congress in 2004).[14] A request to restore funds (after their cancellation in 2004) to reduce the time required to restart nuclear underground testing from thirty-six to eighteen months was also included.

In canceling the Advanced Concepts Initiative funding in 2004, Congress redirected the funding ($9 million for fiscal 2005) to a new program, the Reliable Replacement Warhead (RRW) Study, which got under way in May 2005. The administration strongly embraced this new program while still insisting that the weapons complex must be prepared (by studying a number of new concepts) to quickly deploy new weapons to meet new military requirements should they arise.[15]

Secretary of Energy Samuel W. Bodman described the purpose and scope of the RRW program:

> In order for the United States to sustain the nuclear weapons stockpile indefinitely, we believe it will be necessary to have the capability to replace most of the components in the weapons in the present stockpile. Therefore, we are beginning a program to understand whether, if we relaxed some of the warhead design constraints imposed on Cold War systems (e.g., high yield to weight ratios), we could provide components for existing stockpile weapons that could be more easily manufactured and whose safety and reliability could be certified with assured high confidence, without nuclear testing. We intend that such an effort will also result in reduced infrastructure costs for supporting the stockpile. ... The focus of the RRW program is to extend the life of those military capabilities provided by existing warheads, not develop warheads for new or different military missions. If, in the future, the DoD [Department of Defense] identifies requirements for new or different military capabilities, it is conceivable that certain of the concepts identified in the RRW program could be applied in the development of warheads to meet those new requirements. That is not, however, the purpose of the RRW program and, in any event, no new warhead could be developed or fielded without the specific authorization of Congress.[16]

The initial effort of the RRW program focuses on an SLBM replacement warhead (RRW-1). This is to be followed by an ICBM replacement warhead (RRW-2). The initial eighteen-month study on RRW-1 is a competition between two laboratory teams—Los Alamos National Laboratory working with Sandia New Mexico, and Lawrence Livermore National Laboratory working with Sandia California—to determine technical feasibility, followed by design definition and cost.[17] The study will also examine whether it will be possible to design a warhead and reentry vehicle that can be used on both

SLBMs and ICBMs (something that is not possible with current warheads). The Department of Defense would like to have the first production unit of RRW-1 completed by about fiscal 2012.

Some members of Congress and many nongovernmental analysts remained skeptical about the purpose of the RRW program, fearing that it might be a Trojan horse that could lead to new nuclear designs and perhaps nuclear testing. Indeed, it is quite clear that an RRW could easily provide capabilities that current deployed weapons do not have. For example, current nuclear-tipped ballistic missiles carry only relatively high-yield warheads, which according to the NPR and other administration statements greatly limit their flexibility and utility in the post–cold war environment. To remedy this "shortcoming," a nuclear design option for the RRW that consisted of only a primary (instead of a primary and a secondary) would provide such a low-yield option for ballistic missiles.[18]

To take advantage of this low-yield option might require that the accuracy of today's ballistic missiles be significantly improved. Moves in this direction are already being made by the administration: "In 2004 the navy began the Enhanced Effectiveness (E2) Reentry Body program to create 'a near-term capability to steer an SLBM warhead to Global Positioning Satellite (GPS)-like accuracy' (within about 10 meters). . . . The program will expand the potential targets that can be attacked with W76 warheads."[19] Accuracy improvements for the Air Force's Minuteman missile are also under consideration.

The future of the Bush administration's drive for the development of new, "usable" nuclear weapons remains uncertain. Although the administration's fiscal 2006 request for funding for RNEP was once again defeated, the RRW program (with its potential for many new weapon variations based on current and old designs) was easily passed by Congress.[20] Moreover, because new weapons concepts are central to the Bush doctrine, the ongoing debate will likely continue, despite any short-term setbacks with Congress. Therefore, to understand and contribute to the debate, it is important to examine possible new nuclear weapon concepts, their effectiveness, and the strategic and political implications of implementing such programs.

The role of the RNEP is to attack hard and deeply buried targets (discussed in the next section). The only current U.S. nuclear earth-penetrating weapon, the B61-Mod 11, is assessed to be of limited effectiveness, not being able to penetrate very hard surfaces and survive. Thus the Departments of Defense and Energy undertook a joint feasibility study to determine whether an existing warhead placed in a 5,000-pound-class penetrator would provide significantly enhanced earth-penetration capabilities. The two warheads under consideration were the B61-7 designed by Los Alamos National Laboratory and the B83 designed by Lawrence Livermore National Laboratory. However, funding was cut off before the study was completed. In its request for funding to complete the study, the administration has indicated that now only one weapon is under consideration, the B83.

In addition, the NPR indicates that under the new doctrine recommending "nuclear attack options that vary in scale, scope, and purpose," there is considerable interest in low-yield nuclear weapons for use against a wide variety of aboveground military targets. For example, low-yield weapons specially designed to attack aboveground facilities for storing biological warfare agents have been discussed. Also, some concept studies have explored alternative yields for ballistic missile warheads (which, as noted, could easily be provided by the RRW program) and possible warheads for a future "enhanced cruise missile." More generally, new weapons might be useful in a warfighting role—to attack massed troops or mobile missiles and artillery, for example. In this context, enhanced radiation weapons and other specialized nuclear weapons that have been developed, deployed, or suggested in the past could eventually be revisited.[21]

A key issue surrounding the development of new nuclear weapons is that of testing. The United States currently observes the prohibition on nuclear testing of the Comprehensive Test Ban Treaty, which it has signed but not ratified. Without testing, the United States would probably find it difficult—perhaps impossible—to build and certify the safety and reliability of entirely new weapons concepts. Thus if new concepts were fully explored and militarily useful designs created, there is likely to be pressure to resume underground testing.

The administration at this point insists that its plans do not include new testing. For example, in a position paper submitted to the UN Disarmament Commission in 2006, the United States argued that "All States should maintain national moratoria on nuclear testing."[22] Moreover, the administration emphasizes that the RRW program will produce designs that do not require nuclear testing in order to certify that they are safe and reliable. Thus if the test moratorium holds, new weapons would generally have to be based on old designs that have been tested in the past or on modifications of current weapons. Of course, with RNEP, RRW, and many other possible designs, this is not a significant limitation on producing weapons with capabilities different from those in the current stockpile.

However, even though in principle new weapon types (based on very conservative designs) could be produced and certified without the necessity of testing, there is considerable concern that if a substantial part of the nuclear stockpile were replaced with these new weapons, at some point there would be strong political (rather than technical) pressure to renew testing. As physicist Richard Garwin has noted, "How many in Congress does it take, or in the military, to say, 'nobody has ever tested this design of nuclear weapon and I will not be responsible for managing the stockpile and assuring that it will work during wartime without at least one test.'"[23] The resulting breakdown in the test-ban moratorium could undermine the nonproliferation regime and militarily work to the disadvantage of the United States, particularly in regard to China, which now has much less sophisticated nuclear weapons designs (owing to only limited testing) than the United States.[24]

Operational and Strategic Considerations

The use of even a small number of nuclear weapons (of whatever kind, new or old) in a regional conflict would raise significant operational and strategic questions. For example:

—If nuclear weapons were to be used in a regional conflict, steps would have to be taken to ensure that if the bomb, cruise missile, or RV went off course it could be safely destroyed without endangering civilians. Another concern is that weapons may sometimes not detonate as planned or an aircraft or cruise missile carrying the weapons could crash, possibly compromising design technology or allowing the retrieval of nuclear materials if the weapon were recovered by hostile forces. In either case, some reliable, probably remotely activated, way to harmlessly destroy the weapons must be found.[25]

—There could be a serious limitation on the use of ICBMs (and to a lesser degree SLBMs, depending on where the strategic submarines are patrolling) in a regional conflict. Warning systems in Russia and elsewhere will detect and raise an alarm if U.S. ICBMs and SLBMs are launched. If U.S. missiles had to fly over Russia or China to reach the regional power that was being attacked, the attack might be mistaken for an attack on Russia or China, which could trigger a retaliatory strike or other adverse action. At the least, such overflights would have to be coordinated with the country in question.

—If the use of nuclear weapons is to be limited, detecting and identifying the small set of targets that if attacked will bring about a decisive conclusion of the war will place unprecedented requirements on U.S. intelligence, communications, and control systems as well as on prewar strategic analysis.[26]

—The decision to use nuclear weapons will presumably have to be made in Washington (predelegation of nuclear-use authority is unlikely to be politically acceptable). It may be extremely difficult to fit such decisionmaking into the current network-centric, rapid-response pattern of U.S. warfighting tactics.[27] Certainly the usual command and control structure for nuclear weapons is incompatible with a prompt decision to use a nuclear weapon in response to intelligence that may have a limited lifetime.[28]

—U.S. use of nuclear weapons against a nuclear-armed enemy is likely to lead to counter-use against the United States in the area of combat (if not the homeland), putting at risk local U.S. bases, carriers, and the other high-value concentrated targets that have been essential for force projection. Furthermore, the announced U.S. policy of preemption gives an incentive to a weaker, nuclear-armed enemy to preempt against the U.S. military targets in the buildup phase with the most effective weapons he has. As in the case of Pearl Harbor, time does not work on a weaker enemy's side.

Effectiveness and Collateral Effects of Proposed New Weapons

The NPR identifies a number of target types that current weapons are unable to kill or unable to kill without excessive collateral damage: HDBTs and chemical warfare (CW) and biological warfare (BW) agents.[29]

Hard and Deeply Buried Targets

"The term 'hard and deeply buried targets' (HDBTs) refers to an adversary's threatening and well protected assets in structures ranging from hardened surface bunker complexes to deep tunnels. These facilities are typically large, complex structures incorporating the attributes of concealment, self-sustainment, multifaceted communications, strong physical security, modern air defenses, and siting in protective (often mountainous or urban) surroundings."[30] Most of the HDBTs of current interest are in fact underground, at depths ranging from a few meters to many hundreds of meters.[31] The Defense Intelligence Agency reports approximately 10,000 HDBTs on the territory of potential U.S. adversaries worldwide, and about 2,000 of these are of strategic significance. About half of these strategic HDBTs are located in or near cities.[32]

Most HDBTs built by regional powers are probably command and control centers that could also house their military and political leadership. Such facilities might also contain biological weapons factories. According to the NPR, current conventional weapons are unable to effectively destroy HDBTs, although they could in some circumstances isolate them by attacking entrances and by destroying their communications links to the outside world.

Effectiveness. Many HDBTs could be destroyed with current surface-burst nuclear weapons. However, because in many cases the yield would have to be very high, the collateral damage from blast, fires, radiation, and fallout could also be very high. A nuclear weapon that can penetrate into the ground and explode will deposit more of its energy into the ground shock wave, reducing the yield required to kill a hardened underground target by a factor of 20 to 30 compared with a surface burst.[33] Hence, because the yield required to kill a hardened underground target could be reduced, the fallout and other weapon effects could also be considerably reduced from that of a surface burst.

Technically, the production of an effective earth-penetrating weapon such as RNEP will present a serious challenge. The accelerations that the system must survive are unprecedented. Not only the warhead, but also the safing (the means of ensuring that the weapon will not explode under any condition until it is intentionally fired) and arming systems, plus possibly a communications antenna to receive a destruct message in case of a misfire, must all survive impact. Moreover, it may be difficult to achieve the desired penetration and ensure that the weapon remains stuck in the ground. Experience with conventional ordnance shows that detailed geophysical knowledge (including the ground slope of the target area and the underlying stratification and other inhomogeneities) and a proper angle of entry of the weapon (almost perpendicular to the surface) are required to achieve these objectives (otherwise the weapon may penetrate but then pop out again). Obstacles such as large rocks can also prevent proper (or any) penetration.

Assuming that the technical challenges can be overcome, a rough estimate of the effectiveness of a penetrating weapon can be made by using past measurements on underground nuclear tests carried out between the 1950s and 1970s for the U.S. civilian nuclear explosion program "Plowshare." These measurements indicate that suitably hardened targets can survive peak stresses in excess of 1 kilobar and that such a peak stress is caused by a 1 kiloton fully contained explosion out to a distance of 60 meters in granite and 40 meters in alluvium. Increasing the yield to 10 kilotons in granite brings the 1-kilobar line out to 140 meters. These numbers represent upper limits of what can be expected from a cratering explosion that vents some of its energy to the surface, as any penetrating munition of such yields would.[34]

More detailed calculations indicate that to achieve a high probability of kill against a target will also require very high accuracy. Generally, the military requires a probability of destruction of 0.95 or greater to be sure of destroying the target. Even with an accuracy of 10 meters, a 10-kiloton weapon (buried at a depth of 3 meters) could achieve this kill capability against a target (buried in granite) with a hardness of 1 kilobar only if the target were at a depth of about 85 meters or less. If the yield were raised to 300 kilotons, a 1-kilobar target could be killed at a depth of about 250 meters if the accuracy were 10 meters. With a weapon accuracy of 100 meters, the probability of destruction for a 10-kiloton weapon against a target buried greater than a depth of 20 meters would never exceed 0.42. Against a target at a depth of 200 meters, the probability of destruction would be only about 0.05. By raising the yield to 300 kilotons, a probability of destruction of 0.95 could be achieved against targets buried at a depth less than 100–150 meters.[35]

These calculations assume that the location of the target is precisely known and that the facility is of modest size. Uncertainties regarding the location of the underground facility (as could easily exist in the case of facilities buried deep under mountains) could severely degrade the effectiveness of an earth-penetrating weapon even if the accuracy of the weapon were perfect. If the facility is large in extent, much-larger-yield weapons will be required to ensure the destruction of the facility than would be required for a small bunker.

On the basis of past tests and detailed calculations, weapons of very low yield (less than 1 kiloton) are likely to be effective against only a small set of underground structures. Even highly accurate weapons with yields of a few tens of kilotons are likely at best to be effective only against facilities that are no more than 100–150 meters deep (depending on many details).

Collateral Effects. While earth-penetrating weapons lower the yield required to kill an HDBT, the collateral effects from these weapons could still be quite large, depending on the depth and hardness of the bunker and thus the yield required. Fallout illustrates the point. A moderately hard underground bunker might require a 1-megaton surface burst to destroy it. A weapon with this yield would produce (in dry rock) a twenty-four-hour dose of radioactivity that would be lethal to about 50 percent of the exposed population (the so-called LD50 dose) over an area of about 700 square kilometers.[36] By contrast, if a 50-kiloton weapon buried at a depth of 5 meters would suffice to kill the target, the fallout area would be reduced to about 100 square kilometers. For softer (or more shallow) targets, an earth-penetrating weapon with a yield of 5 or 10 kilotons might suffice. These yields will produce an LD50 fallout area of about 14–28 square kilometers, which could still cause significant casualties unless the target was isolated far from urban areas.[37]

Of course, lower but often still dangerous levels of radiation fallout (causing death, illness, or latent cancers) would cover a much larger area than indicated in these examples. In general, to reduce fallout to an "acceptable" (negligible) level would require the use of very small yields (which would be ineffective against most hardened, buried targets), or the weapon would have to be buried at a very great depth, which is impractical since nuclear earth-penetrating weapons can probably penetrate only meters into hard rock and perhaps tens of meters into softer soil.[38]

In wars fought against countries that are geographically close to U.S. allies or neutrals, it will in general not be possible to keep at least noticeable, if not dangerous, amounts of fallout from reaching these countries, depending on wind conditions and other changeable factors. (Indeed, distinctive traces of radioactivity, along with a seismic signal, would be detected all around the world for any presently possible burial depth.) Recall in this connection that, despite the best precautions that could be taken at the time, fallout from U.S. tests carried out in Nevada caused thyroid cancers in Utah and elsewhere, especially among children.[39] These tests were surface events of moderate yield. Fallout from a single, low-yield penetrating weapon explosion would be much reduced, as just outlined, but could nevertheless easily lead to claims that the United States was endangering the health of allies and neutrals, especially that of children and pregnant women, who are more susceptible to the effects of radiation.

The blast wave from a nuclear explosion would also produce damage on the surface. For example, the burst from a 10-kiloton weapon (comparable to the 13-kiloton bomb dropped at Hiroshima and capable of causing similar damage if exploded in an urban area) on or near the surface will produce overpressure of 5 pounds per square inch, which would be capable of destroying masonry apartment buildings at a range of about 1 kilometer.[40] If instead the explosion were buried, the reduction in surface blast would generally be quite modest. To reduce the range of any particular overpressure by even a factor of two for a 10-kiloton explosion would require burial to a depth of about 75 meters in granite or about 125 meters in alluvium—which again is impractical.[41]

Countermeasures. The reason that many countries have built HDBTs is to escape destruction from the threat posed by current and past weapons of their potential adversaries. If it becomes clear that the United States is pursuing nuclear earth-penetrating weapons to attack bunkers, these countries may react by simply building them at a greater depth in the future. The additional costs of going deeper are not likely to be a significant barrier if one's national security is thought to be at stake. This would cause the United States to have to use larger weapons with an ensuing significant increase in collateral effects. At sufficient depth, even the largest U.S. nuclear earth-penetrating weapon would not suffice.[42]

Alternative. Command posts are useless without communication, at least to the units that they command. They also need some link to the outside world. These links, whatever their nature, are likely to come closer to the surface than the facility itself and therefore to be more vulnerable, if they can be found, to conventional munitions. Destruction of these communications links is generally called "functional" kill of the command post, and while not the preferred method of kill (because of the uncertainty involved), it may suffice in many cases. If the bunkers are very deep or hard, it may be the only way to attack them, since even nuclear weapons may not be able to destroy such structures.

BW Agents

Biological weapons are thought to be stored primarily in surface-located warehouses or shallow-buried bunkers (probably no more than 10–20 meters below the surface, if that).[43] Since current conventional "agent defeat weapons" (ADW) have insufficient energy to heat to lethal temperatures the large masses of agent stored in moderate-sized or large facilities, significant quantities of live agent could survive and be dispersed over very large areas, potentially causing the deaths of tens or hundreds of thousands of civilians (depending on the location of the facility and the wind direction at the time of attack). Nuclear weapons have therefore been suggested as an alternative attack weapon.

Information drawn from catalogues of global biological and chemical weapons programs identifies "20+ suspected sites in Iraq prior to the 2003 war, 20+ in DPRK [Democratic Peoples Republic of Korea], 7 in Iran, 5 in China, and 75+ in Russia,"[44] As the recent war in Iraq demonstrated, however, it is very difficult to estimate the number of such targets, let alone their locations. The nature of the targets can also vary widely. They could range from small factories and laboratories to small amounts of agents perhaps stored directly in the ground, to substantial facilities with separate rooms and corridors. The more elaborate the facility, the more likely it is that intelligence resources would be able to locate it. On the other hand, more elaborate facilities are also less likely to have all of the BW agent destroyed by a given nuclear explosion. Small facilities are likely to be more numerous and harder to find, though also more vulnerable if they can be pinpointed.

Buried Storage. Whether a low-yield nuclear weapon can destroy the large mass of biological agent in a large storage site with negligible live bio-agent dispersal depends sensitively on the storage configuration, the depth of the emplacement targeted, and the accuracy of targeting. For shallow-buried bunkers (which would require an earth-penetrating weapon, but not necessarily an RNEP), the agent would be neutralized primarily by the thermal effects (with contributions from the prompt radiation released by the weapon and radiation emitted from bomb debris). The weapon would have to explode inside the storage bunker to be effective, making for very stringent intelligence and targeting requirements. Only the agent within the hot gas cavity created by the explosion—a few to perhaps 20 meters in most materials for yields of 1 to 10 kilotons—would be neutralized with certainty, and then only if the exposure lasts long enough before venting to the outside cools the cavity. For shallow sites, the exposure to high temperatures and radiation fields may only last milliseconds. Complete sterilization in such a short time has not been demonstrated.[45]

If the agents were stored in underground bunkers buried at depths of about 10 meters or more in hard rock or about 30 meters in softer soil material, the nuclear weapon could not destroy the agents (since it could not penetrate that deeply), but could (depending on the depth of the bunker and the yield of the weapon) possibly crush the bunker and the entrances to the bunker. It is not known whether this would contain the material or perhaps increase the likelihood of breaking the containers and releasing the materials through fissures created by the nuclear explosion.[46]

Surface Storage. An earth-penetrating weapon would not be necessary to target BW agents stored on the surface, in the open or in warehouses. The agent would be neutralized primarily by neutron-induced radiation (along with fireball thermal effects and debris radiation).[47] For this mission, if a fusion weapon were built and deployed (such warheads, while deployed in the past, are no longer in the stockpile), the yield could be an order of magnitude lower than that of a fission warhead to produce the same result (or alternatively the lethal range would be larger for the same yield). The reason for this is that fusion warheads typically produce ten times the number of neutrons per unit yield as fission weapons and most of the neutrons produced are in the high-energy range (14 million electron volts) in comparison with the low energy of fission neutrons. For example, a 10-kiloton explosion would produce a lethal range of about 10 meters if the yield comes from fission and about 50 meters if the yield comes from fusion.[48]

If a nuclear attack on BW were successful, the net collateral damage would arguably be lower than from an unsuccessful conventional attack. However, the suggested reduction in collateral damage will result only if the storage facility is located far from urban areas. In that case, the collateral damage caused by the nuclear explosion itself could (in principle) be small compared with possible BW agent dispersal by a conventional ADW attack. For a 10-kiloton fission warhead, the lethal prompt nuclear effects of near-surface bursts could extend out a few kilometers (depending on wind conditions).[49] Dangerous nuclear fallout effects from surface or shallow-buried bursts could extend a few tens of kilometers downwind from the explosion. By comparison, a release of 200 kilograms of anthrax (out of perhaps a total of 1,000 kilograms in storage) from a conventional attack can produce a lethal dose hundreds of kilometers downwind, if it is effectively dispersed and the particle size is in the effective range. Even the release of 20 kilograms of anthrax might spread a lethal dose greater than 150 kilometers downwind.

In practice, there could be serious technical difficulties in implementing this nuclear solution. In the case of buried storage, the many technical problems of a successful attack have already been noted. For aboveground storage, if the yield is to be kept relatively low (10 kilotons or less), the delivery system will have to have at least GPS-like accuracy (approximately 10 meters)—or even better, if the warhead is a fission weapon. Even with precise accuracy, if the storage building is large and the position of the BW material uncertain, or if there is a long stack of barrels (greater than 20 meters), or if there is more than one shed separated by some distance, a 10-kiloton nuclear weapon (fission or fusion) might not kill all the material.[50] Instead of containing the threat, some of the barrels could be broken by the explosion and the BW agent widely dispersed (in addition to the nuclear fallout and other effects).

Utility of Nuclear Weapons for Attacking BW. The trade-off in deciding whether to use a nuclear weapon to attack BW storage sites should be between the risk involved in the nuclear attack (the number of people exposed to lethal nuclear effects plus the probability of BW agent being released times the number of people potentially exposed to a lethal BW dose) versus the risk of a later BW attack against U.S. and allied forces or their homelands (the probability of the stored BW agent being used times the number of people at risk from such an attack). Unfortunately, such probabilities and trade-offs would be almost impossible to ascertain.

What is clear, however, is that using a nuclear weapon *preemptively* for this purpose would *ensure* some collateral damage from the explosion (and possibly from a dispersed agent), while the BW agent in storage represents only the *possibility* of later damage. Indeed, if war is imminent, BW storage sites might pose very little risk, since the BW agent is likely to be "weaponized" to the extent that it can be (that is, loaded in special dispersal mechanisms, bombs, or missile warheads) and dispersed among the forces in the field. Thus the BW agent left in storage is unlikely to be the major consideration in the ensuing war and may indeed only constitute a marginal threat to U.S. forces or other targets.

Perhaps more important, collateral damage comparisons do not capture the human and political impact of a U.S. first use of a nuclear weapon. This impact could be particularly significant if no BW agent had yet been used (because such an attack was being deterred). In that case, the United States would be in the position of arguing that because a country *might* use a biological weapon (an act that would be universally condemned by the international community), it is acceptable for the United States to break the nuclear taboo (an act that would also be condemned by the international community).

Summary

Nuclear weapons detonated on the surface or in the atmosphere can be effective against very hard targets (on the surface or near the surface) such as missile and artillery emplacements (if the accuracy is sufficient), soft military targets (such as troops or mobile missiles in the field), and targets such as surface BW storage sites that require high heat. In many cases, however, low-yield weapons may be inadequate for the task if the delivery system is not very accurate, the location of the target is not known precisely, or the target is spread over a large area.

If all the technical difficulties in designing and employing (particularly in hard rock) nuclear earth-penetrating weapons can be overcome, weapons detonated underground within currently feasible penetration distances could be relatively effective against hardened underground facilities within about 100 meters or so of the surface for moderate-yield weapons. As the NPR notes, however, "for defeat of very deep or larger underground facilities, penetrating weapons with large yields would be needed to collapse the facility."[51] As time passes and countries become aware of U.S. nuclear earth-penetrating weapon plans (assuming that they were reinstated), most will likely build their facilities much deeper. This in turn will increase the need for larger weapons or perhaps put the target beyond the reach of nuclear weapons.

Against BW and CW agents stored underground, earth-penetrating nuclear weapons would be effective down to at most a few tens of meters from the point of the explosion, which is to say that they would only be effective against shallow-buried storage sites. Even then, precise information about the facility location and design may be required to ensure the destruction of the entire agent (although using larger nuclear weapons could compensate for some lack of information—but at the cost of more collateral damage). Delivery of any nuclear weapon in today's network-centric, prompt-response tactical environment—not to mention the engineering design and associated firing, safing, and locating systems—would pose unprecedented command, control, communication, and intelligence problems.

One of the primary objectives of developing new low-yield weapons concepts is to reduce the collateral effects (fallout, blast, fires, and direct radiation) from nuclear explosions. While many targets may be effectively destroyed with yields of a few kilotons, many more will likely require tens of kilotons and some even hundreds of kilotons, particularly if an opponent has the time to assume an effective responsive posture during the years that weapon development, acquisition, and training will take. Even with relatively low-yield weapons, collateral effects would be significant unless the targets are located in isolated areas. Fallout could drift over other countries and cause cancers there. Thus there are significant reasons to question whether the new weapons concepts, if implemented, would have more than marginal utility or would prove much more "acceptable" than the weapons in the current stockpile.

Contribution of New Weapon Concepts to Fulfilling Strategic Missions

The NPR suggests that not only are there targets that the U.S. military cannot kill at present (or cannot kill without excessive collateral damage), but that having the capability to kill these targets is essential to an effective deterrent capability.[52] However, since (according to the Bush administration) the yields of the current U.S. stockpile of weapons are too large and the weapons too inaccurate, large collateral damage would result, bringing into question the credibility of their use and likelihood of deterrence. Hence the Bush administration has pushed for research on low-yield nuclear weapons, arguing that any restriction on such research undercuts efforts that could strengthen our ability to deter, or respond to, new or emerging threats. . . . [D]eterrence is in the eye of the adversary leadership. . . . In light of the widely-held view that the United States goes to great lengths to limit collateral damage, would a rogue state leader contemplating the use of WMD consider credible a response employing warheads with yields in the range of tens to hundreds of kilotons that could cause considerable collateral blast damage and radioactive contamination to civilian populations?[53]

Similarly, Keith Payne, who as deputy assistant secretary of defense was intimately involved in the formulation of the 2001 NPR, offers two reasons for studying new, low-yield nuclear weapons and the feasibility of threatening hardened and deeply buried facilities:

> First, to deter weapons of mass destruction (WMD) attacks on us and our allies and second, to dissuade rogues from investing in further WMD. . . . If we want to deter an opponent from attacking, the opponent must actually believe our threats to some degree. . . . Our existing arsenal's generally high yields and limited precision could inflict so many casualties that enemies may believe the U.S. president would be paralyzed by "self deterrence." America's popular aversion to causing "collateral damage" is well known. Precision, low-yield weapons that would inflict a much lower level of civilian casualties will appear much more credible to some opponents, and thus constitute a better deterrent to war. . . . Do we want rogue leaders to believe that they can create a sanctuary for themselves and their WMD just by digging? The point is to show the Saddam Husseins of the world that if they use WMD, there will be no place on—or under—the earth for them to hide.[54]

Payne's argument for being able to dissuade "rogue" states from further investment in WMD is that since the United States would have a credible deterrent to respond to their use, it would be pointless to continue to build such weapons.

Are these new weapons really necessary for deterrence and dissuasion, and if so, deterrence of what? Are they not perhaps even more suited for warfighting in general and particularly for a role in the "proactive counterproliferation" mission envisioned by the Bush preemption doctrine?

Deterrence of WMD Attacks

Just as during the cold war, the primary mission of U.S. nuclear weapons is to prevent a nuclear (or other WMD) attack on the U.S. homeland or upon its allies. This was accomplished in the past against a hostile Soviet Union in possession of tens of thousands of nuclear weapons. The threat of retaliation was real and credible as long as the United States maintained survivable forces. However, the National Security Strategy, the NPR, and the statements by Payne and others in the administration imply that in this post–cold war world, hostile regional powers in the possession of a few WMD may not be deterred from launching such attacks unless the United States develops new nuclear weapons capabilities.

Indeed (if the assertion is true), this cannot be considered some distant threat. Today, a number of potentially hostile states already have chemical and biological weapons and at least one (North Korea) very likely has nuclear weapons. The Bush administration appears to be arguing that until the United States develops new weapons concepts—which will be at least some five to ten years in the future—it may not be able to deter a nuclear or a BW/CW attack.[55] This would be frightening if it were true, but this assertion is not self-evident, and we believe it to be incorrect.

Central Deterrence. Would an identifiable regional power initiate an unprovoked WMD attack on the U.S. homeland thinking the United States did not have the "appropriate" nuclear weapons? It seems very unlikely. The credibility of an overwhelming U.S. response that would severely punish the state would be extremely high. This could not only take the form of retaliatory strikes (nuclear and non-nuclear), but would also likely be followed by an invasion and destruction of the regime (depending on the country and the circumstances). It would seem that nothing could be gained by such an attack and much (perhaps everything) could be lost.

If the enemy's attack were nuclear, he could certainly anticipate a nuclear strike in retaliation. Any reservations that the U.S. public might have about the use of nuclear weapons would likely disappear if the U.S. homeland had been struck with nuclear weapons. The same might be true of a nuclear retaliation to a biological or chemical attack that caused massive U.S. casualties.

This is not to argue that the most appropriate strategy in response would be a massive use of nuclear weapons, but simply that the attacker could not count on the United States not responding with massive force and thus would be deterred. Any lack of U.S. capability to attack hard and deeply buried targets or BW storage facilities would likely play no role in the decision by the aggressor, because the aggressor would be aware that the United States would have a wide range of other retaliatory options available from the current stockpile (including bombs and cruise missiles with low-yield capabilities).

Another argument (perhaps meant to be decisive) made for a new weapon to attack HDBTs is that the only thing that would restrain a Saddam Hussein–like dictator is a personal threat to his life.[56] Such a leader might launch a nuclear attack on the United States from the safety of his underground bunker no matter what the consequences to his country. Hence the only way to ensure that an attack on the United States will be deterred is to have an earth-penetrating weapon capable of destroying his bunker (preferably without collateral damage).

This seems implausible.[57] It assumes an adversary willing to lose country and power in order to have a chance at individual survival following a likely U.S. nuclear attack. On the contrary, U.S. opponents such as Saddam Hussein have exercised rational options to oppose the United States as effectively as their situations permitted and have evidenced no tendency to such suicidal Götterdämmerung. In addition, even if the premise were true, a leader may have other options for survival. For example, he could choose to hide in places other than HDBT sites that may be impossible for the United States to locate in wartime, as demonstrated by the difficulty of finding Osama bin Laden and Saddam Hussein. Or, since it will be some time before RNEPs can be available to attack HDBTs, an adversary may in the meantime build bunkers so deep that they would be beyond the reach of U.S. nuclear earth-penetrating weapons.

Deterrence of Assistance to Terrorists. The president and many others have also expressed the concern that some rogue state might give or sell nuclear weapons (or other WMD) to some terrorist organization, which could then use them on the U.S. homeland (presumably by smuggling the weapons into the country, since terrorist organizations do not have intercontinental missiles). The United States has stated that it would hold the cooperating state responsible if such an attack occurred. Since no state could be sure that the United States would not learn the identity of the state that supplied the weapons, much the same deterrence threats, nuclear and conventional, should apply as in the case of a direct attack. Even if a state cooperating with terrorists might rationally count on some degree of deniability, the new weapons under consideration would not diminish that expectation or in any way enhance deterrence against cooperation with terrorists (although they might be useful in a "preemptive" attack, as explained shortly).

Extended Deterrence. Extended deterrence is a situation in which the U.S. protective "nuclear umbrella" over its allies persuades the allies not to procure nuclear weapons to deter nuclear (and other WMD) attacks on them. In many ways, the extended deterrence requirements are the same as the central deterrence requirements, and the contribution of the new weapons under consideration would seem to be marginal.

If the regional power did not have the capability to reach the U.S. homeland with WMD, and the United States were sure of this fact (although there is always the possibility of unconventional means of delivery, for example, in the holds of cargo ships), then the U.S. extended deterrent could appear quite credible. In the case of most regional powers, the United States could respond to an attack on its allies with an overwhelming conventional attack that could severely damage the attacker's forces and infrastructure, perhaps causing its government to collapse, as in Iraq, even without resorting to nuclear weapons. This in itself is likely to be a sufficient deterrent from such WMD threats or attacks against U.S. allies.

In addition, the United States has a wide variety of nuclear weapons available, including, as noted, relatively low-yield bombs and cruise missiles. The aggressor could not count on U.S. reluctance to use these weapons, since if he struck at a U.S. ally or U.S. troops with WMD, the world would be horrified, and the onus of first use and the consequences of the war would be on the aggressor, not the responder. Hence restraints on the type of weapon available for U.S. response would be greatly diminished (if not lifted entirely), and the aggressor would know this—again providing a strong disincentive to the use of WMD.

In practice, if deterrence failed and WMD were used, the primary objective of a U.S. retaliatory strike would be to remove any immediate threat of further attacks with WMD or other weapons. Since it is likely that most of the WMD warheads and stockpiles would have been dispersed by this time, earth-penetrating weapons against storage or production sites would not be of much tactical value. WMD production facilities (if they could be found) are important military targets, but only in the longer time frame. In the interim, conventional attacks could block access to these facilities or storage sites (assuming the stockpile of materials had not been dispersed). Lack of a U.S. nuclear capability to attack these facilities would seem to be at most a marginal factor in an aggressor's decision to initiate a WMD attack on a U.S. ally.

If a regional power had a capability to strike at the U.S. homeland with nuclear weapons (or other WMD), the issue would become more complicated, and extended deterrence might be weakened.[58] Under these circumstances, a U.S. assessment and decision to intervene might hinge to a large degree on whether the president had extremely high confidence that an attack on the United States could be intercepted and defeated or that it had the capability to preemptively destroy (with high confidence) the aggressor's weapons before they could be launched.[59]

Under some circumstances, even without a capability to prevent an attack, the United States might still intervene in the hope that the threat of its overwhelming retaliatory power would deter a WMD attack on the U.S. homeland or its allies. At this point, the regional power's decision to resort to the use of WMD may well depend on whether he thinks that U.S. war aims are limited or the U.S. is intent on destroying the regime.[60] The capability of the United States to deter the use of WMD only applies to the case where its war aims are limited and there is no expressed or actual intent to overthrow the regime. If a hostile regime is convinced that the United States will overthrow it no matter what it does, any kind of deterrence is likely to be less effective, if it is effective at all. In that case, a hostile regime might resort to drastic means (such as a nuclear warning shot at the U.S. homeland) to try to forestall its destruction.

In short, the credibility and efficacy of extended deterrence, as of central deterrence, is not likely to depend on the development of new nuclear weapons concepts, but on such matters as U.S. conventional capabilities, the long-range weapon capabilities of the adversary, U.S. defenses, and U.S. war aims.

Deterrence of Conventional Attacks

The United States could in principle use nuclear threats against nuclear-armed regional powers in order to deter conventional aggression against their neighbors.[61] The credibility and effectiveness of such threats would, as just discussed, depend in part on whether the subject country might have a survivable capability to strike at the United States in retaliation and on the nature of U.S. war aims. Even without the capability to strike at the U.S. homeland, the regional power would likely have the capability to strike with nuclear weapons (and other WMDs) at U.S. forces or U.S. allies in the region if the United States initiated nuclear warfare.[62] To prevent this potentially disastrous escalation, the United States would have to initiate a broad counterforce strike throughout the country. But since the aggressor would have the initiative, he could likely protect these weapons by dispersal before the war begins, and hence new nuclear weapons might be of little value.

Deterring a conventional attack with nuclear threats is in many ways just a subset of the extended deterrence problem. However, an additional complication is that if the United States has an announced policy of initiating the use of nuclear weapons to defeat a conventional attack by a nuclear state, it might tend to cause the other side (if it were determined to attack) to use nuclear weapons (as well as CW and BW) from the beginning, since it would have nothing to lose. This could put the United States at a larger disadvantage than if it tried to deter a conventional attack with conventional weapons. Furthermore, the country being defended might think it is not in its best interest to become a nuclear battlefield (as did America's European allies in the North Atlantic Treaty Organization [NATO] during the cold war) and reject this nuclear warfighting strategy and perhaps distance itself from the United States.

In any event, beyond the technical and strategy problems, many political issues would arise from a publicly announced U.S. policy—which would be necessary if it were to act as a deterrent—of threatening to *initiate* a nuclear war against a country (see chapters 2 and 3). To compound these problems, the U.S. policy might also lead other countries to adopt similar policies.

Preventive War

Today many analysts and policymakers argue that the primary security interest of the United States is to prevent the proliferation of nuclear and other WMD to hostile states and to states that might cooperate with terrorists or insufficiently police their territory against WMD activities on the part of terrorists.[63] Since nuclear weapons (and, to a lesser degree, biological weapons) could inflict enormous damage on the United States, the concern is well justified. In the past, there have been many international efforts to prevent proliferation, including the Nuclear Non-Proliferation Treaty and the Chemical and Biological Weapons Conventions.

Some observers believe that these past methods have failed and that the United States must in the future take preemptive "proactive counterproliferation" military measures to disarm hostile countries. Such an approach, as noted in the introduction, is implied in the NPR and made explicit in both of President Bush's National Security Strategy reports and his National Strategy to Combat Weapons of Mass Destruction. Although it is not explicitly stated in any of these documents that nuclear weapons would be used for this task, statements by Payne and others imply that the only way to destroy certain WMD sites as well as other high-value targets would be to employ new nuclear weapons concepts. Moreover, since an enemy can disperse his stockpile of WMD if he feels war is imminent, following the administration's logic, the only way for the United States to destroy these weapons might be through a surprise nuclear attack.

The possibility that the administration may indeed be considering a policy of preemptive nuclear strikes is reflected in reported changes to U.S. war plans. Although no U.S. administration has agreed to completely forswear the first use of nuclear weapons, beginning with the Carter administration the United States generally agreed not to use nuclear weapons against non-nuclear states. The Clinton administration loosened this restriction by implying that it might retaliate with nuclear weapons against a non-nuclear state that used chemical or biological weapons against the United States or its allies. The Bush administration seems to have broadened this policy beyond one of retaliation against chemical or biological weapons to one of preemption—to prevent an attack by such weapons or perhaps even to destroy weapons production facilities before the weapons can be built.

A draft Doctrine for Joint Nuclear Operations written under the direction of Air Force general Richard B. Myers, chairman of the Joint Chiefs of Staff, and dated March 15, 2005, "envisions commanders requesting presidential approval to use them [nuclear weapons] to preempt an attack by a nation or a terrorist group using weapons of mass destruction." It also mentions "the option of using nuclear arms to destroy known enemy stockpiles of nuclear, biological or chemical weapons."[64] The draft "represents the Pentagon's first attempt to revise procedures to reflect the Bush preemption doctrine. A previous version, completed in 1995 during the Clinton administration, contains no mention of using nuclear weapons preemptively or specifically against threats from weapons of mass destruction."[65]

The new document argues that a preemptive attack could be undertaken in order to prevent the use of WMD by an enemy. But the document goes even further, suggesting it might be legitimate to use nuclear weapons preemptively merely as a "demonstration of U.S. intent and capability to use nuclear weapons to deter adversary WMD use."[66] The document "acknowledges that 'the belligerent that initiates nuclear warfare may find itself the target of world condemnation' but adds that 'no customary or conventional international law prohibits nations from employing nuclear weapons in armed conflict.'"[67]

The Bush administration has refused to acknowledge that it has adopted these specific changes in U.S. policy. While the document in question was unclassified and posted on a Pentagon website, General Myers, at a press briefing on September 20, 2005, with Secretary of Defense Donald Rumsfeld, insisted that it was not authoritative, being just a draft by colonels and not having been through the final approval stages in the Pentagon. The general made no effort to clarify what the new Doctrine for Joint Nuclear Operations is likely to look like when finally adopted. Since then, the document has been removed from the website and no further clarifying comments have been made by the administration.

However, previous reports that the United States has included nuclear options in contingency war plans drawn up against Iran and North Korea (as part of the worldwide Global Strike Plan developed by Strategic Command [Stratcom], which is responsible for U.S. nuclear planning) may lend credence to this policy change: "The global strike plan holds the nuclear option in reserve if intelligence suggests an 'imminent' launch of an enemy nuclear strike on the United States or if there is a need to destroy hard-to-reach targets." This plan, completed in November 2003, put in place "for the first time a preemptive and offensive strike capability against Iran and North Korea," which two months later was certified to the defense secretary and the president.[68]

In the case of Iran, the United States acknowledges that Iran does not now have nuclear weapons and could not produce them for a number of years. However, it has condemned Iran's effort to develop a civilian nuclear power program as a cover for it to build nuclear weapons. While trying to organize the world to force Iran to abandon its nuclear enrichment and nuclear reactor programs, the United States has reportedly drawn up war plans to attack these nuclear facilities before they become operational. Because some of these facilities are deep underground, it is reported that the Pentagon was ordered to draw up plans to use the earth-penetrating B-61 nuclear bomb to attack these facilities. Despite misgivings on the part of the military about a nuclear option, the White House reportedly is unwilling to remove this option from its war plans.[69]

The world seems to have taken the apparent new nuclear preemption doctrine seriously. For example, Andrei Kokoshin, former secretary of the Russian Security Council, expressed alarm at the direction U.S. policy appeared to be taking. He warned that an attempt to remove any distinction between nuclear and conventional weapons in combat could lead Russia to reconsider its basic policies and expenditures.[70] Other countries may also take note of this apparent shift in U.S. policy and act accordingly.

In practice, whether or not nuclear weapons are used, a "disarming counterforce first strike" designed to destroy an adversary's WMD could prove ineffective.[71] In some cases, such as nuclear reactors used to produce nuclear weapons materials, the target may be obvious and easy to destroy with conventional weapons, although at the risk of creating considerable fallout. But more generally, intelligence on the extent of the WMD program (particularly

CW and BW) may be incomplete, since programs can be dispersed and hard to identify. If weapons had already been produced, implementation would be even more difficult, since the weapons could be protected by dispersal, deception, hardening, or placing them in urban areas where they would be politically difficult to attack (because of likely civilian deaths), even if they could be located.

Even if the attack were fairly successful (as against a nuclear reactor), it might mean only a delay in the program, while driving it into less targetable channels (perhaps underground or in hidden gas centrifuges). Moreover, the destruction caused by the U.S. attack would likely increase the hostility toward the United States, both by the leadership and the people who had suffered "collateral damage," persuading the adversary to redouble its efforts.

Thus it seems likely that the only way to ensure that the proactive counterproliferation doctrine would work would be to invade and overthrow the regime. In some cases, the United States may have no choice, since a counterforce strike (particularly if it was not completely successful) could provoke a retaliatory attack or perhaps a general war on U.S. forces or allies in the region (or on the U.S. homeland if the country had the capability to deliver the weapons).[72]

Consider the case of North Korea. Under the Agreed Framework of 1994, drawn up during the Clinton administration, North Korea promised to halt its nuclear program, but progress became very slow after a Republican majority was elected to Congress late that year. Some commitments on both sides were not met; others were delayed. The Bush administration abandoned the overall negotiating approach, and no meaningful negotiations occurred at first. Late in 2002 the United States received intelligence to the effect that North Korea had begun a uranium-enrichment program. Following this, both parties acknowledged the Agreed Framework was essentially defunct. Before the signing of the Agreed Framework, North Korea was suspected of having reprocessed enough fuel rods from its nuclear reactors to produce plutonium for one or two nuclear weapons. This issue was to have been resolved by International Atomic Energy Agency (IAEA) inspections at a later time but never was. After the agreement broke down, North Korea started reprocessing again, perhaps extracting enough plutonium to produce six or more nuclear warheads.[73]

President Bush and Japan's prime minister Junichiro Koizumi, following their summit in 2003, stated that they "would not tolerate" a nuclear-armed North Korea. A six-party negotiation was undertaken (by North Korea, the United States, South Korea, China, Japan, and Russia) to resolve the issue. In

September 2005, after lengthy negotiations in the course of which the United States showed more flexibility, a breakthrough appeared to have occurred, with North Korea agreeing to give up its nuclear weapons, rejoin the Nuclear Non-Proliferation Treaty (NPT), and allow inspections of its facilities in exchange for normalization of relations, security guarantees, and economic aid, to include assistance in developing a civilian nuclear program. The proposed agreement essentially follows proposals made by China and South Korea. However, the details of a final agreement (at the time of this writing) have yet to be resolved, the provision for a North Korean civilian nuclear program being particularly contentious. Negotiations could break down, as they have in the past.

If negotiations ultimately fail, the implication of the Bush doctrine is that the United States might try to disarm North Korea of its nuclear weapons by a military strike. Intermediate steps such as a blockade of North Korea appear more likely in the beginning, but these are acts of war, and North Korea has stated it would construe them as such. As a result, escalation is a clear possibility if negotiations break down.

North Korea already has a stockpile of CW and BW weapons and, as noted, is thought to have perhaps six or more nuclear weapons, a number that may well grow with time.[74] Locating North Korea's nuclear weapons would be very difficult, if not impossible (as would obviously be the case with CW or BW warheads that could be dispersed with or without their delivery systems). At best, the United States might be able to strike at the identified nuclear production reactor and reprocessing plant in Yongbyon and a number of suspect military sites. In retaliation for such an attack, North Korea has stated that it would unleash a massive attack (presumably with its whole arsenal of conventional and unconventional weapons) on South Korea and the U.S. troops stationed there.[75]

In addition, North Korea might launch CW, BW, or nuclear missile attacks on U.S. bases in Japan or even threaten Japanese cities to try to persuade them to not let the United States use Japanese military bases (and could attack them if Japan did not acquiesce).[76] Nuclear attacks on the relatively small number of U.S. bases in Japan and South Korea could prove crippling to U.S. military operations in the area for some time. In addition, the consequences of such a confrontation for U.S.-Japanese relations or for the military balance in Asia could be significant, particularly if Japan lost confidence in the United States and sought to defend itself in the future through a larger conventional force or perhaps nuclear weapons. Much the same rationale holds for South Korea, whose support of U.S. operations would be essential.

Also of concern are the thousands of artillery pieces and hundreds of missiles that North Korea possesses that are within striking range of the more than 10 million people in Seoul, which is within 40 kilometers of the Demilitarized Zone (DMZ) separating the North from the South. To act as a deterrent against a U.S. preventive war, the North could threaten (and execute if necessary) a retaliatory attack against Seoul. Unless this North Korean firepower could be suppressed, the immediate consequences could be devastating, since this array of artillery is capable of killing "literally millions" in the city within a very short time.[77]

To have a chance, the United States would probably have to procure perhaps hundreds of new missiles with small nuclear weapons, maintain them on high alert, and maintain constant surveillance of the area. Even then the task would be difficult, since during the initial U.S. attack most of the North Korean artillery might be in hardened shelters. Even if only 10 or 20 percent of its artillery and short-range missiles survived, it could still devastate Seoul. Since longer-range missiles in its rear might also survive, a nuclear or chemical attack would not even have to rely on close-in artillery or missiles.

Thus even with the procurement of many new nuclear weapons and missiles and the likelihood of eventual "victory," a U.S.-initiated war could still result in many thousands of American casualties and destruction in South and North Korea on a massive scale.[78] (A war today, when the United States has very limited capability to destroy the threatening armaments, would bring much worse results.)

North Korea might be considered an extreme case. In other situations involving other countries, the consequences of a preventive war aimed at disarmament might not be so adverse or immediate. On the other hand, countries such as Iran and Pakistan, which are much larger and more populous, could be more difficult to disarm before devastating retaliatory action in some form is taken. A long, bloody, and perhaps inconclusive war would also be a likely consequence. If the country's weapons were dispersed beforehand, it is not clear that nuclear weapons (new or old) would be at all helpful in preventing either retaliation or a long destructive war.

Dissuasion

The NPR argues that "systems capable of striking a wide range of targets throughout an adversary's territory may dissuade a potential adversary from pursuing threatening capabilities" (p. 12). If the United States fields HDBT-killers and/or other low-yield weapons, so the argument goes, a regional power will desist in procuring and deploying further WMD because it will be deterred from attacking the United States or its allies by these new weapons. Since the WMD would then have no utility, it would be futile to procure the weapons.[79] Previously, we argued that a regional power may indeed be deterred from attacking the United States or its allies with WMD, but it probably has little to do with any new weapons concepts, since the current stockpile as well as the formidable conventional power of the United States would be a sufficient deterrent.

A more candid (but politically risky) argument for dissuasion might be advanced. Because the United States will have the capability to launch a preventive nuclear attack to destroy the rogue's WMD (with supposedly limited collateral damage), possessing WMD will be of no value to the rogue or could even be counterproductive since possession would likely increase the possibility of a nuclear attack by the United States.

In general, either argument assumes a historically unlikely premise, namely, that an opponent will not build otherwise effective weapons because the United States has a weapon that can destroy certain storage or deployment sites. The usual historical outcome has been, as during the cold war and the tense periods leading up to other wars, that arms competition has been enhanced and possibly focused in certain directions. More specifically, in the current international environment, the dissuasion argument for new nuclear weapons overlooks the deterrence role of WMD from a regional power's point of view, particularly if the United States is hostile toward it. The Bush doctrine of preventive war (even without a nuclear threat) provides a strong incentive for such powers to try to obtain WMD to defend themselves by providing a potential deterrent to a U.S. attack, since a conventional deterrent is unlikely to be sufficient against massive U.S. conventional power.[80] If, in addition, the U.S. nuclear posture contemplates using nuclear weapons against such states, they may be further encouraged to build such weapons and to take measures (dispersal, mobility, placing them near cities, deception, and so on) to protect them from a U.S. preventive attack. Thus if the United States maintains a policy of preventive war and were actually to proceed with its plans to develop and deploy new "usable" nuclear weapons, the result may be more proliferation rather than dissuasion.

Strategic Implications of New Nuclear Weapons and the Bush Doctrine

In sum, the new nuclear weapons concepts are unlikely to achieve their announced objectives and would achieve any U.S. objective only at high cost in collateral effects and operational problems. Though these weapons will not exist for some time, and thus could not be expected to affect current problems of proliferation directly, if restarted, the new nuclear weapons program could, coupled with a preventive war doctrine, send strong signals about the direction of U.S. policy.

Strategic Consequences of the New Nuclear Declaratory Posture

In general, the principal means used to stop the spread of nuclear weapons to date have been a combination of the multilateral nuclear nonproliferation regime discussed in preceding chapters and the threat or use of force. The United States has been in the forefront of the nonproliferation effort for decades. U.S. actions were important in preventing nuclear proliferation in South Korea, Taiwan, Ukraine, Argentina, and Brazil, and most recently, Iraq and (with the United Kingdom's assistance) Libya. Indeed, had the United States and other states not proposed and pushed the negotiation of the Nuclear Non-Proliferation Treaty in the 1960s and then worked hard to gain adherence to that treaty by countries around the world, many more countries than the present eight or nine would have nuclear weapons today.

Adherence to a nonproliferation regime is conditional on a state's judgment that its security situation and domestic politics are better served by adherence than otherwise. When states do not take that view, the United States and other concerned countries can choose to make no response (as has been the case with France, China, Israel, India, and Pakistan) or to resort to "coercive diplomacy," which consists of combining military, economic, and related threats "with diplomatic efforts to persuade an opponent to stop or undo his effort to alter a status quo situation that itself endangers the peace."[81] These can be enforcement efforts supported by the UN Security Council, as in the case of Iraq from 1991 to March 2003; multilateral attempts at persuasion by several concerned countries in conjunction with the IAEA, as in the case of North Korea in 1994; or unilateral measures, as in earlier cases of U.S. pressure on Taiwan and South Korea. This coercive diplomacy may involve positive incentives as well as threats, as was the case when the United States and Russia persuaded Ukraine to abandon its large stock of deployed nuclear weapons systems after the breakup of the Soviet Union.

In the extreme, coercive diplomacy can become a policy of counterproliferation, with military force used to prevent or reverse proliferation. Such acts if undertaken without international sanction would not be universally accepted as part of the normal approaches to nonproliferation. They would more likely be considered acts of aggression (see chapter 2).

The Bush administration's new Nuclear Posture, as noted earlier, calls for broadening possible nuclear missions, increasing support to the nuclear infrastructure, and shortening the interval before any resumption of nuclear testing. Many analysts consider this inconsistent with the NPT requirement that the United States and other nuclear weapon NPT members rely on negotiations to reduce and eventually eliminate their nuclear weapons, as discussed in chapter 3. Thereby the new posture may weaken the nonproliferation regime, both because the United States would be seen as not meeting its obligations and because its projection capabilities would make it more dangerous to present or future opponents. The question then is does the doctrine provide any countervailing positive benefits to the nuclear nonproliferation regime?

Reaction of Other States.   The NPR mentions certain countries specifically as being of concern in connection with the nuclear posture: North Korea, Iraq, Iran, Syria, Libya, and China (primarily because of a conflict over Taiwan). In addition, the National Strategy implicitly warns Russia (or any other state) not to challenge U.S. hegemony. Are there any discernible consequences yet?

Russia is modernizing its nuclear force and has retained a large stockpile of tactical nuclear weapons.[82] In October 2003 Minister of Defense Sergei Ivanov issued a "White Paper" providing an elaboration of the Russian Military Doctrine issued in 2000.[83] Both documents indicate that there are two roles for Russia's nuclear weapons: deterrence of an attack on Russia and, if deterrence fails, the use of a small number of weapons to "de-escalate" the conflict. This latter role is believed necessary because of the weakness of Russian conventional forces. If Russia were attacked and its conventional defense was failing, Russia might use a small number of nuclear weapons to demonstrate its resolve and to shock the other side into stopping the conflict. This policy is similar to NATO's Flexible Response Doctrine during the cold war when the use of limited nuclear strikes was contemplated because of the fear that the Warsaw Pact could overrun Western Europe with its superior conventional forces.

One new element to Russia's defense policy introduced by Ivanov (apparently following the example of the United States) was that Russia "can no longer completely rule out preventive use of force if demanded by the interests of Russia or its alliance commitments."[84] While this statement does not refer to nuclear weapons explicitly, it seems likely any U.S. move to develop new, more "usable" weapons would give Russia an impetus to reintegrate nuclear weapons into its general fighting forces and to consider wider use of these weapons.

China may be less concerned about new U.S. nuclear weapons than about U.S. ballistic missile defense systems, particularly the National Missile Defense (NMD) system (designed to protect the U.S. homeland), but also theater defenses if they are given to Taiwan. Although the idea of NMD is not new, it was strongly emphasized in the NPR, particularly as a shield to allow U.S. intervention abroad, and it is one of the "legs" of the New Triad. In order to sustain its deterrence capability, China (currently with only about twenty vulnerable ICBMs) has an incentive from the NPR to expand its ICBM force and perhaps to develop and deploy MIRVs, SLBMs, and cruise missiles to overcome or go around any future U.S. NMD system. From all evidence to date, these are programs that the recent and current Chinese leaderships would rather not have to pay for, in view of the very large and costly tasks the domestic economy faces, but the combination of new U.S. policies with respect to nuclear weapons and renewed commitment to the defense of Taiwan may have reinforced the hand of those within the Chinese government who argue for more nuclear weapons programs. Perhaps the least surprising outcome, given Chinese caution in security matters, is that China will lay the groundwork for a larger, less vulnerable missile force of various types but will await actual developments in the United States before sizing its own nuclear weapons programs.[85]

The Iraq and Libya situations have been "resolved," at least temporarily, without recourse to any of the systems or initiatives spelled out in the NPR, since those are not yet in service. To all appearances, Iran and North Korea have speeded up their nuclear programs.[86] Syria may not be an immediate problem, given the presence for now at least of U.S. troops in Iraq. The United States is building what appear to be major bases in Iraq and may have a long-term military presence there. Such a presence would surely have an influence, positive and negative, on developments in the Middle East. To the extent that Iran feels the continuing threat from U.S. military forces in the entire region, these forces could cause Iran to abandon its nuclear program (which Iran claims is for peaceful energy purposes but the United States claims to be for the development of nuclear weapons) or to determine that its only protection against a U.S. attack lies in the pursuit of nuclear weapons.

Not mentioned in the NPR are some other states of concern, principally Pakistan and Saudi Arabia. Saudi Arabia stated on at least two occasions in 2003 that it was reconsidering its adherence to the NPT.[87] Given the country's resources and the ambiguous record of its government (and the Saudi elite) toward extremist groups, this should be cause for concern. It is certainly not an indication of increased support for the nonproliferation regime.

Pakistan has long been of concern as well, for the obvious reasons: presence of nuclear weapons and a nuclear weapon infrastructure; leading participation in the nuclear weapon black market, perhaps now at an end; presence of organized extremist groups, including al Qaeda; and a fragile, if cooperative, dictatorial government. Although Pakistan may have become more cooperative with the United States on important counterterrorism objectives in the course of the past year or two, as far as public knowledge goes, it has not become more transparent in its nuclear weapons operations, nor has it made any move to support the nuclear nonproliferation regime broadly, other than minimal action, under considerable U.S. pressure, to stop the A. Q. Khan operation (see chapter 4). Whatever Pakistan has done, there seems to be little or no impact from the change in U.S. declaratory nuclear policy yet, as distinct from other U.S. policies.

All of the countries just discussed except perhaps Saudi Arabia are believed to have some form of WMD capabilities.[88] Most of them have HDBTs.

Domestic Support. The importance of domestic support for foreign and security policies cannot be overemphasized, but its salience probably depends on whether the electorate and its various elites connect those policies with their immediate safety. In the past, the American electorate resoundingly rejected nuclear policies that were perceived to be dangerous. One may debate whether the new U.S. nuclear and associated policies have increased or decreased the nuclear danger at least to U.S. forces abroad and perhaps (assuming a risk of nuclear terrorism) to people within the United States. That debate, however, has not yet begun to take place in the broader public. The recent changes in nuclear posture (force structure, concepts of operations, and nuclear missions) and in national strategy have only had a modest political impact in the United States. This probably stems partly from ignorance of the new U.S. nuclear posture and partly from the security-first attitude generated by the terrorist attacks of September 11, 2001, coupled perhaps with some confusion in the public's mind regarding the need for nuclear weapons to deal with hostile WMD capabilities. However, the fact that Congress for the second year failed to fund RNEP, new weapons concepts, or preparations for greater readiness for nuclear testing (although congressional action was not accompanied by a general public awareness of the issues) may demonstrate a widening opposition in Congress to at least the new nuclear weapons aspects of the Bush doctrine.

The broader administration strategic posture, characterized by its stands in Afghanistan and especially Iraq, and by its downgrading or rejection of most forms of arms control and cooperative security, have on the other hand generated considerable political controversy, deepening the split within the U.S. electorate and Congress, as well as within U.S. alliances. An aggressive strategic posture, given its costs in lives and money, will be difficult to sustain in any case, and adding to it an aggressive nuclear element that has no obvious deterrent role may make the overall policy even more controversial and difficult to sustain. This will particularly be the case if the public sees what it regards as unnecessary chances taken against other nuclear weapons–armed states.

This conundrum highlights the need for more carefully thought-out tools for dealing with the nuclear threat in a world where very insecure, sometimes isolated countries, some with fragile governance, have acquired nuclear weapons and where a network of largely less developed countries was able to maintain an effective black market in nuclear weapons technology and materials for a number of years. The United States may have to devise a strategy for dealing with a world where such countries in fact have nuclear weapons or at least can acquire them relatively quickly. That strategy may involve the present tools but will probably need to include some new ones. To the extent that the Bush administration has recognized that the situation has changed from that what it was in the first fifty years of the nuclear age, we believe that it is to be commended. The tools devised, however, for the reasons argued in this chapter, are inadequate to the challenge, most particularly on two counts: they fail to enlist effectively the cooperation of other countries, and they provide incentives for the spread of nuclear weapons capabilities, despite the administration's intentions.

Strategic Consequences of the Use of Nuclear Weapons

If new low-yield nuclear weapons (or, for that matter, current low-yield nuclear bombs and cruise missiles) were actually used by the United States, what would be the likely consequences? Aside from collateral damage in general, discussed earlier, there are physical, social, and economic effects to consider from the use of five to ten 10-kiloton weapons outside of cities in some potential future conflict, perhaps in North Korea or Iran. The range of five to ten seems appropriate because, given the number of HDBTs and possible sites containing biological warfare agents, we think it unlikely that fewer nuclear weapons would achieve much of a tactical advantage. On the other hand, the political consequences will not be proportional to the number of weapons used. Indeed, they are very difficult to predict in other than general terms.

Five to ten nuclear explosions of 10 kilotons each a few meters below ground would physically destroy most buildings within 1–2 kilometers of each explosion; force prompt evacuation to save lives within about 100 square kilometers of each explosion; contaminate buildings, grounds, livestock, and crops over thousands of square kilometers (a significant fraction of some countries, such as North Korea); and, depending on wind and rain, create sufficient fallout to cause evacuation or sheltering as much as thousands of kilometers downwind. In the example of North Korea, precautionary evacuation or decontamination measures would probably be deemed necessary in South Korea and Japan. Measurable radioactivity would be detected around the world.

If active nuclear reactors or spent fuel storage sites were part of the target set, the contamination would be multiplied several fold, depending on the history of the reactor or fuel storage. If biological weapon materials were targeted, it would be all but impossible to guarantee that none of the material would survive and be dispersed, although, with more precise targeting than is now known to be available, and not too deep burial, most of it probably would be destroyed.

These effects, while destructive and dramatic, are probably comparable to those of an all-out conventional war in terms of deaths and direct costs to the country struck, though not in terms of the psychological and political impact. The extent to which radioactive fallout will add to the chemical contamination caused by war and its attendant destruction will depend on the situation. Certainly, the three-year-long war in Korea in the 1950s was far more destructive than five or ten nuclear explosions outside of cities would be if they brought an end to the hostilities and were all that happened. Of course, wars seldom end on any predictable schedule. If the nuclear weapons are not decisive, further conventional and nuclear damage will occur.

While the physical effects of a few nuclear explosions may be comparable to the physical effects of a large-scale conventional war, the social effects of atomic bombing cannot be overestimated and are likely to multiply the economic effects due to the physical consequences of the bombing alone. People in large numbers may leave areas that remain livable, compounding the problems of dealing with the aftermath. There would be lasting concerns over the carcinogenic and mutagenic effects of radiation exposure. Those concerns, which would extend to neighboring countries, would affect the economics and politics of recovery whether they were medically warranted or not.

Militarily, the use of nuclear weapons by the United States may or may not be decisive and indeed could prove counterproductive, as discussed in the early sections of this chapter. If the weapons were targeted against isolated bunkers and storage sites of weapons that had already been dispersed, the military impact could be minimal. On the other hand, if the country targeted already has nuclear weapons and they are in a deliverable and survivable configuration, those weapons could be used quite effectively against U.S. targets, particularly against U.S. targets in the region essential to U.S. prosecution of the war. Should such use occur, either preemptively or in response to U.S. use of nuclear weapons, the successful prosecution of the war with conventional forces would be in question. The United States could go on to devastate the country with a broad use of nuclear weapons, but the human costs there and the physical damage in neighboring countries could be extremely severe, vastly worse than the damage due to one or a few explosions on military targets away from cities.

Proliferation and Stability. Actual combat use of nuclear weapons by the United States could have a significant effect on nuclear proliferation and world stability. Some non-nuclear countries might react by being cowed, cooperative, and submissive for a time at least, whereas others might determine that they should themselves be armed with nuclear weapons. The horrors of Hiroshima and Nagasaki did not prevent some other countries from acquiring nuclear forces as soon as they were able. Many more refrained, but they did so in the presence of and explicitly relying on a security regime (such as NATO and, in some cases, other alliances or guarantees) that seemed preferable to them to acquiring nuclear weapons. Thus it is likely that the consequences of U.S. or other use of a nuclear weapon would depend heavily on the circumstances and on what security arrangements other than acquiring individual nuclear deterrents were available and credible.

If not only the devastation attendant were made obvious, as after Hiroshima, but also the military effectiveness against concentrated targets, the next use of nuclear weapons would seem unlikely to be the last. Given that the U.S. homeland and, to a lesser extent, U.S. projection capabilities can only effectively be threatened by other states through the use of nuclear weapons, the United States would likely find the world a much more dangerous and less secure place after any effective use of nuclear weapons. This is a strong argument in our view for subordinating any new nuclear weapon development to the needs of establishing a nuclear nonproliferation regime that provides security to all adherents.

Other Political Consequences of Nuclear Use

The effect of nuclear weapons use on nuclear weapon–armed states such as Russia, China, and India will also depend on circumstances, although nationalistic and militaristic elements are likely to be strengthened in these countries as in others. Since the United States is the leading model in military matters for most countries, U.S. use of nuclear weapons will almost surely prompt nuclear advocates everywhere to press for the modernization of nuclear weapons systems, expansion of nuclear missions, and nuclear testing.

The community of democratic states committed to increasing the effectiveness of international law and observing the primacy of nonviolent means of settling disputes, a community that includes the most effective and powerful U.S. allies, would surely split from the United States on any use of nuclear weapons that did not seem warranted to them by the urgency of the situation, whether first use or not. Lower yields and other means of minimizing casualties would probably help assuage the reaction if the community considered nuclear weapon use justified in the first place. On the other hand, there have been no nuclear weapons detonated on or near people in sixty years, and no atmospheric tests in a decade, so media coverage of whatever effects do occur is likely to emphasize the damage.

U.S. first use would very likely divide the U.S. electorate more deeply along the current fault lines. U.S. second use would be far more generally accepted, but there still would be considerable revulsion as the human damage done became clear. The factions within the U.S. electorate referred to in the previous section could become quite embittered, especially in the event of U.S. first use. One side, in order to justify the U.S. action, would have to appeal even more to public fears than was the case in defending the U.S. invasion of Iraq, while the other side would condemn the U.S. action even more strongly than it condemned the Iraq invasion. The middle ground in the public mind, which is occupied by deterrence assisted by arms control that nuclear policy successfully espoused from Hiroshima on, could be replaced by essentially unbridgeable divides between those who would consider nuclear weapons as ordinary, indeed necessary, instruments of war and those who would continue to look at them as posing a danger to the whole human race. Any strategy that requires long-term commitments of lives and money but that produces deep and bitter splits in public opinion is likely to falter.

Conclusion

George W. Bush's National Security Strategy asserts that the United States has a global duty to maintain world peace and spread liberal democracy. To carry out this mission, the United States must (it is argued) maintain global military hegemony permanently and must block any challenge to its power. States that are seeking weapons of mass destruction can pose a significant threat to these goals and must in some cases be dealt with by preventive war ("proactive counterproliferation").

The Bush administration undertook the Nuclear Posture Review to refocus the military to meet the challenges of the post–cold war world. It created a New Triad (integrating conventional and nuclear forces as well as offensive and defensive forces) and announced new broad missions. To meet the declared inadequacies of the current nuclear arsenal, it argued, the United States needed new, smaller nuclear weapons that could lower collateral civilian damage and thus make the use of nuclear weapons more "credible" to opponents to be deterred or dissuaded from acquiring WMD or taking other actions hostile to the United States.

However, the new proposed weapons may not be effective for destroying WMD, since most of the adversary's WMD would likely be dispersed or hidden before any military confrontation with the United States. For hard underground targets, relatively small nuclear weapons (perhaps with yields of 10–50 kilotons) could be effective if the bunkers are not buried too deeply. But potential adversaries could build deeper bunkers that would require larger weapons or (if deep enough) even make the bunkers invulnerable to nuclear weapons. Even if small nuclear weapons were effective, unless the targets are isolated far from urban areas, there could be considerable collateral damage to civilian populations, which would call into question the fundamental rationale for new weapons.

Our analysis indicates that the new weapons concepts advanced to date seem to have little to do with deterrence of a nuclear (or other WMD) attack on the United States or its allies. Instead, they appear to be geared toward a warfighting role. Nuclear warfighting, however, could only give the United States a temporary and probably marginal advantage over the forces it already has. In the longer term, such a warfighting posture could lead more countries to seek nuclear armaments and to integrate them into their fighting forces, so as to limit U.S. reach and also to keep up with dangerous neighbors.

Actual use of such new weapons in combat in theaters where the United States is attempting to intervene is likely to produce dire consequences there, particularly if the other side retaliates with nuclear weapons. Ports, airbases, and aircraft carriers in or near the area targeted could be wiped out, and the country to be occupied by the United States is likely to be contaminated—as may neighboring countries. Beyond the area subjected to a nuclear attack, the reaction to U.S. nuclear use will almost surely be to strengthen the hand of those—in Russia, China, India, and elsewhere—who argue that a modern, integrated, tested nuclear force is necessary for their security. Both in the

United States and abroad, U.S. nuclear use, depending on the circumstances, could be attended by considerable revulsion and controversy, and a deeper political split than has occurred to date.

Thus a strategy that makes the use of nuclear weapons more acceptable would seem to run counter to U.S. strategic interests. Nuclear weapons are increasingly easy to acquire and have a significant capability to neutralize conventional advantages. An administration committed to having a free hand in intervening abroad militarily should want to do everything it can to remove nuclear weapons from any possible conflict and to line up as much help as possible in making their acquisition less easy. Yet the overt new threat of using nuclear weapons for military objectives, coupled with the Bush administration's devaluing of international instruments, is likely to have just the opposite effect: incentives to acquire nuclear weapons to deter U.S. military actions will increase while U.S. capabilities to monitor and get cooperation in preventing nuclear weapon development will decrease. The dominant incentive in decisions having to do with nuclear weapons acquisition, deployment, and transfer will continue to be security, with domestic politics an important factor, as has been the case to date. What will be different is that those decisions will be made in the realization that the United States no longer supports or rewards adherence to the prior nuclear norms of behavior, but rather reemphasizes the military utility of nuclear weapons as tools of warfare. Although a case can certainly be made that the international nonproliferation regime needs strengthening to prevent the spread of nuclear weapons (and other WMD), a National Security Strategy that contemplates preventive war, coupled with a policy that integrates nuclear weapons better into the armed forces and gives them more missions, runs counter to this goal.

Notes

1. The National Security Strategy of the United States of America (White House, September 2002 and March 2006). The 2006 version of the document reviewed the progress made by the administration in implementing the strategy in the ensuing four years, since 2002. No fundamental changes in the strategy were suggested in the latest version. Quotation from National Security Strategy (2006), p. 1. Since there are about fifty countries in the world that are not democracies, and many others that are largely democracies in name only, a formidable—and very expensive—job would seem to lie ahead for America. For a detailed discussion of the doctrine see, for example, Edward Rhodes, "The Imperial Logic of Bush's Liberal Agenda," *Survival* 45 (Spring 2003): 131–54.

2. "Our forces will be strong enough to dissuade potential adversaries from pursuing a military build-up in hopes of surpassing, or equaling, the power of the United States." The National Security Strategy (2002), pp. 29–30. "America has, and intends to keep, military strength beyond challenge—thereby making the destabilizing arms races

of other eras pointless, and limiting rivalries to trade and other pursuits of peace." President George W. Bush, West Point, New York, July 1, 2002.

3. Weapons of mass destruction are usually defined as nuclear, biological, and chemical weapons. However, many analysts argue that nuclear weapons are the only true weapon of mass destruction. See, for example, Greg Easterbrook, "The Meaninglessness of 'WMD,'" *New Republic,* October 7, 2002, pp. 22–25.

4. Bush, West Point, New York, July 1, 2002; and The National Security Strategy (2002), p. 17.

5. All references and quotations from the Nuclear Posture Review (hereafter cited as NPR) throughout this chapter are from the leaked excerpts of the report posted on the Global Security website (www.globalsecurity.org/wmd/library/policy/dod/npr.htm). For the Pentagon's unclassified briefing describing the major points of the NPR, see *Findings of the Nuclear Posture Review,* January 9, 2002 (www.defenselink.mil/news/Jan2002/ 020109-D-6570C-001.pdf).

6. Possible future conflict with a number of regional powers was envisioned, notably North Korea, Iraq, Iran, Syria, and Libya, all of which at that time were thought to be sponsoring or harboring terrorists and to have active WMD and missile programs. NPR, p. 6.

7. "The greater the threat, the greater is the risk of inaction—and the more compelling the case for taking anticipatory action to defend ourselves, even if uncertainty remains as to the time and place of the enemy's attack. To forestall or prevent such hostile acts by our adversaries, the United States will, if necessary, act preemptively." The National Security Strategy (2002), p. 14.

8. "U.S. Nuclear Forces, 2006," *Bulletin of the Atomic Scientists* 62 (January/February 2006): 68–71.

9. Ibid. According to the NPR, there were almost 8,000 warheads in the active stockpile in 2001, plus an undisclosed additional number in the inactive stockpile (p. 32). The active stockpile includes deployed weapons (strategic and nonstrategic) and those that are not deployed but are maintained in a ready-for-use mode. Inactive stockpile weapons do not have tritium and other limited life components installed and would take longer to deploy.

10. See NPR, p. 19: "The planned force structure for 2012 comprises 14 Trident SSBNs (with two of the 14 in overhaul at any time), 500 Minuteman III ICBMs, 76 B-52H bombers, and 21 B-2 bombers." The Bush administration has stated that "operationally deployed" does not apply to warheads associated with delivery vehicles that are being overhauled or undergoing repairs. Under the treaty, the warheads in the inactive stockpile or reserve need not be destroyed and can be redeployed after 2012 when the treaty expires, assuming no subsequent agreement deals with them.

11. See, for example, "U.S. Nuclear Forces, 2005," and "U.S. Nuclear Weapons Stockpile, July 1998," *Bulletin of the Atomic Scientists* 54 (July/August 1998): 70.

12. "Statement by Senator Dianne Feinstein (CA) on Low-Yield Nuclear Weapons," *Congressional Record* (May 20, 2003), p. S6664 (frwebgate.access.gpo.gov/cgi-bin/ getpage.cgi?position=all&page=S6664&dbname=2003_record).

13. "Nuclear Weapons Database: United States Arsenal," Center for Defense Information (www.cdi.org/issues/nukef&f/database/usnukes.html).

14. This facility would be able to produce approximately 100–200 plutonium pits per year. A plutonium pit, when combined with high explosives, is the "primary" or "trigger" for a thermonuclear weapon. It can also be an atomic weapon in its own right.

15. For example, the following statement by Mira R. Ricardel, the acting assistant secretary of defense for international security policy, was placed in the record at a congressional hearing in April 2005: "We don't need a smaller Cold War era nuclear stockpile; we need capabilities appropriate for 21st century threats. That means we need to conduct a range of studies on potential weapon concepts including the completion of the Robust Nuclear Earth Penetrator study." Walter Pincus, "Plan to Study Nuclear Warheads Stirs Concern: Arms-Control Advocates Worried about Possible Development of New Weapons," *Washington Post*, April 6, 2005, p. A02.

16. Secretary Samuel W. Bodman, letter to Senator Dianne Feinstein, March 4, 2005.

17. Jonathan Medalia, "Nuclear Weapons: The Reliable Replacement Warhead Program," Report RL32929 (Congressional Research Service, updated March 9, 2006), pp. 51–53. The design decision is scheduled for the fall of 2006.

18. Most of the yield of a modern nuclear weapon comes from the explosion of the "secondary" (the second stage of the weapon). The primary can be designed to give multiple, selectable yields that vary from less than a kiloton to tens of kilotons (see "Statement by Senator Feinstein"). Of course, this low-yield option could be available even without an RRW. For example, Ambassador C. Paul Robinson, president of the Sandia National Laboratories and adviser to the U.S. Strategic Command (STRATCOM), has suggested that the United States could obtain a wide variety of low-kiloton weapons "by depending on the features inherent in many designs in the current U.S. stockpile. An obvious and also very effective approach to obtain low-yield devices would be to use dummy secondaries as a way of quickly achieving single-stage yields (primary-only yields) without having to modify the devices, or to repeat flight tests for the delivery systems, or to conduct nuclear testing." C. Paul Robinson, *A White Paper: Pursuing a New Nuclear Weapons Policy for the 21st Century* (Albuquerque, N. Mex.: Sandia National Laboratory, March 22, 2001), p. 10. Similarly, the NPR states that one way to enhance deterrence might be the "possible modifications to existing weapons to provide additional yield flexibility in the stockpile" (pp. 34–35).

19. "U.S. Nuclear Forces, 2005," pp. 73–75. The W76 is the most numerous of U.S. strategic nuclear warheads and is carried on Trident I (C4) and Trident II (D5) SLBMs.

20. Although direct funding for the RNEP was eliminated, $4 million was appropriated for the Department of Defense to study a conventional "bunker buster" weapon, which might (depending on the nature of the program) have some utility for determining the feasibility of an RNEP weapon's capability to survive a high-speed impact with the ground. In addition to not funding RNEP, Congress denied the administration's request for funding for a Modern Pit Facility and for money to reduce the time required to restart nuclear testing.

21. For an example of a low-yield weapon proposal, see Thomas W. Dowler and Joseph S. Howard II, "Countering the Threat of the Well-Armed Tyrant: A Modest Proposal for Small Nuclear Weapons," *Strategic Review* 19 (Fall 1991): 34–40. An example of an enhanced radiation warhead is the W70 warhead deployed on the Lance missile in 1981, which was developed primarily as a tactical weapon to defeat Soviet tanks. This warhead was called a "neutron bomb" because most of its energy came from the fusion reaction and was released as high-energy neutrons. The W70 is no longer in the stockpile.

22. Disarmament Commission 2006 substantive session, "Recommendations for Achieving the Objective of Nuclear Disarmament and Non-proliferation of Nuclear

Weapons," New York, April 10-28, 2006, agenda item 4, submitted by the United States of America, A/CN.10/2006/WG.I/WP.1.

23. Arms Control Association Panel Discussion, "Reliable Replacement Warhead: Does the United States Need a New Breed of Nuclear Weapon?" April 25, 2006, transcript by Federal News Service, Washington (www.armscontrol.org/events/20060425_RRW_Transcript.asp).

24. As Dr. Garwin further notes in the cited ACA Panel Discussion, if there are political calls for U.S. testing, this "will open the floodgates to the Russians testing and the Chinese testing. The Chinese can make real improvements in their nuclear weaponry with a few tests because they've had only 43 compared with our more than a thousand nuclear tests. Planning ahead, these folks (the Chinese and the Russians) are not going to wait, they will make the same calculation I do; they will prepare to test. We will see them preparing to test. We will not allow them to test first, and so we will have, for absolutely no good reason and much to our security detriment, an outbreak of nuclear testing that will then legitimize the acquisition of nuclear weapons by those people who don't have any." Ibid.

25. The problem of a weapon that has gone off course can only be solved with a self-destruct system on board. Remote activation might not be required if there was a system on board that measured the deviation from the set course and then activated a self-destruct signal. For the case in which the weapon was on course but did not explode, if there were a homing beacon on board the weapon, Special Forces (or other units) might be sent to retrieve the weapon. However, since this approach could not be counted on to succeed in all cases, a remotely activated destruct system would probably be required.

26. For example, "As forces are incrementally changed to meet the New Triad force requirements, command and control (C2) becomes more critical to ensure the effectiveness of the elements of the residual force structure. . . . Strike options will require intricate planning, flexibility, and interface with decision makers throughout the engagement process. Command and control will become more complex and the supporting systems and platforms will require augmentation, modernization, and replacement" (NPR, p. 15).

27. See, for example, Vice Admiral Arthur K. Cebrowsk and John J. Garstka, "Network-Centric Warfare: Its Origin and Future," *Proceedings,* January 1998 (www.usni.org/Proceedings/Articles98/PROcebrowski.htm).

28. Jay Davis, former director, Defense Threat Reduction Agency, personal communication. We are indebted to Davis for several important technical commentaries.

29. The NPR also notes that mobile targets (missiles, communications, command posts, and so forth) are difficult to kill. However, mobile targets in a regional conflict are probably not appropriate targets for nuclear weapons, since they can readily be destroyed by the sophisticated conventional munitions in the U.S. arsenal. The problem has been (and remains) finding concealed mobile targets, a problem for which nuclear weapons offer little if any help. For an excellent review of all of these issues, see National Research Council, *Effects of Nuclear Earth-Penetrator and Other Weapons* (Washington: National Academies Press, 2005) (www.nap.edu/catalog/11282.html).

30. Secretary of Defense, *Report to Congress on Hard and Deeply Buried Targets (HDBTs)* (July 2001), quoted at www.globalsecurity.org/wmd/intro/bunker.htm.

31. "Many underground command, control, and communications (C3) complexes and missile tunnels are between 100 and 400 meters deep, with the majority less than 250 meters deep. A few are as deep as 500 meters or even 700 meters, in competent granite or limestone rock." National Research Council, *Effects of Nuclear Earth-Penetrator and Other Weapons*, p. 2-2.

32. Ibid.

33. As the depth of burial of the warhead increases, the coupling of the nuclear explosion's energy into the earth increases (although the exact relationship between the depth of burial and the amount of coupling is still somewhat uncertain). Thus, in principle, deeper penetration allows lower yields to be used. However, most of the coupling appears to occur in the first few meters of penetration, with the effect dropping off rapidly at greater penetration depths. The "coupling curve" is shown in Robert W. Nelson, "Low-Yield Earth-Penetrating Nuclear Weapons," *Science and Global Security* 10 (2002): 1–20, fig. 1, p. 4; and in National Research Council, *Effects of Nuclear Earth-Penetrator and Other Weapons*, p. 4-3.

34. Edward Teller and others, *The Constructive Uses of Nuclear Explosives* (New York: McGraw-Hill, 1968), pp. 165–75. Calculations by Levi (based on work done for the Defense Nuclear Agency in 1977) show that for a 1-kiloton warhead detonated at a depth of 5 meters, an underground bunker will be destroyed at about 35 meters in hard rock and at about 45 meters in dry earth. Michael A. Levi, *Fire in the Hole: Nuclear and Non-nuclear Options for Counterproliferation* (Washington: Carnegie Endowment for Peace, November 2002), p. 12.

35. National Research Council, *Effects of Nuclear Earth-Penetrator and Other Weapons*, p. 4-16.

36. The LD50 dose is assumed here to be 450 rads, the rad being a measure of the amount of energy absorbed as a result of exposure to radiation. Death will usually occur within four to six weeks of this exposure level.

37. Frank Serduke, *Standard KDFOC4 Fallout Calculations for Buried Nuclear Detonations*, UCRL-ID-146937 (Lawrence Livermore National Laboratory, September 14, 2001). There is an uncertainty of about a factor of two in these calculations. In general, for a given yield, fallout increases somewhat at shallow depths before it begins to diminish as the burial depth is increased. For example, a 10-kiloton surface-burst weapon will produce a 24-hour LD50 fallout area of about 20 square kilometers. If the warhead were buried 5 meters in dry rock, it is calculated that it would produce a fallout area of about 28 square kilometers (about a 40 percent increase). The area of dispersal depends, of course, on wind velocities and can thus vary widely with local conditions.

38. Even calculations that indicate that fallout would be limited if the explosion were buried at great depth ignore the fact that the weapon will leave a hole behind it as it penetrates deep into the earth. For example, at least one cratering explosion conducted by the United States, Palanquin, a 4.3-kiloton event detonated at a depth of 85.3 meters in 1965, had an opening to the surface owing to the ejection of a plug (a strong cylindrical steel casing used to seal the shaft drilled to insert the explosive device). The radioactive material emitted by that shot greatly exceeded what would have been expected without the hole. The radioactive cloud topped out at a height of 4 kilometers. Spenst M. Hansen,

"A Crater Formed by Gas Erosion of a Nuclear Explosion Vent," *Meteoritics* 4 (October 1968): 61–87. For details of the fallout, see the National Cancer Institute database on Underground Era Test Series (www2.nci.nih.gov/I131/intros/BK0.html).

39. *Exposure of the American Population to Radioactive Fallout from Nuclear Weapons Tests: A Review of the CDC-NCI Draft Report on a Feasibility Study of the Health Consequences to the American Population from Nuclear Weapons Tests Conducted by the United States and Other Nations* (Washington: National Academies Press, 2003). A summary describing the publication states: "The CDC-NCI study claims that the fallout might have led to approximately 11,000 excess deaths, most caused by thyroid cancer linked to exposure to iodine-131. The committee noted that CDC and NCI used the best available data to estimate exposure and health hazards" (www.nap.edu/catalog/10621.html?onpi_newsdoc021103).

40. Samuel Glasstone and Philip J. Dolan, *The Effects of Nuclear Weapons* (U.S. Department of Defense and U.S. Department of Energy, 1977), p. 115. For 10 pounds per square inch, which is enough overpressure to cause moderate damage to reinforced concrete buildings, the range would be about three-quarters of a kilometer.

41. Ibid., p. 258. On the other hand, thermal radiation could be significantly reduced because a large amount of the energy is absorbed by the earth and the fireball that does develop is obscured to a great extent by earth thrown from the crater.

42. According to the NPR (p. 47), the criterion for destroying an HDBT is to collapse the bunker. Of course, even for the deepest bunkers, a nuclear weapon could destroy the entrance or exit to a bunker. (Multiple nuclear weapons could be required for bunkers with many exits.) However, conventional weapons could also destroy the entrances and exits, although in a long war, it might require multiple attacks to keep the tunnels closed. Since the central argument for RNEP is that nuclear weapons are a necessity not just a more efficient means of attacking a target, using them just to close tunnels would not seem to meet this requirement.

43. Chemical weapon facilities might also be attacked, but since these weapons are generally a much smaller threat (compared with biological weapons), the use of a nuclear weapon to attack them might not be considered justified.

44. Zachary Haldeman, "New Roles for Nuclear Weapons: Bunker Busting and Agent Defeat" (Center for International Security and Cooperation, Honors Thesis, Stanford University, 2003), quoting globalsecurity.org.

45. For a more elaborate treatment, see Michael May and Zachary Haldeman, "Effectiveness of Nuclear Weapons against Buried Biological Agents," *Science and Global Security* 12 (2004): 1–23, long version (www.princeton.edu/~globsec/publications/SciGloSec.shtml).

46. A safer alternative might be to try to block the entrances using conventional weapons. This might suffice to make stored agents or a weapons factory useless for the duration of the war, unless the war proved to be quite long and the United States for some reason could not restrike the sites.

47. The following discussion is taken primarily from Hans Kruger, *Radiation-Neutralization of Stored Biological Warfare Agents with Low-Yield Nuclear Warheads*, UCRL-ID-140193 (Lawrence Livermore National Laboratory, August 21, 2000), and from private communications with Dr. Kruger.

48. Ibid. These calculations are for an explosion with a 10-meter height of burst against a double-layer running stack of 200-liter barrels of liquid BW agent located in a metal roof building on the surface. The radii are based on a 1-megarad neutralization criterion. Different configurations of barrels would give somewhat different results.

49. Ibid. As noted, a fusion weapon might reduce the requirement to a few kilotons or less. However, the higher yield might still be needed to account for delivery inaccuracies or position uncertainties (see the following discussion in the text).

50. The alternative for separated sheds or large buildings might be to use more than one 10-kiloton warhead, but this would require very precise timing to avoid fratricide problems (to prevent one warhead from killing the other) and would, of course, increase the fallout.

51. NPR, p. 47. Presumably, this means hundreds of kilotons, if not more.

52. For example, see NPR, p. 46, quoted earlier in "Perceived Shortcomings of U.S. Nuclear Weapons" section. Also, "Deterrence requires we be able to hold at risk that which an adversary values. Our efforts to determine the potential effectiveness of an earth penetrating weapon reflect a continued emphasis on enhancing deterrence." Ambassador Linton F. Brooks, under secretary of energy for nuclear security and administrator, National Nuclear Security Administration, statement before the Senate Armed Services Committee, Subcommittee on Strategic Forces, 108th Cong., 2nd sess. (Government Printing Office, March 24, 2004), p. 6. The idea that the United States has to be able to kill all possible target types in a country or else deterrence will be threatened evolved during the cold war. However, there is no logical necessity to the idea (and never has been). For example, even though the United States could never destroy all of the Soviet Union's strategic forces or command posts, deterrence prevailed because U.S. strategic forces were also survivable, providing a capability to retaliate against a wide range of other Soviet targets, delivering a punishment far beyond any advantage that the Soviets might have ever hoped to achieve by an attack on the United States.

53. Department of Energy, Department of Defense, Department of State, *An Assessment of the Impact of Repeal of the Prohibition on Low Yield Warhead Development on the Ability of the United States to Achieve Its Nonproliferation Objectives,* Joint Report to Congress (GPO, March 2004), p. 2.

54. Keith B. Payne, "The Nuclear Jitters," *National Review* 12 (June 30, 2003): 22–25.

55. One might also wonder why deterrence has not yet failed, since these states have had WMD for some time.

56. See Payne, "The Nuclear Jitters"; and NPR, p. 17: "The types of targets to be held at risk include leadership and military capabilities"; Robinson, *White Paper*: "Targeting the leadership, along with military forces and military capabilities—the very tools of aggression—as was done against the Soviet Union; these are the appropriate primary targets that should be held at risk under any U.S. deterrent policy." Also Dowler and Howard, "Countering the Threat."

57. Similar arguments were made during the cold war, when it was argued that even though the United States could completely destroy the Soviet Union, this would not be enough to deter the Soviet leadership from attacking. The United States also had to be able to destroy Soviet hardened command posts and thus threaten the leadership personally. As late as 2000, the U.S. strategic nuclear war plan reportedly still contained 160

Russian leadership targets. See Bruce Blair, "Cold War Era Assumptions Drive U.S. Nuclear Force Levels: Why the Target List Should Shrink," *Coalition to Reduce Nuclear Dangers* (www.clw.org/pub/clw/coalition/briefv4n7.htm).

58. The U.S. decision to retaliate for its allies would be all the more difficult if the regional power had nuclear weapons capable of reaching the United States, since BW and certainly CW are likely to produce much less damage.

59. If the opponent had long-range ballistic missiles, this would require the development of an extremely effective missile defense system. But other means of delivery such as cruise missiles or less conventional approaches (for example, weapons smuggled into ports on ships) would also have to be accounted for and defeated.

60. Since a war would be going on, the regional power could have dispersed its weapons and stockpiles, and U.S. earth-penetrating weapons would not likely be central to its decision to resort to the use of WMD.

61. The NPR states: "Nuclear weapons . . . provide credible military options to deter a wide range of threats, including WMD and large-scale conventional military force" (p. 7). Presumably, deterring conventional attack means only against nuclear states since the United States, in connection with the NPT, has pledged since 1978 not to initiate the use of nuclear weapons against non-nuclear states (if they were not aligned with nuclear states at war with the United States). Beginning with the Clinton administration, the United States has stated that this pledge does not preclude nuclear retaliation after the use of CW or BW weapons against the United States or its allies (although no exceptions for CW or BW use were made in the original declaration).

62. Short- and medium-range missiles capable of carrying CW/BW warheads as well as nuclear warheads (depending on the sophistication of the design) are possessed by a number of countries throughout the world, for example, North Korea, Iran, Syria, Pakistan, India, and China. National Intelligence Council, *Foreign Missile Developments and the Ballistic Missile Threat through 2015* (December 2001) (www.cia.gov/nic/special_missilethreat2001.html). The technology for missiles to strike neighboring countries is not particularly sophisticated. Other means of delivery, such as aircraft, cruise missiles, ships, and trucks, could also be used. It is unlikely that a state willing to develop WMD would not also deploy a means of threatening its potential adversaries with such weapons.

63. However, it should be noted that terrorists could also acquire such materials from friendly or reasonably friendly states. For instance, terrorists might acquire weapons sold by disgruntled or impoverished guards or employees in such states. Moreover, small, well-financed groups operating in friendly countries can produce small (but significant) quantities of CW and perhaps BW on their own, as was demonstrated by the Aum Shinrikyo cult in Japan in 1995.

64. Walter Pincus, "Pentagon Revises Nuclear Strike Plan Strategy; Includes Preemptive Use against Banned Weapons," *Washington Post*, September 11, 2005, p. A01.

65. Ibid.

66. Hans M. Kristensen, "The Role of U.S. Nuclear Weapons: New Doctrine Falls Short of Bush Pledge," *Arms Control Today* 35 (September 2005) (http://www.armscontrol.org/act/2005_09/Kristensen.asp).

67. Ibid.

68. William Arkin, "Not Just A Last Resort? A Global Strike Plan, With a Nuclear Option," *Washington Post,* May 15, 2005, p. B01.

69. Seymour M. Hersh, "The Iran Plans," *New Yorker,* April 17, 2006 (www. newyorker.com/fact/content/articles/060417fa_fact). For a more general discussion of how the United States might deal with Iran and other emerging threats, see "U.S. Military Options against Emerging Nuclear Threats," *International Institute for Strategic Studies* 12, no. 3 (April 2006) (http://www.iiss.org/publications/strategic-comments/past-issues/volume-12—2006/volume-12—issue-3).

70. Interview in the Central Organ of the Defense Ministry of the Russian Federation, *Red Star,* September 21, 2005.

71. For one thing, as noted earlier, even if an attack were completely effective against all hostile states, it might not preclude terrorists from attaining CW or BW materials from other, more friendly states.

72. In the past, one could assume that dispersal of weapons would be highly likely, since the United States, being a democracy where Congress is involved in such questions, would be unlikely to strike with nuclear (or conventional) weapons completely out of the blue, giving the regional power time to react. However, under the new powers assumed by President Bush to fight the War on Terror, this assumption of democratic participation in a decision to attack another country may no longer be valid.

73. "We assess that North Korea has produced enough plutonium for at least one, and possibly two, nuclear weapons. Spent fuel rods canned in accordance with the 1994 Agreed Framework contain enough plutonium for several more weapons." Central Intelligence Agency, *Unclassified Report to Congress on the Acquisition of Technology Relating to Weapons of Mass Destruction and Advanced Conventional Munitions, 1 January through 30 June 2001,* released in January 2003 (www.fas.org/irp/threat/bian_apr_2003.html), p. 4. In October 2003, the North Koreans claimed to have reprocessed the spent fuel rods noted in the report. According to Mohamed ElBaradei, director general of the IAEA, North Korea had the capability by the end of 2004 to have reprocessed these 8,000 fuel rods into enough material for an extra four to six nuclear weapons (this is in addition to the previously suspected material for one to two nuclear weapons). David E. Sanger and William J. Broad, "North Korea Said to Expand Arms Program," *New York Times,* December 3, 2004.

74. "We assess North Korea is self-sufficient in the production of chemical components for first generation chemical agents. They have produced munitions stockpiles estimated at up to 5,000 metric tons of several types of chemical agents, including nerve, choking, blister, and blood. We assess that North Korea has the capability to develop, produce, and weaponize biological warfare agents, to include bacterial spores causing anthrax and smallpox and the bacteria causing the plague and cholera." Secretary of Defense, *2000 Report to Congress: Military Situation on the Korean Peninsula* (Department of Defense, September 12, 2000), sec. 2 (www.defenselink.mil/news/Sep2000/korea09122000.html).

75. North Korea has also threatened to retaliate against the U.S. homeland, but probably does not have the capability at this date to do this directly—although unconventional delivery means are a possibility.

76. North Korea has hundreds of short- and medium-range ballistic missiles.

77. Senator Jon Kyl (R–Ariz.), *Congressional Record Weekly Update,* January 6–10, 2003. North Korea's artillery force of over 12,000 self-propelled and towed weapon systems, without moving any artillery pieces, could sustain up to 500,000 rounds an hour against targets south of the DMZ for several hours. Secretary of Defense, *2000 Report to Congress.*

78. Even a strictly conventional war would be devastating. For example, the former commander of U.S. Forces Korea, General Gary Luck, estimated that a war on the Korean peninsula could cost $1 trillion in economic damage and result in 1 million casualties, including 52,000 U.S. military casualties. Quoted in Victor D. Cha and David C. Kang, "The Korea Crisis," *Foreign Policy* 136 (May/June 2003): 20–28.

79. "A working U.S. nuclear deterrent . . . can help to devalue rogue WMD, by credibly threatening a costly reply if those WMD were ever used." Payne, "The Nuclear Jitters," p. 25.

80. The Bush administration agrees that the overwhelming U.S. conventional capability and demonstrated willingness of the United States to use this power encourages proliferation among "rogue" states but argues that these rogue states acquire weapons not to deter the United States from aggression, but only in order to commit aggression themselves (and to deter the United States from protecting itself or its allies). *An Assessment of the Impact of Repeal of the Prohibition on Low-Yield Warhead Development,* p. 4. This argument might be taken more seriously if the administration did not couple its military power with a strategy of preventive war, a strategy recently demonstrated in Iraq.

81. Alexander L. George, *Forceful Persuasion: Coercive Diplomacy as an Alternative to War* (Washington: United States Institute of Peace, 1991), p. xi.

82. "Russian Nuclear Forces, 2003," *Bulletin of the Atomic Scientists* 59 (July/August 2003): 31–35.

83. Sergei Ivanov, "Immediate Tasks of Development of the Armed Forces of the Russian Federation" (Aktualnye Zadachi Razvitiya Vooruzhennykh Sil RF) (www.rian.ru), cited in Nikolai Sokov, "Russian Ministry of Defense's New Policy Paper: The Nuclear Angle," CNS Report (cns.miis.edu/pubs/reports/sok1003.htm).

84. Sokov, "Russian Ministry of Defense's New Policy Paper."

85. "The IC [Intelligence Community] projects that by 2015, most of China's strategic missile force will be mobile. China has three new, mobile, solid propellant strategic missiles in development—the road-mobile CSS-X-10 ICBM (also called the DF-31), which is now in the flight-test stage; a longer range version of the DF-31; and the JL-2 SLBM. This modernization effort, which dates from the mid-1980s, forms the foundation of Beijing's efforts to field a modern, mobile, and more survivable strategic missile force. . . . China has had the capability to develop and deploy a multiple reentry vehicle system for many years, including a MIRV system. The IC assesses that China could develop a multiple RV system for the [current silo-based] CSS-4 ICBM in a few years." Central Intelligence Agency, *Foreign Missile Developments and the Ballistic Missile Threat through 2015* (December 2001), p. 6.

86. For Iran, see, for example, the summer 2004 FAS nuclear guide on Iran at www.fas.org/nuke/guide/iran/nuke/ and references therein; also the 2003 Council on Foreign Relations background information at www.cfr.org/background/iran_nuclear.php. For current updates, see the series issued by the Harvard University Belfer Center

from annaliis_abrego@harvard.edu. For North Korea, see Larry A. Knisch, "North Korea's Nuclear Weapons Program," Issue Brief for Congress (Congressional Research Service, 2003).

87. Saudi Arabia has stated that "in response to the current upheaval in the Middle East, [it] has embarked on a strategic review that includes looking at the option of acquiring nuclear weapons," according to a report in the *London Guardian*, September 19, 2003 (www.dailytimes.com.pk/print.asp?page=story_19-9-2003_pg7_6).

88. See www.fas.org/irp/threat/wmd_state.htm, and references therein.

eight

U.S. Nuclear Weapons Policies for a New Era

George Bunn and Christopher F. Chyba

National decisions about the construction and employment of nuclear weapons are among the most consequential that any government, and any national leader, can make. Hundreds of thousands of lives, possibly many millions, rest on making these decisions well. While the consequences of a wrong decision may be smaller today than during the cold war, the context for these decisions is now more complex and uncertain, as is the manner in which they may ramify through the entire international system.

What role should U.S. nuclear weapons play in the world today? What related policies should the United States follow to promote international security while safeguarding its national interests? This book has sketched the technical and international political environment in which nuclear weapons decisions must now be made and has confronted U.S. nuclear weapons policy with the present and future context of international security risks. These risks include dangers left over from the cold war era, challenges posed by states that are newly growing in power, and the dramatic new presence of nonstate actors such as terrorists. These factors are dynamic, so will require a regular reassessment of the changing landscape.

The preceding chapters represent an effort to provide one such assessment, although they reflect not a consensus but the views of the individual authors. Nevertheless, the main features of their arguments form a coherent statement about U.S. nuclear weapons policy in a new world of risk.

U.S. Nuclear Weapons Policies before September 11

During the cold war, U.S. nuclear weapons policies were focused on protecting the country and its allies against the armed forces and nuclear stockpiles of its rivals, the Soviet Union and China, and on preventing the spread of nuclear weapons to yet more countries. Because the Soviet Union had so many more nuclear weapons than China (at their peak, tens of thousands compared to hundreds) and because Soviet missiles were capable of reaching and devastating the entire Western world, the Soviet threat dominated U.S. thinking.

The fundamental mode of protection against the nuclear weapons of the Soviet Union was nuclear deterrence through the threat of punishment—the adversary would be deterred from launching a nuclear attack on the United States or its allies by the expectation that the United States would retaliate in kind. The United States and Soviet Union used arms control treaties in an effort to manage this deterrence relationship, to limit its greatest risks and to limit its financial burdens.

The United States negotiated treaties with the Soviet Union to limit and then reduce strategic offensive arms (the SALT and START treaties placed restrictions or limits on the land- and sea-launched ballistic missiles and bomber aircraft that could deliver strategic nuclear weapons), and to strongly restrict defenses against such missiles (through the Anti-Ballistic Missile or ABM Treaty). Since any ABM system could be overcome by a set of less costly countermeasures, including building more and more missiles, policymakers reasoned that it would be better to limit the extent of ABM systems to begin with in order to save the cost and risk to each side of building the additional missiles, warheads, and decoys needed to overcome each other's defenses. Moreover, some feared that if either side ever did believe it had achieved an effective defense, this belief (or the other side's fears of this belief) might increase the chances of misguided nuclear war. Despite the ABM Treaty and the partial limitations on offensive strategic weapons, however, the arms race continued throughout most of the cold war.

With the end of the cold war, major improvements took place in the U.S. relationship with what became Russia after the collapse of the Soviet Union. Nevertheless, nuclear deterrence between the United States and Russia did not end altogether. But the prospects for nuclear war between the two countries seemed far less likely. Indeed, the Pentagon's 2001 Nuclear Posture Review (NPR) argued that major changes in the U.S. nuclear posture were necessary because Russia was much less threatening than the Soviet Union had been; future defense against possible nuclear attacks on the United States should rely less on deterrence of Russia and more on ballistic missile defense against attacks by hostile states; and non-nuclear weapons would be increasingly important for U.S. and allied defense.[1] The NPR therefore proposed significant changes in U.S. nuclear weapons policy, but these dealt primarily with potential attacks by hostile nations, not by terrorists. Among the policy suggestions were the possible targeting of states having biological or chemical but not nuclear weapons, and possible new uses for tactical nuclear weapons.

U.S. nuclear nonproliferation policies before the end of the cold war were similarly focused on preventing states, rather than terrorists, from acquiring nuclear weapons. After the collapse of the Soviet Union, the threat of nuclear terrorism began receiving increased attention, and throughout the 1990s substantial efforts were made to secure "loose nukes" and nuclear explosive material in the former Soviet Union. September 11 accentuated U.S. fears of all forms of mass-casualty terrorism, including the horrifying prospect of a nuclear weapon in terrorist hands. The global nuclear nonproliferation regime put in place to control the spread of nuclear weapons during the cold war did not seem adequate to meet this newly appreciated threat.

This regime is anchored in the Nuclear Non-Proliferation Treaty (NPT), which by the beginning of President George W. Bush's administration had been joined by 188 nations, more than had participated in any other treaty apart from the UN Charter.[2] Since this treaty went into effect in 1970, far fewer additional countries—three or four—have acquired and retained nuclear weapons than was imagined would be the case prior to the treaty's existence.[3] But the treaty is primarily concerned with state behavior, not with that of substate groups. The treaty addresses terrorists' acquisition of nuclear weapons only insofar as it prohibits nuclear weapon states from transferring nuclear weapons to "any recipient whatsoever," and by requiring NPT state parties not having nuclear weapons to account for all their nuclear materials to a multilateral inspection agency, the International Atomic Energy Agency (IAEA).[4]

U.S. Nuclear Policies in a Post–September 11 World

After September 11, 2001, the Bush administration placed a new emphasis on the utility of preventive war, calling it "preemption" in national strategy statements issued by the White House.[5] This emphasis was explained in presidential speeches and three administration policy reports released during the seventeen months following the September 11 attacks: the National Security Strategy of the United States of America (September 2002), the National Strategy to Combat Weapons of Mass Destruction (December 2002), and the

National Strategy for Combating Terrorism (February 2003). The arguments of the 2002 National Security Strategy have been affirmed in the March 2006 National Security Strategy.

The 2002 National Security Strategy (NSS) warned that "our enemies," including both terrorists and "rogue states," are seeking "weapons of mass destruction."[6] Supporting the idea of preventive war, President Bush wrote in the preface to the NSS that, "as a matter of common sense and self-defense, America will act against these emerging threats before they are fully formed."[7] The NSS itself, ambivalent about the role of deterrence in the post–September 11 world, warned that "deterrence based only on the threat of retaliation is less likely to work against leaders of rogue states more willing to take risks" than was true for deterrence against the Soviet Union during the cold war.[8] The December 2002 National Strategy to Combat Weapons of Mass Destruction called for "capabilities to detect and destroy an adversary's WMD [Weapons of Mass Destruction] before those weapons are used." The February 2003 National Strategy for Combating Terrorism stated: "We cannot wait for the terrorists to attack and then respond."[9] All three strategy documents declared a willingness to strike first against terrorists or "rogue states."

A feature of counterproliferation in the first Clinton administration, according to then secretary of defense William Perry, was "disabling or destroying WMD assets in time of conflict if necessary through counterforce attacks."[10] The Bush administration has at times considered going a step further—to contemplate the use of *nuclear* weapons in preemptive or preventive attacks to destroy a potential enemy's underground bunkers believed to contain either biological or chemical weapons.[11]

The Bush administration has extended counterproliferation actions that the United States may take outside times of conflict. An example is the drafting and implementation of the Proliferation Security Initiative (PSI), discussed in chapters 3 and 5. Under PSI, the threat of force can be used to stop merchant ships at sea for inspection to see if they are carrying "weapons of mass destruction" or the equipment, technology, or materials for making them.

The United States continues to support the NPT, which was intended to prevent additional countries from acquiring nuclear weapons. The Bush administration has not, however, followed the U.S. cold war practice of seeking detailed, verified nuclear arms reduction agreements, at the time with the Soviet Union. It did negotiate a nuclear weapons reduction treaty with Russia (the Moscow Treaty of 2002) that specified (without agreed verification measures) American and Russian strategic warhead numerical limits to be achieved by 2012.[12] The treaty requires the reduction of the number of operationally deployed strategic nuclear warheads but does not require the destruction of the warheads that are not deployed, such as warheads that are in storage, held in reserve, or undergoing maintenance. The number of operationally deployed strategic warheads in Russia and the United States in 2012 must, according to the treaty, lie between 1,700 and 2,200. This would represent about an 80 percent reduction from 1991 levels for the United States.[13] However, the total number of nuclear warheads held by each side is expected to be several times this amount.

In 2002 the United States withdrew from the ABM Treaty with Russia and began building a national missile defense against nuclear warheads on incoming intercontinental missiles.[14] While the United States had previously contemplated space-based weapons that could be used to attack incoming enemy missiles, the termination of the ABM Treaty also formally ended the prohibition on the development, testing, or deployment of such weapons.[15]

A New World of Risk: The Threat from Nuclear Terrorists and "Rogue States"

The February 2003 National Strategy for Combating Terrorism draws attention to the "changing nature of terrorism" in today's global environment, in which "terrorists increasingly enjoy a force-multiplier effect by establishing links with other like-minded organizations around the globe. Now, with WMD capability, they have the potential to magnify the effects of their actions manyfold." Furthermore, these actions are being abetted by leaders such as Osama bin Laden, who consider "the acquisition of WMD a religious duty."[16]

The United Nations Secretary-General's High-Level Panel on Threats, Challenges and Change reached a similar conclusion: "Two new dynamics give the terrorist threat greater urgency. Al-Qaida is the first—not likely to be the last—of an armed non-State network with global reach and sophisticated capacity. . . . [T]he threat that terrorism—of whatever type, with whatever motivation—will seek to cause mass casualties, creates unprecedented dangers."[17]

The September 11, 2001, al Qaeda attacks in New York City and Washington emphasized that group's interest in causing mass casualties. Several years earlier, Osama bin Laden had accused an American "Crusader–Zionist alliance" of killing "millions of Muslims," and he issued an edict calling on Muslims "to comply with God's order to kill the Americans and plunder their money wherever and whenever they find it."[18] The September 11 mass-casualty attacks, combined with these statements by bin Laden, imply that he would use nuclear weapons in attacks on the United States were he able to acquire them. While nuclear weapons acquisition through theft of warheads or, more likely, nuclear explosive materials (NEM) would not be easy for a terrorist group, it cannot be ruled out (see chapters 1 and 4).[19] Former secretary of defense William Perry warned in 2005: "I fear that we're headed toward an unprecedented catastrophe where a nuclear bomb is detonated in an American city. The bomb will not come in a missile at the hands of a hostile nation. It will come in a truck or a freighter at the hands of a terrorist group."[20] Other former U.S. officials, analysts, and politicians have issued similar warnings.[21]

At the end of the cold war, the collapse of the Soviet Union radically reduced the security for former Soviet nuclear weapons and nuclear explosive material, security that had relied heavily on strong police, secret service, and military control. Subsequent revelations about poor Russian nuclear security and illicit trafficking in nuclear materials produced new efforts to better protect military and peaceful nuclear programs around the world from terrorists and thieves. Then director of Central Intelligence Porter Goss testified before a Senate committee in 2005 that "there is sufficient material unaccounted for [from Russia] so it would be possible for those with know-how to construct a nuclear weapon" from that material.[22] A U.S. National Intelligence Council report found it "highly unlikely that Russian authorities would have been able to recover all the [weapons-usable nuclear] material reportedly stolen."[23]

Preventing Terrorists and Rogue States from Acquiring Nuclear Weapons

Making nuclear weapons would not be impossible for terrorists if they could acquire weapons-usable nuclear material. Therefore the world needs better security, policing, and export controls for the components, technology, and materials that are useful for making nuclear weapons. As a result of legislation first adopted by the U.S. Congress in 1991, the Nunn-Lugar program has provided financial assistance to Russia both for better security of nuclear materials and weapons against terrorists and thieves, and for better peaceful employment opportunities for Russian weapons scientists. The program was subsequently expanded to other former Soviet republics that had insufficiently secured nuclear materials. In 2002 the Group of Eight Industrialized Nations (G-8) agreed to cooperate in expanding similar programs around the world, for example, to countries that had poorly protected highly enriched uranium in research reactors (see chapter 5).

The threat of acquisition of nuclear weapons by additional countries hostile to the United States is not new, but it has worsened in recent years. North Korea withdrew from the NPT in January 2003, has reprocessed sufficient plutonium for perhaps as many as eight nuclear weapons, and may be trying to enrich uranium in a parallel uranium-based program. While now participating in discussions with its neighbors and the United States about relinquishing its nuclear weapons capacities, North Korea had, by mid-2006, agreed only in principle to do so if its other demands were met.[24]

Latent Proliferation. The North Korean experience is an example of a major problem facing the nuclear nonproliferation regime, sometimes known as latent proliferation. North Korea resisted Soviet requests that it join the NPT until 1985, then resisted signing the NPT-required safeguards agreement with the IAEA until 1992, and then hid some of its nuclear activities from IAEA inspectors. It built reactors said to be for peaceful purposes and burned uranium fuel rods in them, producing spent fuel containing plutonium mixed with other elements. Its nuclear scientists learned how to separate ("reprocess") the plutonium from these other elements, and the plutonium could then be used either for nuclear reactors or in nuclear weapons. This is an example of latent proliferation: North Korea's development of nuclear technology, while ostensibly for peaceful (nuclear power) purposes, gave it a latent capability to make plutonium for nuclear weapons. It chose to do so, and its efforts were discovered. It withdrew from the NPT and has claimed to have nuclear weapons (see chapter 4). That is, while working within, or appearing to work within, the restrictions of the NPT for peaceful use of nuclear technology, it is possible for a country to develop many of the capacities required for a nuclear weapons program.

This was also the course that Libya followed until it gave up its nuclear-weapon efforts. Libya turned over its nuclear equipment and designs to the United Kingdom and the United States as part of a deal to escape the sanctions that had been imposed on it for earlier transgressions.[25]

Latent proliferation is also the path that Iran may now be pursuing to nuclear weapons. Its negotiations under way with Britain, France, and Germany as well as China, Russia, and the United States may help determine which way it will go: toward peaceful nuclear uses, nuclear weapons, or both. So far, it appears to want to keep all its options open.

Because the NPT has been interpreted as permitting its non-nuclear weapon state members to enrich uranium and separate plutonium to make reactor fuel for peaceful purposes, the danger will remain that countries that have enrichment or separation technology and equipment will use it to make nuclear weapons.[26] What can be done to mitigate the threat posed by latent proliferation?

Recent Proposals from the IAEA and the United States. Various proposals have been put forth to address the challenge of latent proliferation (see chapter 3). In 2004 and 2005, Mohamed ElBaradei, director general of the IAEA, proposed that:

—The separation of plutonium and the enrichment of uranium take place only under some form of bilateral or multilateral consortium that requires international monitoring to ensure that no material is diverted to a nuclear weapons program. An early example of this is the enrichment efforts in Germany and the Netherlands that are under inspection by European Atomic Energy Community (Euratom) monitors stationed at the plants and checked periodically by IAEA inspectors.[27]

—Existing enrichment facilities operated by non-nuclear weapon state members of the NPT should all be limited to producing low-enriched uranium (LEU) unsuitable for making nuclear weapons.

—Agreement should be reached on a five-year moratorium on building uranium-enrichment facilities. To supply enriched uranium to countries like Iran that would be asked to give up national enrichment efforts, an international consortium of countries already having multilateral enrichment facilities with multilateral monitoring and periodic IAEA inspections could supply LEU at reasonable prices. Indeed, the IAEA has the authority to provide a guarantee of supply of LEU to Iran or a similar country.[28]

In February 2004 President Bush proposed that the Nuclear Suppliers Group (NSG) refuse enrichment and reprocessing equipment "to any state that does not already possess full-scale, functioning, enrichment and reprocessing plants." At the G-8 2004 Sea Island Summit meeting, the G-8 leaders agreed to a resolution calling on all of them to refuse for a year (to allow more time to achieve a better solution) to export enrichment or reprocessing equipment to any country not already in possession of such equipment. At their 2005 Gleneagles Summit, the G-8 said:

> We welcome the decision at the recent Plenary Session of the Nuclear Suppliers' Group . . . to work actively with a view to reaching consensus on this issue. In aid of this process, we continue to agree, as we did at Sea Island, that it would be prudent in the next year not to inaugurate new initiatives involving transfer of enrichment or reprocessing technologies to additional states. . . . We also welcome the adoption by the NSG of important measures which restrict nuclear transfers to States which have violated their nonproliferation and safeguards obligations.[29]

The G-8 governments are clearly striving to prevent further proliferation of uranium-enrichment and plutonium-separation technologies. They welcomed the efforts of ElBaradei's IAEA Expert Group to describe possible "multinational approaches" to enrichment and reprocessing, but they did not favor one of these approaches over others. They did, however, call for "assured access to the market for nuclear fuel and related services" by non-nuclear weapon states that meet their NPT obligations.[30] Brazil has a new uranium-enrichment plant that the IAEA has accepted as meeting ElBaradei's call for multilateral enrichment facilities inspected by the IAEA periodically and monitored regularly by personnel from other countries. Brazil's plant will be verified bilaterally by the Argentina-Brazil Agency for Accounting and Control of Nuclear Materials (ABACC) as well as by the IAEA. With regular monitoring by ABACC and periodic inspections by the IAEA, this arrangement was accepted by the IAEA after lengthy negotiations.[31]

Nuclear Proliferation Rings. The past decade has seen the elaboration, and partial dismantlement, of illicit "proliferation rings" of individuals and companies that trade in components, technology, and materials useful for making nuclear weapons. When there were only a few nuclear suppliers, control of such exports was easier. The suppliers generally agreed to NSG criteria for nuclear exports, particularly exports useful for enriching uranium and separating plutonium. But countries that are not members of the NSG are now acquiring nuclear technology and components not fully controlled by NSG members. Nonmember governments such as those of Pakistan, North Korea, Iran, and Libya, as well as individuals and companies from these and other countries (including Malaysia, South Africa, and Turkey, but also many European nations), have traded in technology, components, or nuclear materials useful for making weapons. Nuclear experts in Pakistan apparently traded uranium-enrichment technology for missile technology from North Korea. Countries such as Iran and Libya acquired nuclear materials, components, and technologies in similar ways. A representative of Pakistan later said that entities in two dozen countries were involved in these proliferation rings (see chapters 3 and 4).

Latent proliferation and proliferation rings represent major challenges to the nonproliferation regime today. Technology transfer among proliferating states and companies has the potential to reduce the difficulty, cost, and time involved in acquiring nuclear weapons. Were such proliferation rings to expand, there would be a greater possibility of nuclear weapons or weapons-usable nuclear materials being stolen by terrorists or intentionally transferred to them by nationals of states having such materials.

New Efforts to Prevent the Spread of Nuclear Weapons. The Bush administration has championed a variety of nonproliferation and counterproliferation measures that are meant to be more quickly implementable and more flexible than the traditional multilateral treaty process. The lack of a full multilateral process leaves these efforts more open to charges of unilateralism, but there is precedent for such approaches, for example, in the formation of the NSG.

Proliferation Security Initiative (PSI). In response to an initiative from the United States, U.S. allies, later joined by Russia and many other states, agreed to cooperate to interdict transfers of nuclear as well as chemical and biological weapons (and equipment and material for making them) "to and from states and non-state actors of proliferation concern." The transfers might be delivered by ground vehicles that could be inspected when crossing land borders, or by aircraft that could be inspected at airports, or by ships that could be inspected in ports or even stopped at sea. On the high seas, the ship commanding the stoppage must be under the national flag of the ship being stopped—unless permitted to take action by the government of the flag nation. Potential legal difficulties have been reduced by two means. First, several small countries that permit a great many ships to fly their national flags may grant advance permission to have their ships stopped (after a short delay during which the flag nation has the chance to permit or decline boarding). Second, the number of countries cooperating in the effort has been increasing. Some eighty countries are said to be cooperating, at least in part. The United States claims as a success of the PSI the interdiction of uranium-enrichment equipment on board the BBC *China*.[32] Other PSI-ascribed successes have not been made public.

UN Security Council Resolution 1540. The UN Security Council adopted Resolution 1540 in 2004 by unanimous agreement after months of negotiations. UNSCR 1540 requires that nations adopt criminal statutes, regulations, export-control standards, and other measures to prevent unauthorized persons from acquiring nuclear materials and equipment in their countries. The Resolution 1540 implementing committee stated that, as of July 2005, its expert staff had begun a "substantive" review of the "first round" of reports submitted by 118 countries, but that 74 UN member states had not reported what they had done to comply with the resolution.[33] Some UN members had complained that much of the information demanded from them was secret, or that they did not have significant problems with terrorists and thieves and therefore did not need to take the required actions. Gaining broad cooperation is important: the tentacles of the Khan network show that countries may have a proliferation-related export problem—perhaps a company that is producing proliferation-relevant components—without their government necessarily being aware of it. Enforcing the resolution is a challenge, but worth major effort.

The Challenge of Enforcement

Historically, unilateral U.S. pressure, U.S. incentives for good behavior, and positive security assurances have played an especially important role in maintaining compliance with the NPT on the part of a number of members.[34] This unilateral activity was perhaps most successful for the United States when dealing with allies such as Germany, Japan, South Korea, or Taiwan. In other cases, such as Ukraine, a more multilateral approach was required. In South Africa, a domestic political change played an important role.[35]

Only the IAEA has the formal authority to determine that an NPT member is in noncompliance with its safeguards agreement under the NPT. Should IAEA inspectors find that an NPT party is not in compliance, the IAEA's charter requires that its Board of Governors report that noncompliance to the Security Council as well as to the party.[36] If the party refuses to comply, the board itself has no authority to order any sanctions, beyond cutting off any benefits that the party may have been receiving from the IAEA. States cooperating to prevent proliferation should then, one hopes, agree to cut off whatever nuclear supplies they provide to the offending NPT member.

The UN Security Council has authority to require compliance if the council finds that a state's noncompliance with its NPT obligations constitutes a threat to international peace. This council authority has, in fact, been used to enforce the nuclear nonproliferation regime in several cases. Examples of this exercise of council authority—or its lack—include the cases of Iraq and North Korea:

—In 1993, after the Gulf War of 1991, the council issued orders commanding Iraq to permit international inspectors to look for and destroy biological, chemical, and nuclear weapons as well as missiles. In 2002 it again ordered inspections of this sort in Iraq. These inspections were, in fact, quite successful, though they were cut short by the start of the 2003 Gulf War.[37]

—When North Korea gave notice of its intention to withdraw from the NPT in 1993 after the IAEA board had found it in noncompliance, China (a permanent member of the UN Security Council) would only agree to a UN

Security Council order calling upon North Korea to correct its violations or face a future order imposing sanctions. When North Korea refused to comply with this order, the council members could not agree to impose sanctions because of China's opposition—suggesting a veto. Subsequently, North Korea stopped its notice of withdrawal from the NPT on the last day of the withdrawal period and then negotiated with the United States to produce the Agreed Framework of 1994. This agreement brought IAEA inspectors in again. However, in January 2003 North Korea renewed its withdrawal from the NPT, and the Security Council took no enforcement action. Further negotiations among North Korea, four of its neighbors, and the United States are ongoing.[38]

The NPT withdrawal clause (pursuant to which North Korea withdrew) was based upon language drawn from the withdrawal clause of the earlier 1963 Limited Test Ban Treaty (LTBT) language, with two key additions: the NPT language requires a withdrawing party to give notice of its withdrawal not just to the other parties, as in the case of the LTBT, but to the Security Council as well; and the NPT withdrawal clause requires the withdrawing party to provide its *reasons* for withdrawal. These two requirements were intended to permit the council to decide whether withdrawal might produce a "threat to the peace" within the meaning of the UN Charter. If so, the Security Council would have power to prevent withdrawal or to take other action. The council could require, for example, that the withdrawing country continue observing the NPT even though it had given notice of withdrawal or actually withdrawn from the treaty. The council could also authorize the use of force to require compliance with IAEA inspection orders.[39] However, the council did not take such actions when North Korea withdrew from the NPT.

The United States is now seen as the principal proponent of NPT enforcement with respect to members' nonproliferation obligations under Articles I and II. But to be successful, the nonproliferation regime needs the cooperation of many countries. The failure of the 2005 NPT Review Conference to reach a consensus on any substantive recommendations and the failure of the 2005 UN General Assembly Summit to agree on any recommendations dealing with nuclear nonproliferation suggest that full multilateral cooperation to strengthen the nonproliferation regime has become more difficult, even as less than fully multilateral approaches to strengthening the regime, such as the PSI and UN Security Council Resolution 1540 (and the NSG, which dates from 1975 and has roots in discussions begun in 1970), continue to be explored and implemented.[40] But the foundation of the regime, and its international legitimacy, remains the NPT.

Defense of the U.S. Homeland from Nuclear Attack

To protect the United States from nuclear attack, the U.S. government has relied upon measures beyond those intended to prevent acquisition of nuclear weapons by potential enemies. In the cold war, the United States relied largely on threats of retaliation against Soviet nuclear attack. In today's post–cold war era, the attacks could come from several sources by many delivery means. Potential attacks could now include not just ballistic missiles, but cruise missiles from nonmilitary ships or explosions of nuclear weapons on vessels in major U.S. ports.

Given this wide variety of potential post–cold war threats, assigning relative priority to defense against intercontinental ballistic missile attack seems unjustified. Terrorists armed with intercontinental ballistic missiles are not a realistic threat. Even if ballistic missile attacks are conceivable from several states, the likelihood of U.S. retaliation, including the possibility of nuclear retaliation, remains a powerful deterrent against such an attack. But terrorist attacks are likely to be very hard to deter, and it is here, therefore, that other means—including defense, but especially measures to prevent terrorists from acquiring nuclear weapons or nuclear explosive material (NEM) to begin with—are especially important.

A comprehensive approach to defense against nuclear attack requires improvements in the security of NEM worldwide and, as a second line of defense, the screening and interdiction of nuclear weapons and NEM in commercial shipping or other covert means for delivery to the United States. Research on potential ballistic missile defenses should continue, but without illusions about its effectiveness against the wide spectrum of threats now challenging the United States. U.S. nuclear weapons policy must continue to face the reality of offensive dominance for the delivery of large nuclear arsenals, and the irrelevance of missile defense against likely terrorist attack scenarios (see chapter 6).

New Uses and Designs for U.S. Nuclear Weapons

The NPR of late 2001 was intended to refocus U.S. military forces to meet the challenges of the post–cold war world. The NPR argued that the stockpile inherited as the legacy of the cold war was inadequate to current U.S. needs. To meet these needs, the NPR argued for new, smaller nuclear weapons so as to lower potential collateral damage to civilians. This would make the use of nuclear weapons more credible to potential adversaries that need to be deterred or dissuaded.[41] In the case of hard and deeply buried targets, such as bunkers housing chemical or biological weapons, the weapons would also have to be able to penetrate underground. In the view of the National Security Strategy of September 2002, countries seeking nuclear, biological, or chemical weapons could be dealt with, if necessary, by preventive war (which the NSS calls "preemptive war"). The justifications for invading Iraq in 2003 that executive branch officials gave to the U.S. Congress, to the UN Security Council, and to the American public were generally consistent with these aspects of the NSS (see chapter 2).

Chapter 7 suggests that these arguments, taken as a whole, have little to do with the *deterrence* of a nuclear (or biological or chemical) weapon attack on the United States or one of its allies. Instead, the idea motivating research into new nuclear weapons was an active kind of preventive defense: to use nuclear weapons to penetrate and destroy bunkers for biological or chemical weapons (including those underground) before they could be used. This could mean being the first to use nuclear weapons. This perception has been reinforced by other administration statements referred to in chapter 7.

The use by the United States of even small, tactical nuclear weapons in war could convince additional countries of their need to acquire nuclear weapons. It would likely not matter that the nuclear weapons used were described by the United States as being of low yield and used in a fashion to limit collateral damage. The first use of nuclear weapons in war since World War II could be catastrophic for the nuclear nonproliferation regime. To assume that other powers would then not subsequently use nuclear weapons themselves would be to commit what political scientists call "the fallacy of the last move."[42] Making the acquisition and use of nuclear weapons more acceptable would not serve U.S. interests.

A U.S. administration desiring to have a free hand to use preventive force abroad, as in the invasion of Iraq, would be wise to avoid suggestions that it would use nuclear weapons in such conflicts. When the U.S. invasion of Iraq actually took place in 2003, there was no statement that the United States would use nuclear weapons to destroy any Iraqi facilities said to exist for making and storing nuclear, chemical, or biological weapons. Suggesting the use of nuclear weapons would have engendered greater foreign and domestic opposition to the Iraq war.

After long consideration, in late 2005 Congress denied fiscal 2006 funds requested by the Department of Energy for future research to produce "bunker-buster" nuclear weapons for attacking underground enemy sites suspected of harboring chemical or biological weapons. Whether this decision to deny funds will be repeated in the next fiscal year remains to be seen.

For fiscal 2006, Congress appropriated $25 million to support further research on "reliable replacement [nuclear] warheads" (RRW). Secretary of Energy Samuel Bodman said that this research was to extend the life of existing warheads. "If in the future," he added, the Department of Defense "identifies requirements for new or different military capabilities, it is conceivable that certain of the concepts identified in the RRW program could be applied in the development of warheads to meet those new requirements."[43] This may suggest that the RRW program could lead to new nuclear weapon designs and perhaps renewed nuclear weapon testing, as some observers have suggested (see chapter 7).

Where Should the United States Go from Here?

This book has documented the great challenges now facing the world's nuclear nonproliferation regime. Historically there has been a succession of such challenges, but the regime has nevertheless survived and contributed to preventing the world of "15 or 20 or 25" nuclear powers that President John Kennedy foresaw in 1963.[44] While wars against some proliferators are possible in the future, after its experience in Iraq, the United States will likely be deterred from exercising the war option unilaterally except as a last resort, and in the face of high costs.

It is therefore greatly in the self-interest of the United States to place a high priority on maintaining a strong nuclear nonproliferation regime, even while acknowledging that no single strand of the evolving regime can, in itself, be sufficient to the challenges faced. The nonproliferation regime requires a web of prevention consisting of many strands.[45] The United States must be attentive not only to the different strands, it must make difficult choices about which ones to emphasize, and it must make these choices strategically because strengthening one strand of the web may sometimes weaken others. In this context, we recommend a nuclear weapons strategy that focuses on the following elements: strengthen the security of nuclear weapons and materials, insist on compliance with nonproliferation obligations, address the demand side as well as the supply side of nuclear proliferation, reduce the salience of nuclear weapons in U.S. foreign policy, and right the balance in homeland defense.

Strengthen the Security of Nuclear Weapons and Materials

It is crucial that the security of nuclear weapons–usable material against theft be strengthened worldwide, and that resolutions to this effect be persistently followed through with financial and political commitment.[46] Measures to prevent the export or illegal trade of nuclear weapons–related equipment and materials must be made more effective, and it is vital that UN Security Council Resolution 1540 be successfully implemented.[47] Greater effort is required in all these areas.

Insist on Compliance with Nonproliferation Obligations

The nuclear nonproliferation regime has proved its worth over the decades since its anchor document, the NPT, entered into force. The NPT should be strengthened, not undermined. The United States must insist that all states party to the NPT, non-nuclear weapon states and nuclear weapon states alike, fulfill their obligations.[48] In addition to UNSCR 1540 and strengthened safeguards resulting from the widespread adoption of the Additional Protocol (see chapter 5), noncompliance can be addressed on an escalating scale of targeted sanctions and bilateral pressure, through the IAEA, and ultimately through the UN Security Council, despite the challenges these paths entail. But to minimize the cases where coercive diplomacy and the threat of military force must be contemplated, the United States must place a high priority on medium- and long-term efforts to circumvent future programs like those of North Korea or Iran before they reach the advanced stages they are at in those countries.

Address the Demand Side as well as the Supply Side of Nuclear Proliferation

The nuclear nonproliferation regime must better address the demand "pull" for nuclear weapons components, know-how, and materials, as well as focus on the supply "push." This will be all the more true as the relevant technologies evolve and become more accessible to more countries. The development of proliferation rings, while greatly slowed by the apparent dismantlement of much of the A. Q. Khan network, is a reminder that in the long term any control regime that relies on restricting the diffusion of technology may ultimately fail. Eventually, virtually all new technologies acquire a dual use and spread around the globe.[49] Therefore one purpose of the nonproliferation regime is to provide time during which alternative approaches may be found to limit the perceived need for nuclear weapons. These approaches will involve both addressing regional security dilemmas and encouraging the evolution of governments that do not see nuclear, biological, or chemical weapons as wise diversions of their society's resources. As technology spreads, addressing demand must become an ever more important component of nonproliferation strategy.

One important contributor to regional security dilemmas is the fear that one's neighbors may be developing nuclear weapons. A key implicit bargain within the NPT is that non-nuclear weapons states forgo nuclear weapons with some confidence that their neighbors and rivals are simultaneously doing so. Fears that this might not be the case push in the direction of a proliferation spiral. The successful reversal of Libya's nascent nuclear weapons program is a substantial victory in this respect. Similar victories, while undoubtedly very different in details, are needed in the cases of Iran and North Korea.

Because of its superpower status and global military reach, the United States is in effect a "regional power" in every area of the world. The United States, and the other nuclear weapons states, must judiciously weigh the effects that their own nuclear weapons programs, and the way they discuss and portray these programs to the world, may have on other countries' nuclear weapons decisions. The willingness of the United States to project and use military power as in Iraq could be important with respect to encouraging nuclear proliferation in certain countries. But there are other drivers of nuclear proliferation that are independent of U.S. military power. Did either Iran or North Korea begin their acquisition of technology to enrich uranium or to separate plutonium because of an imminent threat of U.S. military power? Both countries began their pursuit of these technologies long before the invasion of Iraq in 2003. In our view, the reasons that likely dominated their thinking were closer to home, though both undoubtedly perceived the United States as a possible threat.

Reduce the Salience of Nuclear Weapons in Foreign Affairs

The United States now enjoys overwhelming dominance in the sophistication and reach of its conventional armed forces. The crushing combat victories it achieved in the First and Second Persian Gulf Wars demonstrated to the world that the ongoing "revolution in military affairs"—the incorporation of "smart" high-technology weapons (including precision-guided munitions, cruise missiles, surveillance, and stealth) into its armed forces and doctrine— had placed the U.S. military on an altogether different plane from that of its potential rivals.[50] This "overwhelming conventional military dominance" has important consequences for U.S. nuclear weapons policy and strategy.[51]

Show discipline in discussions of nuclear weapons policy. There are now very few, if any, military requirements apart from deterrence for which it is credible to imagine the United States choosing to use nuclear weapons.[52] This implies that it is in the interest of the United States to reduce the visibility of its nuclear weapons, in order not to undermine U.S. national security objectives in nuclear nonproliferation. While it may be true that U.S. conventional dominance may push some adversaries to pursue "asymmetric" responses to U.S. conventional dominance, possibly including nuclear, biological, or chemical weapons, U.S. conventional power coupled with the implicit threat of nuclear deterrence provide it with powerful replies.[53] With such big sticks, the United States can afford to speak more softly in order to pursue other important national security objectives.

The United States needs the discipline to avoid careless rhetoric that signals that it is not living up to its NPT obligations, and thus undermines its ability to attract partners in its efforts to achieve nonproliferation compliance. It should take visible steps to reduce the salience of nuclear weapons in its foreign policy, and to reduce the role of nuclear weapons globally. Beyond choices about how U.S. policymakers publicly speak of the role of U.S. nuclear weapons, substantive implementation of this goal would include several steps.

Affirm that the core mission of nuclear weapons remains deterrence. The central purpose of U.S. nuclear weapons during the cold war was to deter attacks on the United States or its allies by the Soviet Union or China. Deterrence was always understood to entail certain risks, but it was nevertheless viewed as central to national security strategy (see chapter 2).[54] Deterrence against the use of nuclear weapons by other states remains the core purpose of U.S. nuclear weapons.

Reaffirm central past nonproliferation commitments. To gain the indefinite extension of the NPT in 1995 (when the treaty was otherwise due to expire), the United States promised not to use nuclear weapons against any NPT member not having nuclear weapons unless such a member attacked it (or one of its allies) while in alliance with a nation having nuclear weapons. Similar promises were made by the other members of the P-5 (see chapter 3). Subsequent to these promises, the Security Council declared that an NPT member not having nuclear weapons had a "legitimate interest" that the Security Council should "act immediately" in the event the NPT member was "the victim of, or the object of, a threat of aggression in which nuclear weapons are used."[55]

The P-5 statements were not the equivalent of "no-first-use" promises. But they were nuclear non-use commitments to NPT members not having nuclear weapons and were later recognized by the International Court of Justice (the principal judicial organ of the UN) as legally binding.[56]

This U.S. nuclear weapon non-use promise has been qualified by U.S. statements considering the use of nuclear weapons to counter attacks using biological or chemical weapons—even if the attacker had no nuclear weapons and was not allied with any country that had nuclear weapons.[57]

Bush administration appropriations requests for research on new nuclear weapon designs that could be used in U.S. attacks against underground bunkers containing biological, chemical, or leadership targets could undermine the nation's 1995 pledge and undercut the statement in the Bush administration's Nuclear Posture Review that nuclear weapons could play a reduced role in the overall U.S. security policy.[58] Moreover, the possibility that U.S. research on new nuclear weapon designs, were they to lead to a resumption of nuclear testing, would undermine a commitment made by the P-5 at the 2000 NPT Review Conference, where the first of thirteen "practical steps" called for in the conference's Final Document was the entry into force of the Comprehensive Test-Ban Treaty.[59]

The United States should reaffirm its intention to reduce the salience of nuclear weapons in national and international security policy. This should include maintaining its current moratorium on nuclear testing and reaffirming that it seeks ratification of the Comprehensive Test Ban Treaty (CTBT) as a long-term goal. In 2006 the United States called upon all governments to refrain from testing, and presumably intends to do so itself.[60] This is a useful step forward toward the goal of full adherence to the CTBT.

Increase the response time for strategic missile systems. Despite the end of the cold war, nuclear risk has not disappeared from the U.S.-Russian relationship. In particular, hundreds of nuclear-armed missiles on both sides remain on high alert, ready to launch on minutes' notice.[61] The possibility that Russia could launch nuclear missiles as a result of a mistaken belief that it is about to be attacked must be taken seriously; this is especially the case given that Russia's early warning system against nuclear surprise attack has substantially deteriorated since the end of the cold war.[62] More broadly, a situation in which thousands of strategic warheads remain ready for launch on only minutes' notice presents the possibility of mistaken or inadvertent launch, especially during some future crisis.

The prompt launch postures are an unnecessarily dangerous residue of the cold war. We recommend negotiations with the Russians to achieve agreement on steps to improve the reliability of warning notifications and increase substantially the time from warning to nuclear missile launch.

Decrease the number of nuclear weapons held by all nuclear weapon states. Since the end of the cold war, there have been substantial reductions in the nuclear weapons arsenals of both the United States and Russia, as well as anticipated cuts to even lower levels, where nuclear weapons would be counted in the thousands rather than the tens of thousands. The United States and the Russian Federation signed the Moscow Treaty in May 2002, committing themselves to reducing their operationally deployed strategic nuclear weapons to between 1,700 and 2,200 by the end of 2012.[63] These numbers do not include strategic nuclear weapons held in reserve or maintenance status. Nor do they include nonstrategic weapons. Moreover, the Moscow Treaty has no verification provisions. In May 2004 President Bush approved a unilateral plan to cut the U.S. nuclear weapon stockpile "almost in half" by 2012.[64] Nongovernmental experts estimate that the current total of U.S. warheads deployed, undergoing maintenance, and in reserve is about 10,000 as of 2005.[65]

The Moscow Treaty remains in force only until the end of 2012, although it may be extended. The United States should build on this treaty with the objective of reducing the number of nuclear weapons of all types even further, ultimately to include reductions in the stockpiles of the world's other nuclear powers. Apart from Russia, no other nuclear power has numbers of weapons comparable to those of the United States, so other nuclear powers are unlikely to agree to negotiated reductions until U.S. and Russian stockpiles shrink considerably more.

Building down to low numbers of warheads will require a near-global regime of verification and monitoring of nuclear warheads and accounting for nuclear explosive materials, because as absolute numbers of warheads decrease, the importance of verifying that nuclear weapons or materials are not being hidden in violation of international commitments will become of even higher consequence.[66] Because of this, the long-standing commitment of the United States and the other NPT parties under Article VI of the NPT "to cessation of the nuclear arms race at an early date and to nuclear disarmament, and on a Treaty on general and complete disarmament under strict and effective international control" would ultimately require a multilateral accounting, monitoring, and verification effort that extends far beyond the nuclear weapon states.[67] It is not too early to begin discussion on how this could be done.

Right the Balance in Homeland Defense

The United States has now deployed a rudimentary national missile defense, and the Bush administration has a continuing commitment to an effective defense against possible missile attack.[68] But there are easier methods for the delivery of nuclear explosives to U.S. soil than by intercontinental missiles, and delivery by terrorists using ballistic missiles is extraordinarily unlikely. Possible intercontinental ballistic missile attacks by other states are still subject to deterrence, as they have been in the past, by the threat of retaliation against the perpetrator. Smuggling in, and detonating, a nuclear weapon in the United States is less likely to reveal who is responsible for the attack than would be the case for an intercontinental missile, and could be within the reach of some terrorist groups as well as nations.

We therefore recommend against giving budget priority to building missile defenses. We recommend a reassessment of defense against nuclear attack that weighs the probabilities of different means of attack against current investments and likely effectiveness of the defensive measures needed to address the different styles of attack. Such a reassessment would lead to greater emphasis on defending the United States against means of nuclear attack beyond that posed by intercontinental ballistic missiles.

Conclusion

This book has focused on U.S. nuclear weapon policies for the early years of the twenty-first century. It has not attempted to see far into the more distant future, to describe all future scenarios, or to assess whether and how to achieve a world without such weapons. It does urge the government and public alike to recognize that nuclear weapons decisions are among the most important that any national leaders can make. They are also complex, because decisions by any one nuclear power ramify through the international system and affect the decisions made by other nuclear, as well as non-nuclear, powers.

Certain long-standing principles, such as the centrality of nuclear non-proliferation, have proven their worth and should not be abandoned without strong efforts to maintain and strengthen their effectiveness—efforts that will, inevitably, mean forgoing or compromising certain other options. Other principles, such as the centrality of deterrence, have indeed been modified—in this case because of the principle's limited role in relation to possible terrorist acts.[69]

The dynamic nature of the technical and political environment in which nuclear weapons decisions must now be made requires an ongoing assessment of this changing landscape, with an eye on history for perspective on how the United States arrived at its current position. Our intention in this book has been to present that history, then to provide something better than a mere sketch, if necessarily less than a detailed plan, for how the United States should pursue its nuclear weapons policy in these early years of the twenty-first century. It is the ongoing burden of U.S. leadership in the coming decades to choose the wisest path forward.

Notes

1. The Nuclear Posture Review was provided to Congress at the end of 2001, but likely reflected thinking largely done prior to September 11. Describing earlier policies, the NPR said: "In the decade since the collapse of the Soviet Union, planning for the employment of U.S. nuclear forces has undergone only modest revision, despite the new relationship between the U.S. and Russia. [The past plans for, and size of, U.S. nuclear forces assumed that] Russia presented merely a smaller version of the threat posed by the former Soviet Union. . . . Defense planning will now shift from the threat-based approach of the Cold War. . . . This new approach should provide, over the coming decades, a credible deterrent at the lowest levels of nuclear weapons consistent with U.S. and allied security." The NPR is a classified document, but portions of it were leaked and are available at wwwglobalsecurity.org/wmd/library/policy/dod/npr.htm.

2. Some countries contend that North Korea's withdrawal from the NPT was legally ineffective. If North Korea is counted as an NPT party, the total is 189 states that are parties to the NPT.

3. Chapter 1 quotes President John Kennedy's remark at a news conference in March 1963 that he feared a world of "15 or 20 or 25" nuclear weapons states by 1975 and notes similar predictions by others in the 1970s.

4. See NPT, arts. I and III.

5. In previous usage, "preemptive" had been a term used for "anticipatory self-defense," an attack on an enemy that was preparing to attack you imminently, so justifiable under the UN Charter. In UN parlance, a "preventive war" was one that came *before* there was an imminent threat by the potential attacker. Administration usage conflates the terms "preventive" and "preemptive." The U.S. "preemption" policy was implemented in the invasion of Iraq owing to the putative threat of Iraqi "weapons of mass destruction." However, the primary justification for the invasion of Iraq given by the State Department legal adviser was general language in previous UN Security Council resolutions that had been adopted for the purpose of authorizing new international inspections in Iraq; this justification for the invasion was not accepted by many UN Security Council members, including France, Germany, Russia, and several others. See William H. Taft IV and Todd F. Buchwald, "Preemption, Iraq and International Law," *American Journal of International Law* 97 (July 2003): 557. These respective authors had been legal adviser of the State Department and the legal adviser's top assistant at the time of the 2003 invasion of Iraq, so presumably their advice to the administration was consistent with their arguments in this article. A senior Justice Department lawyer at the time expressed a similar view; see John Yoo, "International Law and the War in Iraq," *American Journal of International Law* 97 (July 2003): 563; conflicting views appear in *American Journal of International Law* 97, nos. 3 and no. 4 (October 2003).

6. We have stated our concern over the misleading aspects of the term "weapons of mass destruction" (WMD) elsewhere; see, for example, Christopher F. Chyba, "Toward Biological Security," *Foreign Affairs* 81 (May/June 2002): 122–36.

7. National Security Strategy of the United States of America, September 17, 2002 (available at www.whitehouse.gov/nsc/nss.html).

8. For an analysis of this point, see the discussion in Dara K. Cohen, "Relative Threat Assessment Working Group Background Briefing Paper," prepared for the Princeton

Project on National Security, March 2005 (www.wws.princeton.edu/ppns/groups/ThreatAssessment/index.html). Francis Gavin comments that this did not always hold for China during the cold war: "U.S. policymakers responsible for assessing international politics following the testing of an atomic device by the People's Republic of China (PRC) on October 16, 1964, would have been puzzled by the Bush administration's characterization of their world. [Four decades ago China appeared] not only irrational but perhaps undeterrable." See Francis J. Gavin, "Blasts from the Past: Proliferation Lessons from the 1960s," *International Security* 29 (Winter 2004/5): 100–01.

9. National Strategy for Combating Terrorism, p. 15 (www.whitehouse.gov/news/releases/2003/02/counter_terrorism/counter_terrorism_strategy.pdf).

10. William J. Perry, *Annual Report to the President and the Congress* (Department of Defense, 1995), p. 73.

11. See chapter 7 for a discussion of the reports and statements by members of the executive branch in the Bush administration that imply consideration of this possibility.

12. George W. Bush, Letter of Transmittal of Moscow Treaty to U.S. Senate, White House, June 20, 2002.

13. See Andrew K. Semmel, principal deputy assistant secretary of state for nuclear nonproliferation, "Universal Compliance with Nuclear Nonproliferation," address to Workshop on Prospects for the 2005 NPT Review Conference, Bali, Indonesia, January 20, 2005 (www.state.gov/t/np/rls/rm/41896.htm).

14. This is discussed at length in chapter 6; see also "Defending Missile Defense: An Interview with Missile Defense Agency Director Lt. Gen. Henry Obering," *Arms Control Today* 35 (November 2005): 6–12.

15. See ABM Treaty, art. V.1. For an argument against the weaponization of space, see Michael Krepon, with Christopher Clary, *Space Assurance or Space Dominance?* (Washington: Henry Stimson Center, 2003).

16. National Strategy for Combating Terrorism, p. 10.

17. See the Secretary-General's High-level Panel on Threats, Challenges and Change, *A More Secure World: Our Shared Responsibility* (New York: United Nations, 2004), par. 146.

18. See "Jihad Against Jews and Crusaders: World Islamic Front Statement," February 23, 1998 (www.fas.org/irp/world/para/docs/980223-fatwa.htm); and "When Terrorist Response Is Justified: An Interview with Osama bin Laden," May 1998 (www.justresponse.net/Bin_Laden3.html). See also Daniel Benjamin and Steven Simon, *The Next Attack: The Failure of the War on Terror and a Strategy for Getting It Right* (New York: Times Books, 2005), pp. 65–72.

19. NEM refers to any mixture of materials that can be made to support an exponentially growing chain reaction triggered by "fast" neutrons, and so is potentially suitable for a nuclear weapon. Highly enriched uranium (HEU) and plutonium are the two most important such materials; see "Physics and Technology of Nuclear Explosive Materials," in *Monitoring Nuclear Weapons and Nuclear-Explosive Materials* (Washington: National Academies Press, 2005), app. A, pp. 221–44.

20. William J. Perry, quoted by Lisa Trei, *Stanford Report*, February 16, 2005, p. 3, which reports on a meeting of the Stanford Institute of Economic Policy Research, February 11, 2005.

21. See, for example, Graham Allison, *Nuclear Terrorism: The Ultimate Preventable Catastrophe* (New York: Times Books, 2004).

22. Douglas Jehl, "U.S. Aides Cite Worry on Qaeda Infiltration from Mexico," *New York Times*, February 17, 2005, quoting Goss's response to a senatorial question.

23. See ibid.

24. See, for example, "Bush Aides Report 'Increasing Doubts' North Korea Will Give Up Nuclear Arms Program," *New York Times*, June 15, 2005; and Steven R. Weisman, "U.S. Says North Korean Demand for Reactor Won't Derail Accord," *New York Times*, September 21, 2005. The latter article describes differing reactions of the two countries to an agreed outline of a possible future agreement by North Korea to give up its nuclear weapons.

25. See Bruce Jentleson and Christopher Whytock, "Who 'Won' Libya? The Force-Diplomacy Debate and Its Implications for Theory and Policy," *International Security* 30 (Winter 2005/06): 47–86.

26. This capability holds for other nations with the nuclear fuel cycle as well as Iran, Libya, and North Korea. In the view of many analysts, Japan, for example, is only a year or less away from a nuclear weapon capability, were it to decide to violate its NPT commitments and pursue nuclear weapons. See Kurt M. Campbell and Tsuyoshi Sunohara, "Japan: Thinking the Unthinkable," in *The Nuclear Tipping Point: Why States Reconsider Their Nuclear Choices*, edited by Kurt M. Campbell, Robert J. Einhorn, and Mitchell B. Reiss (Brookings, 2004), pp. 218–53.

27. Euratom is a multilateral nuclear operating and inspection agency with inspectors from several West European countries.

28. See Mohamed ElBaradei, "Tackling the Nuclear Dilemma," *Arms Control Today* 35 (March 2005) (www.armscontrol.org/act/2005_03/ElBaredei.asp).

29. G-8 Gleneagles Statement on Non-Proliferation, July 2005, par. 13.

30. Ibid.

31. See Erik Asplund, "Brazil: Enrichment Safeguards but No Additional Protocol," *Trust & Verify* 117 (November/December 2004): 2.

32. For a skeptical view of the role of the PSI in the BBC *China* case, see Wade Boese, "Key U.S. Interdiction Initiative Claim Misrepresented," *Arms Control Today* 35 (July/August 2005) (www.armscontrol.org/act/2005_07-08/Interdiction_Misrepresented.asp).

33. See statement of Mihnea Ioan Motoc, chairman of the 1540 Committee, UN Security Council, Press Release SC/8454 (July 20, 2005).

34. Positive security assurances refer to assurances given by the United States to defend nations subject to nuclear attack.

35. For a description of the importance of the U.S. unilateral role in some particular cases, see *The Nuclear Tipping Point*, edited by Campbell and others; Don Oberdorfer, *The Two Koreas: A Contemporary History* (New York: Basic Books, 2001), pp. 68–74; and Ariel L. Levite, "Never Say Never Again: Nuclear Reversal Revisited," *International Security* 27 (Winter 2002/3): 59–88. See also Peter Liberman, "The Rise and Fall of the South African Bomb," *International Security* 26 (Fall 2001): 45–86.

36. See Statute of the International Atomic Energy Association, art. XII, par. C.

37. See, for example, the account by the retired deputy director of the U.S. On-Site Inspection Agency, Edward Ifft, "Iraq and the Value of On-Site Inspection," *Arms Control Today* 34 (November 2004): 21–27. For an international perspective, see Hans Blix, *Disarming Iraq* (New York: Pantheon, 2004).

38. For a brief history of these events, see Michael O'Hanlon and Mike Mochizuki, *Crisis on the Korean Peninsula* (Brookings, 2003).

39. See George Bunn and John Rhinelander, "The Right to Withdraw from the NPT: Article X Is Not Unconditional," *Disarmament Diplomacy* 79 (April/May 2005): 39.

40. A history of the NSG may be found in Leonard S. Spector with Jacqueline R. Smith, *Nuclear Ambitions: The Spread of Nuclear Weapons 1989–1990* (Boulder, Colo.: Westview Press, 1990), app. F.

41. This argument is made in the administration's *Report to Congress on an Assessment of the Impact of Repeal of the Prohibition on Low Yield Warhead Development on the Ability of the United States to Achieve Its Nonproliferation Objectives,* jointly submitted to Congress in March 2004 by the secretaries of State, Defense, and Energy.

42. See Herbert York, *Race to Oblivion* (New York: Simon & Schuster, 1970), p. 211.

43. Secretary Samuel W. Bodman, letter to Senator Dianne Feinstein, March 4, 2005.

44. See President John F. Kennedy, News Conference 52, March 21, 1963, John F. Kennedy Library and Museum, Boston.

45. This argument was made by Chyba and Greninger in the biological weapons and terrorism context, but it applies as well—with very different characteristics—to the nuclear nonproliferation regime. See Christopher F. Chyba and Alex L. Greninger, "Biotechnology and Bioterrorism: An Unprecedented World," *Survival* 46 (Summer 2004): 147. See also Chaim Braun and Christopher F. Chyba, "Proliferation Rings: New Challenges to the Nuclear Nonproliferation Regime," *International Security* 29 (Fall 2004): 49.

46. For a recent summary of the extent of progress in many of these areas, see Matthew Bunn and Anthony Wier, *Securing the Bomb 2005: The New Global Imperatives* (Harvard University, Project on Managing the Atom, May 2005). For a more thorough discussion of new multilateral initiatives, see chapters 3 to 5 of this book.

47. A State Department indicator of the U.S. government's success through 2004 in preventing nuclear weapons–related exports by other countries to Iran and North Korea acknowledged showing mixed results, and in some cases "little progress" for 2003 and 2004. See U.S. Department of State and U.S. Agency for International Development, *FY 2006 Performance Summary, Strategic Goal 4: Weapons of Mass Destruction*, pp.110–11 (www.state.gov/documents/organization/41605.pdf).

48. For a separate approach to this issue, see George Perkovich and others, *Universal Compliance: A Strategy for Nuclear Security* (Washington: Carnegie Endowment for International Peace, 2005).

49. This point, among others, is made by Wolfgang K. H. Panofsky, "Nuclear Proliferation Risks, New and Old," *Issues in Science and Technology Online* (Summer 2003) (www.nap.edu/issues/19.4/panofsky.html).

50. For a review and historical context, see MacGregor Knox and Williamson Murray, eds., *The Dynamics of Military Revolution, 1300–2050* (Cambridge University Press, 2001). The U.S. victories in initial combat operations did not, of course, speak to its ability to manage the Iraqi occupation.

51. The implications of this dominance are discussed in greater detail in chapter 1. The quotation is from Ian Roxborough, "Globalization, Unreason and the Dilemmas of American Military Strategy," *International Sociology* 17 (September 2002): 339–59.

52. This view is widely, though of course not universally, shared; as just one example, Major General (Ret.) William Burns has commented, "It would be difficult to conceive of a situation today in which nuclear weapons would be a serious military or political option." See William F. Burns, "Is There a Role for Nuclear Weapons Today?" *Arms Control Today* 35 (July/August 2005): 12.

53. After the U.S. conventional victory in the First Gulf War, India's chief of army staff was famously quoted as saying that the lesson of the war was "Don't fight the Americans without nuclear weapons." Quoted by Patrick J. Garrity, *Why the Gulf War Still Matters: Foreign Perspectives on the War and the Future of International Security*, Report 16 (Center for National Security Studies, July 1993), p. xiv.

54. For U.S. fears that China would prove undeterrable, see Gavin, "Blasts from the Past."

55. UN Security Council Resolution 984 (1995).

56. International Court of Justice, "Legality of the Threat or Use of Nuclear Weapons, Advisory Opinion to the UN General Assembly," July 8, 1996, *International Legal Materials*, 35 (1996): 609. See George Bunn, "The Legal Status of U.S. Negative Security Assurances to Non-Nuclear-Weapon States," *Nonproliferation Review* 4 (Spring/Summer 1997): 1.

57. See, for example, George Bunn, "Expanding Nuclear Options: Is the U.S. Negating Its Non-Use Pledges?" *Arms Control Today* 26 (May/June 1996): 7.

58. For example, the leaked Nuclear Posture Review asserts that "the establishment of this New Triad can both reduce our dependence on nuclear weapons and improve our ability to deter attack in the face of proliferating WMD capabilities" (www.global security.org/wmd/library/policy/dod/npr.htm).

59. See *2000 Review Conference of the Parties to the Treaty on the Non-Proliferation of Nuclear Weapons: Final Document*, May 24, 2000, (www.iaea.org/NewsCenter/Focus/ Npt/NPT_Conferences/npt2000_final_doc.pdf).

60. United States, "Recommendations for Achieving the Objective of Nuclear Disarmament and Non-proliferation of Nuclear Weapons," A/CN.10/2006/WG.I/WP.1 (UN Disarmament Commission, April 18 2006). This U.S. statement said that "all states should maintain national moratoria on nuclear testing."

61. See, for example, remarks by former senator Sam Nunn, cochairman of the Nuclear Threat Initiative, "U.S. Nuclear Weapons Policies and Programs," delivered to the Carnegie Endowment for International Peace Nonproliferation Conference, June 21, 2004 (www.nti.org/c_press/statement_nunnceip_062104.pdf).

62. See Pavel Podvig, "History and the Current Status of the Russian Early-Warning System," *Science and Global Security* 10 (2002): 21–60.

63. The Moscow Treaty was ratified by the U.S. Senate in March 2003, with some reporting conditions attached. The text of the Moscow Treaty is available at www.state.gov/t/ac/trt/18016.htm.

64. See remarks by Linton F. Brooks, administrator of the National Nuclear Security Administration, "A New Triumph of Sanity," delivered to the Carnegie Endowment for International Peace Nonproliferation Conference, June 21, 2004 (www.nnsa.doe.gov/ docs/speeches/2004/speech_%20Carnegie_Nuclear%20_Policy_(6-04).pdf).

65. See, for example, Robert S. Norris and Hans M. Kristensen, "NRDC Nuclear Notebook: Dismantling U.S. Nuclear Warheads," *Bulletin of the Atomic Scientists* 60 (January/February 2004): 72, 73; Norris and Kristensen, "NRDC Nuclear Notebook: U.S. Nuclear Forces, 2005," *Bulletin of the Atomic Scientists* 61 (January/February 2005): 73.

66. For a detailed technical study of the kinds of monitoring that would need to be achieved to support the reductions of nuclear weapons to low or very low levels, see Committee on International Security and Arms Control, *Monitoring Nuclear Weapons and Nuclear-Explosive Materials* (Washington: National Academies Press, 2005).

67. Article VI of the NPT reads in full: "Each of the Parties to the Treaty undertakes to pursue negotiations in good faith on effective measures relating to cessation of the nuclear arms race at an early date and to nuclear disarmament, and on a Treaty on general and complete disarmament under strict and effective international control" (www.state.gov/t/np/trty/16281.htm).

68. See "Defending Missile Defense: An Interview with Missile Defense Agency Director Lt. Gen. Henry Obering," *Arms Control Today* 35 (November 2005): 6–12.

69. Limited does not mean nonexistent. For an analysis of the circumstances under which terrorism may be deterrable, see Robert Trager and Dessislava Zagorcheva, "Deterring Terrorism: It Can Be Done," *International Security* 30 (Winter 2005/06), pp. 87–123.

About the Authors

CHAIM BRAUN is a vice president of Altos Management Partners, Inc., and a science fellow at the Center for International Security and Cooperation (CISAC) at Stanford University. He has led or contributed to many studies on economic and security aspects of nuclear energy. With Christopher F. Chyba he wrote "Proliferation Rings: New Challenges to the Nuclear Nonproliferation Regime," in the fall 2004 *International Security*. His current long-term research project is entitled "The Energy Security Initiative and a Nuclear Fuel Cycle Center: Two Enhancement Options for the Current Non-Proliferation Regime."

GEORGE BUNN helped negotiate the Nuclear Non-Proliferation Treaty (NPT) as the lawyer for the negotiating delegation. He served as general counsel for the arms control agency, now in the State Department, from 1961 to 1968, and as U.S. ambassador to the Geneva Disarmament Conference for the last of those years. He has also worked for the U.S. Atomic Energy Commission, the U.S. Nuclear Regulatory Commission, and a Washington law firm. Later, he became a law teacher and then dean of the Law School at the University of Wisconsin. At CISAC for the past twenty years, he has focused on nuclear subjects. His book *Arms Control by Committee: Managing Negotiations with the Russians* provides a history of the negotiation of the NPT. Recent articles have appeared in *Arms Control Today*, *The Nonproliferation Review*, *Science and Global Security*, the *IAEA Bulletin*, and *Disarmament Diplomacy*.

CHRISTOPHER F. CHYBA is a professor of astrophysical sciences and international affairs at Princeton University, where he directs the Program on Science and Global Security at the Woodrow Wilson School. Previously, he was co-director of CISAC at Stanford University. He was a member of the White House staff from 1993 to 1995, entering as a White House fellow, serving on the National Security Council staff and then in the Office of Science and Technology Policy. He is a member of the Committee on International Security and Arms Control of the National Academy of Sciences. His research focuses on nuclear proliferation, nuclear weapons policy, and biological terrorism as well as solar system exploration and the search for life elsewhere. Recent articles have appeared in *International Security, Foreign Affairs, Survival, Science,* and *Annual Review of Astronomy and Astrophysics.* In October 2001 he was named a MacArthur Fellow for his work in both planetary sciences and international security.

DAVID HOLLOWAY is the Raymond A. Spruance Professor of International History, a professor of political science, and a senior fellow with the Freeman Spogli Institute for International Studies (FSI) at Stanford University, CISAC's parent organization. He co-directed CISAC from 1991 to 1997 and directed FSI from 1998 to 2003. His book *Stalin and the Bomb: The Soviet Union and Atomic Energy, 1939–1956* was chosen by the *New York Times Book Review* as one of the eleven best books of 1994 and won the Vucinich and Shulman prizes of the American Association for the Advancement of Slavic Studies. He is at work on an international history of nuclear weapons and a biography of Yulii Khariton, scientific director of the Soviet Union's first nuclear bomb project.

MICHAEL MAY is an emeritus director of the Lawrence Livermore National Laboratory, an emeritus research professor in the Stanford University School of Engineering, a senior fellow at FSI, and former co-director of CISAC. He was a technical adviser to the Threshold Test Ban Treaty negotiating team, a member of the U.S. delegation to the Strategic Arms Limitation Talks, and at various times has been a member of the Defense Science Board, the General Advisory Committee to the AEC, the Secretary of the Energy Advisory Board, the RAND Corporation Board of Trustees, and the Committee on International Security and Arms Control of the National Academy of Sciences. His current research addresses nuclear weapons and terrorism; energy, security, and environment; and the relation of nuclear weapons and foreign policy.

W. K. H. Panofsky is an emeritus professor of physics and emeritus director of the Stanford Linear Accelerator Center (SLAC). He served as a consultant to the Manhattan Project, the U.S. Arms Control and Disarmament Agency, and the White House, and, through the National Academy of Sciences (NAS), has advised many other projects and agencies on nuclear science issues. A longtime member of the NAS Committee for International Security and Arms Control, he chaired the committee for eight years. As the first director of SLAC, Panofsky pressed the case for basic accelerator research. His role in the Manhattan Project profoundly influenced his thinking on scientists' ethical and social responsibilities. He helped secure the Atmospheric Test Ban Treaty during the Kennedy administration and the Anti-Ballistic Missile Treaty of 1972, and he helped found the Arms Control and Disarmament program at Stanford, from which CISAC developed.

Karthika Sasikumar is a Simons Postdoctoral Fellow at the Simons Centre for Disarmament and Nonproliferation Research at the University of British Columbia. She earned her Ph.D. from Cornell University's Department of Government in 2006. Her dissertation is titled "Regimes at Work: The Nonproliferation Regime and the Case of India." She has an M.A. in international studies and an M.Phil. in disarmament from Jawaharlal Nehru University, New Delhi, and an M.A. in French. Sasikumar was a predoctoral fellow at CISAC in 2004–05.

Roger Speed is a physicist formerly with the Lawrence Livermore National Laboratory and now an affiliate of CISAC. He has also worked at the National Academy of Sciences, at R&D Associates, and, as a Peace Fellow, at the Hoover Institution, where he wrote a book on strategic nuclear policy. He has served on a number of defense-related committees, including ones for the Office of Undersecretary of Defense for Policy, the American Physical Society, the U.S. Navy (Non-Acoustic ASW Panel), the National Academy of Sciences, and the Air Force Space and Missile Systems Organization. He has conducted a broad range of national security studies for the Department of Defense, Department of Energy, and Central Intelligence Agency in such areas as arms control, strategic deterrence, nuclear war, ballistic missile defense, nuclear weapons safety, and the survivability of strategic systems.

Dean A. Wilkening directs the Science Program at CISAC. He holds a Ph.D. in physics from Harvard University and spent thirteen years at the RAND

Corporation before coming to Stanford in 1996. His research interests include nuclear strategy and policy; arms control; the proliferation of nuclear, biological, and chemical weapons; ballistic missile defense; and biological terrorism. His work on missile defense focuses on the broad strategic and political implications of deploying national and theater missile defenses, in particular the impact of theater missile defense in Northeast Asia, and the technical feasibility of boost-phase interceptors for national and theater missile defense.

Index

ABM Treaty. *See* Anti-Ballistic Missile (ABM) Treaty

Acheson–Lilienthal Report, 36, 45

Additional Protocol inspections: acceptance and ratification of, 79–81, 163–65; creation of, 45, 47; ElBaradei on, 171; and EU, 95, 185; and export controls, 95, 177; and Iran, 190–91; and UN Security Council enforcement, 200

Advanced Concepts Initiative, 251

Advanced Passenger Manifest, 228

Advance Electronic Cargo Manifest, 228

Agreed Framework. *See* North Korea

Ahmadinejad, Mahmoud, 62, 141, 145, 191–93

Airborne Laser Program, 239

Air defense, 232–34

Airline security, 228

Al Qaeda, 1, 48, 129, 280, 301

Alternatives to nuclear energy, 179–81

Annan, Kofi, 201

Anti-Ballistic Missile (ABM) Treaty of *1972*, 42, 235, 298; U.S. withdrawal from, 34–35, 56, 59, 89, 106, 108, 236, 301

Anti-nuclear blackmail strategy, 16

Argentina: and mutual monitoring agreement with Brazil, 93, 305; as nonnuclear state, 277; and NPT, 111, 132

Assessing U.S. nuclear posture, 11–12, 183–84, 248–96; and biological weapons, 260–64; and countermeasures, 259–60; and dissuasion, 265, 275–76; and domestic support for security policy, 280–81; and hard and deeply buried targets, 256–60; new U.S. strategic doctrine, 249–50; and new weapon concepts, 251–55, 264–76; operational and strategic considerations in, 255–56; and perceived shortcomings, 250–51; political consequences of, 283–84; and preventive war, 270–75; and proposed new weapons, 256–64; and reaction of other states, 278–80; strategic consequences of new posture, 277–81; strategic consequences of use of nuclear weapons, 281–83; and weapons and military targets, 250–56. *See also* Deterrence; Preventive war and preemption

Atomic Energy Act of *1946* (U.S.), 43–44, 195, 196

CENTER FOR INTERNATIONAL SECURITY AND COOPERATION

The Center for International Security and Cooperation, part of Stanford University's Freeman Spogli Institute for International Studies, is a multidisciplinary community dedicated to producing policy-relevant research, influencing policy, and training the next generation of specialists in international security. The Center brings together scholars, policymakers, area specialists, business people, and other experts to focus on a wide range of pressing security concerns.

BROOKINGS INSTITUTION

The Brookings Institution is a private nonprofit organization devoted to research, education, and publication on important issues of domestic and foreign policy. Its principal purpose is to bring the highest quality independent research and analysis to bear on current and emerging policy problems. Interpretations or conclusions in Brookings publications should be understood to be solely those of the authors.